Time in the Wilderness

Time in the Wilderness

The Formative Years *of* John "Black Jack" Pershing *in the* American West

TIM MCNEESE

Potomac Books
An imprint of the University of Nebraska Press

© 2021 by Tim McNeese

Portions of the book previously appeared in Tim McNeese, *John J. Pershing*, © 2003 by Chelsea House Publishers, an imprint of Infobase; and Tim McNeese, *The Gilded Age and Progressivism, 1891–1913*, © 2010 by Chelsea House Publishers, an imprint of Infobase. Reprinted with permission of the publisher.

All rights reserved. Potomac Books is an imprint of the University of Nebraska Press.
Manufactured in the United States of America.

♾

Library of Congress Cataloging-in-Publication Data
Names: McNeese, Tim, author.
Title: Time in the wilderness: the formative years of John "Black Jack" Pershing in the American West / Tim McNeese.
Other titles: Formative years of John "Black Jack" Pershing in the American West
Description: Lincoln: Potomac Books, an imprint of the University of Nebraska Press, [2021] | Includes bibliographical references and index.
Identifiers: LCCN 2021009497
ISBN 9781640124066 (hardback)
ISBN 9781640124950 (epub)
ISBN 9781640124967 (pdf)
Subjects: LCSH: Pershing, John J. (John Joseph), 1860–1948. | Indians of North America—Wars—1866–1895. | Spanish-American War, 1898—Campaigns—Cuba. | Philippines—History—1898–1946. | United States. Army—History—Punitive Expedition into Mexico, 1916. | Generals—United States—Biography. | United States. Army—Biography. | BISAC: BIOGRAPHY & AUTOBIOGRAPHY / Military | HISTORY / United States / State & Local / Southwest (AZ, NM, OK, TX)
Classification: LCC E181.P495 M36 2021 | DDC 355.0092 [B]—dc23
LC record available at https://lccn.loc.gov/2021009497

Set in Questa by Laura Buis.

To Beverly, who read every word
and whose opinion matters most

Contents

List of Illustrations | ix

Introduction: Canyon, June 1889 | 1

1. Childhood, 1860–73 | 23
2. Community, 1873–82 | 39
3. Cadets, 1882–87 | 61
4. Cavalry, 1887–90 | 85
5. Cloak, 1890–91 | 109
6. College, 1891–95 | 137
7. Cree, 1895–98 | 163
8. Cuba, 1898 | 193
9. Colony, 1898–1903 | 221
10. Courtship, 1903–9 | 253
11. Conquest, 1909–13 | 277
12. Calamity, 1913–16 | 295
13. Chase, 1916–17 | 309

Conclusion: Civilian, 1917–48 | 349

Acknowledgments | 357
Notes | 361
Bibliography | 393
Index | 405

Illustrations

Following page 136
1. Pershing family home in Laclede, Missouri
2. Sixth Cavalry at Ford Bayard
3. Gen. Nelson Miles
4. Gen. Eugene Carr
5. Troop B of Ogallala Indian Scouts
6. University of Nebraska's University Hall
7. James Hulme Canfield
8. Charles G. Dawes
9. William Jennings Bryan
10. Willa Cather
11. George Meiklejohn
12. Pershing during the Spanish-American War
13. Theodore Roosevelt as a member of the Rough Riders
14. Helen Frances "Frankie" Warren
15. Pershing at Camp Vicars
16. Pershing family in the Philippines
17. Brigadier General Pershing
18. Pershing family's burned-out home at the Presidio
19. Pershing with his son, Francis Warren
20. Pershing and Pancho Villa

Illustrations

21. Pancho Villa
22. Pershing with his officers at Casas Grandes
23. Cartoon of Pershing's Punitive Expedition
24. Pershing during the Punitive Expedition in Mexico

Time in the Wilderness

Introduction

Canyon, June 1889

Accessing its rims is elementary, the challenge nonexistent. Today, millions of Americans and tourists from around the world visit Arizona's Grand Canyon, the geological jewel of the American Southwest. Modern highways and airports provide easy, comfortable access to the various rims of the vast chasm. But during the late nineteenth century, more than twenty years before President Theodore Roosevelt declared this leg of the rock-red Colorado River and the deep sandstone mega cut it carved over eons of time a national monument, a stalwart, if naive, pair of young U.S. cavalrymen attempted a visit that nearly ended in tragedy. Save for the kindness of strangers and a large dose of luck, this pair of blue-clad second lieutenants might have perished, their lives cut short and their bones left to bleach anonymously on some lonesome malpais outcropping in a desert they had misjudged. And the implications could have had a profound effect on U.S. history.

In June 1889 twenty-eight-year-old John Joseph Pershing and his comrade in arms John Miller Stotsenburg, age thirty, set out on a journey across the high Great Basin Desert fraught with peril they did not foresee. Pershing, born in Missouri, had called the American Southwest his professional home following his graduation from the U.S. Military Academy at West Point in 1886. Stotsenburg, an Indiana Hoosier, had graduated five years earlier from the military academy and had seen service at remote fort assignments in both New Mexico and Arizona. The two junior officers were not new to the frontier realities of the Southwest that summer when they finally decided to take the trip they had talked about for some time—a visit to one of the most exotic, sublime, and remote places on Earth. But they soon discovered the desert logistics involved in crossing this particular bit of frontier backcountry were much more complex than they thought.

They did not head off into the wilderness without some element of planning, however. Having spent a handful of years stationed at a string of federal army posts planted in this barren land as monitoring stations to keep watch on the region's various Indian nations, Pershing and Stotsenburg had a grudging respect for the desert and its challenges. They began their five-hundred-mile trip at Arizona's Fort Defiance, located on the southern perimeter of the Navajo Indian Reservation, a desert outpost that hugged the Arizona side of the border it shared with New Mexico. From there, with compasses in hand and a rudimentary knowledge of how to identify trails in remote places, the men's journey represented largely a straight arrow shot westward to a destination along the south rim of the canyon—a lonely log cabin occupied by the first Anglo-American to make his home on the edges of the Grand Canyon, a muleteer and part-time asbestos miner named John Hance.

From the relative safety of Fort Defiance, the second lieutenants charted a path that would leapfrog them through Keams Canyon to a pair of Indian settlements—the Hopi villages of Walpi and Oraibi, both on the Moqui Indian Reservation—and to the Mormon community of Tuba City. Then, if their plan went smoothly, they would find themselves standing in awe on some remote precipice of the greatest of American canyons.[1]

But maps can be deceiving. Sometimes it is what one doesn't see in two dimensions that really matters. Between Tuba City and the Grand Canyon, only one known water hole awaited them, and it would prove easy to miss.

Of course, Pershing and Stotsenburg did not plan on failing,

Introduction

and their preliminary arrangements seemed, to them, quite reasonable. They purchased mountain ponies from the local Indians. They arranged for three, seemingly sturdy mules to carry their supplies and hired as a scout a local Navajo named Sam, a graduate of the Carlisle Indian School in Pennsylvania who had served the U.S. Army for years. He knew a portion of the region through which they intended to pass. They took on another Native American, a veteran packer everyone referred to as "Minus," a name that, in time, would seem perfectly appropriate, for he ultimately detracted more than he contributed to the expedition. They loaded their mules lightly to avoid undo strain on their pack animals and were careful to bring along enough rations for themselves and grain for their four-footed comrades. They even packed a single extra blanket just on the off chance they might need it. The American soldiers could only imagine the adventure of a lifetime ahead of them. But as Stotsenburg would later write, "We were not after all the adventures that we found before we reached home." He would add to his analysis: "The plans that we made were perhaps not very well matured."[2]

Once they set out on the first day of their trip, problems began to crowd their path. Their ponies proved unreliable. Stotsenburg's mount, Spike, had been sold to him as a "gentle, tough, and sure-footed" animal, but it ultimately proved balky and kicked and bit at both soldiers.[3] In addition, the Indian who sold Spike to the unwitting Stotsenburg had included in the deal a promise to lead the small party along a stretch of the planned route unfamiliar to even Sam. His failure to show up as promised would create a significant challenge to Pershing and his companion.

The first important stop on the trail was Keams Canyon, approximately eighty rugged miles west of Fort Defiance. Stotsenburg described the canyon as "a beautiful spot," a teaser for the great chasm they were intending to visit. Here, a local named Tom Keam, a former soldier-turned-prospector-turned-proprietor, ran a trading post for local Indians, including the Hopis and Navajos. The desert outpost also included a Christian Indian school operated by a small cadre of Eastern women. The ladies showed off their charges by having them sing a variety of gospel songs, including one written by P. P. Bliss, a master hymnist of the era in Protestant circles, titled "Hold the Fort." Its words perhaps signaled more to Pershing and Stotsenburg than they could possibly know at that point in their trip: "We'll join our hands in union strong / To battle or to die" and "Side by side we battle onward; / Victory will come." When the impromptu frontier concert ended, so did the school day, and the two officers watched with surprise as the children scampered out of the school, "regaining their liberty by running up the perpendicular walls of the Canyon like so many goats."[4] The men experienced one profound disappointment at Keams Canyon: Tom Keams—a font of local information who could have given Pershing and Stotsenburg crucial advice about the trail to the Grand Canyon—was not at the settlement.[5] At a minimum, he likely could have provided them with a local guide. His absence was a significant loss for the soldiers.

The lieutenants and their party headed out of the canyon the following morning, a bright, sunny Sunday. The sky was clear, and off in the distance, a hundred miles to the southwest, rose the San Francisco Mountain, which would mark the group's flank for the next two days. In her novel *The Song of the Lark* (1915), the Pulitzer Prize–winning Nebraska writer Willa Cather, whom John Pershing would encounter repeatedly during his lifetime, describes a landscape reflective of the one through which the two young lieutenants passed: "The San Francisco Mountain lies in Northern Arizona, above Flagstaff, and its blue slopes and snowy summit entice the eye for a hundred miles across the desert. About its base lie the pine forests of the Navajos, where the great red-trunked trees live out their peaceful centuries in that sparkling air. The piñons and scrub begin only where the forest ends, where the country breaks into open, stony clearings and the surface of the earth cracks into deep canyons."[6]

For certain, the two soldier-explorers saw interesting, even picturesque sights along their way. When they reached First

Mesa and the Walpi Hopi village, population two hundred, Pershing and Stotsenburg visited the Natives' mud-clay, cliff-perched pueblo situated on top of a three-hundred-foot mesa, which was only accessible by a steep, ribbon-thin trail ascending the cliff wall.[7] The mesa was home to the descendants of the long-vanished Anasazis. In the light of the setting sun, the pueblo and the tumbledown rocks blended into a single natural landscape, as if the adobe houses had simply sprung out of the red clay spontaneously. Somewhere in the village lived a female potter named Nampeyo, whose Sikyátki pottery would one day sell for hundreds of thousands of dollars.

The smell of burning sheep manure permeated the air, since the local Hopis used it for fuel to heat and cook. The party remained long enough in the village to take a meal inside the tumbledown adobe, even if the Indian dishes put before them were hardly to their liking. The repast included a sweet bread whose preparation involved the cook chewing up the bluish-black cornmeal first and then spitting it on the hot rocks to cook. In the village, the army officers were appalled to see twenty or so bald eagles held in small cages. Many of their feathers had been stripped from them, as the Hopis used them in their ceremonial garb during ritual dances. Pershing wondered why the army had not been dispatched to put a stop to the desecration of the national bird.

At noon, the men moved on a short distance and reached Third Mesa and Oraibi, a second Hopi village, where they camped for the night. For eight hundred years, the Hopis had lived on the mesa; nearly a thousand still called it home. When the local Natives approached them, Pershing and Stotsenburg traded some of their coffee, tobacco, and much-prized matches. The meal that evening consisted of bread Stotsenburg cooked Indian style, placing the dough in a hole in the desert sand that was preheated with coals. It was serviceable for their army palates, even if "it was a bit heavy and a trifle gritty."[8]

As they moved westward from the village, Pershing and Stotsenburg were in unfamiliar territory. The Native American who had sold Spike to Stotsenburg and promised to meet them at the Hopi settlement never arrived. This turn of events placed the party in jeopardy. As Stotsenburg described it: "The breaking of this promise caused us much trouble and suffering, as the following mishaps show."[9]

But such disappointing mile markers did not deter Pershing and Stotsenburg from continuing on their journey. The men, after all, had covered more than thirty miles that day despite the inhospitable environment. They saw themselves as veterans of the West, men who had become accustomed to the challenges of the desert and its extreme conditions. Their naivete likely shielded them from considering their trip might actually become a matter of life and death. Perhaps they felt the invulnerability of youth, the tendency toward a bulletproof presumption that should have been tempered by their own previous experiences as soldiers. Still, they pressed on.

The fourth day on the trail brought them to Tuba City, a small Mormon settlement and frontier outpost. They arranged for their ponies to be shod, but Stotsenburg's Spike was so cantankerous the blacksmith could not get shoes on him. This would prove a costly problem down the trail as the party passed through a region where the landscape turned treacherous, blanketed with a flinty malpais. In Spanish, the word means "badlands." Such land is covered with the remnants of volcanic lava flows that, over time, became excessively eroded, creating a rough, hard-edged landform that makes a crossing on horse or mule difficult, even dangerous. On this topography, little vegetation can grow, rendering it unsuitable for farming. Whether Pershing or Stotsenburg knew this before reaching the hard-ground malpais field is unclear. But on such ground, they could hardly rely on an unshod, balky pony.

At the crude Mormon hotel, the men sat down to a spartan meal of stewed gooseberries and soda biscuits. At the table, they met a Mr. Ruggles, a traveling showman who was in town with a frontier circus troupe. Later that day, his performers entertained all with a flying trapeze act and a Punch and Judy puppet show that brought down the house, with the majority in the audience having never seen anything of the like. At the end of the show, Mr. Ruggles passed a hat for contributions. The next morning, Pershing, Stotsenburg, and Ruggles shared another meal at the hotel, with the lieutenants providing the flour, coffee, and bacon to make a decent breakfast.

Despite such diversions, Tuba City delivered several disappointments to the two young officers. Sam, their guide, left them. He told his comrades he had relatives in the region whom he wanted to visit and that he would return soon. He said his pony was nearly exhausted, and his own people could provide him with a replacement. But when they prepared to leave the next day, Sam was still absent. With no reliable guide at their disposal and with the most difficult portion of their trip ahead of them, here the two officers likely made one of their most serious critical errors. Several of the local Mormons knew the way to the Grand Canyon, and some were willing to provide direction as guides. But they expected to be paid well for their services—to the minds of the pair of lieutenants, too well. Pershing and Stotsenburg decided they could not afford the cost, leaving them on their own initiative to continue the journey. Circumstances were stacking up against them: no guide, no clear path before them, and a harsh, flinty landscape waiting to torment them. An additional problem would nearly prove their undoing: the Mormons informed them that only one water hole was between Tuba City and the Grand Canyon. If they located it, they might have enough water to reach their goal. Miss it, and peril would stalk their steps.

The next day, a Tuesday, they set their eyes westward toward the absolute unknown. Despite the challenges that had presented themselves in rapid succession and boded a difficult march to the great canyon, as Pershing—for some inexplicable reason, Stotsenburg had a habit of referring to his comrade as "Jackson"—and his companion left Tuba City, the pair were "very much refreshed" and "in high spirits."[10] Sam proved as elusive as the desert wind, but the lieutenants felt they had a pretty good idea of what trail to follow toward the northwest to the South Rim.

The weather proved another challenge as the small party

experienced "one of the hottest and most disagreeable rides" along the Moenkopi Wash that led them to the banks of the Little Colorado River.[11] During their lunch stop in the canyon, Pershing and Spike, the recalcitrant pony, experienced a clash of wills. When the young lieutenant tried to adjust the horse's saddle after hours on the trail, the pony thanked him with a hard kick, followed by a bite on his arm. Pershing lost his temper, telling the animal "that since he could not return the bite he would include it in the kick." He soon followed his words with a booted blow to the animal's ribs, causing the cantankerous pony to fall to the ground.[12]

Later that afternoon, the trail the lieutenants followed into the canyon appeared to be leading them further down into a long, narrow sandstone defile, but by sundown, they managed to find their way out. After supper, a rifle shot rang out, the report bouncing along the canyon walls. More shots soon followed. Their concern was soon alleviated when their packer, Minus, appeared. He explained he had become lost; his shots served as distress signals. But Sam was still missing, and the officers believed they had seen the last of their guide and interpreter.

The following morning, they set out under a predawn sky, heading along the trail they had rediscovered the previous evening. Soon they realized they had not found the right path and for several hours crossed over sharp, flinty malpais. By midmorning, fortunately, they hit on the right trail once again, leaving one concern behind them, at least for the moment.

But despite a trail seeming to appear, then disappear, one problem soon overrode all others—their lack of water. Warned that a single water hole was along the trail leading to the Grand Canyon, they had filled their canteens at the river, as well as an old, beaten-up coffee pot. Uncertain where, exactly, or when they would reach significant water once they left the canyon and the Little Colorado, they agreed to refrain from taking a drink until noon. What a surprise to the young officers to discover, not long after hitting the trail, Minus had already consumed his canteen and the entire coffee pot of emergency water! Things soon began to unravel for the small party. Minus pan-

Introduction

icked, afraid he would die of thirst in short order (although he had already consumed more water than either of the officers), so he left them in search of a source. At the same time, Spike turned up lame and developed a bad sore on his back, making riding him impossible. With Minus gone and Stotsenburg without a mount, the party was soon split three ways, with the second lieutenant heading out on foot to gain ground, while Pershing waited for Minus. Once the Indian finally returned, he and Pershing tried to catch up with Stotsenburg. By the time they reconnoitered, an argument developed over whether Stotsenburg had followed the correct trail. Ultimately, they stayed on Stotsenburg's path until they reached the rim of a box canyon. Peering over the brink, the party could see the Little Colorado, its reddish waters snaking between canyon lands two thousand feet down. The only known water was now less than half a mile away, but for the party of thirsty men, it may as well have been on the other side of the globe.

Stotsenburg's insistence regarding the trail had landed them seven miles off course. The footsore second lieutenant was worn to a frazzle, and Minus was still panicking over their lack of water. His concern was greater than simple uncertainty. Stotsenburg wrote in his diary: "We experienced the shock of seeing a strong and hearty man changed into a cowardly beast. We could not tell what rash act Minus would commit after we had gone to bed."[13]

After a short rest beneath the shade of a handful of thinly leaved bushes, the men set out again in search of the trail. Their situation relentlessly deteriorated. Pershing's pony also played out, leaving both lieutenants to mount a pair of pack mules. They did manage to reach the fork that Pershing had suggested they take when he caught up with Stotsenburg, and soon they were riding along the Buckskin Mountains, which Stotsenburg considered well named since "they were so tough."[14] Then, in a hopeful sign, doves flew overhead, having emerged from a nearby canyon. The party knew enough to realize such birds gathered at water holes at eventide, so they dispatched Minus to check the canyon for a spring.

Introduction

But as had already happened, Minus seemed to disappear completely as the hours passed, and the thirst of the two officers increased. Evening fell into night. The men fired their guns, the reports reverberating across the seemingly endless canyon walls, but elicited no response from Minus. Parched and uncertain when they might again drink water, they fell asleep exhausted.

The following morning dawned threateningly. The men not only were dry throated but also knew they were facing complete dehydration. The Arizona desert takes no prisoners. Seventeen years following Pershing and Stotsenburg's ordeal across the malpais of northeastern Arizona, a published study on the effects of extreme dehydration focused on the experiences of Pablo Valencia, a forty-year-old desert prospector who went seven days without water and drank only his own urine and the moisture squeezed from a scorpion. His ordeal included some of the same physical responses the lieutenants were experiencing.

Dehydration begins to manifest itself in obvious ways, including the expected dry mouth, or "cotton mouth," due to a lack of water beyond mere thirst. A victim's saliva thickens as his breath turns sour. The tongue begins to swell, and the throat dries up, causing one's speech to slur or to turn into a hoarse, cracking sound. The study refers to the tongue becoming so hardened due to a lack of moisture that it feels like "a senseless weight, swinging on the still-soft root and striking foreignly against the teeth."[15] Even swallowing becomes difficult to impossible. And the resulting pain spreads throughout the head and neck. The skin dries up and even shrinks. In its extreme form, dehydration—true, full-throated dehydration—affects the senses, causing difficulties in hearing and even manifestations of hallucinations. Valencia's symptoms went far beyond his throat and mouth. His lips had disappeared, his gums had turned hard as jerky, and "his eyes were set in a winkless stare."[16] His skin had turned purple and blotchy, and where his legs had been gashed and cut by thorns and sharp rocks, the wounds were dry and bloodless. For all purposes, Pablo Valencia, after a week without water, had taken on the look of a living mummy.

Introduction

It is no wonder Minus, who had spent nearly his entire life battling the harsh realities of the Arizona desert, began to panic over a lack of water.

Discounting Minus's overwrought concerns regarding where his next drink of water might come from, Pershing and Stotsenburg were facing many problems on their trek without adequate training and field experience. While they were veterans of western fort postings, their service did not guarantee they had the appropriate endurance skills needed to handle all desert challenges. These two Anglos were out of their depth. By comparison, consider the skill set of those Natives of the Southwest most recognized for such abilities, the Apaches, whom U.S. Army troops had only recently fully subdued. Apache warriors were men of the desert, fighters who moved across the barren landscape with disciplined ease. Having trained since adolescence to meet the challenges of a hard-edged land, Apache warriors carried little except their weapons, expecting to live off the land and to find water where available. As historian Steve Kemper notes, "They could walk forty miles without eating or drinking. If provisioned, they could cover 120 miles by foot in two days."[17] The problem Pershing and Stotsenburg faced during their trek across the desert was that despite their experiences to date as cavalrymen in the West, this venture in the heart of a heartless environment had pushed them beyond their skill set. They were left with only two options—succeed or perish.

Other Anglos with greater experience and the appropriate regard for the arid landscape and its challenges could have handled the problems Pershing and Stotsenburg faced. They had surely heard of Kit Carson, whose reputation as a mountain man, trapper, and scout had turned him into a "blood and thunder" western legend fifty years earlier in frontier New Mexico and Arizona. But were they aware of Carson's capacity to move across an uninviting western topography and survive? Historian Hampton Sides notes a panoply of Carson's required skills: "As a tracker, he was unequaled. He knew from experience how to read the watersheds, where to find grazing grass, what to do when encountering a grizzly. He could locate water in the driest arroyo and strain it into potability. In a crisis he knew little tricks for staving off thirst—such as opening the fruit of a cactus or clipping a mule's ears and drinking its blood."[18] Nowhere in Stotsenburg's diary does either lieutenant suggest clipping a mule's ear to quench their thirst.

Further complicating matters, the party's mounts had bolted in the night and scattered, having literally pulled up from their roots the small bushes to which they had been tied. The already-thirsty and tired men now had to track down their animals. Stotsenburg summed up their morning with agonizing accuracy: "It would be impossible to picture our dismay when we got up at daylight and found that we had been left on foot in the heart of an unfrequented desert and twenty-five miles from the nearest known water. We were even then weak and exhausted, and there was not half a gill [four ounces] of water in our canteens."[19]

A desperate reassessment of their situation was upon them, and the decisions they began to make were difficult. Traveling light was a necessity, so they began to leave items behind. They took the short provisions they had remaining, including "a little coffee, sugar, bacon, and biscuits," and placed them in a cotton sack.[20] Breakfast was a bit of biscuit soaked in whiskey, which Pershing found refreshing, but it made Stotsenburg ill. As they set out under an early morning sky, the mountains still shrouded the sun. The first five miles of walking were bearable, yet they stopped often to rest.

Their discomfort intensified as the sun rose over the crest of the mountains. The heat was unbearable, and their lack of water excruciating, as the men felt their dried faces blister and crack. The two lieutenants, who had started off the day tired and thirsty, were now under siege from the sun itself. They were on a course for the only water source they knew with certainty, the Little Colorado River, but just reaching its red-water banks would be difficult. Stotsenburg's diary noted the absence of a single cloud in the unmerciful heavens above and "the sun's glare bouncing off the rocks," which only dried their bodies and their tongues further. He described how their "lips and tongues began to swell and turn black."[21] Their feet were on fire from the

Introduction

heat and the harsh, unforgiving flinty malpais, but they knew they must continue, that to linger too long could signal the end. Resting under the few available scrubby shade bushes produced dreams of verdant valleys flowing with rushing streams of cool water cascading in the shadow of shade trees. Waking up was a horrible experience, as the dreams faded and their senses returned to reality. At some points, Pershing had to force his comrade to his feet and continue moving. As Stotsenburg summed things up, "Every step that we took was only with the greatest exertion, knowing that if we gave it up it meant death."[22]

As the day lurched forward, the men had trouble staying awake, their energy sapped, burned up. The last of the whiskey was not consumed but rubbed on their exposed skin: the face, the neck, the upper chest. Then came the last of the water, consisting of only enough to fill a pair of canteen screw tops. These were their last drops, literally. Pershing offered to his companion his half, which Stotsenburg refused with equal gallantry. It was here they could imagine the end. The lieutenants decided they would continue until one or the other could go no farther; then his friend would proceed alone in a desperate search of water, another human, or anything that could bring them relief. Reality was unavoidable, as Stotsenburg wrote: "We ... agreed to these resolutions because both of us now considered that our case was desperate."[23]

They threw off every item that might lighten their load or slow them down. They discarded any unnecessary clothing. Pershing "mournfully" left on the rocks his Winchester rifle, a gift he had received from a fellow soldier. When Stotsenburg whispered to Pershing, "Things looked a little grim," a form of gallows humor, they smiled at one another, "no easy task with lips and tongues swollen like ours."[24] What possible encouragement could these men find in their life-threatening predicament but the comradeship they had shared for so long as young American soldiers? Perhaps one of the verses of Bliss's "Hold the Fort" hymn entered the mind of one or the other of the struggling lieutenants as they faced increasing threats to their very existence:

Introduction

> Fierce and long the battle rages
> But we will not fear.
> Help will come whene'er it's needed.
> Cheer, my comrades, cheer.

Death approached like a pale rider. The men stumbled forward, desperate to reach the Little Colorado and its reviving waters. But their strength was nearly gone. Sheer will was their soul motivation, a desperate survival instinct driving them toward nothing but water.

Then, a mirage in the distance. A man on a horse. Dreams crossed the path of reality. Their throaty shouts tumbled down the hill separating the dying from the vision. To their delight, the image did not vanish as they gathered their strength and hurried into yet another canyon toward rescue.

It was Sam, their missing guide.

When the lieutenants reached him, a single word passed through their lips: "Water! Water!"[25] The fortuitous rendezvous in the desert signaled a second chance for Pershing and Stotsenburg as they drank from Sam's oversized canteen, practically draining it. They made an impromptu camp in a scattering of shade as Sam lit a fire and prepared them a resuscitative meal of coffee and bacon.[26] Sam's rescue was not yet complete. He left his comrades and went in search of additional water, which he soon located in a lower canyon. He found in the seclusion of some large boulders a beautiful rock tank of rainwater.[27] This became a sanctuary for the next couple of days as the two lieutenants recovered from their near-fatal ordeal and did little else but sleep, their dreams of valley shade and cool streams banished.

Sam further redeemed his absence by tracking down the missing ponies, abandoned saddles, discarded clothes, and even Pershing's prized Winchester. Then, reaching the main trail, Sam spotted the long-missing Minus and the two mules. Reaching him, Sam saw a specter of a man driven half mad with anxiety and confusion. Stotsenburg describes him in his diary: "He was a ghastly sight when Sam brought him into camp.... he had been eating mud and his face and lips were covered with it."[28]

Having become separated from the lieutenants, Minus had lost his way. Without knowing, he had nearly stumbled back into the lieutenants' campsite. He also had accidentally stampeded their mules, and catching them had proven a nightmare. He lost the trail and even his direction; at one point, after catching the mules, Minus had decided to head back to Tuba City but had actually headed west instead of east. Now, the men gave him his own day to recover before they set out on their ultimate quest for the Grand Canyon.

The next morning, the men rose hopeful that their drama was behind them. They decided to send Minus back to Tuba City, for he had proven more of a detriment than a help to the group. Early that afternoon, having found a suitable trail, they encountered a Havasupai Indian named Burro and a boy who were out hunting. Burro was quite a sight to the men as he was wearing an antelope's head and a camouflaged shirt to lure his prey. The path to the Grand Canyon beckoned invitingly as the party entered the Kaibab Forest, where the ponderosa pine trees provided a cooling shade and a sweet scent. Along their way, they found articles that Minus had discarded in his delirium.

Up ahead, the yawning South Rim of the Grand Canyon, rimmed by pinon juniper trees, rose up to meet the weary party. The men reached a log cabin nestled near the rim, and Stotsenburg knew the owner, John Hance. He had served as a freight conductor at Fort Verde—Pershing described him as "a mule driver with the Sixth Cavalry in Arizona"[29]—and had arrived at the canyon in the early 1880s to mine gold, silver, and even asbestos. Once the mine had played out, he remained at the canyon rim, where he served as a guide to occasional, would-be tourists such as Pershing and Stotsenburg. Hance advertised in a Flagstaff newspaper: "Being thoroughly conversant with all the trails leading to the Grand Canyon of the Colorado, I am prepared to conduct parties thereto at any time."[30] Arizona sheriff Buckey O'Neill, who rode with Roosevelt's Rough Riders and was killed on San Juan Hill, Cuba, during the Spanish-American

War, said of Hance in 1893: "God made the canyon, John Hance the trails. Without the other, neither would be complete."[31]

Hance greeted the weary men heartily and prepared them food. Then they made their way to the canyon and saw for the first time the sublime vision they had sought across more than two hundred miles of unforgiving desert. Stotsenburg was captivated by what he saw: "We sat on the hill, awed by the wonders of nature now spread out before us. The magnificence of this view cannot be described. It was a long while before we could realize the grandeur of it."[32]

Pershing included in his autobiography his own response to the wonders of the Grand Canyon: "The impression of awe created in my mind at this first view has never been equaled. Since that day I have seen the highest peaks of the Rockies, stately, snowcapped Fujiyama in Japan, and the towering masses of the Andes and the Alps, but never have I witnessed a sight so marvelous as the Grand Canyon of the Colorado."[33]

The men tromped along the canyon, breathed in the sights, and enjoyed lunch on the trail prepared by Hance. Despite their earlier ordeals, they mustered the stamina to explore and climb until they reached a gurgling spring where they cooked their coffee. Stotsenburg later wrote, "The day was a most enjoyable one and we will never forget it."[34]

Again, in Willa Cather's *Song of the Lark*—the second novel of her Prairie Trilogy, which includes *O Pioneers!* and *My Ántonia*—the Nebraska author describes a scene the two army officers, who had nearly perished to reach the rim of the Grand Canyon, might have recognized. Having reached their destination, the challenges of their past days faded, replaced by the solid footing of assurance that they were safe:

> At last a kind of hopefulness broke in the air. In a moment the pine trees up on the edge of the rim were flashing with coppery fire. The thin red clouds which hung above their pointed tops began to boil and move rapidly, weaving in and out like smoke.... Little birds began to chirp in the bushes along the watercourse down at the bottom of the ravine, where every-

Introduction

thing was still dusky and pale. At first the golden light seemed to hang like a wave upon the rim of the canyon; the trees and bushes up there, which one scarcely notices at noon, stood out magnified by the slanting rays. Long, thin streaks of light began to reach quiveringly down into the canyon. The red sun rose rapidly above the tops of the blazing pines, and its glow burst into the gulf.... It bored into the wet, dark underbrush. The dripping cherry bushes, the pale aspens, and the frosty PINONS were glittering and trembling, swimming in the liquid gold.... The arch of sky overhead, heavy as lead a little while before, lifted, became more and more transparent, and one could look up into depths of pearly blue.[35]

After reaching the canyon bottom and the sandstone-red Colorado River, they hiked back out, having gained two perspectives of the canyon from the extremes of top to bottom. As for Sam, he was not impressed with what he called "the big hole" and, despite the challenges of completing their two-hundred-mile journey, chose not to enter the canyon. Instead, he killed a deer, Burro killed an antelope, and the party of white men and Native Americans feasted on a supper like none the lieutenants had eaten in some time. That evening, they washed their clothes and enjoyed sunset at the Grand Canyon. Stotsenburg recalled in his diary, "The grand red cliffs and peaks clothed in the deep green of the pines were wonderfully sublime in these lights."[36]

After less than two days at the canyon, the lieutenants set out on their return trip, perhaps a bit wiser, certainly better informed, and knowing Minus was ahead of them somewhere on his way back to Tuba City. While the return did not include the same, life-threatening dramas as the westward trip, there were additional mishaps. Reaching an abandoned Indian dam along the Moenkopi Wash, Pershing tried to lead a mule over the barrier, only to have the animal sink up to its ears in quicksand. The men worked for hours to rescue the beast, finally utilizing one of the tired ponies to pull the mule to safety. The lieutenants were covered in mud, sand, and alkali water, and moving hurriedly on to Tuba City seemed a good idea. (One concern was they would not catch up with Minus, who might beat them back to Fort Defiance, tell a tale about the missing officers, and produce a panic at the fort.)

They did reach the Mormon settlement before nightfall and slept soundly on a haystack. Before breakfast, they found Minus. The next day, the party reached Oraibi Spring without significant incident except Minus disappeared for the last time, along with nearly all of the food they had picked up from the Mormon women who had cooked for them in Tuba City. Repeatedly, Pershing showed himself to be a poor cook, unable to even make a decent cup of coffee. As they camped that day, Pershing burned the last of their bacon. As a final insult, their animals escaped one more time, and to catch them, the weary lieutenants "had to chase them around in the dark in their stocking feet, cutting themselves on sharp stones and bushes."[37] In his diary, Stotsenburg explains why the soldiers kept losing their stock: "There were no trees in that country and we could only find bunch grass or greasewood to tie up to, and it was easy for the mules to pull this up if they wished to do so."[38]

The next day, they covered ground to the Hopi settlement at Oraibi and dined on soft-boiled eggs, flapjacks, and coffee, all prepared by Indian women, who ground the corn on a stone metate. It was a pleasant moment after so many difficulties, and as Stotsenburg stated, they "felt for once like blessing everything and everybody except Minus."[39] Suddenly, water was no longer a scarce commodity to the lieutenants, who only days earlier had experienced full-throated dehydration. After washing their hands and morning dishes, they threw the soapy water onto the ground, raising a howl from the Indians. The lieutenants observed that the Indians "are very careful of their water," believing "after they have carried it so far that it is too precious to use for washing purposes."[40]

After a ride of thirty-five miles, Pershing and Stotsenburg reached Keams Canyon and finished their trip back to Fort Defiance the same day (July 3). They returned with tales to tell. To their comrades at the fort, they appeared worn out, desperate, mud caked, rank, and bound for the sleep of the dead. For the

Introduction

next two or three days, all they could manage was sleep. While they were proud of their difficult march, they also "felt perfectly satisfied that we knew how not to go to the Grand Canyon."[41]

Young John J. Pershing and his companion had, indeed, completed a five-hundred-mile round trip to the Grand Canyon, and the memories of their adventure would never fade. But this trip had proven to be more misadventure than adventure. While the men had survived, they had grossly miscalculated the circumstances of their endeavor, and it had almost cost them their lives.[42]

John Pershing had other destinies to fulfill, even if he could not have known so as a twenty-eight-year-old second lieutenant stationed in the remote, hostile environs of the American Southwest. He and his companion had proven themselves too impetuous and overly self-assured. They had gone into their experience without proper planning, having failed to even accommodate their own personal logistics. Had Pershing died in the desert during the sweltering summer of 1889, U.S. history—and perhaps the history of the twentieth century—would have turned on a completely different axis.

Nearly thirty years later, 2nd Lt. John Joseph Pershing had risen in the ranks to general of the armies, the highest possible rank in the U.S. military. World War I had been underway for nearly three years before Pershing and hundreds of thousands of doughboys, all of whom served under his command, arrived on the western front. When Pershing first led American forces into battle in September 1918 at the long-held German salient at St. Mihiel, he was in command of more men on a single battlefield than had ever been gathered previously in U.S. history. What had changed for Pershing during those three decades between those early days in the American West to Europe's battle-scarred killing fields?

During those thirty years from West Point to the western front, Pershing experienced a colorful and varied military career: action during the Spanish-American War in 1898; postings in Asia, including subduing the fanatical Filipino Moros in 1903;

Introduction

an appointment as a military attaché in 1905 during the Russo-Japanese War; and a return to the Philippines with service as the commander of the Military Department of Mindanao and the governor of the Moro Province in 1909–13.

While overseas service became an important aspect of Pershing's pre–World War I experiences, he gained another, perhaps more formative experience during various service points in the American West. In fact, when Pershing received word from his father-in-law, Sen. Francis Emory Warren (R-WY), in May 1917 informing him that he had been tapped to command U.S. forces in Europe, he was stationed at Fort Sam Houston outside San Antonio, Texas.

Much of his time out west found Pershing serving as a young cavalry officer, beginning with post assignments in 1886 to New Mexico at Forts Wingate, Stanton, and Bayard. These years constituted a colorful chapter in the life of John Pershing; his personal tale of the American West included adventures as a young, horse soldier-officer during the final days of Apache resistance in the Southwest. They were the last days of Geronimo and other Apache leaders, when Arizona and New Mexico still represented an untamed frontier of blue-clad soldiers, Native Americans, cowboys, rustlers, miners—all battling a hostile desert environment set against a rough-and-tumble landscape of mountains, mesas, rocky outcroppings, arroyos, and endless vistas dotted with cacti and Spanish Bayonet. For Pershing, the Southwest was a land where a young cavalryman could cut his military teeth.

But his experiences in the Southwest were just the beginning of Pershing's exploits in the West. He saw assignments over the years in the Dakotas, during the Ghost Dance uprising and the battle of Wounded Knee, and a posting at Montana's Fort Assinniboine. Following his years in Asia, Pershing returned to the West with a command at the Presidio in San Francisco and a prolonged assignment on the Mexican-U.S. border in El Paso. That led to his command of the Punitive Expedition, tasked with riding deep into northern Mexico to neutralize the threat of Pancho Villa and his fellow pistoleros.

Introduction

Essentially, all these experiences spent in the American West were formative for Pershing, since they served as preparatory precursors to his ultimate assignment as the top American commander during the Great War. If, in fact, the American frontier and, in a larger context, the West provided a cauldron in which Americans tested themselves during the nineteenth century, it is no less true for John Pershing. His story is, in a sense, a historical western.

Essentially, all these earlier experiences of John J. Pershing's were, in their own way, *frontier* experiences. He took to the saddle as a uniformed cavalryman and guerrilla campaigner in the American West. His service in Cuba during the Spanish-American War was in a similar vein, notes Pershing historian Donald Smythe, as Cuba (and soon the Philippines) represented an "extension of America's frontier as she moved out to make the Caribbean an American lake.... The Philippines was really the frontier, America's farthest-flung possession, containing strange people with strange customs."[43] Each represented another frontier environ, a new American West, as Pershing engaged in additional guerrilla fighting. For Pershing, even Europe and the Great War would prove to be yet another West, with another frontier experience—the western front—where the fight was different and more complex but still represented something new.

Time in the Wilderness tells the story of Pershing's experiences and his time spent in the wilderness of the American frontier, wherever it moved, throughout the late nineteenth and early twentieth centuries. How the West formed one of the greatest U.S. military commanders and how he adapted to life on a variety of frontiers, including his misplaced Grand Canyon adventure, is a tale filled with drama and challenge, with lessons learned, and with experiences that provided the "iron sharpening iron" backdrop of a soldier in the making, while presenting the good, the bad, and the ugly of Pershing's experiences in the West. There is a compelling story here, one littered with heroism and challenge, insight and vision, and a series of experiences that ultimately formed a young Missourian into the military commander he was destined to become.

Introduction

It is a story that needs retelling. A century ago, the name of John J. Pershing crossed the lips of every American. At the end of World War I and for years to follow, he continued to loom large in the American psyche. But time and other history have left him in the shadows. For those who don't regularly peruse the secondary history holdings of university libraries, a quick trip to one's local bookshop tells a version of the story. Shelves contain dozens and even scores of books on the Civil War and World War II, including entire biographies on their generals, such as Grant and Sherman, Lee and Stonewall, Eisenhower and Patton. Wedged in between these works, one might find no more books on World War I than could be counted on one or maybe two hands. As for John Joseph Pershing, few fully framed biographies have been written about him in the past thirty years. My goal with this book has been to write a biography of Pershing's life to the verge of his involvement in World War I, the culmination of a military career that began to take shape thirty years earlier in the deserts of New Mexico. Although he served in the U.S. Army for decades, he did not enter military service as a man ready to meet all the challenges set before him in 1917–18. Like all soldiers, he had to grow into that role. And much of that growth took place in the wilderness of the American West.

ONE

Childhood, 1860–73

During the Great War, the sprawling worldwide conflict that provided the backdrop for the culminating years of John J. Pershing's lengthy military career, the general of the army penned a letter to a comrade that included the following philosophical musings: "Strange things do happen in the world. Is it not fortunate that none of us knows what is going to happen to him?"[1] He understood how the ultimate plan for one's life depends on not simply one's self but also others who may well have laid a groundwork on which the next generation stands. Pershing knew that before he could become a successful, even famed American, four generations of Pershings had preceded him and made their own marks on the American landscape. So self-conscious was he that his success began by standing on the shoulders of previous Pershings, the opening lines of his memoirs state that very sentiment: "It is a matter of no little pride that my forebears were made of the fiber, mental as well as physical, found in the common people that form the backbone of this country. Originally of upstanding, though humble, European stock, we like to think they brought to America a worthwhile heritage of human traditions and achievements."[2]

With the first generation of Pershings arriving from Europe in America around the mid-eighteenth century, John Pershing links his predecessors with the movement of the American frontier. They were unremarkable as American pioneers, notes Pershing, just common folks. "Like millions of other Americans, both the men and women were great in their simple, honest, wholesome way." They endured the challenges, hardships, dangers that accompanied life in the howling wilderness of early America. For Pershing, his people could be counted among the many who were "found in the columns that settled the Western Reserve," the frontier that included the six thousand square miles of land stretching along the south shore of Lake Erie, colonial land that would become northeastern Ohio.[3]

From the mid-eighteenth century and through the century that followed, various and sundry Pershings migrated westward, settling in the Northwest Territory; then they headed to Missouri and the Trans-Mississippi West, only to leapfrog across the Great Plains in wagon trains bound for land in Oregon and gold in California. Pershings fought the Indians on whose lands they encroached, defended their families against outlaws, and engaged in virtually every war between the French and Indian War and the Civil War. While the Pershings represented his paternal family roots, Pershing also recognized other families on his mother's side, including the Thompsons and the Brothertons. Nearly all ancestors on both sides helped settle the American frontier as farmers.

John Joseph Pershing experienced the final stage of frontier America, and the experience altered him as much as it had his ancestors. As for the direct Pershing line in America, John was a son of the fifth generation. The name "Pershing" was the result of an eventual anglicizing of the medieval Germanic family name of Pfoershing or some other European variant.[4] Pershing begins his family tree with a Frederick Pfoerschin born in 1724 in Alsace, a region long disputed between the French and the Germans not far from the banks of the Rhine River.[5] Growing up, Frederick spoke both French and German but little English. When John Pershing reached Europe in 1917 to lead American troops, his arrival symbolized a full circle of history for the Pershing family. U.S. forces would battle across ground that was inherently the Pershing family's homeland.

Due to royal oppression, particularly at the hands of the French king Louis XIV, Pershing's people began abandoning their central European roots for dreams of freedom in other lands, including colonial America. These French Protestants, called Huguenots, were Christian exiles in search of new homes. Frederick left Alsace, migrated to Holland, and took passage out of Amsterdam on board the immigrant ship *Jacob*. Since Frederick had little money and no one waiting for him in America to ensure his success, he surrendered himself to the temporary life of a "redemptioner," a type of indentured servant who paid off his ship's passage through hard labor. After a miserable voyage that included poor food, unsanitary conditions, and sleeping in a swaying hammock, Frederick and 249 fellow passengers arrived in 1749 in Philadelphia, where he found plenty of other immigrants of German extraction. The history of the Pershings in America had begun.

Within a year of his arrival in colonial America, Frederick married Maria Elizabeth Weygandt, and the couple settled in York County. Maria eventually produced nine children, and the sixth provided the second generation of Pershings leading to John Joseph. His great-grandfather Daniel was born in 1769. He became a Methodist minister, representing an early convert to a new Protestant sect in America. He married Christena Milliron, and they had a dozen children, including John's grandfather (number seven among his siblings), one Joseph M., born in 1810. In his maturity, Pershing's grandfather married Elizabeth Davis. Then came John Fletcher Pershing, born in 1834 in Westmoreland County, Pennsylvania. But while the first three generations of Pershings had called Pennsylvania home, John Fletcher, as an adult, was caught up in yet another era of Americans moving farther west. The West represented "the land of opportunity, the land that beaconed irresistibly to every adventurous spirit." With no more financial wealth than his great-grandfather had brought to America, John Fletcher—"a strapping, broad-shouldered six-footer"—lit out for the western territories with wanderlust as his only companion.[6]

This John Pershing grew up with little opportunity for an

Childhood, 1860–73

extensive book-based education, but he was a student of the Scriptures who took dual pleasure in studying theology and the law. He was also a hearty man of the frontier, having grown up working the family farm. As he moved westward in search of his destiny, John Fletcher labored in a logging camp bordering the banks of the Ohio River and experienced an early adventure floating a raft of lumber from Ohio to New Orleans. His son, John Joseph, retained many memories of the stories his father told of his boyhood adventures. Young Pershing imagined his father as a latter-day western explorer, likening him to the French colonizer La Salle.

After more than a century of Pershings staking their livelihoods in Pennsylvania, Pershing's father became a man of the West, seeking adventure and opportunity in a new frontier. In 1857 John Fletcher landed in St. Louis, where he worked as a produce broker. While hardly a job filled with adventure, it was steady work, and St. Louis was an exciting metropolis of the West, a busy river port with a bustling riverfront of warehouses and trading outlets. The city boasted a population close to 160,000 during the 1850s, having experienced significant growth since its early days as little more than a trading post established by the French explorer Pierre Laclède.

In time, the restless John Fletcher sought new opportunities farther west in north-central Missouri and went into business with friends. The partnership of Stone, Pershing, and Jennings subcontracted with the North Missouri Railroad, then building a line between St. Charles, Missouri, and the outpost settlement of Macon, a town located on a line of the Hannibal and St. Joseph Railroad, itself a sub-line of the greater Chicago, Burlington and Quincy Railroad. John Fletcher took a job as a section manager along a seven-mile stretch of track extending from Laclede, Missouri—named for the same French explorer—westward to Meadville. Soon, the half-settled John Fletcher met a girl in nearby Warrenton whose family had migrated to Missouri from Kentucky. Then in her midtwenties, Anne Elizabeth Thompson, who would one day become the mother of a great American general, "combined the charm of Kentucky with the self-reliance of the West."[7] The couple married in March 1859. Their first home was a humble clapboard house near the railroad line that John Fletcher helped maintain as a section boss. It belonged to a local judge and had previously served as housing for his slaves. Starting out simply in their marriage, the Pershings were not above living in such a simple dwelling.

The Pershings did have to accommodate themselves to one serious consideration, given the turn of events unfolding on the American political stage in 1860. With the nation seriously divided over the issue of slavery and its expansion into the western territories, the Pershings came from entirely different backgrounds. John Fletcher's family had always lived in the North, and Anne's people were longtime Southerners. The Thompson clan had called North Carolina its home during the Revolutionary War and moved to Tennessee during the 1820s. There, in Blount County, Anne was born in 1835. She was only two years old when her father packed up and placed his family in a covered wagon and moved to Warren County, Missouri, where slavery existed, even if to a lesser extent than in the Deep South. Northern Missouri during the 1830s represented a region of frontier living. As John Joseph describes it in his autobiography, "During those earlier years in Missouri life was very primitive."[8]

Pershing had vivid memories of his mother as a gentle Southern woman in manners, speech, and bearing. He adored his maternal grandfather and could recall riding on his shoulders down to the family sawmill. Once the Civil War erupted, the Thompsons were not simply strident supporters of the Southern cause. Two of Anne's brothers held opposite sympathies during the conflict. One of young Pershing's uncles joined the Union Army and served under General Grant during the 1863 siege of Vicksburg; a second uncle supported the Confederacy, at least in spirit, never donning a uniform during the divisive conflict. As for the Pershing household, John Fletcher remained a staunch Union man. But even as a young boy, John Joseph Pershing "used to hear alternately both Unionists and Southern sympathizers air their views or relate their experiences."[9]

John and Anne Pershing proved quite suited to one another, and, despite the outbreak of war, there was no division at home. Instead, they proved themselves to be as upwardly mobile as any other man and woman starting out in life together in an unsettled section of northern Missouri. Laclede became their home. Several children came along, with John Joseph Pershing the first, entering the world on September 13, 1860. Eight additional siblings followed over the next sixteen years, all of whom were born in Laclede. Three died in infancy. His three surviving sisters—Mary Elizabeth, Anna May, and Grace—would each impact his life in special ways. The eldest, Elizabeth, played a crucial role in encouraging her older brother to attend the U.S. Military Academy at West Point. May became a caregiver to her aged, ailing, hero-brother, and Grace, the youngest, married a friend of Pershing's, a fellow cavalry officer.

Although born and raised in Missouri, Pershing, along with his family, would eventually develop extraordinary roots in Nebraska. One day, as a thirty-year-old army officer, he would teach at the University of Nebraska–Lincoln, where one of his young students was destined to become one of the state's most popular writers. Willa Cather was also a child of the midwestern frontier and thirteen years younger. She grew up in Red Cloud, Nebraska, a small town she would immortalize through such fictional works as *O Pioneers!* and *My Ántonia*.[10] In the latter novel, published in the last year of the Great War, Cather renames her fictional town Black Hawk, exchanging one Native American leader for another. Her Black Hawk is reminiscent of Pershing's Laclede, which she describes early in the novel. Sharing a train ride with Jim Burden—"as we still call him in the West"—the narrator observes:

> While the train flashed through never-ending miles of ripe wheat, by country towns and bright-flowered pastures and oak groves wilting in the sun.... The dust and heat, the burning wind, reminded us of many things. We were talking about what it is like to spend one's childhood in little towns like these, buried in wheat and corn, under stimulating extremes

of climate: burning summers when the world lies green and billowy beneath a brilliant sky, when one is fairly stifled in vegetation, in the color and smell of strong weeds and heavy harvests; blustery winters with little snow, when the whole country is stripped bare and gray as sheet-iron. We agreed that no one who had not grown up in a little prairie town could know anything about it. It was a kind of freemasonry, we said.[11]

Like Cather, Pershing never completely outgrew his small-town roots, and the adult versions of both the writer and the soldier knew they owed much to their respective days spent in Red Cloud and Laclede.

The Civil War overshadowed Pershing's first five years. Early settlers, including the Thompsons, had migrated westward from Kentucky, Tennessee, and Virginia, and some of them brought their slaves with them. Even though Missouri was admitted as a slave state in 1821, it did not secede from the Union forty years later but remained one of four such states identified as "border states." Perhaps more than the others—Kentucky, Maryland, and Delaware—Missouri was seriously divided, and the sympathies held by advocates on both sides of the slavery issue tended to run deep. During the 1850s, something of a dress rehearsal for the Civil War had unfolded in the borderlands between Missouri and the Kansas Territory. These violent days were known as "Bleeding Kansas," as partisans on both sides fought one another over how much farther west slavery should be extended. Between 1854 and 1859, hundreds of Missourians and Kansans had raided one another's settlements and towns, shot one another, and burned their cabins across the dark and bloody border ground. Pro-slavery Missouri "border ruffians" voted illegally to turn Kansas into a slave state, as Kansas "Jayhawkers" (the rabid, abolitionist-martyr John Brown could be counted among them) struck Missouri farms and "kidnapped" slaves away to freer soil in the West.

During the early days of the war, though, the violence did not find its way to Laclede, and the conflict actually provided opportunities for John and Anne. As early as October 1861, John managed to save enough money to abandon his work as a section boss and go into business as a storekeeper. The family moved to a house in Laclede, one a bit larger and more suited to a family on the rise in their frontier community. The local general store owned by the Lomax family was up for sale. Pershing purchased the store's inventory and soon gained an appointment as a sutler to the Eighteenth Missouri Volunteer Infantry, which was stationed outside Laclede. Through his services, he provided soldiers with those items that Uncle Sam or the state of Missouri did not, including tobacco, cookies, cakes, fruits, knives, wooden combs, medicines, and even joke books. By 1863 he made available the same service to the First Regiment of the Missouri State Militia. This business proved lucrative for John Fletcher, and his general store became such an important mercantile business that he even began to serve as a wholesaler for other, smaller general store owners in the outlying area. After a year or so, he left his sutler work, which required him to leave home several times and follow the soldiers wherever their unit was assigned, to concentrate solely on his business dealings in Laclede. With customers frequenting his store, John Fletcher also became the local postmaster. His expanding prosperity allowed him to buy a lumberyard, and he invested in a pair of nearby farms—one with 80 acres and the other of 160 acres (the typical quarter-section of a frontier township)—situated near Laclede. He also moved his family to yet another house—a long-term family home, as things turned out—that was previously known as the DeGrew House. Framed by a requisite white picket fence, it signaled a midwestern, middle-class prosperity with its white clapboard siding and a roof featuring a trio of gables.

While the Pershing family had gradually made its mark on Laclede, the sphere of its midwestern world was a small one. The community was a frontier settlement of six hundred local citizens, nearly all white, with little to suggest a significant future. But as was often the case among the pioneering immigrants of the nineteenth century, hope almost always sprang eternal. The arrival of two railroad lines was important. If a railroad bypassed a community, it could easily mean no growth or even eventual unacceptability as an attractive settlement site for later arrivals. Otherwise, Laclede did not have much to offer beyond easy rail access. Its streets were unpaved; there were no sidewalks or even a church building in the community until after the Civil War had ended, even though it boasted several saloons. At that time, Laclede's one-room school did not even have a permanent teacher.[12]

But during the Civil War, such a small town could prove a tempting target for one faction of fighters or another. With guerrilla, or irregular, units moving throughout the countryside as semi-military gangs, it should have been expected that eventually one would find its way to Laclede. Such an attack came to the sleepy Missouri town on the afternoon of June 18, 1864.

About four o'clock, Henry Lomax, who worked as a clerk in John Fletcher's general store and was the son of the store's original owner, suddenly burst into the mercantile. Breathing heavily, he shouted excitedly, "Bushwhackers are riding into town! They're headed right this way."[13] Lomax was announcing a gang of Confederate sympathizers, but the townspeople could only imagine which ones. Multiple groups of bushwhackers were known throughout northern Missouri, and most filled their would-be victims with fear. Such men as William C. Quantrill, William "Bloody Bill" Anderson, the Younger brothers, and Frank and Jesse James had garnered notorious reputations among those who remained loyal to the Union. John Fletcher Pershing was one such citizen of Laclede. His sutler service made it clear which side he supported in the war. In his youth, the elder Pershing had been a passive supporter of slavery, but he had changed his mind on that issue years ago. With the war on, he only redoubled his loyalty to the Union, flying an American flag over his storefront every business day, a banner Anne had sewn with her own hands. When some of his Confederacy-supporting neighbors complained and even threatened him for his obvious loyalties, John Fletcher was clear, stating unequivocally he would shoot any man who tried to take down the Stars and

Stripes outside his store. The flag elicited cheers from trainloads of Union soldiers as they passed through Laclede. On this particular mid-June day, that flag marked him and his store as targets for the Confederate bushwhackers headed toward Laclede.

Soon, fifteen bushwhackers rode into town and began terrorizing the frightened citizenry. Their leader was known in the region. Capt. Clifton Holtzclaw had carried out other such raids on neighboring towns that supported the Union. As his force rampaged down the town's main street, it took only seconds for pandemonium to become the order of the day. Many citizens hid, knowing that such bushwhacker gangs were always well armed and did not hesitate to kill.

Within minutes of their arrival, they did just that, rounding up everyone they could find and corralling them on the town square directly opposite the Pershing family home. Holtzclaw explained that he and his gang were raiding the town in retribution for a Union raid on Keytesville, another northern Missouri hamlet thirty miles to the south. He shouted that Laclede harbored abolitionist sympathizers and that such men needed hanging. When a local named David Crowder, a discharged veteran of the First Missouri State Militia and one of Laclede's leading citizens, fired at the Holtzclaw gang from a nearby building, he wounded gang member Jim Nave, who then killed Crowder. When Laclede resident and local attorney Jonathan Jones tried to make a run for it, he, too, was shot down in cold blood. With most of the townspeople isolated and under guard, members of the bushwhacking gang began to fan out. One immediate target was John Fletcher's store. (The Pershing home was just five doors down the block, with both buildings situated on the north side of the town square.)

John Fletcher was not a man to surrender his livelihood that easily. More was at stake than met the eye, for many residents of Laclede utilized Pershing's store safe to keep their most valuable items, since the community had no bank. His store was the largest in town, plus the challenging American flag drew the bushwhackers' attention immediately as they headed toward its front door.

Pershing was in his store that afternoon, heard the shots, and hurriedly grabbed his shotgun to defend his own but cursed his luck. Although typically he kept the gun loaded, earlier that day he had removed the shells since three-year-old John had been playing under the store counter. Pershing had no choice but to slip out the back door and head quietly through an alley homeward, where he could load his shotgun. In the meantime, a pair of Holtzclaw's raiders was at the Pershing house, questioning Anne Pershing about her husband's whereabouts. She claimed she did not know and offered to let them in to search. They had just left, satisfied Mr. Pershing was elsewhere, when John Fletcher entered the back door. He loaded his gun and looked out the front window to the street, where he observed Holtzclaw's men were not hanging anyone, fortunately, but were looting the town's business fronts instead.

With what he saw before him, including the bodies of two Laclede men dead in the street, John Fletcher was ready to return the favor to Holtzclaw's men. John raised his shotgun and prepared to exact a cost to the bushwhackers. Before he pulled the trigger, a frightened Anne rushed to her husband, threw her arms around him, and pleaded with him to stop.

"Please don't shoot," she begged. "You're only one against all of them. You'll be killed, and maybe us too. Let the money go."[14]

Her words rang true, of course, and her angry husband lowered his gun. He helplessly watched the Holtzclaw men raiding his store, stealing his goods and his pride at the same moment. John and his siblings would grow up with a father. While the raid went on, Holtzclaw swaggered in the street, shouting that "if any of his southern friends were abused . . . he would deal with them severely, killing two for one."[15]

At its center, the Holtzclaw attack on Laclede served as another example of the kind of activity that unfolded across rural northern Missouri and eastern Kansas during the Civil War. Such irregular units moved about on horseback, held no local loyalties other than a spirit of revenge toward those who served and supported the Union. They regularly "embraced frontier-style warfare."[16]

While many such gangs supported the Confederate cause, there were also pro-Union guerrilla fighters—even if unofficially (through the decades following the war, irregular fighters were almost never included in official military reunions)—including the Kansas-based "Red Legs." These irregulars included between fifty and a hundred men, even some teenagers, whose actions became as notorious as those of the Confederate supporters. At times, they raided as far east as Columbus, Missouri, less than a hundred miles from Laclede. Some in the group made up the "buckskin scouts," who at times included those destined for frontier stardom, such as James "Wild Bill" Hickok and William "Buffalo Bill" Cody, whom John Joseph Pershing would meet years later as a young cavalry officer. Cody once summed up the actions of the Red Legs, admitting, "We were the biggest thieves on record."[17]

The Holtzclaw raid on Laclede was not simply a story told around the family dinner table years later for the young John. He thereafter counted the attack as among his first clear memories as a child, even if he had "only a hazy recollection" of the attackers themselves, as he likely never even saw them. "I clearly recall that I was badly scared for fear father would be killed," he wrote in his memoirs, "and that mother made me and my small brother lie flat on the floor until the raiders disappeared."[18]

Sectional rivalry, national politics, and simple human greed nearly brought the town of Laclede to its knees that day. It suffered great losses, of course, in blood and treasure. Two men familiar to their neighbors were dead. Most of the raiders escaped with pilfered funds taken from business cash drawers amounting to approximately $4,000—no small sum for such a small town—plus a few firearms; a quantity of alcohol; other valuables, including jewelry and watches; and some of the best horses in Laclede. Pershing would claim a loss of $811 in money and goods. Not all ended in Holtzclaw's favor. When Nave was shot, his captain sent him out of town in a local mail delivery buggy with four comrades, two in the buggy and another pair on horseback.[19] They would have their own problems.

When the raid opened, a few locals managed to escape and

reached the Union outpost at Brookfield, less than three miles away. The commanding lieutenant dispatched some of his men on a train for Laclede, while he and others mounted their horses and whipped them toward the town under siege. The soldiers on the train managed to catch up with the five fleeing Holtzclaw men. Racing alongside the buggy on the road running parallel to the tracks, the soldiers fired rifles and shotguns from the train, and the bushwhackers returned fire since the fleeing men "had some distance to go by the side of the track, before they could turn off."[20] All five bushwhackers were hit. Nave and two of his comrades died, while two others were wounded and captured. As for the mounted soldiers, by the time they reached Laclede, Holtzclaw had scattered his men in every direction. None were ever captured even though Union troops chased various targets in a circuit that ran sixty miles until they ended back in Laclede where the terror attack had begun.

Throughout the raid, under the orders of their frightened mother, three-year-old John "and his two-year-old brother, James, had huddled on the floor until the raiders departed." They had watched their father load his gun as their mother begged him not to risk his life and theirs. John Fletcher had wisely taken her counsel, and the family remained intact to recover and rebuild from their losses and the scars that violence had placed on them that June day in their little frontier town.[21]

What had happened that day that would have a lifelong impact on the Pershing toddler who would one day grow up to see more violence and bloodshed both in the context of war and outside of it? The adult Pershing always remembered the fear, both his own and his mother's, and the event remained permanently seared in his mind's eye. Young Pershing had been introduced to some of the ugliest versions of humanity—those who kill for revenge, who kill indiscriminately. He became aware that day of human death and the tragedy that accompanies it. He saw the aftermath of the attack, perhaps even saw his first human corpse, lying in the street, blood staining the earth. That day, Pershing heard his first gunshots fired in anger, in the name of revenge, and knew that innocent people had been hurt. Historian Donald Smythe imagines what all this might have meant to both the young and the adult John Pershing: "He was to know fear again in later life, although not, it seems, as much as the average man. He was to hear the crack of rifles thousands and thousands of times. He was to have experience of men taking from one another, and hurting one another, and killing one another. He was to see many, many men die before he himself came to pass on eighty-four years later."[22]

How many times during the days following the attack did Anne Pershing take her two boys in her arms and thank her God that her family had survived this bloody, violent raid will never be known. But it is unimaginable that the family, including John, was ever the same again.

Following the Holtzclaw raid, a detachment of Union troops began to encamp close to the ravaged Missouri town. Little John Joseph was already fascinated with the blue-clad soldiers he saw coming and going in his little hamlet, and, perhaps ironically, Anne even agreed to sew her boy his own blue uniform so he could mimic the look of his military protectors. It would prove the first of many military uniforms he would don over the decades. Those troops he visited thought him quite the precocious boy and were delighted with his youthful admiration. "I certainly saw a lot of soldiers as a child," Pershing later recalled, "and liked to be with them."[23] Other than his parents, these men in uniform would represent Pershing's earliest heroes.

In time, the Civil War and such attacks on civilians as the Holtzclaw raid came to an end, even if the memories would linger for decades. For the Pershings, the opportunity came to put the war behind them and get back to the dual business of raising a family and becoming more prosperous. But even as the war receded into the past, the conflict continued to impact the small sphere of Laclede. As Pershing recalled, "The flotsam of war left in this borderland many good for nothing characters." The frontier element in Pershing's neck of northern Missouri continued even as he moved from toddler to teenager. His town became home to a "worthless sort of whites," including "criminals and even desperadoes" who would have "an unwholesome influence upon the younger generation, and long after the war respect for the law and order continued at a low ebb."[24]

As the war ended and guerrilla fighting lost its relevance, such irregulars as the James brothers and Cole Younger and his siblings represented prime examples of what Pershing would later call "proof of the degenerating contagion that existed in that part of the country"—lawless elements that were still applauded in "the sensational press" and elevated to folklore status. Bank robbing and horse stealing seemingly became the fallback options of Laclede's "general lawlessness," as local boys joined gangs of horse thieves. Several eventually "landed in the state penitentiary."[25]

Laclede, during the days of Pershing's youth, became known as a "wild and woolly" town, and the greater region of northern Missouri gained an unsavory reputation of frontier lawlessness that continued for most of a decade following the Civil War. The hamlet became known for its "unsavory characters" who would "come to town on Saturdays, carouse at the two saloons, and then gallop through the streets yelling and firing their pistols in the traditional manner of the wild west," noted Pershing, who actually witnessed such activity firsthand. "As a boy I saw such exhibitions." These same years marked the early cattle drives along the Sedalia and Baxter Springs Trail from southern Texas to railheads in Sedalia, Missouri, just eighty miles south of Laclede, before the Chisholm Trail and advancing railroads westward shifted the cattle drive business over into neighboring Kansas. In the end, life on the frontier had the capacity to either break a man or make him. In Pershing's case, it would be the latter.[26]

TWO

Community, 1873–82

As the Civil War receded into memory, Laclede and the surrounding region outpaced its lawless reputation as new families of eastern emigrants from Illinois, Indiana, and Ohio reached Linn County, expanded the population, established new farms, and developed the commercial potential of north-central Missouri. Pershing's father still ran his general store and even began selling the latest agricultural equipment. His store remained a mecca for the bustling community—the post office was still located there—and John Fletcher was one of the town's leading citizens. Always interested in Republican politics, he was approached to run for the state legislature and later for Congress, but he turned down both offers. His loyalty was to the town he had called home since before the war and to the rearing of his six children.

Three girls and two boys ran in and out of the Pershing household each day, five siblings who could count their parents among the best they could possibly have had. (A sixth sibling, Ward, was born in 1874. He survived into adulthood, while three others—twins Rose and Ruth, born in 1872, and Frederick, born in 1876—all died in infancy.) The Pershing children were expected to do their assigned chores, as a good work ethic was one of the most important lessons their father wished to instill in them. In his younger days, John was assigned to pull weeds from the family garden and later to work in the family stable. Henry Lomax, who had worked as a clerk in Pershing's store and later became one of the town's most influential bankers, remembered the family dynamic: "I didn't regard Pershing as an autocrat in his family. He was for discipline in his family, and so was Mrs. Pershing. They were good parents and the children were fond of them."[1] But even as young John proved himself a hard worker, while his mother and father meted out regular lessons on obedience and responsibility, John also gained a reputation among some neighborhood observers as a spirited lad. As one recalled years later, "Oh yes, John had devilment in him—nothing mean about it—just a little quiet, sly devilment."[2]

With the frontier element always little more than a stone's throw away from the adolescent John, for a time he fell under the influence of the local Huckleberry Finn, a street lad named "Feather" Hawkins. He invited eleven-year-old John to join him behind "Old Man Biggers" tobacco barn outside town to enjoy his first chew of tobacco. John spent the remainder of the day lying on a haystack "as sick and sorry as a boy can be only at his first taste of tobacco."[3] (It would be a lesson ultimately forgotten, for the adult Pershing proved a regular smoker.) On another occasion, Feather encouraged a small cadre of boys, including John, to join him for a daring daytime raid on a local peach orchard, with the ringleader insisting he had received permission of the owner, "Old Margrave," as long as they did not give the trees a shake. The owner's brother caught the pack in the act, their pockets full of fruit, and the boys scattered to the winds, but only after being recognized to the last man. The boys held a subsequent council to determine how they should handle the situation, and Pershing was appointed to deliver the group's apology. "With a meekness that I can never forget," he remembered, "I told him how sorry we were, and with the promise not to repeat the offense he let us off."[4] Such were the innocent adventures of Laclede's version of a Tom Sawyer gang.

As young Pershing moved from adolescence into his early teen years, he became a reasonably good-looking man. In his preteens, he still had curly, light-colored hair. In time, he grew to nearly six feet in height and strong, the result of working hard on the family farm. Education was always important in the Pershing household, and school was a constant for him and his siblings. His first teacher, outside his parents—Anne had already taught him to write two-syllable words—was Sally Crowder, who ran something similar to a kindergarten out of her home. (Her father had been killed during the Holtzclaw raid.) Then he was sent to Miss Ella Seward's school, which was also home centered. Her father was the local Congregationalist minister (by this time Laclede boasted several churches) and would read scripture and lead prayers with the children. But it seems that Pershing's most memorable experience was when Miss Seward required her young charge to recite the simple lines of "Mary Had a Little Lamb." This exercise in early elocution would prove terrorizing to Pershing, who, dressed in his best, muffed his public appearance. He recalled, "The words would not come. They had left me. After a dreadful pause, mother, who sat well up in the front, came to the rescue." Unbelievably, writing seventy years later, Pershing still became clammy at the mere memory, claiming, "Often to this day when I get up to speak the latent memory of that first experience comes over me with distinctly unpleasant effects."[5]

Young Pershing was an avid reader. His parents modeled the interest first—Anne was more educated than the average woman of her time and place—and the family library had enough books to John's liking to keep him busy between chores, school, and his various outdoor games and play. At the center of the library were the Bible and biblical commentaries, as well as classical literature including *Pilgrim's Progress*, *Aesop's Fables*, *Robinson Crusoe*, and biographies of such frontier heroes as Daniel Boone and Davy Crockett. Shakespeare's plays proved popular with young John, who "used to learn and dramatically recite for the family and at school long passages from his works."[6] (Perhaps Mary and her lambs had not completely halted Pershing from public speaking after all.) He enjoyed his *McGuffey's Eclectic Readers*, especially the fifth and sixth readers, which contained "a collection of literary gems." But even if such books drew the young Pershing's interest, as a boy of the frontier he was drawn to the popular adolescent literature of his day, Beadle's "dime novels," which featured enough adventure, heroic action, and western storytelling to fill the dreams of even the most unimaginative of boys. Since these "blood and thunder" storybooks—they served as the graphic novels of the late nineteenth century—were not as popular with adults, Pershing, like other boys, sometimes enjoyed "the hairbreadth escapes of the heroes of these blood-curdling tales" surreptitiously, including at school, and was occasionally "caught with a novel hidden behind my history or geography."[7]

One of the most important family influences for young Pershing was religion. The local Methodist Church was established in 1866, and the Pershings were members, with John Fletcher taking the lead in getting the church building finally constructed. Willa Cather again would have recognized the significance of a small church in a small prairie town, as she reminisced of a winter's walk in *My Ántonia*:

> The children, in their bright hoods and comforters, never walked, but always ran from the moment they left their door, beating their mittens against their sides. When I got as far as the Methodist Church, I was about halfway home, I can remember how glad I was when there happened to be a light in the church, and the painted glass window shone out at us as we came along the frozen street. In the winter bleakness a hunger for color came over people, like the Laplander's craving for fats and sugar. Without knowing why, we used to linger on the sidewalk outside the church when the lamps were lighted early for choir practice or prayer meeting, shivering and talking until our feet were like lumps of ice. The crude reds and greens and blues of that colored glass held us there.[8]

Circuit Methodist ministers stayed the night at the Pershing household regularly. Young Pershing fondly remembered the local pastor, Brother Sidebottom, whom many called "Old Side," even if never to his face. While the pastor was very devout, he also smoked and chewed tobacco, but John appreciated the minister's personal storehouse of stories. "We children loved him and respected him above all the others who came to our home," Pershing would later write, "but we were not always as reverent as we should have been."[9] One example of this lack of reverence occurred when Old Side came to visit the family on one occasion, and Pershing's eldest sister pasted circus posters all over the minister's horse. Though Anne Pershing was mortified at the prank, "Old Side" took it well, and all gained a laugh over it.

Anne drilled lessons on faith and morality into her children with relentless intent. Historian Frank Vandiver observes, "Mother knew her Bible, believed in it, and expected her family to believe. Johnny accepted the form but worried little about the faith. And yet there was one essential about life that his mother taught him, one that would linger with him always: 'There were moral obligations that it was the duty of everyone to fulfill.'"[10]

This observation by the adult Pershing is important, not so much for how it explains or relates to his views on religion, but for how important it was for him to perform his adult duties, which generally remained focused on the military.

While a portion of John's youth was spent in mischief shared with boys of a like mind—often innocent enough but still unacceptable to his religious and civic-minded parents—much of his childhood was taken up with shared familial adventures. After the war, John and his siblings played among the dilapidated breastworks that Union troops and Home Guard militia had erected as defensive lines to repel a storming enemy. Fourth of July celebrations took on an added meaning with the fight over the state of the Union settled. When John was nine years old, he and his father shared dual honors as John Fletcher donned a heavy frock coat and requisite red sash to serve as the town's grand marshal for the midsummer parade while his son carried the American flag. John Joseph later recalled how he "felt the burden of the nation resting upon my diminutive shoulders."[11] It was a grand day for the young Pershing as the whole town turned out to cheer the local veterans marching along, wearing their uniforms again even as the guns of war remained silent. The people of Laclede did not segregate their celebration, and those recognized for their service included "the colored men who had been soldiers," remembered John.[12] The parade ended at Glovers Grove, a great copse of hickory trees a mile west of town, where the crowd gathered, ministers prayed, and John continued to hold up the flag "though weary from the march."[13] Speakers extolled the virtues of George Washington, Abraham Lincoln, and then-president Ulysses S. Grant, and the crowd sang martial songs including "John Brown's Body" and "Union Forever." Pershing mused on the festivities in his memoirs: "The pleasure that marked such celebrations was evidence of the return to normal existence that had been so violently disturbed by four years of civil war."[14]

Glovers Grove carried other warm memories for young Pershing. In the summer, it was the site for Methodist camp meetings. Such religious doings were generally for adults only, so the children usually wandered at will as the evening sermons droned loudly in the distance, and mystery danced in the dark trees, the light from torches flickering against their branches. For one camp meeting, John and his brother James (Jim) talked their father into bankrolling a concession stand for them to run. The rough shack had a plank counter and shelves stocked with tempting merchandise from the store, including candy, peanuts, and other refreshments. While they did a brisk business among the faithful, when the accounting was done, they had "barely come out even." Everyone in the family agreed, Pershing recalled, "that Jim and I had eaten up the profits."[15]

As a boy growing up in the rugged rural countryside of north-central Missouri, John could not possibly have avoided one of the common rites of passage—exposure to guns. "I was especially keen about firearms," he remembered. His favorite gun as a youth was the shotgun his father had brandished during the Holtzclaw raid. John and brother Jim came to possess some rifles that evacuating troops had abandoned during the war, and the boys took a couple of them to the local blacksmith to have converted into shotguns. They utilized them for hunting everything that moved in the local woods, including waterfowl, prairie chickens, quail, wild turkeys, squirrels, and rabbits. Occasionally, deer became targets, as well. As young teens, the two boys spent countless Saturdays trolling the local creek banks. Late nights were for coon hunting, which Pershing found great sport and exciting. "There was an eerie character about such adventures, and in imagination we could see wild animals of enormous size in the darkness of the woods and sometimes even things that looked like ghosts."[16]

Pershing learned some awkward lessons concerning firearms as a young handler. He once found a pair of old army revolvers and promptly took them home for cleaning and oiling. Once he had them spiffed up, he loaded one and fitted the gun's nipples with caps, as one of his sisters looked on. When he turned the cylinder to see if the weapon was in working order, the hammer slipped from his finger. The gun went off with a loud bang. Since Pershing was indoors, the .45 caliber ball "went tearing through the outside railing of mother's best mahogany bed." His sister screamed. The door to the bedroom soon burst open, and Anne ran in, certain one of her children had been shot. Pershing was chagrined and disciplined. "Thereafter I was forbidden play with loaded revolvers." Nevertheless, guns were destined to become a significant presence in the life of John J. Pershing.[17]

Pershing's exposure to guns at an early age, plus his memories of the Civil War and of the soldiers who had fascinated him as a toddler, did not point him toward a life in the military. Even as early as age ten, he had dreams of becoming a lawyer. As he grew, he observed such men in his hometown. He sometimes accompanied his father on trips to the family's attorney over in Linneus, the Linn County capital, just a few miles north of Laclede. John Fletcher's business doings sometimes put him in court with his son watching from the gallery. The law seemed to intrigue the youth, and such a degree could be gained at the University of Missouri's School of Law in Columbia.

But that dream was deferred for a distant day. For now, young Pershing studied the art of hunting, wandering creek bottoms regularly. Pershing and his brother also often fished together, taking their poles to a variety of fishing holes. Sometimes they participated in fishing expeditions in the spring after the seasonal rains finally receded, leaving schools of fish stranded in isolated pools. Locals seined their prey and "caught more fish in one day by that means than during the whole season with our lines," wrote Pershing. They caught so many fish that the boys took home plenty for their family and handed off the remaining catch to neighbors and friends.[18]

Among those neighbors and friends, the Pershing family counted African Americans. As noted previously, the elder Pershing was loyal to the Union and, despite an earlier opinion, felt slavery to be immoral. As the Pershings prospered, they employed Black servants, including a married couple, the Robinsons. Martha Robinson was the family cook, and her husband, Dave, performed chores around the Pershing household while also serving as a part-time janitor at the Methodist Church where John Fletcher and Anne were leading parishioners. The Robinsons were also members, as the congregation opened its arms to Black congregants, even as many Missouri Protestants attended segregated churches. In John's younger days, the family employed Sooky, another African American woman, who saw after the children and was a loyal nurse to all. Anne Pershing regularly sewed clothing for her children and then reworked Pershing hand-me-downs for Martha to dole out to her children. The Pershing children regularly played with the Robinson kids, seemingly on an equal footing.

But such relationships were often based on a racial-social etiquette that might seem retrograde by modern standards. As historian Frank Vandiver notes, "In these easy relationships there was no strain or prejudice—place kept to place and friends were friends in a social order war did not wholly change. White and black worked together where the chores demanded. Goodness earned respect."[19] While the adult John Pershing sometimes described Blacks as "darkies," these early experiences provided him with strong, positive feelings for African Americans. He did not balk at rubbing shoulders with Blacks and did not exhibit the same prejudices common among white Americans of his era. In time, he served as a teacher at an all-Black school and commanded an all-Black cavalry unit, the Tenth. That service alone earned him the nickname that stuck with him during his years of military service—"Black Jack."

As John grew into honorable manhood, his family remained a bastion of love, respect, and shared experience. He grew up in a positive family atmosphere, one he appreciated all his life. He developed strong affinities for his siblings, his parents, and others who called Laclede home and represented positive role models for him: ministers, civic leaders, businessmen, hardworking farmers, and others who helped to turn a formerly frontier Laclede into a place of civilized interaction and accumulated prosperity. Yet those rougher, earlier "wild and woolly" years of war, bitter political wrangling, bushwhacking, hardscrabble homesteading, and pioneer sod busting provided a cauldron in which Pershing's basic character and life's outlook were formed and nurtured.

As Pershing grew into a strong, strapping teen, he watched as his father also grew in social status in his community. His mercantile, his lumberyard, his land holdings—all turned John Fletcher into one of the wealthiest men in Laclede. He was one of five civic leaders who helped incorporate the community in 1866. He was a key leader in the Methodist Church, where he served as superintendent of the Sunday school. Neighbors remembered him in later years as the "first man to observe Memorial Day in Laclede, taking his own children and the children of his neighborhood, with flowers from his own garden, to decorate the graves of the soldiers."[20] Politics remained an important outlet, even as he turned down opportunities for public office. Postwar farming saw solid commodity prices that led to increasing land values. A man might purchase land at five dollars an acre, and a few boom years might increase its value five times over. New industries spread here and there across the region, and railroads moved people, produce, and products through Laclede, taking away the hard frontier edge.

Despite his father's relative wealth, young Pershing was constantly expected to work hard, mostly on the family's lands outside Laclede, where he plowed fields, planted long rows of corn, and saw to livestock, including hogs and cattle. Raised on the maxim of doing one's best at all times, Pershing was a perfectionist, a hardworking lad who would "sweat and strain for an hour to remove a rock from the path of his plow and keep his rows straight."[21] In 1873 John became a teenager, and long-term dreams of a college education seemed within the family's grasp.

But that same year proved a turning point for him and his entire family as the prosperity they relied on suddenly slipped away. The Panic of 1873 caught many Americans up short as an economic depression spread across the country. In distant Europe, several German states united to defeat the emperor Napoleon III. When they did, the Germans received a large amount of gold from the defeated French, prompting Germany to halt the minting of silver coinage. This had a severe impact on silver mining in the United States. Then, the U.S. government moved to a gold standard for its money supply, leading to high interest rates that hit debtors, including farmers, hard. These circumstances triggered other problems: large-framed monetary issues over greenbacks, poor commodity prices, and overextended land speculation. By 1875 eighteen thousand American banks and other businesses collapsed, and the national unemployment rate hit a staggering 14 percent.[22]

These economic problems nearly destroyed the Pershings' economy of scale. Suddenly, John Fletcher had no choice but to sell off most of his farmland, including his farm implements and even his livestock. He liquidated his general store, the original centerpiece of his family's hard-earned financial success. What the war and Holtzclaw's raid failed to destroy, a shaky U.S. economy did. When the dust settled, all that remained was the family house and the adjacent farm, a heavily mortgaged spread of 160 acres. Spare rooms were opened to boarders, and the Pershing's New England–style home became the Palace Hotel. For a few years, John's father tried teaching school. Then, in 1876, he was reduced to the status of traveling salesman, taking a position with a clothing company based in St. Joseph, Missouri.

In his father's absence, the eldest son—along with his younger brother James—was expected to work the remaining family farm. As all things fell to John and his young brother, his earlier years of peach orchard raids and guns misfiring into bedposts largely faded in the face of constant work. These years proved hard beyond any previous experience. In 1875 a plague of locusts destroyed the family's corn crop and those of countless other farmers. That year, the long-winged insects destroyed half the crops in the American West. As their numbers accumulated to an estimated three trillion, they flew in a massive swarm that ultimately stretched out a hundred miles wide, a thousand miles in length, and half a mile high—all representing Armageddon for farmers.[23] Another season later, drought stunted the harvest. Even when crops were plentiful—one season Pershing managed to bring in forty acres of timothy—the market proved less so. Sale of the hay barely produced enough profit to cover the cost of rail freight.

Yet, through these years of teenage adversity, John did not curse his family's luck. After his father informed him that "he was practically broke," he also explained that any dream his son had of attending college would have to be placed on hold (at best) and that young Johnny must continue farming for the sake of the family. The son took the father's news as well as could be expected: "I felt at the same time a certain pride that the responsibilities of manhood had been thrust upon me, and I was ambitious to meet them."[24]

Even as Pershing received all of this bad news, it should not be said that he suddenly became a man at that moment, even if he thought in those terms. He understood that his upbringing on the frontier of northern Missouri had helped prepare him for the vicissitudes that suddenly altered his world. His father and mother raised him, as they had all their children, to become a responsible adult. Despite his father's successes prior to 1873, John was never coddled. His parents had expectations of him, and he worked his best to make them proud. Childhood play came only after chores were completed. His mother had instilled that strong sense of duty in her young son, and this expectation remained with him throughout his life. John Joseph Pershing, like the generations of Pershings who preceded him, was a product of the American Midwest and a time when nothing came easy, and redoubled his efforts in the face of adversity. He was, indeed, a product of the frontier.

But the transition from boyhood to manhood was inevitable for John. His youthful days included hard work, but he also enjoyed his boyhood of fun and adventure. In Willa Cather's short story "The Enchanted Bluff," a tight cadre of youthful pals spend a final summer evening outdoors beside a favorite swimming hole. They take turns talking of their future and adult adventures and places they would like to see: Chicago, Kansas City, and a remote Native American mesa in New Mexico, the story's "enchanted bluff." The narrator's immediate plans are to commence a career teaching in a small country school. For him, boyhood was ending, just as it was for John:

> I dropped off to sleep. I must have dreamed about a race for the Bluff, for I awoke in a kind of fear that other people were getting ahead of me and that I was losing my chance. I sat up in my damp clothes and looked at the other boys, who lay tumbled in uneasy attitudes about the dead fire. It was still dark, but the sky was blue with the last wonderful azure of night. The stars glistened like crystal globes, and trembled as if they shone through a depth of clear water. Even as I watched, they began to pale and the sky brightened. Day came suddenly, almost instantaneously. I turned for another look at the blue night, and it was gone. Everywhere the birds began to call, and all manner of little insects began to chirp and hop about in the willows. A breeze sprang up from the west and brought the heavy smell of ripened corn. The boys rolled over and shook themselves. We stripped and plunged into the river just as the sun came up over the windy bluffs.[25]

The original story was illustrated with sketches of boys engaging in the activities of Pershing's youth: boys wearing Huck Finn–style straw hats, fishing beneath a wooden bridge; a barefoot lad sweeping out his father's general store; youths trekking through the tall grass, hunting birds, guns shouldered in anticipation. With the downturn in his father's fortunes, Pershing's dreams of a college education and a law degree seemingly escaped him. As with the story's narrator, he, too, would soon settle for teaching in a one-room schoolhouse.

John Fletcher's clothing salesman job did pay reasonably well for the time—$2,000 annually—but it was not enough to sustain the family and the remaining farm. John Joseph took work as a janitor at the town's public school, for by then, at age sixteen, John had completed his public school studies. Yet all this triangulating of various jobs and work by the Pershing men did not place the family on a solid financial footing. By 1878 John decided to become a teacher. He passed the examination for his teaching certification and began looking for a position. But the only opening available within reasonable distance of his town was one that many white teachers would find unacceptable; it was at the Laclede Negro School.

Young Pershing was raised in a way that supported education for African American students, a tribute to his parents. He was always comfortable among Blacks, working and playing with them as if race did not matter in his world. But it did matter in that era of increasing segregation and Jim Crow laws. One day a white youth appeared at the ramshackle Black school and challenged Pershing for teaching African American students. Pershing responded to the interloper by reminding him that President Lincoln had supported education for Black Americans, and that was what he had been hired to provide. The intruder soon shuffled out. The white teacher had some discipline problems among his forty Black students, some of which he handled with words, others with a switching. Years later, when a former student was interviewed, he noted Pershing's ways: "John Pershing, he got that school in order. Yes, sir, he did. He had a quiet way, but he meant business."[26]

His experience at the school, though, was short lived. At first, African American parents took umbrage with the employment of a white teacher for *their* school, leading some to refuse to send their children. Then, local whites criticized John for even deigning to teach Black students. Some mornings, as he walked to the Negro school, Laclede boys shouted a pejorative all too common at the time: "N——!" The word was thrown at him several times during his life.

Within months, Pershing had another opportunity to teach, this time at Prairie Mound, a hamlet ten miles outside of Laclede. On Sunday evenings, he rode a horse for seven miles south of Laclede and then two miles west to Prairie Mound, where he boarded with a farming family throughout the week; then he headed home on Friday evening. He received thirty-five dollars a month, a decent wage for a northern Missouri teacher, and paid for his room and board. Pershing taught everything in the curriculum from *McGuffey's First Reader* to geometry and algebra.[27]

Here, the eighteen-year-old teacher was in a lion's den of forty-five students, all crowded in a one-room schoolhouse. Their ages ranged from six to twenty-one, with some of the students being larger and taller, not to mention older, than he. Some believed themselves to be tougher, including an incorrigible, large-framed female student, who proved a challenge. When John ordered her to remain inside during a recess lunch, she climbed out a window instead and ran home. The next day, she repeated her misbehavior. She remained in the school at lunch but sent a note home with her younger sister, who returned with their red-whiskered father. As he burst onto the school grounds, carrying a shotgun, the children scattered, screaming. Facing an angry, armed parent, young Pershing grabbed a stove poker and met him at the schoolhouse door. The father blustered as he waved his gun menacingly, ordering the teacher to let his daughter out of the schoolhouse. Pershing stood his ground, refusing to comply, all while the daughter in question shouted, "Shoot him, Pa! Shoot him!" But the angry parent judged his opponent and rode away, shotgun in hand.[28]

Undisciplined boys also challenged young Pershing. Sturdy, muscular farm boys were common in such schools, and the toughs at Prairie Mound had run off the previous schoolmaster in short order. But Pershing proved himself of stronger fiber.

Tug Wilson was older than nearly all the other students, as well as John, and he regularly bullied classmates. Pershing had no room for such mistreatment of his students. When he ordered the large boy to remain after school, Tug defied him and prepared to leave with the others. The teacher moved quickly toward the student, standing inches from his face, and informed him, "Wilson, I am here to run this school, and you must obey my orders." He ordered Tug to return to his seat or face a whipping. Sensing his teacher meant business, Tug sat down.

Guns and parents seemed to repeat themselves when another irate father showed up at school with a shotgun to challenge Pershing's authority concerning his child. When talking over the problem failed, John challenged the father to a fistfight outside the schoolhouse. The teacher bettered the father, then "spent time putting balm on his vanquished foe's wounds."[29] Young Pershing was not one to back down from a fight. As a youth, he saw plenty of scrapes with other boys. One recalled, "I've had many a fight with him and I could always whip him because I was bigger, but he was always ready to keep right on fighting. Whip him one day and he would be right back to tackle you the next. He was the gamest boy I ever knew."[30] Even Pershing's father had admonished him as a youth: "John, my boy, you should not pick a fight, but do not allow other boys to impose upon you." Regarding such fights, Pershing wrote in his memoirs, "I was usually able to hold my own."[31]

There was much more to Pershing as a teacher than a revolving door of student-parent challenges and awkward encounters. He studied hard for his classes, sometimes only remaining a single lesson ahead of his brightest charges. He interacted with them in the classroom and on the playground, where he encouraged active play, the kind he had grown up with, including sports. Pershing often "used to join the boys in their games."[32]

He worked as hard in his role as teacher as he ever had working his father's farm. It was a different kind of labor, of course, one that placed others in his hands, giving him an early opportunity to serve as a leader, a director of people. "My experience in teaching was most valuable," he later wrote, "and there is no doubt that I learned more than any of my pupils, especially in the practical lessons of managing others."[33] Before his lengthy career ended, John J. Pershing would have the opportunity to manage millions of men.

Landing a series of teaching jobs did not cause Pershing to surrender his dream of becoming a lawyer. His intended life's work had shifted as he had grown up, starting with his imagining himself as a blacksmith fashioning horseshoes. (One day he would do just that as a cavalry officer stationed in the West, and he taught the skill to his recruits.) But the law had remained stuck in his mind. And John had a plan.

Gradually, he put some of his teacher pay aside until the spring of 1880; then, between teaching terms, he enrolled for three months in the Missouri State Normal School at Kirksville, sixty miles northeast of Laclede.[34] During his early Kirksville stints, he lived with his uncle William Griffith. Pershing's goal was to gain enough credits to graduate; that would increase his employability in better schools in the future and would bring better pay, which would provide him enough monies to attend the University of Missouri Law School in Columbia. At the normal school, he rubbed shoulders with serious-minded students even as the Latin professor's blackboard instructions included an important academic play on words: "Those who expectorate on the floor must not expect to rate high in the class."[35]

Pershing took to his studies, achieving good grades even if they were not exceptional. He had spent his high school years studying hard. He had also engaged in several pranks, including one incident when he locked the teacher out of the school. Still, as a public school student, Pershing had a reputation, even among his schoolmates, as a hard worker. Through those years, while also working the farm for his father, he had managed to balance all his responsibilities. One childhood friend remembered, "He was a steady worker and never fell down in his lessons. He went ahead step by step in his school life, making sure of his way and holding every inch of progress."[36] The constant stick-to-itiveness that he nurtured as a boy never left him as an adult. Childhood friend and college roommate Charlie

Spurgeon extolled the virtues of his friend in later interviews: "John was no sissy, even if he was clean and well behaved. He was a manly, upstanding boy. In his classes he had his lessons, and when asked to work a problem he would step promptly to the blackboard and do it in a way that proved his heart was in the work."[37]

John began a new seasonal pattern to his life as both teacher and student. From fall to spring, he donned the cap of the instructor at Prairie Mound and then became the student for three months while still lending a serious hand at the family farm. Kirksville was a north-central Missouri metropolis of three thousand people and was surrounded by prime farmland. Flanked by a large lake and surrounded by copses of hardwoods, the college was a smallish campus dominated by a three-story "Old Main," with its four-story front tower. The building spanned 180 feet by 90 feet and featured high windows and a commanding gabled roof. For a young man from rural Laclede, the college—with its faculty of ten and a compact library of a thousand volumes, with many of the classics—must have represented great possibilities for an upwardly mobile farm boy.

After terms spent in 1879 and 1880 at the Kirksville normal school, he was awarded a bachelor's degree in scientific didactics, a program of study that has since gone the way of the dodo, plus a certification that allowed him to teach in any Missouri school. With a degree in hand, Pershing then shifted his studies to the law, even if on his own, reading the requisite *Blackstone's Commentaries on the Laws of England* and nurturing his longtime goal of becoming an attorney. Never, it seems, did he ever have any consideration for becoming a soldier.[38]

By the spring of 1880, John's brother Jim joined him at the Kirksville college. In the fall of 1881, their eldest sister, Mary Elizabeth, whom John called "Bessie," was also a student at the Normal School. John had turned twenty-one years old and taken lodgings on the campus, sharing a room with Spurgeon. Classes ran five weeks at a session, and Pershing immersed himself in English, American literature, civil government, general history, rhetoric, elocution, Latin, drawing, and music, plus a variety of courses in mathematics and the sciences. His grades ran mostly in the ninetieth percentile range. Vocal music was his worst subject at 70 percent. Still, his average was a solid 91 percent through his time of study at Kirksville.

Campus life specifically and college life in Kirksville generally offered little excitement for students at the normal school. Few social outlets were available. The town proudly boasted no saloons to corrupt the morals of the young. The college considered dancing a negative "moral influence." Partying had to remain tame. The college offered sports, especially baseball, as a distraction. Classes began promptly as scheduled, due in part to the installation of the first campus clock-bell system in all the United States. As with many American colleges of that era, one of the chief non-sports activities on campus was the various literary societies, which students could join and then meet, hear speeches, and engage in debates. Pershing joined one, but his sister Bessie noted later, "John was not much of a speaker." She recalled of her college days at Kirksville: "I'm afraid it was a prosy old place."[39]

James's days at the college were limited. The studies did not appeal to him, causing him to drop out and take a job. This gave John and Bessie the opportunity to become closer. She was a light soul to her brother, and the two shared time and dreams as John helped her with her studies. One day, he was lounging in her campus room, reading a local newspaper, when John spotted an advertisement that caught his imagination: "Notice is hereby given that there will be a competitive examination held at Trenton, Missouri . . . for the purpose of selecting one Cadet for the Military Academy at West Point. All honest, strong, God-fearing boys of this district may take part."[40] Checking the details, he saw the exam was scheduled for two weeks later. He turned to his sister, read the ad to her, and asked if she thought he should give the test a try. Her answer would affect the trajectory of the remainder of Pershing's life. To become a soldier had never entered his mind, his sister knew. Despite the martial legacies of the Civil War, soldiers had become stereotyped as hard-edged brawlers, failures at everything else, drunks.

John had once been offered an appointment at the U.S. Naval Academy but had turned it down flat. West Point—she knew what that meant. Yes, her older brother might become an army officer, but he would also have an opportunity for an education few young men in America could expect. His dream of becoming a lawyer might actually have a fighting chance. The U.S. government would provide the education he could not afford. She encouraged him to apply.

Pershing, in fact, did not know much about West Point. All he knew was what most Americans knew: the military academy had served as the training ground for many of the nation's best generals, including Robert E. Lee, Ulysses S. Grant, William Tecumseh Sherman, and Thomas "Stonewall" Jackson. But once John committed to taking the test, he and Bessie researched the subjects that such an exam typically covered, and the list was daunting. With less than two weeks to prepare, brother and sister spent evenings together, studying by lamplight, with Bessie asking questions and Pershing trying to form answers accordingly.

The day of the exam, Pershing was surprised and daunted when he realized that he was among eighteen young men seeking the appointment to West Point.[41] Some of the contenders were eliminated early on due to medical disabilities. The majority of the testing included written questions for all the remaining boys, but some questions were asked of individuals, with one after another failing to answer properly, leading to their elimination. Eighteen was winnowed down to two, including Pershing. After both boys fielded questions on geography, the topic shifted to English grammar. Ironically, things came down to identifying the parts of speech found in the simple sentence "I love to run." For both applicants, the subject and verb were clear. But while the other lad identified "to run" as the adverbial phrase, Pershing saw it as the object of the verb. He was right. The appointment to West Point was his. More than twenty years later, he confided to fellow military officer Col. Frederick Palmer: "I had been at a hard job of plowing when I received word I had been appointed a cadet at West Point." With this appointment, John could begin putting the farming life behind him.[42]

At least in theory. Passing the examination in one's state only qualified applicants such as Pershing to travel to the academy in upstate New York to take the actual entrance exam. Not only did that hurdle stand before him, but he also had to jump another—convincing his parents that attending West Point and becoming a soldier was the right thing for him. He took a train home and broke the news.

Anne was surprised and immediately concerned. "You are not going into the army, are you?" she asked her son.[43]

He played his best cards. Attending West Point and graduating did not mean that he would have to remain in the army for long. He assured her of his safety, claiming, "There would not be a gun fired for a hundred years."[44] It was an opportunity for a good education, he explained. His mother did not stand in his way. Pershing notes in his memoirs, "She was skeptical about the undertaking . . . and in later years she became distinctly proud of having a son serving with the colors and followed my career with the utmost interest."[45]

On December 28, 1881, a few months following Pershing's examination, his hometown newspaper, the *Laclede News*, announced with pride the plans of one of its native sons: "John J. Pershing will take leave of home and friends this week for West Point. . . . May success crown your efforts and a long life be yours!"[46] No one, including John, could have known at the time how much his qualifying examination in Trenton would redirect the course of his entire life. He was proud of what he had accomplished on that September test day. He recalled such thirty years later when he and his West Point classmates celebrated their twenty-fifth reunion: "The proudest days of my life, with one exception, have come to me in connection with West Point days that stand out clear and distinct from all others. The first of these was the day I won my appointment at Trenton, Missouri, in a competitive examination with seventeen competitors."[47] Still, as he prepared to leave by train for New York and the academy, West Point represented a simple stepping-stone for his future. He thought he would attend West Point, gain a valuable education and specialized training on the government dime, perhaps put in a few years of service, and then return to his studies. He hoped to gain his law degree, maybe open his own legal practice somewhere—perhaps Laclede—and prove himself a success, a product of the midwestern frontier and the hard work, drive, discipline, and sense of duty instilled in him through his time spent in rural America. Little could he realize that the vision of his future would follow a completely different path, one that had not yet reached germination in his fertile, young imagination.

THREE

Cadets, 1882–87

Just traveling by train to West Point proved an adventure unlike any Pershing had ever experienced. Growing up in Laclede, he had never traveled at length and had not seen much of the country. He saw wonderful things as he traveled east. He spent time walking around Chicago and New York City and rode on horse-drawn streetcars and atop omnibuses. For the young man who had grown up in the rough country of the rural Midwest, Lake Michigan seemed endless, and the buildings in New York loomed to the sky. He saw the Brooklyn Bridge still under construction and people watched as he strolled down Broadway. Pershing was finally discovering a wider world.

For twenty-two-year-old John J. Pershing, everything about the U.S. Military Academy at West Point was new. He was suddenly thrown into a world different from his own as he rubbed shoulders with young men from every corner of the Union. Their accents, their manners, their personalities, their personal prejudices, and their preconceptions presented their own challenges to the young man from Missouri. Ironically, he was one of the oldest among the other 103 members of his class.[1] (Only 77 would ultimately graduate four years later.) John was uncertain that he was prepared to take the entrance examination at the academy, so he arrived in town several months early and took preparatory studies at a nearby academy headed by a former army colonel to help ready him (and eleven other would-be cadets) for the final hurdle to walk through the gates of West Point. Pershing remembered studying "page after page of stuff that we forgot completely before plebe [freshman] camp was over."[2] The prep school was just outside those gates, and as the dozen young men watched the evening parade marches and the retiring of the flag, Pershing longed even more to become a cadet. During one visit to West Point, Pershing thrilled to see the aging general Ulysses S. Grant attending a dedication ceremony for a new statue on the grounds.

All twelve of the young men did manage to pass the West Point examination and become part of the class of 1886 entering the elite military academy, their lives soon following a course set by others for the next four years. Among the larger group taking the exam, many struggled with their reading. Pershing could thank his rural education and his parents' rudimentary library, with those works of Shakespeare he sometimes recited aloud to his family, for he had few troubles with the exam, which also included mathematics, grammar, history, and geography.

When Pershing began his freshman year as a plebe, West Point was under the direction of Superintendent Oliver Otis Howard, a fervent Christian soldier who had lost an arm during the Civil War. (Later he received the Medal of Honor.)[3] He was replaced within months by Wesley Merritt, another Civil War veteran who, at twenty-seven, had commanded a cavalry division along with an even younger George Armstrong Custer. Merritt ran a tight ship, putting the plebes through their paces, including drill, marching, and constant studying. Courses ranged from mathematics—at which Pershing generally excelled—to history to French (with which he struggled) to the arts more closely relating to the military, such as fencing, musketry, gunnery, and horsemanship. Horses had always been part of Pershing's world, a rural advantage, and he proved himself the best marksman in his class.

Pershing and his fellow plebes lived in a part of the barracks complex that upperclassmen referred to as "Beast Barracks," and there the newest cadets received their first instructions, the basic wiring of military discipline that would set the tone for their future at the academy. Pershing recalled these early lessons: "Each of us in turn was told how to stand at attention, how to address the older cadets, how to enter and leave an office, and so on, all of which is doubtless still vivid in the minds of all who have had the experience."[4]

The West Point program proved intense academically, physically, and even emotionally. The cadets were divided into four companies (or one battalion), and an army officer called a tactical officer, or "tac," led each company. The other class officers and noncommissioned officers were chosen from among the cadets themselves. Cadets in the third class could become corporals; the second class, sergeants; and the first (or graduating) class, captains or lieutenants.

Pershing was soon recognized as a leader among his classmates. After only a few months at the academy, he was chosen as the class president, the only nominated candidate. During every year at West Point, he managed to achieve the available rank. In fact, when he could do so under the academy regulations, he became the ranking corporal of the battalion; next, the ranking first sergeant; and then the first captain, the highest rank available for a cadet at West Point.

Such appointments were not typically about achieving the highest academic standing among one's fellow cadets. It was about other qualities that are difficult to test on paper, the qualities considered essential for a soldier: his overall personality, his bearing, his capacity to lead and command, and his ability to instill confidence and discipline among his fellow cadets. Pershing quickly appeared to his peers to have such qualities. The young man who had grown up on the Missouri frontier, who had never seriously considered the life of a soldier, was proving himself up to the challenges of West Point and soldiering.

He faced plenty of challenges, of course, as did all plebes at the academy. One of the duties of tactical officers was to constantly harass their charges, making their lives difficult to help them develop coping skills while disciplining them. During his four years at West Point, Pershing accumulated two hundred demerits (informally they were known as "skins"), or nearly one a week, for infractions of the academy's rules. (Twenty of his classmates did not receive a single demerit during their four years at the academy!) The majority of these infractions were for tardiness, a lifelong problem for John, a personal shortfall that he never conquered. (A day came when as the general of the armies, he required kings to await his arrival.) Some were small violations of the rules, and others were nothing more than simple harassments. An askew cap, mud on one's boots, swinging one's arms too much while walking—anything a tac wanted to make a point of, a plebe could receive a demerit for it. One night Pershing was studying his French after hours, hiding the lamplight under a bedcover. Hearing an approaching tac officer, he furtively doused the lamp and scrambled under his bedcovers in his clothes. Failing to fool the tac, he received demerits and was meted several "punishment tours," including marching outside with a rifle. In the end, such demerits did not automatically detract from the positive attributes a cadet might exhibit. Where things really counted, the boy from Missouri excelled: "As an immaculate and snappy and severe and disciplined soldier of perfect military bearing, he was unsurpassable."[5]

Discipline was the order of the day, every day. Plebes were hounded and yelled at regularly, and everything was scrutinized, including how one stood at attention—chins on chests, shoulders square. Uniforms were constantly eyed for a mud spot here or a missing button there. (It was a lesson learned for Pershing, who, even when visiting battle-weary American doughboys at the front during the Great War, gave a soldier trouble for a misbuttoned tunic.) Plebes soon knew not to talk back to tac officers, not to question orders, and not to take too much time between receiving an order and obeying it. Plebes were expected to spin lots of plates in the air at any given moment, with an equal importance placed on marching, drills, taking care of equipment, and maintaining the tidiness of their barracks—all within a narrow response range that always included an enthusiastic "Sir, yes, sir." Often, through the years, those who observed Pershing in uniform were struck by his rigidity, how he held himself ramrod straight, giving him the bearing of a soldier.

Through all of these rigors and seemingly unreasonable expectations, Pershing understood it was all part of his professional training. Despite its difficulties, attending West Point was a source of pride for Pershing: "I was . . . a student at the institution that had trained such soldiers as Grant, Lee, Sherman, Jackson, Sheridan, and other great figures of the Civil War."[6] When Grant died in upstate New York in 1885, his funeral train passed West Point, where the cadets lined up to "present arms." Pershing remembered it was the greatest thrill of his life.

Twenty years earlier, the toddler Pershing had only experienced the war remotely, save for the Holtzclaw raid, and his memories were dim and few. Now he was in the very institution that had prepared that generation of men for military service. Some of those same heroes of the war paid occasional visits to West Point during Pershing's tenure there, giving him the opportunity to see them up close. Several times, an aging general William Tecumseh Sherman came to West Point to see the cadets.

Pershing poured himself into his plebe year at the academy. The rigors were relentless, with classes moving swiftly; once completed, they were immediately replaced by the next round of academics. Pershing's first roommate, William M. Wright, did not make it past January, failing to grasp the essentials of Euclidean geometry. As for Pershing's overall academic record, he finished West Point ranked at number 30 out of seventy-seven graduates, close to the same ranking Ulysses S. Grant had achieved at West Point. The classroom was only part of the training. During the winter months, the plebes received indoor instruction in fencing and participated in gymnastics. (West Point at that time did not have organized athletics such as baseball or football, thus no sports rivalry between the army and the navy existed.) A fellow cadet remembered Pershing's athleticism: "John was a splendid horseman. Many's the time I've watched him. He would do anything that required grit and strength and skill. But I never saw him do anything spectacular, never anything that required foolhardiness.... At gymnastics John excelled in all things that require great strength of arms and shoulders."[7] There were even classes in dancing, as officers were expected to perform well at post soirees and parties as much as they were expected to know the ways of the battlefield. They were, after all, receiving training in how to become both officers and gentlemen.

By the end of the second semester of the first-year term, the ranks of the plebes were reduced. During that first year, of the 104 new cadets, a dozen dropped out. The next year, another nine fell out, followed by five in the third year. Only one left the academy during the fourth year of Pershing's class of '86. Later, Pershing was able to take stock of those who remained. He selected several to serve under him during World War I, many of them as generals.

Some of Pershing's accumulated demerits over four years of training at West Point were the result of his tendency to enjoy the fellowship of his comrades. While he remained a dutiful cadet, one who studied and drilled with the best of them, he also liked having a good time. As historian John Perry notes, "As an individual and as a friend, Pershing was warm, cordial, fun-loving, adventurous, and willing to risk punishment for the chance to enjoy himself."[8] Despite the rigors of his family's religious training and expectations of Christian virtue, John enjoyed a good smoke and liked a strong drink, and dancing was a favorite pastime. The latter meant ladies, an enjoyable distraction for the young man from Missouri. The opportunities for interactions with young women were limited during plebe year—plebes could not attend Saturday night hops—but a cadet's third-class year opened with new possibilities. As Pershing remembered, "When we became yearlings [second-year cadets] we were given our first opportunity to attend cadet hops, which were held twice or three times a week. Many young ladies visited West Point during the summer and that added much to our pleasure."[9]

Pershing did not have any problem attracting the attention

of the young ladies who frequented either the hops or Flirtation Walk, "where tradition held that a girl could not refuse a cadet's request for a kiss."[10] He arrived at West Point in the summer of 1882 as a well-built farm boy, weighing 155 pounds and standing five feet nine. Within two years, he was nearly six feet tall and had gained twenty-five pounds. He was still trim and reasonably handsome although still with clean-shaven, boyish looks. Girls were drawn to him. Robert Lee Bullard—West Point class of '85 who served with Pershing in a variety of military theaters, including the Philippines and the western front, where Bullard commanded the Second Army—remembered his friend as "a hop-goer, what cadets called a 'spoony' man. He loved the society of women."[11]

Each new year at West Point meant additional opportunities for the cadets. During Pershing's second year, he was riding horses twice weekly, allowing him to further develop a childhood skill. He loved horses, and the cavalry began to form in his mind as the assignment he would accept at graduation. Academy regulations allowed cadets in their third and fourth years to take a three-day leave, and Pershing took advantage of his after two years away from home. He returned to Laclede to see his family. One of the first locals he met when he arrived in his hometown was an elderly African American woman who loudly greeted him: "Land o' mercy, Johnny, I sho' is glad to see you. The Lord has been mighty good to you, boy, to bring you back here to your mother." The reunion was pleasant, indeed; as Pershing later noted, "I have to confess sharing her joy."[12]

John's third and fourth years at West Point brought him closer with his fellow classmates, who honored him with rank and election as the class president. His classes included physics, chemistry, and drawing, as well as studies in tactics. Horsemanship remained a beloved activity. Pershing recalled a third-year highlight as a visit to the academy by Civil War commander Gen. William S. Rosecrans, who sat alongside Pershing's physics professor and participated in John's oral presentation on the subject. At the end of the third year, his classmates voted him as the senior cadet captain of the corps, a singular honor.

Pershing enjoyed his senior year more than any other. The end of studying and training was finally within sight, and the threats of tac officers receded into memory. During that year, a special guest arrived at the academy—the famed American writer and humorist Mark Twain. Twain's visit occurred on a Sunday when no classes would interfere. John was perfectly familiar with Twain's novels, including *The Adventures of Tom Sawyer* and *Huckleberry Finn*, whose fictional adventures were sufficiently reminiscent of his own childhood days in rural Missouri. Since Twain hailed from Pershing's home state, the boy from Laclede obtained permission for the writer to visit his barracks following church service, which was compulsory each Sunday at the academy. Pershing hosted Twain in his room, with several of his fellow classmates also attending, and for a full hour Twain told amusing stories to the gathered cadets. Before he left, he honored Pershing by referring to him as a "fellow Missourian."[13]

Through four years at West Point, Pershing experienced the most rigorous training available in America for would-be army officers, those who would lead the enlisted ranks. Even though John was proud to attend the academy for what it represented, the West Point of his day, removed from the Civil War by more than a generation, tended to offer a curriculum based on the past rather than a future in which wars might be fought differently. Most of the program was still extremely European, with the lion's share of the training consisting of classroom studies, few field exercises, and virtually nothing in the way of tactical studies. West Point was an insular bubble, one that ran on repeated lessons in discipline. Command opportunities for the cadets were extremely limited, representing a place where "no cadet ever had a chance to command so much as a platoon in a simulated problem of reconnaissance, attack, or defense."[14] It is not an exaggeration to suggest that the West Point cadets of Pershing's experience studied many subjects but with one exception, war itself. The program did offer one course of study on the Civil War during a cadet's senior year.

All this is not to say that Pershing's four-year study at West

Point represented a complete waste of time. One of the key elements was the human element—that is, the formation and the molding of young men into soldiers by honing their capacity for discipline and obeying orders. The academy's motto of "Duty, Honor, Country" was drilled into them. This view suggests that the emphasis was not on the specifics of war but on the training of the soldier's mind so that no matter what conflict he found himself in, he was, at a minimum, mentally prepared. In later years, Pershing expressed this sentiment succinctly: "If they won't soldier, they won't fight."[15] This is no small accomplishment. But throughout Pershing's long career in the military, the training future officers would receive changed dramatically, just as the elements of war would change. For Pershing then, once he graduated, his success in the field as a young second lieutenant would continue a learning curve that his training at West Point had only begun.

Pershing was always supportive of West Point and even protective of his cadet experiences, which he considered valuable. One key significance of Pershing's time at West Point was the opportunity it provided him to meet young men of talent who would one day serve their country under his command. For those who ultimately graduated as the class of '86, he had lived with them for four years, came to know them personally and professionally, understood their personalities, knew their faults, and maintained connections with them after their West Point days. His class proved itself extraordinary, and its ranks eventually included ten brigadier generals, fifteen major generals, and Pershing, who became general of the armies during World War I. One out of three in his class achieved a general's rank. During the Great War, American men composed forty-two divisions, and fourteen of Pershing's classmates served as their commanders. Among classmates in the years directly ahead of and behind Pershing's, another sixteen served as divisional commanders under his command. World War I included 474 American generals, and a quarter of them attended West Point at one time or another during Pershing's four years as a cadet. When Pershing selected such commanders for the American

Expeditionary Forces (AEF), his decisions took him back to West Point graduates.

Pershing never outgrew his days at the academy. In a letter he penned to the then-superintendent of the academy in 1929, more than a decade following the climax of World War I, the general of the armies was still nostalgic about West Point: "The longer I live, and the further I have gone on in the service, the more I reverence the things that inspire the heart and soul of young men at West Point."[16]

But for all of Pershing's long-term attachment to West Point, at the approach of his graduation from the academy in 1886, the senior cadet did not seem ready to strike out on a long-term career in the military. As graduation approached, he confided to a friend, "I'll graduate, but afterwards I may resign and take up law."[17] Pershing would eventually gain a law degree later, but his years of military service became a full-life career. Graduation day was June 11, 1886, and Pershing finished his years at West Point as a leader of his class. The graduation speaker that day was the aging Civil War hero Phil Sheridan. Pershing and his classmates put aside their cadet gray uniforms and exchanged them for the blue uniforms of the U.S. Army. West Point graduates entered the army and chose their branch of service according to their class rank.

But choosing between the infantry, cavalry, or artillery was never a question for Pershing. He was set on the cavalry, the branch that would keep him in the saddle, the branch that he considered the most colorful and romantic. He chose the Sixth Cavalry specifically "for the reason that it was then active in the Southwest against the Apache Indians."[18] The Sixth had an exceptional record beginning with its organization in 1861 in the early days of the Civil War, followed by action at Antietam, Fredericksburg, Gettysburg, the Wilderness, Cold Harbor, and Appomattox Courthouse. Over the years following the war, the Sixth saw service in the American West, stationed at outposts in Texas, Kansas, Colorado, and Arizona. As Pershing prepared to head west, the Sixth was stationed at a remote post in New

Mexico. That summer of 1886 had already seen cavalry campaigns to capture the renegade Apache leader Geronimo. As far as Pershing knew, he was to soon find himself immersed in a field of action, one that might have conjured up in his mind the plots of so many of Beadle's dime novels, the kind he had surreptitiously hid behind his textbooks in school long ago.

With graduation behind them, Pershing and his classmates took a few days to bid farewell to one another. They settled their debts at the academy, packed up their personal things, and readied to leave their four-year home. Three days following graduation, the class of '86 boarded the local steamer *Mary Powell*, which for many years plied the Hudson River, carrying endless classes of cadets between the academy and New York City. The party gathered at the legendary Martinelli's, one of the swankiest restaurants in New York City, and repeated toasts left many graduates with hangovers the following morning. Then they were off, touring the sites of the city, taking in the skyscape with its new skyscrapers. They visited the Eden Musée, where the graduates saw wax renderings of Thomas Edison, Abraham Lincoln, Ulysses Grant, and Queen Victoria. The museum's Chamber of Horrors included a display labeled "Indian Barbarities," which piqued Pershing's interest, since his first assignment was to New Mexico, where cavalry units were frantically galloping all over the northern region in search of Geronimo.

The party walked across the recently completed Brooklyn Bridge—Pershing remembered how many of the young men "walked across feeling quite shaky"—and rode the city's sooty elevated railway.[19] Some went shopping, others continued to drink, and all understood that with their West Point days completed, many would never fully cross one another's paths again. On the group's second night in the city, they went to Delmonico's. By the following day, their reverie was winding down, and the young men began to scatter as they caught trains taking them to their family homes. A few stayed together and rode a train down to Washington DC to tour the sights there. By June 24 Pershing was finally headed west to return to his family. But the trains did not deliver him to Laclede.

After calling the small Missouri town home for years, John Fletcher had found employment elsewhere during John's years of study at West Point. Laclede had lost its luster for the Pershings, as the region no longer represented a place of opportunity. Pershing's father was determined to find his fortune in another semi-frontier town, the promising Nebraska capital of Lincoln. The state university was an additional lure, and John Frederick hoped his remaining children might have the opportunity to attend there.

Young second lieutenant John J. Pershing's trip took nearly five days, as he arrived in Lincoln on June 29. Lincoln instantly impressed Pershing as "a handsome, clean, and remarkably stimulating city on the Nebraska prairie."[20] The moment was golden when he returned to his family. Soon he caught up on family news and met their new Nebraska friends. Over the following five weeks, John reacquainted himself with those who had framed his youth. He found his mother completely reconciled to her son's becoming a full-fledged member of the U.S. Army, especially as an officer. The summer was his own, for he did not have to report to his new station until September. But by early August, he was bored and took a trip to Chicago to rendezvous with comrades who were equally bored. For several days, a handful of his classmates shared one more urban adventure with their class president and friend.

Pershing spent the remainder of August in Lincoln with his family. Wiley Bean, one of John's West Point classmates, came to visit Pershing and his family before both comrades headed westward. September arrived, and John and Wiley took a train east to Omaha and boarded an Atchison, Topeka and Santa Fe (AT&SF) train headed ultimately into the sprawling American Southwest and the rugged backcountry of New Mexico.

The train trip became yet another adventure for members of the class of '86, as Bean and Pershing were joined by a handful of other graduates at various western stations, including Kansas City and Fort Dodge, Kansas—all bound for western assignments. Pershing recalled the days on the AT&SF train fondly: "A jollier crowd than ours never traveled. We told stories, sang class songs, cleaned out eating houses, fired at prairie dogs, hazed the peanut boy, and practically ran the train."[21]

A few of his comrades remained on the train as the tracks turned southward across Colorado and into New Mexico. Viewing the passing landscape from the train window, Pershing saw before him a region like no other he had ever viewed. Mountains and mesas rose majestically in every direction, their ranges broken by rolling desert floors dotted with scrub brush and patches of blue-green sage and scarred by twisting arroyos. The southwestern ranges of the Rockies—the Culebra Range and the Sangre de Cristo Mountains—stood off in the western distance. The landscape was a painted desert of earth tones and ancient dark folds etched along the low-slung ranges carved over eons of time and by water. Just the land alone likely suggested adventure to young Pershing.

In her novel *Death Comes for the Archbishop* (1927), Willa Cather describes this landscape, the Truchas Mountains of the Sangre de Cristo, and paints a colorful panorama of a territory that must have seemed to Lieutenant Pershing as the most exotic and sublime he had ever witnessed as a young man from Laclede, Missouri: "On every side lay ridges covered with blue-green fir trees; above them rose the horny backbones of mountains. The sky was very low; purplish lead-coloured clouds let down curtains of mist into the valleys between the pine ridges. There was not a glimmer of white light in the dark vapours working overhead—rather, they took on the cold green of the evergreens."[22]

Towns loomed periodically into view—Raton, Las Vegas, Santa Fe, Albuquerque, and smaller southwestern communities—with a comrade occasionally disembarking until John got off at Deming, where the Mexico border lay a mere fifty miles farther south. (Pancho Villa would lead a guerrilla raid on Columbus, New Mexico, just forty miles south of Deming, that would summon Pershing back to New Mexico thirty years later.)

From Deming, Pershing headed northwest toward Silver City, then a prosperous mining community and the widest place in the road between the AT&SF line and his final destination, the lonely fort to which the newly minted second lieutenant had been assigned—Fort Bayard. Pershing was now a citizen of the American Southwest.

Bayard was a typical, remotely planted U.S. Army post of the American West. Established twenty years earlier (1866), the original building had been constructed from the local clays by Company B, 125th U.S. Colored Infantry and named for Brig. Gen. George D. Bayard, a Union officer killed in the battle of Fredericksburg. Those who erected the original adobe buildings had met with hostile Apaches, who had boldly raided the post before its completion, rampaging on horseback across the fort's unfinished parade ground. Fortunately, by the time Pershing arrived, the fort had undergone significant improvements, "until Bayard became one of the most attractive posts in the Southwest."[23] As early as 1877, thirteen duplexes of officers' quarters had been constructed in tidy rows surrounding the post's parade grounds. Adobe barracks provided accommodations for four companies of enlisted men. The grounds included a headquarters flanked on both sides by officers' quarters. On the south side of the grounds were the commissary and storehouses, while the library and hospital took up the northern perimeter of the quadrangle. An 1879 report identified Bayard as having one brevet lieutenant colonel, a major, four captains, eleven lieutenants, 325 enlisted men, fourteen laundresses, fourteen civilian workers, and twenty-five Navajo scouts, along with 280 cavalry horses and eighty-nine mules. As western forts of the era went, Bayard represented the best that any new cavalry officer might have expected. "Instead of a desolate Siberia [Fort Bayard] became a pleasant and popular assignment."[24]

Bayard was a much-improved version of itself when Pershing arrived. But some forts were absolute hellholes. As Gen. Tecumseh Sherman observed in 1874, "Some of what are called military posts are mere collections of huts made of logs, adobes, or mere holes in the ground, and are about as much *forts* as prairie dog villages might be called *forts*."[25] With the heavy controls and financial restrictions Congress had placed on the army during the 1870s, the cost of building a fort was kept to an absolute minimum. To keep the cost down, soldiers themselves built nearly all frontier forts and army posts. Not until the 1880s did the conditions of western forts begin to improve. But even as late as 1884, soldiers stationed out west "quipped that if they wanted to be well cared for, they must become inmates of either the military prison or a national cemetery."[26]

When Pershing arrived in September 1886, he joined the Sixth Cavalry in the final days of a protracted Indian campaign. The commanding officer of the Sixth was Col. Eugene A. Carr, known among his Indian opponents as "War Eagle." Carr had served the army for decades, beginning with Indian wars during the 1850s, followed by duty during the Civil War, and then years spent in the West fighting Indians during Sheridan's winter campaign of 1868–69, the Republican River Expedition, and the campaigns in the Dakota Territory. He had fought Apaches in Arizona and had only been assigned to Fort Bayard in May 1884. Carr's career came with some controversy, but he was known as a capable commander.[27]

Pershing was joining thousands of other regular army troops stationed in the West in those latter days of the frontier who "saw themselves as the advance guard of civilization," a constabulary force assigned to secure the wavering line between the advance of farmers, miners, cattlemen, and mercantile men (as Pershing's father had been nearly a generation earlier on the frontier of north-central Missouri) and a defiant, yet ever-retreating population of Native Americans.[28] In 1886 the extended campaign of conquest appeared to be nearly won. But battles, skirmishes, chases, and surrenders, as well as massacres—such as Wounded Knee (1890), a debacle that placed a tragic period at the end of the sentence describing the ultimate settlement of the West—still occurred.

During the month before Pershing's arrival at Bayard, the Apache leader Geronimo had finally been captured. During the twenty years since the final shots of the Civil War had been fired, the U.S. Army had engaged almost constantly in fighting Native Americans. At that time, the troops assigned across the

West, stationed in 255 military outposts, had numbered between twenty-four thousand and twenty-seven thousand men, and had become "a rugged, disciplined, professional force."[29] After several years, veteran officers of the conflict between the North and the South became accustomed to the hit-and-run guerrilla tactics of western Indian warriors and learned hard-fought lessons, adapting their own tactics and limiting their campaign forces to only a few hundred men per march, at best, while relying on the organization and discipline inherent in the army's structure—both of which Pershing had learned at West Point. Such elements as warm clothing and the maintaining of complicated logistical structures that kept western forts supplied during harsh, western winters provided the army with a singular advantage that proved difficult for Indian fighting units to overcome. Even Geronimo had been pursued until he could fight no more.

Still, the Apaches had proven intractable warriors. No one knew that better in 1886 than Lt. Col. George Crook, who was assigned as the commander of the Department of Arizona in 1871 at the age of forty-one and spent the next two years engaging them in battle and through diplomacy. Crook's words provide a clear understanding of his dogged protagonist: "The Apaches only fight with Regulars when they choose and when the advantages are all on their side. . . . The bucks absolutely without impediments swarm your column, avoid or attack as their interests dictate, dispute every foot of your advance, harass your rear, and surround you on all sides. Under such conditions Regular troops are as helpless as a whale attacked by a school of swordfish."[30]

By 1873 Crook was promoted to brigadier general and given command of the Department of the Platte in Omaha, Nebraska. By 1876 he was commanding troops engaging the Lakotas, whose land in the Black Hills had been overrun by gold seekers. That campaign saw Custer's Seventh Cavalry wiped out on the treeless ridges along the Little Big Horn River, followed by Crook's ultimate success against the Lakotas, Cheyennes, and other Native nations in 1877. By 1882 he was back in the Southwest again and over the next four years pursued warriors led by his old nemesis Geronimo. By the time Pershing arrived at Fort Bayard, Crook had been replaced by Brig. Gen. Nelson A. Miles the previous April and reassigned again to command of the Department of the Platte. Miles had completed that campaign by summer's end, taking far more credit for bagging Geronimo than Crook believed he should have.

Although Crook was no longer in the southwestern theater when Pershing walked onto the barren parade grounds at Bayard, John would meet him later in his career. He also became aware of Crook's legacy; his personal approach to handling Apache renegades and those tactics would inform Pershing in his later years of service. Those who admired Crook, including those who had fought against him and the U.S. Army, considered him "one of the most absolutely just and true friends the Indian had ever known."[31]

Crook had not singularly approached the Apaches as enemies but had sought to negotiate, to utilize diplomacy. He also fought his enemy across the trackless deserts of Arizona, often doggedly, in part so that he could then turn to the negotiating council. For years, he sought to understand his enemy, to educate him, to bargain with him, to convince him that resistance would only prolong the inevitable. Additionally, Crook was savvy about engaging other Indian peoples to help him fight the Apaches, who were often their enemies as well. He frequently exerted a level of patience with the Apaches that irritated many in his command, but through his dual approach of hard fighting and fair treatment, he won over his enemy.

Although Pershing missed the opportunity to observe Crook firsthand in the Southwest, he came to understand just how the general had managed to ultimately bring such intractable opponents as Cochise and Geronimo to bear. Through the years Pershing was stationed with the army in the American West, he developed a skill set practically identical to that of Crook: fight hard, negotiate when necessary, rely on Native allies, educate, and show respect. Not only would such an approach inform Pershing of how to handle American Indians in the West, it would also serve as his approach to handling other indigenous opponents in other fields of military service, especially during his protracted years in the Philippines following the Spanish-American War. Crook created a template that Pershing utilized repeatedly. John's parents raised him to be empathetic, with a sense of putting himself in the shoes of others, of trying to meet them on their terms. As historian Mitchell Yockelson notes, "Pershing firmly believed that educating oneself about other cultures was an essential part of leadership, and he remained dedicated to this approach for the rest of his Army service."[32]

Pershing did not have to wait long before receiving his first assignment at Bayard. While Geronimo had already surrendered, at least one additional subchief, a warrior-leader named Mangus, had not. In October a pair of cavalry units, including Pershing's L Troop, were dispatched on a reconnaissance mission to search the nearby Mogollon Mountains, located immediately northwest of Bayard and just south of the San Francisco River. The new lieutenant was soon immersed in responsibility: "The details of preparation of the troop were left to me, and with the assistance of the first sergeant and the other noncommissioned officers, many with years of experience, everything, including ten days' rations, was made ready."[33] Pershing was smart enough to know that he needed help in organizing such a march and did not hesitate to rely on his sergeant and others. Such a concession on his part clearly shows that he was not led by his ego despite being a recent graduate of West Point.

Pershing's first assignment was likely formed with the same simple mathematics that usually fit such short campaigns, referred to as "emergency calls." A typical troop consisted of sixty men, carrying the simplest of rations including sowbelly— the bacon of the day—flour, coffee, sugar, salt, and pepper. Each man in the troop packed a blanket, a saddle blanket for his mount, and a cache of fifty rounds of ammunition. Pack mules carried supplies, including an additional 120 rounds of ammunition per man. The men did not carry tents, so equipment was kept to such a minimum that "ten pack mules could carry the impedimenta for a whole troop on a ten days' scout."[34]

As troops gathered in the late October morning light, Pershing was surprised to see that many of his men were either drunk or still hungover from having lingered in the post trader's grog shop too long. He did not like their appearance otherwise, noting how "the variety of uniforms, including hats and leggings, fell far below standard" and "was not in accord with my conception of how troops of the Regular Army should appear."[35] But Pershing merely filed his concerns in a mental drawer. After all, he was new to the field, and he served under commanders of his own.

The march had its difficulties. The men left the fort and soon reached Silver City; then they followed a trail paralleling the Mogollons until they made camp at Mangus Springs.[36] That evening, Pershing and his comrades failed to hobble their horses, and dawn revealed an encampment without any mounts. Pershing's men did not recover their horses and mules until noon the following day. He later noted, "It was a somewhat embarrassing situation in which to find ourselves—cavalrymen afoot in such a wild country with not a horse in sight."[37] Eventually, Pershing received word that a troop of the Tenth Cavalry, an African American cavalry unit that Pershing himself would one day command, had captured Mangus in Arizona. The lieutenant and his detachment returned to Bayard without seeing a single Apache or firing a single shot.[38]

But such marches served as learning curves for the newly assigned Pershing. Riding across the desert was like nothing he had ever experienced. He began to understand the nature of the environment he was in, how quickly water became precious, and how the sun could dry a man up in no time, searing his skin and blistering his lips, hands, and face. Shade in the open desert was rare. Men scrambled during rest breaks under rock outcroppings and beneath thin stands of cacti, or, in desperation, they would lie face down on the hard earthen floor with their hats covering their necks and heads. At times, the troop camped where no water was available—the term was "dry camp"—and their horses became almost wild with thirst. Pershing's first march proved a challenge, but he took the lessons as they came to him.

Immediately after Pershing's troop returned to Bayard on November 7, minus the renegade Mangus, he was assigned a complicated, even dangerous mission involving communications equipment. Post Order 171 instructed Pershing to install a series of heliograph stations across the New Mexico landscape to connect Fort Bayard and Fort Stanton, located more than 175 miles to the east near the Capitan Mountains. The territory between the two forts resembled "some of the roughest, most inhospitable country in the Southwest."[39] Such an assignment was usually reserved for more experienced officers, especially those familiar with the rugged landscape, but the lot fell to Pershing regardless. Amazingly, he seemed up to the challenge despite having only been stationed at Bayard for a mere matter of months.

The heliographic system that Pershing was tasked to create across the barren New Mexican landscape was based on a simple technology. Invented in the late 1860s by a British electrical engineer named Henry Mance, it was essentially a wireless solar telegraph utilizing mirrors. First developed by the British during the Second Anglo-Afghan War (1878–80), the technology proved effective and even remained in use through World War II.

The heliograph represented a cutting-edge technology for the American West of the 1880s, a means of nearly instantaneous communication that turned the blazing desert sun into a useful tool. By means of a series of large mirrors, signalmen could flash, literally, Morse code–based messages across vast distances; they were something akin to Indian smoke signals, only more technologically advanced. Such mirrored devices needed to be set up at intervals of approximately twenty-five miles. Creating the system might seem deceptively easy. In fact, the mirrors were installed across mountainous terrain, typically on high ground to be seen at a greater distance, but each site had to accommodate a line of sight that went both ways, from peak to peak. Putting up such a system might prove a difficult trick.

Organizing his expedition was easier the second time around, and Pershing took care of many details himself. He collected a detachment of sixteen men, some of whom he likely had come to know and trusted with such an assignment. One question was in regard to the time: how long should he expect such a mission to take? He estimated a month and planned accordingly in taking supplies and the appropriate number of pack mules.

Through those weeks, Pershing and his men worked under an endless sun as the winds slipped down the southernmost part of the Black Range to the Mimbres Mountains, an escarpment of igneous rock running north–south, east of Fort Bayard. Farther east, the landscape flattened out to a lonely plateau named centuries earlier as Jornada del Muerto, "Journey of the Dead Man," a forbidding landscape encompassing a route passing through a hundred miles of particularly dry ground. Men on horseback could cross this desolate piece of ground in two days, but locating water was always a problem. Homesteaders as early as the 1860s had dug a few wells here and there along the route, but several of them had already been abandoned by the mid-1880s. Also, the region was heavy with alkali deposits that burned flesh and sometimes rendered water undrinkable. Since Pershing's detachment was working in November and December, nights were cold, cutting through the layers of clothing the men wore and further damaging their skin.

But the work went on as Pershing selected sites for heliographic stations, riding back and forth between designated locations to make certain their signals were visible along the ever-expanding route. After weeks in the field, the detachment reached Fort Stanton, situated on the northern edge of the Mescalero Apache Reservation. Stanton appeared grand to the weary men under Pershing's command. The fort was well placed against the dramatic backdrop of the Capitan Mountains. The land was less austere, boasting a green zone of grasslands watered by the meandering Rio Bonito. Pershing and his men remained at the fort for a few days, recovering before their return trip to Fort Bayard. Stanton also provided John with a one-man reunion with Julius Augustus Penn, a West Point classmate who was posted at the fort.

The return trip still included harsh sun by day and bone-chilling temperatures at night, but at least the detachment could make progress in a relatively straight line without having to climb up and down endless mountain ranges. The day Pershing's men returned to Fort Bayard the calendar marked an exact month since their original departure. Through those challenging weeks, the men had crossed three hundred miles in difficult conditions and under the command of Second Lieutenant Pershing, who had learned more lessons about leading men in uniform in the Southwest. With the heliographic system in place, the distance between Bayard and Stanton had been dramatically reduced.

Superior officers soon took notice of Pershing. What, exactly, drew men of greater rank and service experience to Pershing is uncertain. Perhaps it was the same mettle, the same human qualities that had caused classmates at West Point to recognize his leadership early on and elect him repeatedly as the class officer and president. But the notice came. One senior officer at Fort Bayard thought well of young Pershing: "Within a very short time after he came to the post, a senior officer would turn to him and say: 'Pershing, what do you think of this?' And his opinion was such that we always listened to it. He was quiet, unobtrusive in his opinions."[40]

So much about frontier life in the backcountry of New Mexico appealed to Pershing and fed his professional drive and his personal preferences. He had received reprimands from superiors, just as he had been corrected by tacs at West Point, but he loved the camaraderie of his desert assignment. He absorbed the lessons of how to fight and otherwise engage the Native Americans. He commanded well and fairly. Just as he had done as a teacher in Laclede and Prairie Mound not so many years earlier, he sometimes dealt with a challenge to his leadership by calling out the unruly subordinate and settling matters with his fists.

Pershing learned a great deal during his first march across the hostile, New Mexican desert. At its most essential, "the excursion taught Pershing how to plan and command an extended campaign in the field. It became one of the many learning experiences he was to absorb during his four years in the Southwest."[41] One aspect of such campaigns related to the animals involved. Pershing became recognized for how well he treated the horses and mules serving under his command. His love of horses translated into his not overworking them, not wearing them out to the point of exhaustion. But he knew how to work with mules too. Growing up in Laclede likely gave him plenty of experiences with "Missouri mules." Even General Miles became aware of Pershing's best practices, praising him during the fall of 1887 for "marching his troops with a pack train of 140 mules in forty-six hours and bringing in every animal in good condition."[42]

FOUR

Cavalry, 1887–90

Following his successful installation of the heliographic system, Pershing fell into a fairly regular routine of activity at Fort Bayard. In a letter he penned on March 9, 1887, he noted that routine: "With General Courts, Garrison Courts, morning and evening stables, drills, recitations in tactics, and Boards of Survey—(arrange with a view to climax) my time is quite well occupied."[1] Through most of the winter months at Bayard, Pershing read and studied often while also engaging in "horsemanship, troop drills, tactical training, and other outdoor work."[2] Days often began with mounting guard, and evenings included dress parade, which provided both distraction and morale building among the men. The Sixth Cavalry had an excellent band and hosted concerts as well as weekly hops that brought out civilians from Silver City, including young ladies.

Nearby Silver City was still a booming frontier mining town where money could be made. The town was experiencing flush times when Pershing arrived, as silver poured in from the mines, prompting the *El Paso (TX) Herald* to claim that "Silver City is the most substantial, beautiful and wealthy city in New Mexico."[3] The town's population included the substantial citizens—merchants, businessmen, farmers—who provided the community's backbone, but one could also find wild cowboys, lawless toughs, rough hombres, rustlers, drunks, prostitutes, gamblers, and a Chinese subcommunity where one could surreptitiously purchase opium. Pershing rubbed shoulders with the townspeople regularly, attended dances, and spent time with comrades during off-hours in bars. Perhaps Silver City reminded Pershing of Laclede's rougher days, only with a southwestern flair, as well as the books he read as a youngster. Pershing was, in fact, living in a western of his own. He had read the exciting literature of the West, and once he arrived in New Mexico, the experience moved from the two-dimensional page into the real world of the frontier.

Springtime was the season for target practice at the fort, an activity considered important for the troopers. In this arena, Pershing was at his best. Having grown up hunting with rifles and shotguns, he was comfortable with both and had done well as a marksman at West Point. When the departmental competition was held in August at Fort Wingate (located in northern New Mexico, Pershing's second post assignment), he was chosen as one of the competitors for his regiment. This training proved important for Pershing, who one day would create a competitive rifle corps while assigned to instruct the cadet-students at the University of Nebraska–Lincoln.[4]

He found time for fun but never shirked his responsibilities. While he took to his duties at Bayard with enthusiasm—Pershing seemed to gain an early appreciation for the Southwest—he also enjoyed himself in the off-hours, the evenings when duty was replaced by leisure. A fellow officer noted of the second lieutenant: "He worked hard, and he played hard; but if he had work to do, he never let play interfere with it."[5]

While poker playing was a common pastime among soldiers stationed at remote forts and other installations in the West, Pershing was not initially a player. When he did play cards growing up, it was usually a game of euchre or seven-up played "on rainy days in the barn loft with other boys." He had never played poker even at West Point. His playing began at Fort Bayard by accident. During evenings spent in the fort's officers' club, Pershing occasionally watched poker matches, which always included limited betting. One night, a friend was called from the table, and he gave Pershing his cards to finish his hand for him. Pershing protested that he knew little about the game, but when his fellow officer returned an hour later, Pershing was up around $125. Soon, he took up the game occasionally but finally quit playing altogether when he found himself "getting interested in it to such an extent that it seemed best to drop that form of amusement."[6]

Growing up, his Beadle's dime novels typically cast Native Americans as ruthless enemies threatening the Anglo-American advance of the young republic. But Pershing began to view the Indians with an open mind, even if the basic reason for his being in the West was to keep tabs on the Native population and ensure the safety of those occupying their traditional lands. He saw the tragedy of what Indian life had become as the last of the Apaches were rounded up and forced onto reservations.

He came to admire much about Indian culture. He watched with fascination as an Indian warrior disguised himself in a white hunting shirt with a set of antlers on his head. It reminded the young officer of "a character out of some fable or legend of ancient times."[7] Pershing ingratiated himself with various Indian leaders, spent time conversing with them (he even learned Native languages, devoting himself to studying with local Apaches and various Indian scouts), listened to their stories, became familiar with their customs, and attended their ceremonies and dances when allowed. In short order, he learned the sign language that provided a common means of communication between Native nations. In so doing, he set himself apart from most other officers. Pershing kept up this practice at future postings, including in the Philippines, where he learned the nuances of the island's indigenous tongues.

So many of the details of the Indians' cultural lives had not yet fallen away when Pershing studied them in the 1880s. They still danced around tribal fires, wore loincloths and moccasins, painted themselves for ceremonies, fashioned their arrowheads by hand, and boiled the occasional dog for dinner. They carried the white man's guns, of course, and sometimes purchased their cotton shirts in local general stores, but their traditional world was still relatively intact for Pershing to study.

Pershing felt it was important to deal with the Native Americans fairly. He knew that was the hallmark of General Crook's dealings with the tribes of the Southwest, especially the Apaches, and he saw no reason to take absolute advantage of their plight simply because he had to the power to do so. While many of his contemporary army regulars typically referred to the Indians they encountered as "savages," Pershing tried to understand them, sought to walk in their proverbial moccasins and to find an honest common ground when he could—all with the understanding that he was a soldier of the Southwest. If necessary, he knew military force was always an option.

After eleven months at Bayard, Pershing transferred to his second posting in the New Mexican backcountry, Fort Stanton, at the end of the line for Pershing's newly placed system of heliographic mirrors. The fort was established in May 1855, just months following the death of Capt. Henry Stanton at the hands of the Apaches. Early during the Civil War, Union forces abandoned the post with the approach of Confederate troops, but the First New Mexico Infantry, led by the legendary Col. Christopher "Kit" Carson, drove out the rebels in October 1862. Following the war, regulars who sought to round up the Mescalero Apaches garrisoned the fort.

By the 1870s Fort Stanton was the base for campaigns against the Mescaleros and Jicarillas, until both Indian groups were finally settled on the Mescalero Reservation.[8] Stanton was a smaller post than Bayard, but Pershing was pleased with his new military home.[9] The officers' work at the fort proved simple enough, and the opportunities for "hunting, fishing, . . . and spooning" were "unsurpassed."[10] Pershing was reacquainted with his old West Point pal Julius Penn, as the two fellow officers shared lodgings at the fort. Pershing also made an early friend in Lt. Richard B. Paddock of the Sixth Cavalry, and the three young officers—Pershing, Penn, and Paddock—soon became known as the "Three Green P's." (Second Lt. Andre W. Brewster also became friends with Pershing, and Brewster later served the AEF commander in France as his inspector general.) These comrades in uniform became close and spent social hours together both on the fort grounds and at the local frontier town of Lincoln situated just nine miles away.

Lincoln was the county seat of Lincoln County, a thirty-thousand-square-mile stretch of southeastern New Mexico. Equivalent to the size of South Carolina, it was home to fewer than two thousand residents. The county featured a mixed geography of rolling, desert plains and mountain ranges including the Sierra Blanca (the White Mountains), Capitan, Sacramento, and Guadalupe. Lincoln was situated in an upland valley of the Rio Bonito, flanked by the Capitan Mountains to the north and the Sierra Blanca off to the southwest. Many of the local Anglo farms and cattle ranches were located along the Ruidoso, which runs south of the Bonito. Both rivers reach a confluence forming the Hondo, which ultimately flows into the Pecos River.

The town was hardly comparable to Silver City. Lincoln consisted of little more than an adobe village boasting a population of four hundred residents, predominantly Hispanic. The town's main street—its only street really—ran a mile in length and was flanked by shade trees. On the edge of town stood the only two-story building, L. G. Murphy & Company, the largest general store in the area. Despite serving as the county seat, Lincoln did not have its own courthouse. Instead, an expansive adobe building served as a courtroom and a dancehall.

Fort Stanton provided crucial lifeblood for the citizens of Lincoln. Troopers came into the town regularly, patronizing its taverns and stores. The fort stood guard over the Mescalero Apache Indians at the local reservation. The town and fort provided dual outposts of frontier settlement, yet Lincoln County had a reputation for cattle rustling and the violence that often went along with it. In addition, racial tensions were always prevalent with issues between Anglos and Hispanics, as well as between the local whites and the African American soldiers garrisoned at Stanton. As for the local Indians, everyone seems to have harbored prejudices against them. With so many young cowboys in Lincoln who drank in the saloons and carried guns, Lincoln

County had a reputation to live down for several decades running, and at its center was a record of cold-blooded murders by Henry McCarty, also known as William Bonney or "Billy the Kid." Ironically, until 1877, Lincoln County did not even have a jail, "only a hole in the ground topped by a log guardroom near the east end of town."[11]

East of Lincoln, the mountain ranges fell away, making room for the extended Pecos Plains. Most of the big cattle spreads were located there, with the maze of smallish rivers feeding the grama grass for miles on end. The greatest cattle baron on these lands was John Simpson Chisum—"the Cattle King of New Mexico"—who had arrived in the territory in 1867, having driven a herd of mealy-nosed longhorn cattle up from Texas along the Goodnight-Loving Trail. Ten years later, he owned eighty thousand head of cattle that ranged for 150 miles along the Pecos River nearly all the way back to Texas.[12]

When Pershing arrived at Fort Stanton, the region was known for its frontier legends. Names such as Billy the Kid and Pat Garrett were either famous or infamous. Pershing, in fact, had the opportunity to meet several of the ranchers and cowboys who owned and worked the farmlands throughout the region of the fort and along nearby Eagle Creek, south and west of the New Mexico garrison. Pat Garrett, the former sheriff of Lincoln County, and John Poe, an ex–cattle detective, were among them. Both men, along with a deputy of Garrett's, had been a part of the 1881 raid that had approached Pete Maxwell's ranch in an effort to locate Billy the Kid, who was wanted for several murders. It was in Maxwell's own ranch house bedroom that Garrett found and killed the eighteen-year-old in a shootout that would become one of the most repeated stories on the New Mexican frontier. Pershing first met Garrett and Poe during their regular visits to the fort to pick up their personal mail. On several occasions, John paid calls at both of their ranches along Eagle Creek. Once again, Pershing was living in the midst of legendary characters worthy of Beadle's novels. Pershing, who had come to New Mexico too late to have encountered Billy the Kid firsthand—he and Billy the Kid were the same age—observed in his memoirs, "But this was before my time, and while the West was by no means entirely law-abiding, it was making definite advances in that direction."[13]

Pershing enjoyed such social encounters with the civilian locals around Fort Stanton. He and the other two Green P's often spent off-hours outside the fort—the threat of Apache raids was next to nil by then—riding along valley floors, across stretches of farmland, and along the foothills of Sierra Blanca. They also shared a Chinese cook. Pershing wrote in a letter: "We are living like kings, we have milk, quail, wild turkey, a wagon load of vegetables, potatoes, carrots, turnips and onions—quails stuffed with them—plenty of grain and hay, good water, plenty of wood. The only thing lacking is—." Penn wrote his own summation of how well the men were eating by observing that their cook "certainly knows how to get up a good dinner."[14]

The trio frequented a local inn maintained by Mr. and Mrs. Frank Lisnet. In the surrounding area, Pershing, Paddock, and Penn sometimes hunted wild boars. During one such hunt, Pershing accidentally shot one of Mrs. Lisnet's pigs, mistaking it for a wild, tusked animal. Mrs. Lisnet was indignant at the death of one of her animals and went into her yard to give the young cavalryman a sharp scolding. Pershing apologized, and the Lisnets proved forgiving.

Nearly thirty years later, Pershing returned to New Mexico for the Punitive Expedition to capture Pancho Villa and took a side trip to the New Mexico Military Institute in Roswell. When he heard the Lisnets were living in the area, he paid them a call. When Pershing reached their homestead, the then–brigadier general approached the elderly Mrs. Lisnet, smiled, and said, "How do you do, Mrs. Lisnet! Remember me?"

The longtime resident of New Mexico responded without missing a beat, "Sure and I do. You're the lieutenant that was always killing me pigs!"[15]

During the fall of 1887, Gen. Nelson A. Miles, the commander of the Department of Arizona, sent out instructions to various posts across the Southwest intended to provide specialized training in Indian fighting and tracking. Although the plan seemed to some a bit late, considering the Apache had all but been rounded up by that time, it went forward. Miles's "field maneuvers" basically amounted to a version of the game "cowboys and Indians," with soldiers serving both roles. The troops called it "rabbit hunting," and the war games consisted of a pair of cavalry teams, one designated "raiders" and the other "pursuers."

The raiding team was provided with an eighteen-hour head start and the goal of reaching another military post—the pursuers were not informed which one—and getting as close as a thousand yards from its flagpole before being detected. Pursuers only had to catch up to the raiding party close enough for it to hear a bugle call. With the game, Miles intended to provide a simulated Indian raid, one of his chief objectives: "At the same time it is an experience from which can be obtained instruction that will be invaluable to the officers in case they should be suddenly called upon for service in civilized warfare."[16]

Such raids allowed the men to gain some skills in tracking and pursuing an enemy, and to become more familiar with hundreds of square miles of the countryside—all while having some fun and friendly rivalry. In no time, men such as Pershing were having the time of their lives, riding the wide, open stretches of frontier New Mexico, sleeping under the canopy of a billion stars, eagerly looking forward to time in tomorrow's saddle. Willa Cather describes an evening on the southwestern prairie, a man's respite, spent drinking coffee around a campfire as the sky shifts from light to dark: "The sun had set now, the yellow rocks were turning grey, down in the pueblo the light of the cook fires made red patches of the glassless windows, and the smell of piñon smoke came softly through the still air. The whole western sky was the colour of golden ashes, with here and there a flush of red on the lip of a little cloud. High above the horizon the evening-star flickered like a lamp just lit, and close beside it was another star of constant light, much smaller."[17]

The cavalry units that participated in the games engaged in every trick they could imagine to win each matchup. It was not a simple game of riding as fast, hard, and long as one could so pursuers could not possibly catch up, for the rules allowed the raiders to move only between noon and midnight. Their pursuers were free to stay in the saddle as long as they wanted, though, so the raiders' eighteen-hour head start eventually did not matter. Strategy was everything. Thinking, planning, imagining what one's "enemy" might be doing—the psychological aspect of these war games was as important as the physical challenges such pursuits required.

So off they rode. The young men in the saddle galloped in pursuit of their quarry, covering desert miles with a focused sharpness and looking for signs, evidence, any disturbance in the landscape, a plume of dust in the distance, anything to provide a clue of where to head next. Pershing fully engaged in the chase and its requisite strategies. If pursuing, he tried to place himself in the mind of the raiders: What were they thinking? What is their objective? What would I do if I were in their boots? His first game unfolded on September 17, 1887, when he was given command of Troop L and designated as pursuers against Lt. George Scott's Troop D, the raiders.

The chase proved spirited as the raiders hightailed it out of Stanton on the morning of the eighteenth with the goal of reaching Fort Bayard. As the chase unfolded, Pershing felt the advantage of having trekked across the ground between Stanton and his old post the previous year when laying out the heliographic line. Pershing envisioned the land before him and worked out a likely route for the raiders he would pursue: "Reaching the Rio Grande bridge at noon on the third day, we saw Scott just leaving the town and overtook him a few miles farther west. My men were overjoyed, as there was considerable rivalry between the two troops."[18]

Here was 2nd Lt. John Joseph Pershing at perhaps his frontier best. He was in the saddle, something he came to love; his time serving with the cavalry in the American West represented something wild and exciting to him, an opportunity to play his own bit part in the drama of taming the frontier. He rode with his men fast and hard, the desert wind whipping his face, his cap strapped firmly to his chin, its crown crested with golden crossed sabers blazoned with the numeral 6. It was the fulfillment of every young boy's dream. Mountains to the north, a menacing expanse of ancient lava ahead, its sharp edges failed to intimidate these dust-covered, blue-clad men of America's army. Leaning forward, boots straining in the stirrups, adrenaline-spiked excitement running high, they scanned the horizon before them, seeking signs of movement. Pershing loved it all and thought such training was formative and worthwhile. As his days in the West stretched before him into years, he was probably right, even if they provided almost no preparation for what he and his millions of doughboys eventually faced on the western front. For the moment, the American West was their essential field of war.

An excited Pershing sent a self-congratulatory telegram to Fort Stanton to inform his commander of his success: "Captured raiding party here to-day one mile from camp at twelve twenty—P.M. Will remain here several days to recuperate stock & return to Post by easy marches unless otherwise ordered. J. J. Pershing."[19] His message was well received, with his commander at Fort Stanton sending a copy to the adjutant general of the department and to the commander at Fort Bayard. Within days, General Miles sent his own congratulations to Pershing, directing him and Scott to continue their war games.

After several days' rest for both the men and the animals, the tables were turned, as Pershing's men became the raiders and Scott's men their pursuers. On September 25, Pershing and the twenty men of his Troop L mounted up and headed hurriedly to the southwest. They galloped as they approached the Magdalena Mountains toward Fort Craig, situated halfway between Forts Bayard and Stanton, along the AT&SF rail line. Pershing and his men knew their ground well and made several river and stream crossings, trying to steer clear of arroyos blocking their path. They put much ground between themselves and their pursuers, covering 110 miles during the first and second days, before they finally camped in the Black Mountains outside the outpost of Chloride, with Fort Bayard to the southwest. In this same country, the army had recently campaigned in search of renegade Apaches. With no sign of Scott's men on the horizon, Pershing felt he had made progress.

The following morning—day 3 of the chase—Pershing and his men prepared a breakfast of bacon, bread, and coffee before saddling up. A local prospector wandered into their encampment, surprised by the presence of the cavalrymen. He asked Pershing if the Apaches were on the warpath again, and the second lieutenant responded with an assuring no.

Suddenly, he and his men heard a war whoop in the distance.

"Good God! Captain, the Indians are on you!" shouted the prospector, who "grabbing his hat from his head took to his heels."

Scott's men then appeared over a ridge, having caught up with their quarry.[20]

Such war games continued through the following months, and Pershing became quite skilled, gaining a reputation among his fellow officers and especially among his own men. These opportunities afforded young officers such as Pershing experience in field command, making decisions on the fly and engaging in real-time maneuvers with clear goals. Through such raid-and-pursuit exercises, Pershing also gained notice from his superiors including Colonel Carr, the commander of the Sixth, who recognized Pershing as one of the best troop commanders during these "rabbit hunts."

These war games based on raid and pursuit would prove invaluable to Pershing thirty years later when he and thousands of U.S. Army troops were dispatched to the New Mexico border frontier to engage in a real game of desert cat and mouse during the Punitive Expedition against the Mexican pistolero Pancho Villa.

The appeal of such maneuvers and life in general at Fort Stanton remained high for Pershing. Photographs taken of him—he was in his late twenties—during his posting at Fort Stanton reveal how much he had taken to army life in the American Southwest. He looks serious—as he often did—sober, tough, a bit harder for the experience. He grew a mustache that made him look the part of the dashing cavalry officer. There is a confidence in his appearance, not the cocksureness of the overly confident, but the look of a man who is comfortable in his own skin, who knows how to command, and who is having a good time.

He was proving himself a worthy commander. Infrequently, he had to explain with his fists why his orders were important, even though such fights between officers and enlisted men were against the rules. He brooked no guff, no slight, taking a disciplinary line he had drawn during his days in Laclede and Prairie Mound as a schoolteacher facing intractable youths. Robert Bullard, who served with Pershing in New Mexico, in the Philippines, and finally in Europe during the Great War, recalled only two occasions when Pershing was reduced to fighting a subordinate to make his point: "Once by one who . . . was convinced by Second Lieutenant Pershing in his shirt-sleeves, and once . . . by one who within forty-eight hours had paid with his life for his disobedience to Captain Pershing—dying of cholera. I buried him."[21]

During Pershing's time in the Southwest, he fostered a reputation that followed him through decades of army service. He was tough but fair. He told his men what to expect, and they understood he meant what he said. But he was more than a gruff officer who barked out orders that he expected to be obeyed. He also gained a reputation for seeing to the needs of his men. As historian Richard O'Connor observes, "Pershing looked after his men more diligently than most officers, keeping a close watch over their food, equipment, living quarters, and sanitation—the mark of the best kind of company officer."[22] He continued to foster this tendency throughout his career in the military, later scrounging food and supplies for the African American troops he commanded in Cuba during the Spanish-American War and, on a massive scale in Europe, ordering his subordinates to route trains of supplies to waiting doughboys (even if the trains did not always arrive in time).

While stationed at Fort Stanton, Pershing made the best of his time, absorbing the training and general post life fully. He and his comrades, especially Paddock and Penn, took up a game new to them—tennis. Pershing, though, preferred another sport often played at the New Mexican outpost. Baseball—sometimes called "rounders" at that time—was a favorite among many of the men, including both the enlisted and the officers. Pershing became quite proficient at the game both in batting and pitching. He was never a fast runner, but he rounded the bases with a young man's competitive enthusiasm. Like everything else he engaged in, he played as hard as he worked.

One highlight that Pershing experienced at Fort Stanton during the fall of 1887 was a visit from his sisters May and Grace, who were then attending the University of Nebraska–Lincoln. They spent an entire month at the fort, and Pershing later remembered he and his siblings "passed many happy hours with the younger set both on the post and on jaunts into the surrounding country."[23] The visit yielded some surprising results. Grace was introduced to Pershing's friend Paddock, and the two became a couple and later married. Their time together was ultimately cut short when Paddock died during the Boxer Rebellion in March 1901. Grace passed away just three years later in 1904. Pershing always considered her "the most talented of our family."[24]

While Pershing spent the final months of 1887 enjoying his sisters' company and engaging in the excitement of repeated rabbit hunts, the winter proved harsher than usual and kept the men of Fort Stanton mostly close to their base. If the number of field maneuvers was cut short, Pershing and other officers found plenty of time to hunt, with Pershing carefully noting the difference between Mrs. Lisnet's pigs and wild boars. Springtime brought new life to the fort, and Pershing turned his attentions from hunting to fishing in several local mountain streams. John and others brought their catches to the post kitchens, where they were prepared, served, and enjoyed by all.

The year 1888 marked two years since Pershing's graduation from West Point. He had enthusiastically adjusted to army life on the New Mexico frontier. At some point during those two years, Pershing seems to have experienced a change in attitude about army service. While he had originally planned to remain in the military for a limited time, he began to have doubts about whether he truly wanted to abandon his military service. He began to ponder his future to the point of near obsession, feeling he was making one of the most important decisions of his entire life. Should he make the wrong decision, he was afraid the die would be cast and that altering that chosen trajectory might prove difficult. He talked with his fellow officers about what to do. Had Pershing not found army life so appealing, the decision might have been easier. But his days in the army did appeal to him, seemed to fit him as perfectly as a pair of handmade gloves. In the end, he felt he needed the input of those who probably knew him the best—his family. In October, he took a short leave of absence and returned by train to Lincoln, Nebraska.

During his visit to the Nebraska capital, Pershing took note of some things about the city that he had not noticed previously. Little had changed during the two years framing his absence. He saw more of the university grounds, met more of his parents' friends, and was introduced to "several prominent citizens of the state and a number of university professors."[25] He became aware that the university had established a new law school. As a land grant college, the University of Nebraska–Lincoln was required to operate a Corps of Cadets program, the late nineteenth-century equivalent to a more modern Reserve Officers' Training Corps program. Someone even proposed to the veteran second lieutenant that he might consider applying for an appointment as the military instructor at the university. The thought had crossed his mind already. The previous June, Pershing had written to the university's board of regents and requested such an appointment, but he had not received an answer. Such a post would mean he could remain in the army, teach in the world of academics, and perhaps even gain the law degree that he had dreamed of for years.

While Pershing was in Lincoln on leave, *Buffalo Bill's Wild West* came rolling into the prairie community and set up a great outdoor arena. Buffalo Bill, whose real name was William F. Cody, had made Nebraska his home for several years;

his ranch, Scout's Rest, was located in the far western reaches of the state in the cattle country around North Platte. Buffalo Bill was a favorite son of the state, an influential voice. It was in North Platte that Cody founded his *Wild West* (the word "show" was not in the original title) in 1883. No name became more synonymous with popular entertainment during the late nineteenth century in America than Buffalo Bill's.[26]

He was a product of multiple frontiers, having been born in 1840s Iowa and raised in 1850s "Bleeding Kansas," where young Cody had ridden as a guerrilla with the Union-supporting Red Legs. His frontier résumé ran a mile long and included the likes of pony express rider, buffalo hunter, army scout, and, more recently, purveyor of the mythology of the American West. Pershing knew about this sort of man of the frontier after experiencing Holtzclaw's guerrilla raid and having spent a couple of eye-opening years in New Mexico, where cowboys and outlaw legends still plied their trades. Cody had fought Indians, just as Pershing anticipated he would do himself in New Mexico. Pershing had grown up on such legends, the mythologized likes of men such as Kit Carson, who represented the generation of frontier heroes prior to Cody. Pershing's Beadle's dime novels were too early to include Buffalo Bill, but the early 1880s saw Cody's exploits—real or imagined—splashed across Beadle's pages, including an 1882 volume titled "Adventures of Buffalo Bill from Boyhood to Manhood."[27]

Pershing encountered Cody during his visit to Lincoln because the showman served Nebraska governor John M. Thayer as a military adviser of sorts. If 2nd Lt. John J. Pershing was no longer captivated by the lure of Beadle's dime novels, he was still vulnerable to the aura that a performer such as William Cody projected. Historian Frank Vandiver sums up the symbolism of Buffalo Bill's legacy: "In legend he served poignantly for every grown man who remembered the West the way it should have been and for every young man who wanted to know a West slipping into history."[28] Pershing was essentially both the young and the grown man all at once. When he met the buckskin-wearing Cody, the young cavalry officer found it difficult to look away.

Cody wore the stylized costume of the West, including a wide-brimmed sombrero. He sported a wispy goatee, and his hair was a full mane of salt and pepper. In his *Wild West* production, he rode gallantly on a beautiful gray mare. Pershing heard him speak in Lincoln, as the former western scout bragged ceaselessly about his days with the Fifth Cavalry in Kansas and Nebraska, his buffalo hunts, and all his other adventures, some that reflected Pershing's current New Mexican experiences enough to seem eerily similar. The second lieutenant wrote later in his memoirs, "The average listener would be inclined to doubt the accuracy of a man who seemed to boast so much about himself, but General Carr told me later that 'Buffalo Bill' had really been in a number of Indian fights with the Fifth Cavalry and had been highly valuable as a scout."[29]

Pershing relished the time spent with his family members in Lincoln and was further introduced to the community they called home. He even asked for an additional month's stay. He did not spend all his time in Nebraska, however; by January 1889 he was in New York, where he was responsible for new army recruits bound for service out west for the Department of Arizona. Pershing accompanied most of them to Fort Wingate, the headquarters for the Sixth Cavalry, located near the Zuni Indian Reservation in the northwestern region of New Mexico, just a few miles east of Gallup. When he arrived at the fort, he was surprised to discover that he had been temporarily transferred to Wingate.

When Pershing arrived at the fort in January 1889, it was the second such army post in New Mexico bearing that name. The original Fort Wingate was erected in October 1862 near the village of San Rafael to serve as a base of operations against the Navajo Indians. The fort was named for brevetted Maj. Benjamin Wingate, who was wounded during the Battle of Valverde, New Mexico, with Confederates. (Wingate subsequently died the following June.) In April 1863 Brig. Gen. James Carleton, the commander of the Department of New Mexico, ordered thousands of Navajo peoples removed from their traditional lands to the Bosque Redondo Reservation on the Pecos River near Fort

Sumner. When many refused, Carleton ordered Col. Kit Carson and a thousand troops—including Ute, Zuni, Jemez, and Hopi auxiliaries—assembled at Wingate to force the Navajos' removal. By the fall of 1864, approximately eight thousand Navajos had surrendered to Carson and were subsequently herded to Bosque Redondo along a trail that became known as the "Long Walk," a southwestern version of the forced removal of the eastern Cherokees known as the "Trail of Tears."[30]

By 1868 the disastrous removal of the Navajos was reversed, and the remaining members of the tribe were returned to their original homelands. At that point, the army decided to build a new post named Fort Wingate near the previously abandoned Fort Lyon adjacent to the Navajo Reservation. This new post was situated closer to Gallup and forty miles northwest of the old Fort Wingate, which was abandoned. Pershing arrived at the new Fort Wingate in January 1889.[31]

In his memoirs, Pershing expresses a positive opinion of his new assignment. The fort was the headquarters of the Sixth Cavalry and was home to five "troops of the regiment," plus a company of Navajo scouts and two companies of the Ninth Infantry. Pershing's immediate superior was Capt. Henry M. Kendell, under whom he had served at Fort Stanton. The fort had its charms, according to Pershing. He noted, "There is an air of gaiety at this station, including riding parties, excursions, hunting, dancing, and all that sort of thing, which, together with the serious work of training, made it more desirable than any other post at which I had served."[32]

The fort featured the typical layout for western army posts of the era, consisting of four rectangular-framed, C-plan buildings, which were the company's quarters. The quarters included a washhouse and sink located at the rear of each building. Across from the parade grounds sat the officers' quarters and the fort's storehouse.[33] Wingate was smaller than either Stanton or Bayard, but it was neatly laid out. With the Sixth only recently reassigned to Wingate, it was a busy beehive of activity with Troops A, C, H, I, and K barracked on the grounds. Colonel Carr was also there and still in command.

The fort had some of New Mexico's best scenery. The compound faced westward in a basin rimmed by the Zuni Mountain lowlands with a ridge of mesas to the south. To the north, a great sandstone formation known as the Navajo Church rose up to the sky. While Pershing had become accustomed to the starkness and beauty of the New Mexico landscape, Fort Wingate offered sometimes breathless sunsets as shafts of unfiltered light struck the surrounding rimrock, causing the men in the fort to halt what they were doing and take stock of God's handiwork.[34]

As Pershing had already done at his two previous New Mexico posts, he made the best of his situation, taking responsibilities as they came while looking for ways to leave his own individual mark. If the second lieutenant's extended trip to Lincoln, Nebraska, to consult with his family about his future—whether to remain in the army or to quit and attend law school—had not ended in a final decision, Pershing's assignment to Fort Wingate and the immediate orders he received upon his arrival likely helped. Soon after he arrived, Captain Kendall left the fort on an extended leave, and John was handed command of Kendall's Troop A.

Still, Pershing knew he had his work cut out for him. Troop A was a lackluster unit in need of improvement. Since Pershing was already recognized as a capable marksman who had performed well at inter-post competition, he took it upon himself to sharpen the overall marksmanship of the men of Troop A. He soon found "the troop had usually stood lowest in the regiment in target practice, mainly because the men had not been given the necessary individual instruction."[35] Soon, they were much improved under Pershing's guidance, with his troop sweeping the regimental competition that year. John trained his men in other skill sets, offering instruction in riding, tactics, and even how to best care for one's animals. Though Pershing met some resistance due to his relentless drilling and instruction, in the end, his men progressed. His experience in training his men in marksmanship was only the first such opportunity of Pershing's career. It helped prepare him to train college cadets at the University of Nebraska in just a few short years. Their marksmanship skills brought intercollegiate recognition to the campus.

In early May 1889 Colonel Carr received important dispatches from the nearby Zuni Reservation. A trio of white men had been caught stealing horses from the Zunis. The Indians had chased them down, and at least a hundred warriors had cornered them in a log cabin on the local Diamond S Ranch. In the exchange of gunfire, the horse thieves had killed three Zuni warriors. The Zunis considered Carr a friend to their people, so they sought his help.

Carr sent orders to Pershing to gather ten men, ride out to the ranch, and place the white men under arrest. Horses were saddled, guns were loaded, and Pershing's men mounted up. They then rode hard for twenty miles until Pershing heard gunfire in the distance. He had no real plan, and his orders were vague. He and his men were entering a firefight with the Zunis massed in much greater numbers than his force. Without any specific training, a contingency plan, or a delineated strategy in place, Pershing jumped immediately into the situation and quickly took command. He found the Zunis understandably agitated and angry. Pershing summed up things as he saw them: "I found the Indians, a hundred or more, greatly excited and determined to take the thieves dead or alive."[36]

Once again, Pershing found himself in the midst of his own dime novel, as a brave cavalry trooper riding with his ten "Yellow Legs" into the midst of a firefight between the cowboys and the Indians. He had likely read of such a plot before as a youth. Perhaps a scene from *Buffalo Bill's Wild West* entered his mind, one that featured the legendary man of the West riding to the rescue of his fellow white men under siege by dozens of bloodthirsty savages. But this frontier encounter was not a fiction. It was real, with Pershing at center stage. He was intent on putting an end to the standoff, not at the expense of the Native Americans but by bringing the three white men to justice.

Tension framed the moment. The Zunis had their own sense of justice, and they had to be convinced Pershing was there to do right by them. When they balked at his plan to take the men in the cabin with him, resistance raised its head. After all, the Indians dramatically outnumbered the soldiers by greater than ten to one. Yet as they judged the cavalry commander standing before them, they understood that he would fight them if necessary to accomplish his mission. The Zunis cleared the way for Pershing to move in.

Pershing and his men rode in closer to the cabin; then they dismounted. He ordered the men to deploy around the log hut. All the while, Pershing kept his Colt navy revolver in its holster until the last minute. Then the moment of truth arrived. He crept up to the cabin, hoping to remain unseen by the desperate men inside. Approaching the door, he kicked it in and threw himself inside, where he came under the aim of three Winchester rifles. Yet Pershing was coolly in control.

"Well, boys, I've come to get you," he stated matter-of-factly.

The men disagreed, showering the second lieutenant with insults and curses. Pershing then explained their situation, making them understand that they were doubly surrounded by both Indians and ten cavalrymen, a circle within a circle.

"What are you going to do with us?" one of the men asked.

"Take you to Fort Wingate."

Negotiations unfolded, with the accused rustlers agreeing to leave under Pershing's custody only if they could retain their guns. Pershing held the most cards. "No, you're going as my prisoners. I'll promise you that the Indians will not touch you."

Soon, the three men surrendered their weapons. Pershing then marched his prisoners out of the cabin but was uncertain how the Indians, who had lost comrades, might respond. He spotted a buckboard nearby and ordered one of his men to retrieve it. He even said to his men, "We are going to take those men away and if these bucks get hostile remember we mean business."[37]

Once Pershing had his prisoners on the buckboard, he and his men rode through the mass of angry Indians without incident. The situation had been defused; the Indians had trusted the young, uniformed representative of their friend, Colonel Carr; and the mission seemed a success. Pershing and his troopers returned to Wingate, and the rustlers were placed in the guardhouse.[38] Pershing had handled the situation much to Carr's satisfaction. Old War Eagle understood the delicate situation into which he had dispatched his second lieutenant, and the colonel gave him a commendation for having successfully threaded a difficult needle.

Pershing's later encounters with the Indians of the Southwest did not turn out as well for him as it had that day with a hundred angry Zuni warriors ready for blood. Despite the subjugation of the Apaches seemingly a fait accompli when Pershing arrived fresh from West Point in 1886, occasionally a handful of renegades left their reservations. An 1889 incident put Pershing on the trail of several roamers who had harassed local settlers. The commander led his detail of troopers across the desert in a pattern of intersecting angles, but the second lieutenant became separated from his men. Alone and isolated, Pershing was soon attacked by eight Apache warriors who emerged on horseback from a nearby arroyo.

The cavalry officer tried to outrun his attackers, but a warrior caught up and struck him on the head, causing Pershing to fall off his mount and sending him sprawling across the desert floor. Pershing had drawn his pistol, but the revolver flew out of his hand, landing twenty feet away. By this time, his men had spotted Pershing and were riding to his aid. Lying on the ground and only half conscious, the cavalry officer could see the Apache attacker kneeling above him, his tomahawk raised to deliver a death blow. But Pershing survived the moment, despite his desperate situation. Inexplicably, the Indian stood up, ran to retrieve Pershing's revolver, jumped on his horse, and sped away with his comrades, leaving Pershing alive. Throughout his lifetime, Pershing believed he was helped by an element of personal luck. Without question, this moment counted as exhibit A.[39] He soon survived another desert drama that included a significant amount of the Pershing luck—his near-fatal trip with Stotsenburg to reach the Grand Canyon.

By September 1889 Pershing was transferred once again, this time back to Fort Stanton, along with his troop. Colonel

Carr made the transfer as well. The move met with Pershing's approval. Wingate had lost some of its charm for him compared with his initial arrival just eight months earlier. In a letter he wrote the following year (1890) to his comrade Julius Penn, Pershing expressed his unvarnished opinion of Wingate: "This post is a S.O.B and no question. . . . Tumbled down, old quarters. . . . The winters are severe. It is always bleak and the surrounding country is barren absolutely."[40]

Soon after the transfer, Pershing had the opportunity to perform a personal service for Carr. War Eagle enjoyed a good bear hunt, and Pershing informed his commander that he had a local source near Stanton who could provide an excellent hunting dog. Carr gave him fifty dollars to buy the animal. Pershing made the purchase and had "it carefully crated and shipped" to the colonel. Receiving the dog specially bred for hunting bear, Carr planned a hunting trip. But when the party of hunters encountered its first bear, "the dog turned tail and fled back to the post." Pershing was extremely chagrined by the affair, having invested Carr's money badly. "It was a long time before I heard the last of it," remembered Pershing.[41]

Nevertheless, Colonel Carr remained a supporter of Pershing's, giving him a "most excellent" rating on his 1890 efficiency report. Somewhere along the way, Pershing made up his mind about the military. He enjoyed the life, found it rewarding, and planned to stick with it. But he did not intend to remain stuck out on the New Mexico frontier forever. Soon after his transfer to Fort Stanton, Pershing requested an opportunity to attend the Infantry and Cavalry School at Fort Leavenworth, Kansas. Although Carr supported him with a recommendation, the coveted assignment did not materialize. Not to be outdone, Pershing then contacted a comrade at Leavenworth, requesting that he send the entire course offered at the school so John could study on his own.

In late October, Pershing saw one of his final assignments in New Mexico. Brig. Gen. Alexander McCook, a department commander, arrived at Wingate intent on visiting with several area tribes. He was accompanied by Lt. Chauncey B. Baker, a West

Point classmate of Pershing's who would eventually serve under him in Europe during World War I. Pershing commanded the escort that Fort Wingate provided to deliver the McCook party to a large council of Navajos and Moquis.

The meeting proved splendid, involving many Indians from the region, including young Native warriors, their faces decorated with war paint, and Indian women wearing colorful, variegated blankets. The great council was the largest Indian-white powwow Pershing ever attended during his time in New Mexico. Along with the sit-down between both parties, there were lots of games, wrestling matches, and races. Once the Indians finished racing one another, they challenged their white visitors to compete with them. Pershing's pal Baker convinced the warriors that Pershing was a strong wrestler. The second lieutenant declined and challenged the Indian men to a footrace, instead. Only after issuing the challenge did Pershing remember he had sprained his right ankle while playing baseball a year earlier and that it had knocked him out of activity for nearly two months.

But the challenge was accepted and the best Indian runner selected. Bets were taken on both sides, and a hundred yards paced off. Pershing "stripped down to almost as little as the Indian wore." Someone fired a pistol, and the two sprinters sprang forward. Pershing describes what happened: "The race was rather even for the first fifty yards, then I began gradually to draw away from him and in the end came out two paces ahead."[42] In his memoirs, Pershing does not include an important detail. As he neared the finish line, his ankle gave out on him, sending him sprawling to the ground, where he rolled across the finish line. The Indians cheered him anyway, even as the betting resulted in their handing off to the winning troopers "a number of blankets, bows and arrows, and other Indian paraphernalia."[43] In the spirit of diplomacy, Pershing instructed his men to return all the items to their Indian owners. When the warriors called for a rematch, he declined.[44]

Despite failing to receive the Leavenworth appointment, a change soon came for Pershing. While the Native Americans of the Southwest were nearly all situated on reservations across Arizona and New Mexico, the year 1890 witnessed a new Indian challenge for the U.S. Army, this time in South Dakota. A strange uprising was unfolding, encouraged by a Native holy man whose visions foretold the decline of whites on the Great Plains, the resurgence of Native populations, and the miraculous return of the buffalo. Tales of ghosts and of elk hide shirts impervious to the white man's bullets spread across the Northern Plains, bearing visions of new hope. Soon Pershing and the Sixth Cavalry received orders to transfer from their remote, desert corner of New Mexico to the treeless plains of the Dakotas. Pershing's days in the desert were over for now, but he had not seen the last of its mysterious mountains.

FIVE

Cloak, 1890–91

On New Year's Day 1889, a total eclipse of the sun blanketed the American West in a shadowy darkness. Out west in modern-day Nevada, a Native American holy man dedicated himself to turning the darkness into light. Wovoka lived forty miles to the northwest of the desolate Paiute Reservation near Walker Lake. Soon after the eclipse, he began preaching a message nearly every American Indian in the West eventually wanted to hear. He considered himself a prophet—in his memoirs, Pershing describes him as "a man impersonating Christ"—whose vision of the Native American future was bright and promising.[1]

Wovoka grew up on a local ranch, raised by a white rancher named David Wilson. He learned English, converted to Christianity, and received the Christian name of Jack Wilson. As Wovoka became an adult, he combined elements of his Christian faith and some Mormon teachings with Indian religious influences. The eclipse appears to have provided him with the sign of authority he was seeking. He felt destined to speak for his people and guide them toward a new light. After all, the world they occupied had fallen on hard times.

Over the preceding decades, much change had come to the Indians living on the Great Plains and farther west. The Anglo-Americans' movement across the Trans-Mississippi West had accelerated since the 1840s, with their endless wagon trains rolling westward along the Oregon Trail, carrying pioneer families bound for either rich farmland in Oregon or the gold-laden streams of Northern California. A half century had passed in the meantime, delivering millions of farmer-settlers to the Great Plains who occupied traditional Indian lands and brought instability to Native populations everywhere. So many Americans and recently arrived European immigrants arrived on the plains by the 1880s that they outnumbered the Native Americans at least forty to one. The tidal wave of migration simply overwhelmed the Indians.

While most of the disruptive influx onto the Great Plains was embodied in countless farmers and their families, other Americans also brought irrevocable change to the Indians. Providing cover for the mass of farmers were soldiers such as young John Pershing. Another group that caused great damage to the traditional Native way of life, the horse and buffalo culture that had unfolded during the early nineteenth century, were professional buffalo hunters. Throughout the 1870s and into the 1880s, bison numbers dwindled dramatically. Prior to such singular slaughter, the number of buffalo on the Plains stood between thirty-five million and forty million head. The federal government had developed a policy of encouraging professional buffalo killers to spread out across the Plains to slaughter as many bison as they possibly could. As Col. Richard Dodge of the U.S. Army encouraged a buffalo hunter in 1867: "Kill every buffalo you can! Every buffalo dead is an Indian gone."[2]

Buffalo hunters carried out their deadly work in short order. Between 1872 and 1874, non-Indian hunters killed off as many as three million bison annually, while hundreds of thousands of Indians killed only 150,000 head. By the mid-1870s, the great bison herds of the Plains were nearly nonexistent, and by the early 1880s, their numbers were reduced to fewer than a thousand, prompting Smithsonian Institution officials to send an expedition out west to kill a few more to taxidermy one for a museum display. The days of the Indians' reliance on bison for their food, shelter, and other purposes were gone. Native Americans had to surrender to the pressures of settling down on federally established and operated reservations, where they often lived as paupers. (The time frame for wiping out the western bison herds corresponded with the movement of cattle up from Texas on the legendary long drives of the 1860s, '70s, and '80s. With their numbers controlled by whites, the cattle replaced the buffalo as the primary animal stock of the Plains.)

In his memoirs, Pershing notes another significance of this great reduction of bison on the Great Plains: "Buffalo hunting became the sport of frontiersmen, and Indians also took part, killing the animals for their hides alone, which they used to cover their tepees and to spread on the dirt floors. The army purchased hides by wholesale and made them into overcoats, the last of which were issued to the cavalry in the Sioux campaign."[3]

Wovoka's vision provided Native Americans on the Northern Plains with a hope they believed had long vanished. He claimed he heard the voice of God. Like a latter-day version of Joseph Smith, the Indian medicine man told everyone that a spirit visited him during the eclipse and ordered him to look toward the darkened sky, where he "saw God and all the people who died a long time ago."[4] God then told Wovoka to "take charge of things in the west" and handed him powers that allowed the seer to control the rain and snow, as well as fire.[5]

His reputation spread far and wide across the Plains. Reservation Indians representing various tribes became curious concerning the rumors of Wovoka and his visions. The timing could not have been better placed for many of them. Tribes from the Cheyenne to the Arapaho to the various Lakota bands seemed leaderless. Sitting Bull and Crazy Horse—the legendary victors of the Battle of the Greasy Grass, or the fight that whites knew as the Battle of the Little Bighorn or Custer's Last Stand—had seen their best days. Crazy Horse was long dead, and Sitting Bull lived on the Standing Rock Reservation. Red Cloud, the greatest of the Lakota leaders, had long ago also accepted reservation life.

Even the one white man who always seemed to represent their best hope, Major General Crook, had died of a heart attack at Chicago's Grand Pacific Hotel in March 1890. His death prompted a sad response by Red Cloud: "Then General Crook came; He, at least, had never lied to us. His words gave the people hope. He died. Their hope died again. Despair came again." It seemed to many Plains Indians that Wovoka's message was their only remaining hope.[6]

By March 1890 a pair of Lakota leaders trekked out to Nevada to find Wovoka, held a council with him, and gained insight into his powerful vision. When Short Bull from the Rosebud Reservation in modern-day South Dakota and Kicking Bear from the Cheyenne River Agency (he had fought alongside Crazy Horse at the Little Bighorn battle) reached Walker Lake, they joined hundreds of Indians from many different tribes who had gathered to hear the words of the self-proclaimed messiah. Kicking Bear was surprised when he saw Wovoka; he had expected to see a white Christ, since that was the image the missionaries had taught him. He also approached the Paiute holy man to examine him and see if he had the scars of crucifixion on his hands (Wovoka did not). When they returned, Kicking Bear and Short Bull only reinforced the rumors that many on the reservations across the Dakotas were hearing.

While Wovoka's reputation as a holy man, seer, visionary, and Christ-substitute figure gained traction across the West from the Great Basin to the Plains, he was a man of mixed motives. A few years earlier, he famously had made a grand and unlikely prediction that appeared to come true. He announced an ice floe on the Walker River in the midst of summer. With many witnesses gathered along the Nevada stream, most were surprised as they watched large chunks of ice bobbing on the water. However, it was all a trick. Wovoka, with help from his adopted Walker brothers, had loaded onto a wagon blocks of ice from the family's icehouse and dumped them upstream to fulfill his prophecy.

But now the Paiute holy man was on to bigger things, the redemption of all Native peoples. He preached that any who followed God's commands (according to Wovoka) could be reunited ultimately with their ancestors in heaven and experience a new

Earth. Just by following a list of guidelines espoused by Wovoka that largely reflected the biblical Ten Commandments, all might be restored as it was before the arrival of whites on the Great Plains. The medicine man also introduced a new dance to the people known as the "Ghost Dance," one of the most important aspects of the new Native religion. Curious visitors such as Kicking Bear and Short Bull introduced the dance to their own people. Still other Native groups on the Plains found out about the dance through the Shoshones in Idaho. The cosmology of this new religion, then, centered on a practice of nonviolence, a circumspect code of behavior, and a special dance. "You must not hurt anybody or do harm to anyone," Wovoka preached. "You must not fight. Do right always."[7]

Wovoka took his message so seriously that he packaged it as a pan-Indian panacea, claiming all Native American brothers who did not accept his visionary movement were doomed. He preached, "All Indians must dance, everywhere, keep on dancing. Pretty soon in next spring Great Spirit come. He bring back all game of every kind. The game be thick everywhere. All dead Indians come back and live again. They all be strong just like young men, be young again."[8]

By mid-November 1890 the Ghost Dance had spread from one Dakota reservation to another. Sitting Bull invited Kicking Bear to come to the Standing Rock Reservation and teach his people the Ghost Dance. Everyone seemed focused on the new religion that assumed the deaths of whites and the revival of Native peoples. Indian children stopped attending reservation schools. Indian farms went untended. Trading posts were empty. On the Pine Ridge Reservation, white Indian agent James McLaughlin sent a concerned telegraph to the Bureau of Indian Affairs in Washington: "Indians are dancing in the snow and are wild and crazy. . . . We need protection and we need it now. The leaders should be arrested and confined at some military post until the matter is quieted, and this should be done at once."[9]

Matters only unraveled further. By November 20 the Indian Bureau in Washington instructed field agents to compile lists of all the local leaders—the words used in the telegram were "fomenters of disturbances"—of any and all Ghost Dances. Once the list was compiled, it was sent to General Miles's headquarters in Chicago. When the list included Sitting Bull, Miles assumed the elderly chief was at the center of the religious conspiracy.[10]

Rather than arresting Sitting Bull outright, a move that Miles knew might prove difficult, he sent a telegram to Buffalo Bill Cody, asking him to visit Sitting Bull and convince the legendary Lakota leader to go to Chicago for a council. But when Cody arrived at Standing Rock, James McLaughlin did not allow the meeting. Cody left, irate that his time had been wasted.

Against this backdrop of Indian drama, Pershing and the Sixth Cavalry received orders on November 23, just a few days following the exchange of telegrams between field Indian agents in South Dakota and those at the bureau in Washington. As commander of the Military Division of the Missouri, General Miles decided that the call for troops was to meet a legitimate threat posed by the Ghost Dance and the religious message it represented. Reports indicated that three thousand Indians had left the Rosebud and Pine Ridge Reservations, situated along the South Dakota–Nebraska border, and had removed themselves into the "barren hills, narrow valleys, ravines, canons, mounds, and buttes" of the Dakota Badlands.[11]

War Eagle Carr gathered a force of 325 enlisted men, eighteen officers, and 339 horses. The company left Fort Wingate on the afternoon of December 1 and, just before midnight, boarded a train at the Wingate Depot that was ready to depart for Rapid City. The route was a bit circuitous, taking the men east to Albuquerque and then north on the AT&SF Railroad into Colorado and across much of Kansas. They skirted west of Omaha, Nebraska, and headed northwest across the state on the Fremont, Elkhorn & Missouri Valley Railroad to Rapid City in the northeastern region of the Black Hills.[12]

Frigid temperatures dominated the talk among the men when their train rolled into Rapid City. The trip had taken longer than a week. The little community of Rapid City boasted a population of just over two thousand residents in 1890, and the locals were soon overrun by similar trainloads of troops. Everyone needed supplies, and army quartermasters had their hands full outfitting units with food, ammunition, and heavy, winter coats, which Pershing and his men had not required in the deserts of New Mexico. The second lieutenant never forgot the Dakota cold he faced during his weeks on patrol east of the Black Hills, even though he received a newly issued blanket-lined canvas overcoat—in his memoirs, Pershing incorrectly remembered his coat was fashioned out of buffalo fur—plus a heavy fur hat, fur-lined gauntlets, heavy felt oversocks, and a pair of Arctic overshoes.[13] The horses were dressed warmly as well, with many "provided with blanket-lined canvas covers and calked shoes."[14]

The Dakota campaign was the last of Colonel Carr's lengthy career in the West that had been spent quelling multiple Indian uprisings and perceived threats during the advance of non-Indian settlement. The Dakotas were familiar ground for him, having campaigned in the Black Hills in 1876 against the Lakotas. That campaign took him out to Wyoming, with Buffalo Bill Cody serving as a scout.

Soon, General Miles set out on a dual strategy to neutralize the Indian threat. As was common among the reservation Indians almost anywhere in the West at that time, government rations were short, causing an additional grievance for the Native population. He tried to round up additional food and deliver it to the reservations. In the meantime, his strategy focused on creating a military perimeter encircling the Dakota Badlands in an effort to keep various bands of Lakotas and others, especially the Cheyennes, from massing together.

Carr and his men deployed east of Rapid City along the Cheyenne River. War Eagle knew how to lay out such a campaign, including the most important consideration of keeping his men adequately supplied. The colonel soon received a well-known visitor, the western artist and writer Frederic Remington, who tagged along with the Sixth Cavalry and made sketches of the men and their mounts. Observing Carr, he later wrote, "I was a guest of General Carr, the colonel commanding the 'Galloping Sixth' Regiment of United States Cavalry, and I assure you that he thought of nothing but 'bacon and forage.' No tramp of steeled hoofs, no floating guidons, no gallant men or plumes or flashing sabres; nothing but 'bacon and forage.'"

When Remington questioned Carr about his emphasis on "bacon and forage," the colonel was adamant: "Sir, the most important things about a cavalry regiment are the stomachs of the men and horses."[15] Perhaps Carr's emphasis on food and supplies rubbed off on Pershing during his assignments under the general's command, for when it was Pershing's turn to rustle up rations for his men in later theaters such as Cuba during the Spanish-American War, he bent all the rules.

Pershing's Company A and the Sixth Cavalry received orders from Carr to establish a line running approximately forty miles, stretching northeast by southwest along the Cheyenne River between the Black Hills to the west and the Badlands immediately east. The assumption was that Indian bands were roaming on both sides of the Cheyenne, and Carr did not want them to meet up with one another.

Overall, he divided the Sixth Cavalry into three detachments covering that lengthy line with no means of communication between them save for horse-bound couriers. As for Pershing's Troop A, they rode along the line between Box Elder Creek and the confluence where Rapid Creek flows into the Cheyenne. The ride involved two brutal days for the men. Since they had not yet received any camping tents, they had to sleep out in the frozen elements, burning campfires to stay warm. Despite the harsh weather and wind, Pershing's men covered thirty miles of hard ground.

By mid-December Miles was in command of nearly 3,500 troops spread out over hundreds of square miles of Dakota Territory, representing one of the largest troop deployments of the U.S. Army since the Civil War. The situation was hardly ideal. Units could not easily communicate with one another, and the Indians proved somewhat elusive. Rumors confounded commanders. On December 14 Miles received information that the Lakotas, Cheyennes, and others were preparing to launch a large attack. He sent out riders to inform all the moving parts of the Sixth Cavalry to ride with haste to reconnoiter. Pershing turned his men toward Rapid Creek, first on a walk, then a trot, and finally a full gallop. His men remained in their saddles for hours, battling the harsh, bone-chilling weather, including a ceaseless prairie wind as threatening to them as the Indian warriors they had not yet encountered.

While moving fast across the Dakota landscape, Pershing and his men spotted a wide-ranging grass fire off in the distance, representing a bad sign. Carr had informed his officers that such fires sometimes signaled the approach of an Indian attack. That night, his men hardly slept, waiting for the howl of warriors, only to face the howling winds. No attack came. Pershing and his men soon reached the relative safety of the remainder of the regiment.

The following day, December 15, brought some mixed news: Sitting Bull was dead. Three days earlier, General Miles had sent an order to Lt. Col. William F. Drum, who served as the commander of troops at Fort Yates in North Dakota, the tribal headquarters for the Standing Rock Reservation. The order informed Drum "to secure the person of Sitting Bull. Call on Indian agent [James McLaughlin] to cooperate and render such assistance as will best promote the purpose in view."[16]

Things had not gone well. At dawn on the fifteenth, forty-three Indian police moved in and surrounded Sitting Bull's log cabin on the reservation. A squadron of cavalry was on alert three miles away in case it was needed. The leader of the reservation police Lt. Henry Bull Head entered the cabin and found the Hunkpapa Lakota leader sleeping on the floor. When Sitting Bull awoke, he asked Bull Head, "What do you want here?"

"You are my prisoner," responded Bull Head. "You must go to the agency."

Sitting Bull seemed ready to cooperate. "All right," he said, "let me put on my clothes and I'll go with you." He then asked Bull Head to go outside and saddle his horse.

But when the Indian policeman emerged into the early morning light, he found a large group of Ghost Dancers gathered around the grounds, numbering four times Bull Head's police force. Catch-the-Bear, one of the dancers, approached the policeman.

"You think you are going to take him," the Ghost Dancer shouted. "You shall not do it!"

Bull Head turned to Sitting Bull, who had come out of his cabin.

"Come now," he said to the old chief, "do not listen to anyone." When Sitting Bull seemed to balk, Bull Head and Sgt. Red Tomahawk moved toward him.

Suddenly, Catch-the-Bear tossed his winter blanket aside, revealing a hidden rifle, and took a shot at Bull Head. The bullet entered his side. When Bull Head fell down, he tried to take a shot at his assassin but accidentally shot Sitting Bull, instead. Sgt. Red Tomahawk then fired at Sitting Bull, shooting him in the head and killing the legendary Lakota veteran of Custer's Last Stand. A gun battle exploded between the Ghost Dancers and the Indian police. A cavalry detachment moved in finally and managed to rescue the remnant of the reservation police force.

During the battle, Sitting Bull's horse acted out a curious dance of its own. The animal had performed in *Buffalo Bill's Wild West* five years earlier as Sitting Bull's mount. As shots rang out across the cold Dakota landscape, the horse began to go through the steps he had performed in the *Wild West* arena: he "sat upright, raised one hoof, and it seemed to those who watched that he was performing the Dance of the Ghosts."[17]

The death of Sitting Bull struck like a lightning bolt in the midst of an already unsettled situation unfolding in and around the Badlands. No western chief was better known, respected, or mourned by the Lakotas. The fear among the troops was that Sitting Bull's death—even at the hands of Indian police, not the army's—might galvanize further those already fervently engaging in the Ghost Dance. In the end, no such cohesive force brought the various bands of Lakotas together during those frigid, late-December Dakota days. Without Sitting Bull to guide them, many Hunkpapas abandoned Standing Rock and sought out various encampments of Ghost Dancers. Some went to the

Pine Ridge Reservation where Red Cloud lived. A remnant of nearly a hundred joined Big Foot's Miniconjous camped near Cherry Creek. Even separated groups of Miniconjous did not manage to gather into a single, united wall of resistance. In the aftermath of Sitting Bull's death, the military turned its primary attention on the Miniconjou leader Big Foot.

Big Foot's people recognized him as one of the greatest of Miniconjou chiefs. When introduced to the Ghost Dance, he embraced it, for he had long memories of the old ways of his people on the Plains and wanted to believe in better days for them. But by mid-December his dream of the dual return of the buffalo and his ancestors began to fade. With his people facing the cold and severe food shortages, he decided to take his followers to the Cheyenne River Agency, located north of Pierre on the Missouri River, where they might receive rations. But he soon changed his mind when on December 18, a pair of Hunkpapas joined his band and informed him of the death of Sitting Bull. They also told him of soldiers headed his way.

The Miniconjou leader suddenly became uncertain of what move to make next. Some warriors argued they should all go back to their reservation, while others insisted on heading south to Pine Ridge. If he joined forces with Short Bull and Kicking Bear—Red Cloud was also there—they might manage to establish a coordinated resistance. The aged leader chose to return to his old village. But with every move he made, leading his people in one direction and then another, the army was close by, shadowing his movements—all of which it considered hostile.

The march home did not unfold as Big Foot had hoped. He contracted pneumonia, which caused his lungs to hemorrhage, requiring him to ride in a wagon rather than walk. Several younger warriors managed to convince him, once again, to alter his course. On the evening of December 23, he and his people headed toward the Badlands, continuing to move even into the night. By the morning of the twenty-fourth, his party was situated along a branch of the Bad River. At noon, they had reached another fork on the Bad. The sun shone brightly that day—a good sign for Indians looking for omens—but the weather was still cold and raw with the wind blowing up thick clouds of alkali dust.

Meanwhile, as day dawned on Christmas Eve, War Eagle Carr received a telegram from Lt. Col. E. V. Sumner, who had arrived at Big Foot's village: "When I approached his village, I found it vacant. . . . If you can move out tomorrow morning you will doubtless intercept him."[18] Carr wasted no time ordering his men to move. Within half an hour of receiving Sumner's message, buglers called the men together. Soon four troops of cavalry scattered in as many directions, some crossing the Cheyenne River while dragging a pair of Hotchkiss guns behind galloping horses. Other units also began to move.

Big Foot's people pushed on through the twenty-fourth until they reached the Badlands Wall and a pass that had not been used for some time, so it was in serious disrepair, especially for wagon passage.[19] Much of the trail was washed out and gullied. The chief's warriors grabbed shovels, spades, and axes, and worked feverishly to repair the trail. That night the band camped along the south bank of the White River.

That same day, Pershing's Troop A rode east toward Porcupine Creek in search of Big Foot, but he discovered no Indians. Soon he and his troopers set up camp and spent a bone-chilling Christmas Eve night. In his memoirs, Pershing recalled the weather as "intensely cold, and we spent it huddling close to the fires."[20] The following day dawned cold and brisk, hardly an ideal Christmas Day, which Pershing's troopers spent in the saddle in search of Big Foot and his people. Troop A received a courier from Colonel Carr at James' Ranch, near Kane Creek, informing Pershing that Big Foot had eluded the Eighth Cavalry and that his band was headed southward. If his men managed to catch up with them, Pershing was to arrest Big Foot. But again, the Miniconjou band proved elusive. On the twenty-sixth, the second lieutenant selected ten of his best men and engaged in far-ranging reconnaissance, again against low temperatures and wind, until they reached "a prominent peak overlooking the country but saw no sign of Indians."[21] Not only had

Big Foot slipped past the Eighth Cavalry but now he had managed to evade the Sixth as well.

By this time, Big Foot's band moved on to Cedar Spring—today's Big Foot Spring—where the people arrived on Christmas Day. The Native leader then dispatched three riders to proceed ahead and inform the anxious chiefs at Pine Ridge of his impending arrival. Those chiefs were to inform any local white officials that the band was coming in peace and that Big Foot was extremely ill. But his progress proved slow, with the band only covering four miles on the twenty-sixth and reaching Redwater Creek by nightfall.

Just miles away, a frustrated Pershing scanned the horizon and managed to locate an unnoticed trail flanking Porcupine Creek, running south from the Badlands. Reading the landscape, he became convinced Big Foot and his people might pass along that trail and informed Maj. Emil Adam, his squadron commander, that "Big Foot would probably come that way."[22] Adam was a Civil War veteran and thirty years Pershing's senior, a commander who had fought Indians from the Nez Perce to the Utes for fifteen years under George Crook. He discounted Pershing's suggestion and led the troopers toward another trail several miles to the west. In the end, Pershing was proven right. Big Foot's band did take the Porcupine Creek trail, and they were caught on December 28 by the Seventh Cavalry—Custer's old unit at the Little Bighorn—under the command of Maj. Samuel M. Whitside. This encounter led to the tragic Wounded Knee Massacre.

When Whitside met with Big Foot, the old chief was in miserable condition, his lungs racked with infection, crimson staining his blankets. He could hardly speak a word beyond a thin whisper, as blood dripped from his nose onto the snow. Whitside informed the chief he and his people must march to the cavalry camp on Wounded Knee Creek. Big Foot agreed, explaining he was already headed in that direction. Whitside then ordered Sgt. John Shangreau, a half-Indian scout, to disarm Big Foot's warriors, but the sergeant told his commander, "Look here, Major, if you do that, there is liable to be a fight here; and if there is, you will kill all those women and children and the men will get away from you." Whitside finally agreed.[23]

The soldiers transferred Big Foot to an army ambulance, while four troops of cavalry formed a column to lead the Indians—two troops at the vanguard, as the other two followed, along with a battery of two Hotchkiss guns. That evening they all encamped along Wounded Knee Creek. The number of Indians included 120 men and 230 women and children. With darkness descending, Whitside decided to wait until the next morning to begin disarming the Native Americans and ordered rations and tents issued to them, since they were short of tepees. Whitside even had a portable stove set up in Big Foot's tent. Later that night, additional units of the Seventh Cavalry arrived and bivouacked north of Whitside's men. Col. James W. Forsyth, in command of the Seventh, informed Whitside of his orders to deliver Big Foot and his people to a Union Pacific Railroad depot for transport to a military prison in Omaha.

One of Big Foot's warriors, Wasumaza, or Iron Tail—who later changed his name to Dewey Beard—later wrote about the tragedy that unfolded the following morning (December 29): "There was a bugle call. Then I saw the soldiers mounting their horses and surrounding us."[24]

After breakfast, Colonel Forsyth ordered the Indians to disarm. Some warriors cooperated; others hesitated. Soldiers began stacking the confiscated guns. Some troopers searched the Indians' tents and tepees, and brought out "axes, knives, and tent stakes and piled them near the guns."[25] Soldiers ordered everyone to open their blankets to reveal any hidden guns or weapons.

Suddenly, the moment began to deteriorate. A medicine man named Yellow Bird began to perform the Ghost Dance and sing one of his holy songs. The reputation of the dance and of the Ghost Shirts the warriors wore was that they were supposed to make them impervious to bullets. Yellow Bird chanted in Lakota: "The bullets will not go toward you. The prairie is large and the bullets will not go toward you."[26] Black Coyote, a young Miniconjou warrior, refused to surrender his new Winchester rifle, waved the weapon above his head, and shouted the gun was his, that he had paid too much money for it to surrender it to the soldiers. A member of his band later described Black Coyote as "a crazy man, a young man of very bad influence and in fact a nobody."[27] He may also have been deaf. Soldiers approached. A struggle ensued. Black Coyote lowered his arms, pointed his rifle off to the east, fired a shot at a forty-five-degree angle toward nothing, and split the day in two, the before and after of the Wounded Knee Massacre.

As Black Coyote fired his Winchester, a half dozen other warriors produced rifles and fired toward the men of Troop K. Immediately, scores of gunshots ensued, as the soldiers' Springfield rifles answered the reports of the Natives' Winchesters.[28] Panic spread among the women and children as the Hotchkiss guns opened up, with artillerymen blasting off a shell a second, cutting the tepees, the tents, and Big Foot's remnant band to shreds. Louise Weasel Bear later remembered, "We tried to run, but they shot us like we were buffalo. I know there are some good white people, but the soldiers must be mean to shoot children and women. Indian soldiers would not do that to white children."[29]

Soldiers quickly cut down Big Foot. White Lance, one of his warriors, recalled, "I looked [and] I saw Big Foot lying down with blood on his forehead and his head to the right side."[30] The Miniconjou chief eventually became the face of the Wounded Knee Massacre. A photograph taken of his blanketed body dead in the snow—his arms locked in surrender, his head raised, his eyes shut—became a silent reminder of a haunting tragedy forever frozen in black and white.

It was all over in minutes, leaving Big Foot and half his band dead or wounded. The official tally included 153 known dead, but it is believed that many of the wounded later died. Among the soldiers, twenty-five were killed and thirty-nine wounded. Several died from friendly fire, including shrapnel from the Hotchkiss shells' explosions. The Indians were left on the field where they fell that day, as a blizzard blew in and blanketed the frozen corpses with snow. Only afterward did a military party return to bury many of the dead in a mass grave.

One of the Indian combatants in the Wounded Knee engagement was an Oglala Lakota warrior named Black Elk, a second cousin of Crazy Horse. Born in 1863, he grew up during some of the most difficult years for the Lakotas. He saw the buffalo herds destroyed by professional hunters and knew well the devastating effect the slaughter had on his people and their way of life. He witnessed repeated warfare between his people and the U.S. Army, and participated at age twelve in the Battle of the Little Bighorn, where he shot and scalped a soldier. Black Elk later described the incident with a matter-of-fact detachment: "I shot him in the forehead and got his scalp. . . . I was not sorry at all. I was a happy boy."[31]

By the late 1880s, Black Elk became a performer with *Buffalo Bill's Wild West*, just as Sitting Bull had. But he could not stay away from his people long and, within two years, returned to Pine Ridge. Just as he had participated in the Battle of the Little Bighorn and the massacre of Custer and the Seventh Cavalry, he was present during the Wounded Knee Massacre, where he charged soldiers and helped remove several wounded Indians from the field of engagement. He had witnessed repeated tragedies impacting his people through his young life, yet he could only see the importance of the Wounded Knee battle through a dark lens: "I did not know then how much was ended. When I look back now from this high hill of my old age, I can still see the butchered women and children lying heaped and scattered all along the crooked gulch as plain as when I saw them with eyes still young. And I can see that something else died there in the bloody mud, and was buried in the blizzard. A people's dream died there. It was a beautiful dream."[32]

Black Elk lived nearly sixty years following Wounded Knee. In his later years, he organized a Native American show, reminiscent of Cody's *Wild West*, in which he turned the tables on Buffalo Bill's mythologizing of the frontier. Black Elk's show presented the Indian perspective, including Lakota culture and folkways such as the Sun Dance, which he performed.

Perhaps it is fortunate for the military career, or at least the historical legacy, of John Pershing that Major Adam did not heed his advice concerning the Porcupine Creek trail as a possible conduit for Big Foot's escaping band of Miniconjous. That he missed the unfortunate—and, some would say, unnecessary—encounter at Wounded Knee, with all of its tragic ramifications, meant he did not have to explain his steps later or justify his involvement or reconcile anyone's actions in his own head. As for Pershing, he never commented publicly, at the time or later, concerning the deaths of Big Foot and those massacred alongside him. Pershing was a soldier engaged in a task for which he was responsible, and he did not presume to judge those who had taken part in the action at Wounded Knee.

The days following the Wounded Knee Massacre were tense for both the troopers and the Indians. Both sides assumed additional fights were possible, and both remained on high alert. Chiefs Short Bull and Kicking Bear no longer believed remaining at the Pine Ridge Agency was safe, and they soon led those who followed them toward the Badlands, with all its peaks, rock formations, and endless places to hide. Miles took steps to hem in all moving Indians and slowly tightened his grip. Within days, the combined efforts of the army's services, including cavalry, infantry, and artillery, locked the region's remaining Ghost Dance advocates into an irregular triangle flanked by the White River to the northwest, White Clay Creek on the southwest perimeter, and Wounded Knee Creek to the east.

Miles then placed himself at the center of the three-sided cordon and waited for the remaining Indians to bring themselves in. All field units, including Pershing's Troop A, were instructed to stand down and allow the Indians to pass if they appeared bound for Pine Ridge. Slowly, Indians reported in, including some of the fiercest resistors, such as the Brules and Oglala Lakotas. Things did not simply fall into place for Miles, however, as the year 1890 slipped into 1891. The day following the Wounded Knee engagement, a fight unfolded along White Clay Creek fifteen miles north of the community of Pine Ridge after units of the Seventh Cavalry arrived near the Drexel Mission, a Catholic outpost, to check on rumors the Indians had burned it. That encounter resulted in one soldier's death, and seven were wounded. Other small attacks involved the death of an army officer and a pair of warriors who were killed by local whites.

Pershing's Troop A engaged in some limited action of its own. On the afternoon of January 1, units of the Sixth Cavalry, including Troop K, were escorting a supply wagon train to an encampment along Wounded Knee Creek. As the wagons passed along the west bank of the White River, a party of Lakotas appeared on a ridge on the opposite side of the stream. The war party rode down the ridge and through the creek's icy waters, yelling war cries as they bore down on the wagons. The men of Troop K dismounted and engaged in a firefight with the warriors. The sound of gunshots and shouting echoed along the low hills, and other elements of the Sixth were soon dispatched to their aid. Pershing and Troop A rode hard over the rolling hillsides, covering a distance of six miles in minutes and arriving in time to witness the Indians attacking a circle of wagons defended by fellow troopers. As the reinforcements arrived, the Lakotas scattered. Pershing and his men rode straight down a ridge, firing their service revolvers as they attacked. While managing to rescue the wagon train and its defenders, Pershing's men arrived too late for a full engagement. After nearly five years in uniform in the American West, John Pershing had experienced his first, limited taste of combat. Afterward, Pershing's record read: "Action near mouth of Little Grass Creek, South Dakota, January 1, 1891." Other "action" awaited Pershing later in his career.

Such skirmishes fought across the frozen landscape of southwestern South Dakota proved significant if only for one important reason: they represented the last gasps of Indian resistance, the final acts of Native wars that had unfolded since America's colonial era. For hundreds of years, Indian nations had fought the advance of Europeans and, later, of Anglo-Americans and the concomitant decline of their own cultures. The nineteenth century had witnessed countless battles, skirmishes, raids, and massacres, as well as endless diplomacy and treaty making. Now, finally, those days were over.

Through the first two weeks of January 1891, the Pine Ridge Reservation became the destination for thousands of Indians whom the Ghost Dance had betrayed. Approximately four thousand men, women, and children reported to Indian agents at the reservation, bringing with them seven thousand horses and five hundred wagons. They were through with resistance. Chief Kicking Bear literally placed his rifle at the feet of the general, a highly significant gesture. General Miles waited for them all and made certain they received adequate rations, since many were starving.

Pershing, ultimately, played a minor role in that history. He had arrived in New Mexico when the Apache wars were nearly at an end, and he only managed to experience the last days of Indian resistance on the Northern Plains. Still, his time in the West, through these early years of military service, had proven extremely formative for him as a soldier and an officer. He saw how Miles had carried out strategy and deployed his men effectively. He understood how his commander had utilized diplomacy in combination with force. Wounded Knee had happened, unfortunately, and its lessons were tragic and difficult to understand. But Pershing was a better soldier because of his days on the cold, rolling prairies and hills of South Dakota.

Through a limited number of weeks of campaigning in South Dakota, Pershing had gained valuable experience in the field. He managed to meet all the challenges placed on himself and his men. He reflected the values of Colonel Carr by making certain his men were properly supplied, clothed, and fed. Writing in his memoirs years later, Pershing reflected on the campaign that ended the Lakotas' resistance: "It was an exemplary lesson in what might well be called preventive action."[33]

Through the weeks of January 1891, the number of troops stationed in South Dakota slowly dwindled, with the threat of Indian uprising definitively neutralized. This mission was General Miles's final active campaign, culminating his long military career, and everyone under his command knew it, as War Eagle Carr became the new commander. Miles was given a final review of troops on January 24. Sitting on his large black horse, the experienced Indian fighter watched from a rolling knoll as more than three thousand troops filed past him, bugles sounding, columns maintaining a tight formation. Ten thousand Indians looked on. When the Sixth regiment passed, the general removed his hat in respect, giving special attention to Pershing's Troop A. Bands played the popular cavalry tune "Garryowen," as the troops, including the Seventh Cavalry, filed past. It was an emotional moment for Miles, who later described his feelings that day: "That scene was possibly the closing one that was to bury in oblivion, decay, and death that once powerful, strong, defiant and resolute race."[34]

It was a final moment for all before the dispersion of forces began. The Sixth Cavalry did not return to New Mexico but remained in the region, with most units assigned to Fort Niobrara, Nebraska, while others headed out to Fort McKinney, Wyoming, and Yellowstone Park. As for Pershing's Troop A, it was off to Fort Niobrara. The ride to this new posting did not take place until early February, when Troop A and four additional troops set out for their destination, a hundred miles away, close to the Rosebud Reservation. A portion of the trail followed the course of the Fremont, Elkhorn & Missouri Railroad to Niobrara.

Their days in South Dakota featured harsh weather, and the cold season was not yet ended. Many in Troop A grew beards "not as personal adornment but as a protection against the weather," Pershing observed, "and the result was a grim-looking group."[35] After five days on the trail, the troop became aware of the advance of poor weather. On February 6, the troopers reached Cody, Nebraska, where they camped near the rail line. The next morning they headed to Crookston, where the small community offered good stables and a local store for personal supplies. That afternoon, the column of troopers crossed the path of a local rancher who gave them a stern warning: "You'd better get into camp soon. A blizzard's coming!"

A curious officer asked him, "What makes you think so?"

The rancher explained, "This mist isn't in the air for nothing. I've lived out in this country long enough to know what it means. I tell you a blizzard's coming and you'd better get into camp."[36]

No one took issue with this local veteran of winters in Nebraska. The troops went into immediate encampment, with special emphasis on pegging tents as solidly as possible. They laid out the tents in a long row behind the town's railroad station. The men picketed their horses in their own long line about fifteen feet from the tents. After the troops' mess wagon served a quick supper, the men fed the horses and covered them with blankets where they could be spared. Everyone hunkered down for the blizzard the local rancher had predicted. By ten o'clock, the winds came in like a beast, cutting the cold air and pushing hard against the tents, their pegs straining but holding firm.

Years later during an interview, Tom Stevenson, a sergeant in the Sixth, was asked, "Who ordered the men to peg the tents firmly?"

The old veteran thought about it and answered, "I can't exactly remember. But I wouldn't be surprised if it was Pershing: he was always busy looking after the men. I do remember him coming, all muffled up, to my tent just before the blizzard broke.

"'Stevenson,' the second lieutenant said, 'we're in for a bad time. You'd better order the men out to get in more firewood. There is a pile of ties over there by the railroad. Have the men use them. And be sure to tell them to tie towels over their mouths and noses before they leave their tents—this wind is blowing so that a man can't get his breath unless he's muffled.'"

Seventy-seven-year-old Stevenson put Pershing's words into context: "That's the sort of an officer Pershing was, always thinking about his men, and that's why the men would do anything for him."[37]

The night proved itself a frigid hell. The wind never let up, turning ever sharper as dawn approached. But everything the men could do to get themselves through the storm had been done. Second Lieutenant Pershing had seen to that. He took refuge in his own tent, a conical Sibley, a standard issue for field officers dating before the Civil War. It came with a collapsible wood-burning stove—called a Sibley stove—which was entirely inefficient, and a length of narrow stovepipe that vented through the tent's top. Pershing cursed the flimsy stoves:

"But for our substantial winter clothing there would probably have been many casualties."[38] Once morning broke, the storm did not, and the men emerged from their tents into three feet of drifting snow. Even though the mess wagon had been placed only six hundred feet from the tent line, it might as well have been on the moon. Those who tried to cover the distance failed to conquer the ever-increasing drifts. Still, the men's primary concern was not for food but rather for their horses. The snow practically covered many mounts until they appeared as large lumps of snow. But Pershing had ordered his men to protect them, and their precautions paid off well. Not a single horse was lost through a full night of the howling, merciless storm.

If the men could not cover the ground to the mess wagon, they managed to create an open line through the drifts to the little store near their encampment. Lacking new supplies, the store only offered up a quantity of frozen butter and ginger cakes. So butter and cakes it was for Pershing, his men, and all the other troopers of the Sixth who were caught in the aftermath of a hard Nebraska blizzard.

The storm did not abate until the morning of February 9. For more than thirty hours, the weather controlled the movements of the cavalry troops. But the snow moved on, and by early morning when the bugles blew, the troopers mounted their frozen steeds and set out once again for Fort Niobrara, approximately twenty cold miles away. Those miles seemed to extend forever, as the men struggled through endless drifts, with the troops each taking turns leading the others. The last miles took nine hours to cover. When they reached the Niobrara River, the column narrowed to cross the local bridge leading straight into the fort. On the bridge, the struggling troopers saw an unfortunate soldier-postman who had frozen to death, reminding all how close they had come to dying themselves in the same storm.

Finding Fort Niobrara blanketed under deep layers of white, Pershing had difficulty getting a clear picture of the facilities, as he noted in his memoirs: "When we got to the post we found the barracks and quarters almost hidden by the heavy snow banks."[39] During the following weeks, the snow remained, and Niobrara resembled an arctic village more than a western fort. Only after weeks had passed did the long-awaited thaw arrive. Already, Pershing had received his next orders: return to the Pine Ridge Reservation to take up a new command. He was to oversee four newly formed companies of Lakota scouts.

In a sense, he had been in this situation before, leading those of another race, serving as an instructor and guide. His days as a teacher at the Black school in Laclede had taken place a dozen years ago, but something about Pershing suggested race did not matter when one human being interacted with another human being. He embraced his new duty even though he was uncertain how the Lakota warriors might respond to him.

The men assigned to him did not resemble soldier material when Pershing first met them. Receiving his muster roll, he read a list of names suggesting experience, manly pride, vision quests, time spent in battle: Thunder Bull, White Crow, Comes-from-Scout, Running Shield, Red Feather, Big Charger, Black Fox, Crow-on-Head, Guy-Three-Stars, Eagle Chief, Has-White-Face-Horse, Yellow Bull, Ghost Bear, Iron Cloud, White Hawk, Wounded Horse, and Kills Alone.[40] They wore uniforms of a sort, but to him they looked wild, veterans of combat who took pride in their warrior culture. Even though their people had been removed from their homelands and placed on reservations, they still saw themselves as fighters, men whose ancestors had raided their enemies and killed for honor. With that came a certain pride, a haughtiness that Pershing instantly saw and knew he needed to tame. The language barriers were significant, and even the simplest of orders had to be explained, something Pershing was not accustomed to doing. One immediate common ground between Pershing and the Lakotas was their horses. The Lakotas prided themselves in their mounts and took pains with them that the second lieutenant appreciated. Each man was provided forty cents a day for the maintenance of his horse, the same amount regular cavalry troops received; in fact, the Lakota scouts also were paid the same as the regular cavalry.

Pershing began working closely with his Indians. While other white officers sometimes kept Native scouts at arm's length, allowing their racism to determine their actions, Pershing began to study their language and their personal habits. During the cold winter weeks, he devoted whole days to language classes. Pershing appreciated his new command. He felt the use of Lakota scouts could prove extremely valuable for the army, providing a link between the Indians and the government. With Lakota scouts at his side, a commander such as Pershing became more accepted when visiting the Pine Ridge Reservation, where memories of Wounded Knee were fresh and personal. His first sergeant was Thunder Bull, a cousin of the great Lakota chief Red Cloud.[41] In his memoirs, Pershing refers to Red Cloud as "the venerable chief, now very friendly," who "came to camp once in a while to pay us a visit."[42]

Overall, Pershing became pleased with the men placed under his command. A photograph taken in late June 1891 shows Pershing posing with three dozen Lakota scouts, all wearing cavalry blue and a variety of campaign hats, and many are proudly holding their rifles. Alcohol was an occasional problem, just it was with white or Black soldiers. Once they understood the nature of specific orders, the Lakotas proved extremely willing to obey and please. Pershing tried to rank his men according to the status they held among themselves; it could be tricky but was ultimately the right call. Among the Native Americans, Pershing wrote, "prestige was an important factor in discipline."[43] He tried to keep them active, providing them with daily assignments to maintain discipline. In many ways, he treated his Indian soldiers as he did any others under his command.

Once the long weeks of winter came to an end, and Pershing's Indian scouts could work outdoors, he understood their true value. He described their skills: "I often took the troop on marches to various points on the reservation for an outing and for instruction. But field work was second nature to them; they would send out advance guards and flankers and cover the main body perfectly, cautiously approaching the crest of a ridge as if actually in hostile country."[44]

In early April, Pershing received an awkward assignment. He and his Indian scouts were to ride out to the Wounded Knee battlefield to police the grounds over a three-day period. Pershing knew the assignment would severely test the discipline of his men. Some of them might even find signs and remnants of their own families on the battle site. When they arrived, they found the haunted remains of the Indian encampment scattered across a wide piece of ground, a place turned sacred to the Lakotas because of the deaths of so many innocents. Artillery shell holes pocked the land. Broken tepees and fire sites dotted the field. Even human remains were uncovered from gullies and other hidden places.

Pershing, when he arrived, viewed the Wounded Knee Massacre site for the first time and immediately felt out of place. Over the days he and his men worked at the desolate encampment, other Indians visited. Some were relatives of lost family members, seeking solace or perhaps even revenge. The danger to a trooper was real.[45] He became aware of a practice he had not witnessed before on the part of some of his men: "Whenever I left [my] tent one of the scouts, without my orders, would follow closely as a bodyguard." Often the scout standing vigil at the door of Pershing's tent was Thunder Bull. Anytime Pershing encamped for a night on the reservation, he was at his commander's door, smoking his pipe. "Every time I moved," noted Pershing, "that old Indian was on my trail."[46] Through such actions, Pershing developed a strong sense of attachment to his Native scouts. He felt secure in their presence, and when visiting dignitaries came to Pine Ridge during that spring and summer, he knew he could trust his men to provide security.

But his command of Lakota scouts did not last more than six months. Money was not earmarked to continue the Indian troopers, and they were disbanded. The experience was an important one for Pershing. He had worked closely with men of another race and had learned much about their ways and their culture. It served him well when the time came to command the African American troops of the Tenth Cavalry, the "buffalo soldiers" of western cavalry legend. Reflecting on his scouts, Pershing noted, "I found much that was fine in Indian character. Once a red man gave his confidence he was entirely trustworthy."[47]

Even before Pershing's Indian scout unit disbanded, he sensed the prevailing winds in the West, certain he would soon be handed another assignment, but he could not know where. In the five years since his graduation from West Point, he had seen assignments in the American West and grown immensely from those experiences. Still, even if he had reconciled himself to a life of service in the military, he continued to nurse that long-standing dream of becoming a lawyer. Considering his possibilities, he proactively began searching out that alternate destiny. Three years earlier, Pershing had written the secretary of the board of regents of the University of Nebraska and applied for a posting as the "Instructor in Military Tactics." But the request never came to anything.

Pershing felt the time had come to dust off his request and resubmit it. On June 1, 1891, he sent another letter to the adjutant general requesting a specific assignment to the university as "Military Professor of the Nebraska State University at Lincoln . . . as a vacancy will exist in September of this year."[48] Pershing explained his qualifications: graduate of West Point; five years' active service in the West, including Indian campaigns; and command of various troops, including his Sioux scouts. He noted that his parents had made Lincoln their home until January 1890. He was a bit forceful in presenting himself, noting confidently: "I think my application should be considered ahead of any other for the reasons above stated."[49]

Pershing did have other voices speak on his behalf concerning a possible appointment to the University of Nebraska. His parents had already moved to Chicago, but his brother James still lived in the Nebraska capital, where he was involved in Republican state politics. Having recently campaigned in support of John C. Allen as the secretary of state of Nebraska, James felt comfortable enough to ask Allen to support his brother's appointment to the military tactics instructor position. Allen responded positively, and he soon wrote a letter to Sen. Charles Manderson (R-NE), who wrote directly to Secretary of War Redfield Proctor: "I respectfully recommend that Lieut. Pershing now with a troop at Pine Ridge be detailed.... He was through the late Indian trouble, graduated in 1886 and has been in the field continuously and it would gratify me and a number of my constituents to see him detailed."[50] Soon two paths converged for Pershing, with political recommendations followed by military approval. In War Eagle Carr's recent efficiency report, dated May 1890, he gave Pershing "Most Excellent" commendations in every category. Under "special duty fitted for," Carr had written "college detail."[51]

While Pershing waited that summer for word of his fate, he wound up his command of the Lakota scouts and requested temporary assignment to a rifle range. He looked ahead to another marksmanship competition, one more prestigious than his earlier competition in New Mexico—the tri-department competition slated for Fort Sheridan, Illinois, in September. To help him prepare, Pershing was assigned to the Bellevue Rifle Range south of Omaha, Nebraska. While at Bellevue, Pershing received the news he had been hoping for—Special Orders No. 184, his appointment "as professor of military science and tactics at the University of Nebraska ... to take effect October 1, 1891. ... Lieutenant Pershing will report in person at the university September 15, 1891."[52]

As excited as Pershing was about the new appointment, one he had massaged for several years, there was a complication. The rifle competition he intended to participate in at Fort Sheridan required his involvement after September 15, the date he was to report to the university. He wrote a letter to the adjutant general and explained his dilemma. Pershing's worries were over when he received word that he could report to the university ten days later than scheduled. The autumn of 1891 proved golden for Pershing. He competed in the U.S. Army's carbine competition at Fort Sheridan and won a pair of medals. He soon took a train from Illinois west to Fort Niobrara, where he packed his belongings. Then he hopped on another train headed east to Lincoln, Nebraska, and his new assignment.

For five years, 2nd Lt. John Joseph Pershing had called the

American West his military home. He had grown taller and a bit heavier, despite his active service on the frontier. He still sported a trim mustache and looked every bit the thirty-one-year-old army officer that he had become. Even his parents, since his graduation from West Point, had put Laclede, Missouri, Pershing's hometown, behind them. Pershing had seen adventure at every turn in the West. He had engaged in war games; ridden hard across the crusty, sun-baked ancient lands of the American Southwest; and seen every character he had ever imagined from the pages of Beadle's dime novels. Indians—the indigenous peoples of the West—were no longer stereotypes cut out of some white man's imagination. Pershing had seen them, run races against them, sat with them at council fires and ate their boiled dogs, fought them, admired them, and pitied them. But he came out of the West understanding them better than he had going in.

Pershing had seen multiple assignments to a string of forts, made new friends, and learned the intricacies of command. He had served as a soldier from the painted deserts of the Southwest to the frigid plains of the Dakotas. Pershing, of course, never put the lessons of Laclede and northern Missouri completely behind him. But the West had formed him into a man who saw the world through the eyes of experience, with all its drama and irreconcilable human tensions; who tried to understand the other man, felt comfortable walking around in his shoes; and who ultimately was completely confident that he could tackle any responsibility ever handed to him. Still, his appointment to the University of Nebraska represented a challenge, an unknown. Would he find his place on a campus where academics, rather than Indians and buffalo, roamed? Would he stand out among his fellow professors as an uncultured frontier soldier? Would he satisfy his dream of receiving a law degree? If so, would he remain in the army?

As Pershing boarded his train for Lincoln, all his questions remained unanswered. In the meantime, the American West awaited the day of his return.

1. The Pershing family lived in three different homes in Laclede, Missouri. This house was the last John Pershing lived in from the age of twelve until his departure for West Point. Library of Congress, Historic American Buildings Survey Collection, HABS MO, 58-LACL, 1-1.

2. Pershing poses with members of the Sixth Cavalry at Fort Bayard, 1886. Pershing is seated on the left end of the steps and holding a young child. University of Nebraska Archives, Barney McCoy Collection.

3. Gen. Nelson Miles. Pershing served under him in the West during the 1880s and as his aide in Washington DC during the 1890s. Library of Congress, Popular Graphic Arts Collection, LC-DIG-ppmsca-46574.

4. Gen. Eugene Carr, circa 1860–70. Pershing served under him during a portion of his service in New Mexico. Library of Congress, Civil War Photographs Collection, LC-DIG-cwpb-06855.

5. Troop B of Ogallala Indian Scouts formed following the Wounded Knee Campaign with Pershing (*standing, far right*) as the commanding officer, 1891. Library of Congress, Miscellaneous Items in High Demand Collection, LC-DIG-ds-09607.

6. This frontier street in Lincoln, Nebraska, includes the University of Nebraska's University Hall (circa the 1870s). University of Nebraska Archives, Barney McCoy Collection.

7. James Hulme Canfield, the chancellor of the University of Nebraska, 1891–95. His tenure included the four years Pershing was assigned to the university as the commandant of the Corps of Cadets program. University of Nebraska Archives.

8. Charles G. Dawes, a Lincoln lawyer and friend of Pershing's during his days as the cadet commandant at the University of Nebraska. Dawes would be elected the vice president of the United States in 1924. Library of Congress, Bain Collection, LC-DIG-ggbain-15579.

9. William Jennings Bryan, October 1896. During Pershing's days at the University of Nebraska, he and Bryan became friends. Library of Congress, LC-USZ62-8425.

10. Willa Cather, circa 1893–94. Cather attended the University of Nebraska while Pershing served as the cadet commandant, 1891–95. Pershing taught her mathematics and fencing. University of Nebraska Archives, Philip L. and Helen Cather Southwick Collection.

11. George Meiklejohn was Pershing's friend from his Lincoln days. In 1898, while serving as the acting secretary of war, he was able to get Pershing assigned to active field duty and see action in Cuba during the Spanish-American War. Meiklejohn later helped Pershing gain his first assignment in the Philippines. Library of Congress, C. M. Bell Studio Collection, LC-DIG-bellcm-07800.

12. Pershing as a young captain during the Spanish-American War, 1898. University of Nebraska Archives.

13. Theodore Roosevelt as a member of the Rough Riders, 1898. He and Pershing saw action in Cuba during the Spanish-American War. Later, as president, he helped advance Pershing from captain to brigadier general. Library of Congress, LC-DIG-ppmsca-35735.

14. Helen Frances "Frankie" Warren, the daughter of Wyoming senator Francis Emory Warren. Frankie and Pershing married in January 1905. Date of photo unknown. Library of Congress, Bain Collection, LC-DIG-ggbain-19840.

15. Pershing (*pictured at top, center of photo*), 1902. Brig. Gen. Samuel S. Sumner, Pershing's commander (*seated at the left*), is meeting with sultans at Camp Vicars in Mindanao. Library of Congress, Miscellaneous Items in High Demand Collection, LC-USZ62-107906.

16. Pershing family in the Philippines, 1911. Along with John and Frankie are their children Anne, Helen (*seated in a wicker chair*), and Francis Warren. Library of Congress, National Photo Company Collection, LC-USZ62-107733.

17. Brigadier General Pershing in formal dress uniform, probably taken in September 1912. The three medals signify his participation in the Indian Campaign, the Spanish Campaign in Cuba, and the Philippine Campaign. Library of Congress, Bain Collection, LC-DIG-ggbain-21134.

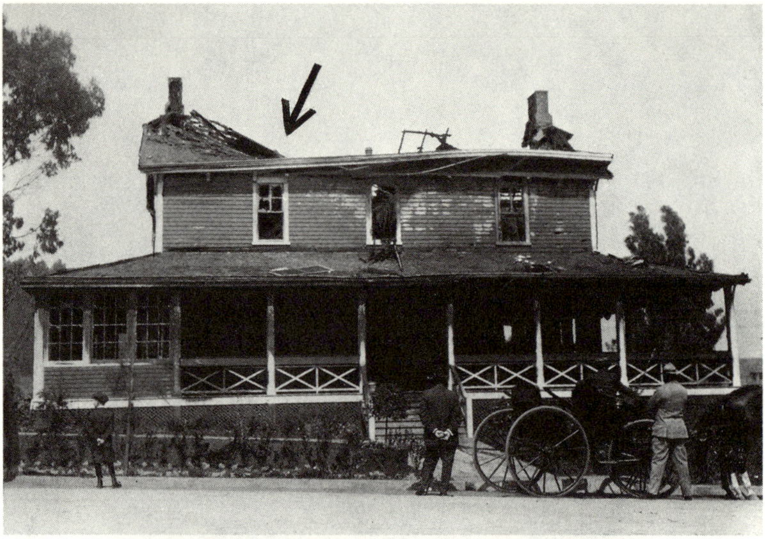

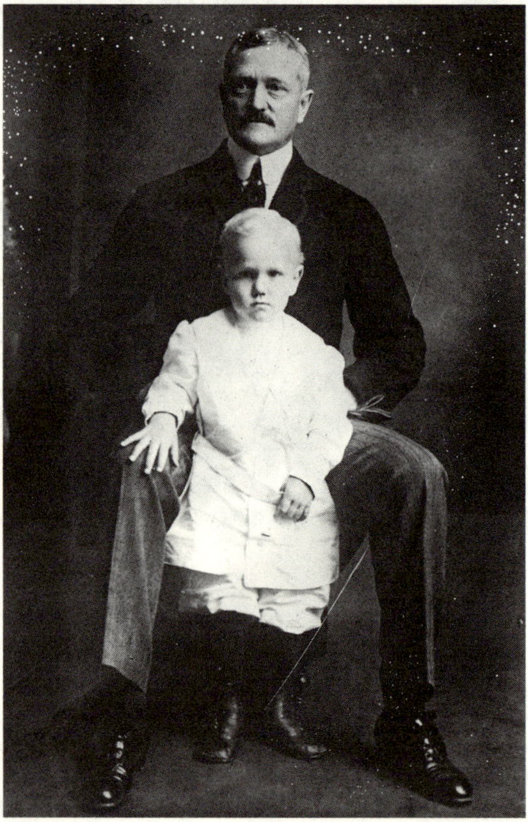

18. (*opposite top*) The Pershing family's burned-out home at the Presidio. Fire destroyed the house on the night of August 26–27, 1915. Frankie, Helen, Anne, and Mary Margaret succumbed to smoke inhalation, while Francis Warren survived. Library of Congress, Historic American Buildings Survey Collection, HABS CAL, 38-SANFRA, 8D-2.

19. (*opposite bottom*) Pershing poses with his son, Francis Warren. The date is likely 1912. Library of Congress, Bain Collection, LC-DIG-ggbain-30234.

20. (*above*) Iconic photograph of Pershing and the Mexican pistolero Pancho Villa during better days between the two. The photo was taken on August 26, 1914, in El Paso, Texas. Accompanying Villa is Gen. Alvaro Obregon (*left*). Behind Pershing is a young Lt. George Patton (*right*). Villa's pockets appear to bulge with concealed pistols. Author's collection.

21. Mexican pistolero Pancho Villa, Pershing's nemesis during the Punitive Expedition (date unknown). Library of Congress, National Photo Company Collection, LC-DIG-npcc-19554.

22. Pershing with his officers at Casas Grandes, Chihuahua, Mexico, during the Punitive Expedition, 1916. Library of Congress, Bain Collection, LC-DIG-ggbain-21382.

23. Political cartoon depicting the difficulties of Pershing's Punitive Expedition, 1916. Library of Congress, Cartoon Drawings Collection, LC-DIG-ds-10810.

24. A stern-faced Pershing during the Punitive Expedition in Mexico, 1916. University of Nebraska Archives.

SIX

College, 1891–95

Lincoln, Nebraska, was the second town of that name Pershing called home. While stationed at Fort Stanton in New Mexico, the first Lincoln represented no more than a local village, home to a few hundred souls, mostly of Hispanic heritage. It was little more than a dusty nowhere, made semi-famous by the gun exploits of Billy the Kid. Pershing's second Lincoln home was a significant step up.

When Pershing returned to Lincoln in the fall of 1891, he was reintroduced to a prairie community younger than himself. Lincoln, situated in the southeastern corner of Nebraska, represented a wider place in the road than most of the young state's towns. At the opening of a new decade, the people of Lincoln aspired to more than they could rightfully lay claim to. Lincoln's history only went back twenty years or so. At the time, residents thought of their town as a genuine midwestern city and bragged of an inflated population of fifty-five thousand citizens. The true number of inhabitants was likely closer to thirty thousand.[1]

But the town was well on its way to outgrowing its earlier, frontier roots. Business was relatively thriving, with O Street serving as the community's main east–west thoroughfare (and even does today). The Haymarket Square, which paralleled Eleventh Street, was a busy beehive of commercial activity. Such main streets were paved with blocks of cedar and were still relatively new. An electric trolley car system zigzagged along tracks in every direction. Adjacent to the main university campus—a tight academic landscape built on four city blocks—trolleys loaded and unloaded passengers at three different depots. A fledging telephone system existed, including a direct line between the state capitol building and the local firehouse.

In its earliest days, Lincoln had a dull brown, monotonous look—similar to the rolling prairie itself—but the immigrants who reached it transplanted new life in it. The town was established too late to be founded only by simple homesteaders seeking new land; instead, Lincoln experienced a different set of frontier elements that were "not of the land but of commerce and the professions: judges, lawyers, merchants, publishers, railroad builders, professors."[2]

Lincoln's founders and the first generation that followed did not live in a true frontier world, despite the saloons and brothels, even though much of the Nebraska land spreading out from this commercial and political hub had been frontier during the 1870s and '80s. The town presented an image of pioneer simplicity—on Lincoln's eastern edge, some folks still only survived in dugouts, and the number of saloons was likely equal to the number of churches—even as the community boasted a variety of social clubs, a reasonably well-stocked public library, and, of course, its own university. The arts-minded could enjoy stage productions at a pair of elaborately appointed theaters: the Funke Opera House, built in 1885 to seat 1,200, and the Lansing Theatre, constructed in 1891, the year of Pershing's arrival, with a capacity of 1,800 patrons.[3] When Pershing came to teach, the Nebraska capital was home to five private schools. An equal number of hotels were available, including the Arlington, which Oscar Wilde extolled after an 1882 visit as "the best hotel west of the Mississippi, not even excepting those in San Francisco."[4]

The university Pershing selected for his academic career as a military professor was still a fairly humble institution but, like the community, was poised for growth and expansion. Originally chartered in 1869 under the Morrill Act as a land grant college, the University of Nebraska–Lincoln (UNL) was built practically from scratch. Its first large-scale building, University Hall, was constructed from sun-dried bricks produced locally, and the wood framing the hall's interior was shipped up from Nebraska City on wagons. In an attempt to establish a bit of European flair to the frontier community, University Hall was built in the "Franco-Italian" style with a red mansard roof. The hall rose three stories above a full basement. Photographs of Lincoln dating to the early 1870s depict a scattering of small, one- or two-story clapboard-framed farmhouses with University Hall otherwise dominating the flat Nebraska landscape like a great red stone outcropping straight from Pershing's New Mexican badlands. Without really understanding what he was saying, one early Nebraska student, who had grown up in a sod house, claimed the expansive building reminded him of the Parthenon.

Early attempts to create an attractive campus included planting hundreds of young trees and building up numerous flowerbeds. But harsh Nebraska winters killed the trees, and hordes of locusts repeatedly consumed the flowers. Still, hearty Nebraska pioneers insisted their university would not only survive but also thrive. University Hall proved a disappointment, though, beginning with its construction. Three workers died in 1870 when a cable holding a section of scaffolding broke, sending the men to their deaths. The building was constructed out of shoddy materials, and even before it opened for the first classes in the fall of 1871, its foundation already needed repair. A whole new foundation was excavated and laid beneath the building's central tower in 1893 during Pershing's tenure on campus. The roof leaked constantly, and when a new slate roof was installed in 1883, the added weight put more stress on the hall's walls and foundation.[5]

Willa Cather attended the University of Nebraska during the years Pershing served as the commandant of the cadet program. She knew the campus intimately, including University Hall. Her novel *The Professor's House* (1925) tells the story of Godfrey St. Peter, a professor of history at a small, unnamed midwestern university in the fictitious town of Hamilton. The location is left otherwise ambiguous except that the university is situated near Lake Michigan, effectively eliminating the possibilities for Nebraska. In the work, she describes a campus building reminiscent of University Hall, one with similar structural issues:

> He walked through the park ... to a building that stood off by itself in a grove of pine-trees. It was constructed of red brick, after an English model. The architect had had a good idea, and he very nearly succeeded in making a good thing, something like the old Smithsonian building in Washington. But after it was begun, the State Legislature had defeated him by grinding down the contractor to cheap execution, and had spoiled everything, outside and in. Ever since it was finished, plumbers and masons and carpenters had been kept busy patching and repairing it. Crane and St. Peter ... had wasted weeks of time with the contractors, and had finally gone before the legislative committee in person to plead for the integrity of that building. But nothing came of all their pains. It was one of many lost causes.[6]

Some of the town's landmarks, including the state capitol and University Hall, still drew visitors' attention just as they had five years earlier when Pershing first arrived to visit his parents. A second building was added to the campus in 1886, the year Pershing graduated from West Point. Soon construction commenced on another university building, a new library, and the new chancellor intended to stand over the builders himself to make certain it was built to specifications.

Beyond University Hall, Cather takes a wider view in *My Ántonia* when describing a UNL-like frontier academic institution through the eyes of the newly matriculated young coed Lena Lingard:

> In those days there were many serious young men among the students who had come up to the University from the farms and the little towns scattered over the thinly settled State.

Some of those boys came straight from the cornfields with only a summer's wages in their pockets, hung on through the four years, shabby and underfed, and completed the course by really heroic self-sacrifice. Our instructors were oddly assorted; wandering pioneer schoolteachers, stranded ministers of the Gospel, a few enthusiastic young men just out of graduate schools. There was an atmosphere of endeavor, of expectancy and bright hopefulness about the young college that had lifted its head from the prairie only a few years before.[7]

Pershing soon made a friend of James H. Canfield, the university's chancellor, who became for the second lieutenant on campus what Colonel Carr had been for Pershing out in New Mexico—a mentor. He was a warm, convivial individual, a leader with whom everyone felt comfortable and who always elicited the best from people. When he and Pershing met, the UNL chancellor took to him immediately, hoping the young army officer could pull the Corps of Cadets program out of the doldrums. The chancellor's daughter, Dorothy Canfield, who became a popular American writer, was only in the eighth grade when Pershing arrived to serve as a professor at the university. (She soon took a mathematics class under Pershing because the local high school was considered too far across town.) She described the relationship between her father and the new cadet commandant: "He did regard Pershing, in a way, as 'one of his students,' and did give him a great deal of good advice about the way to manage his life, which I think the rather stiff West Pointer needed."[8] As it turned out, Chancellor Canfield and Pershing's time at the University of Nebraska proved nearly exact footprints of one another, with both arriving in 1891 and leaving four years later for other opportunities. In a letter Canfield penned in 1895 at the end of Pershing's service at UNL, he described the state of the program the young officer had inherited: "He found a few men, the interest in the battalion weak, the discipline next to nothing, and the instincts of the faculty and the precedent of the University against the corps."[9]

With Pershing on campus, Canfield had high hopes for the university's lackluster cadet program. He had attended a military school as a young man and was a strong advocate for such training. As a land grant institution, the university was required to operate a cadet program, with military training compulsory for male students, but the program had become a punch line by the time Pershing arrived. Excuses to avoid such training were common, and the faculty was complicit. Overall, "the sentiment of the community, of the faculty, and of the student-body was pacifist."[10] War was old-fashioned, an unlikely reality for America's future. Even if war did break out involving the United States, the consensus was that such military training would likely not matter. The young Nebraska politician William Jennings Bryan, who carried the banners of both the Democratic Party and the Populist Party during the presidential campaign in 1896, suggested that in the case of war, "a million men will spring to arms over night."[11] His meaning was clear: the university cadet program was a waste of time, money, and youthful energy.

Despite such prominent negative views across campus regarding the cadet program, Pershing promised Canfield he would revitalize the program. He certainly had the youthful bearing to take on the task, a look that his students might appreciate. Pershing's military training taught him to stand ramrod straight. He appeared handsome, at least many women thought so, with his neat mustache and slightly curling, blondish hair. His eyes pierced through anyone who looked at him long enough. Pershing had the look of young gravitas, which fit him perfectly for his new role on the university campus. His clothes were always spotless, something he could manage on a university campus but was otherwise difficult on assignment in the desert lands of New Mexico. His shirt collar was an exact quarter inch above his coat collar. His coat's brass buttons reflected constant polishing. His shoes shone.

Pershing's presence on campus received immediate notice by many, and opinions of him soon turned positive. The campus newspaper, *The Hesperian*, ran a short editorial on the second lieutenant in the October 1 issue: "J. J. Pershing, Second Lieutenant 6th Cavalry, who takes charge of the Military Department, is a graduate of West Point and brother of the Misses May and Grace Pershing. Our guess is that he will prove very popular with the cadets."[12] For those students who reported as cadets, he made it clear he meant business from day one. From some students, the ones used to something less rigorous, Pershing received some pushback. One cadet stated to another, "This sort of thing may be all right in the Regular Army, but it won't go here."[13]

Pershing set out on his new mission with high hopes and tight-jawed determination. Outdoor training took place during the fall and spring months when the university was in session, allowing the cadets to avoid the harsh Nebraska winter weather. Grant Hall was the main facility, a state-funded armory. The building was fairly expansive, standing three and a half stories high, crafted from red brick, and trimmed in white stone. As Pershing searched its rooms, he found a bowling alley, a spacious gymnasium, a "drill room," a great room for storing artillery pieces—including a couple of muzzle-loading Civil War–era cannon—a room of band equipment, and lockers and dressing rooms. He located a cache of 125 rifles in relatively good condition.

Male students at the university were expected to pay for their own uniforms; that excused several from service, since they simply could not afford the cost. Many students who attended UNL came with little or no money and typically worked to pay their tuition and board by "selling newspapers, serving as waiters in restaurants, cleaning offices, or doing whatever odd jobs they could get."[14] A good number were farm boys straight from the fields, young men who had attended one-room schoolhouses and had hardly read a single book their entire lives. (One of Pershing's first students admitted he had only read one, *The Adventures of Robinson Crusoe*, but he suspected that much of the plot had never actually happened.) Pershing had a soft heart for such students, as they reminded him of his younger days of hard labor and early teaching jobs. During his second year at the university, he actually redesigned the cadet uniform that UNL students wore and fashioned it after the West Point model, including the braided jacket, striped trousers, and dark-blue cloth. But it was expensive, costing cadets $14.50. On one occasion, Pershing nearly lost a senior cadet who was appointed as an officer, only because the lad could not afford the new uniform. Pershing insisted the senior cadet accept the appointment, assuring him that "some way will be found to pay for it." Then Pershing paid for it himself without the cadet's knowledge.[15]

Pershing proved relentless. He knew the cadet program could only improve on a foundation of discipline and swift obedience to orders. Inspections were exacting for the young cadets, as the second lieutenant demanded spit-and-polish appearances and straight backs when at attention. He told boys who slouched, "Cut out that farm walk!"[16]

In some ways, Pershing first had to teach the basics to his college cadets, much as he had done with his early trooper assignments and especially with his Lakota scouts, who sometimes had to unlearn old ways and replace them with new ones. The young military professor fell back on methods he recalled from West Point. He selected his corporals from the sophomores and his sergeants from the junior class, and the seniors were his commissioned officers. In Pershing's view, "this system gave the different grades the prestige of class seniority. Many of the details of training and discipline were left to these cadet officers and noncommissioned officers, who were thus given useful experience in leadership which could be obtained in no other course at the university."[17]

Pershing's push and professionalism won over nearly all the cadets who showed up for drill. He impressed them early on with his ability to call the roll one time and remember names with faces. Throughout his life, Pershing retained an absorptive memory. Cadet Alvin Johnson, who later became the editor of the *New Republic*, recalled how Pershing offered him a corporal's rank during his second year at the university, but Johnson turned it down. Nearly fifty years later, both Johnson and Pershing met again at a party hosted by Bernard Baruch, an American financier and statesman who advised Presidents Woodrow Wilson and Franklin Roosevelt. Pershing approached Johnson: "I think I have met you before."

"Certainly," replied an incredulous Johnson. "You have met hundreds of thousands, who all remember you, but you can't remember the hundreds of thousands."

Pershing proved him wrong: "Was it in Nebraska, when I was commandant of Cadets?"

"It was," said Johnson, dumbfounded.

"And you were the cadet who refused to be a corporal," recalled Pershing. "I never did understand your reasoning."[18]

Pershing did not attempt to ingratiate himself to his charges. Instead, his expectations began to rub off on them. The second lieutenant was able to finagle more equipment for his cadets, including sixty-five brand new Springfield rifles and fifty cavalry sabers, courtesy of the War Department. One aspect of the training that Pershing emphasized early on was target practice. He had a target range set up in the armory basement where the cadets could improve their rifle skills. As a veteran, he understood that such practice was not a simple matter of aiming a rifle and squeezing a trigger. Rifle training could translate well into warfare, and he sought to discipline his boys even on the rifle range.

During one practice, Pershing's cadets were firing at a masked battery concealed in an orchard. The cadets were ordered to fire repeated volleys under the commands of "Load! Ready! Aim! Fire!" Pershing stood immediately behind his cadets, shouting the first three commands, only to tap a cadet with his boot and whisper only to him, "Fire your piece." The cadet was Pvt. William Hayward, who eventually became a colonel in command of the Fifteenth New York Infantry, an African American regiment that served with distinction in France during the Great War as the renamed 369th U.S. Infantry Regiment.

As Hayward obeyed, firing his .45-70, single-shot Springfield, the entire line of rifles blasted off shots in quick response.[19] Pershing's game was on. He moved quickly in front of one cadet, put his face in the lad's face, and turned him into a target. Pershing inquired, "Did you hear the command 'Fire!'?"

The cadet knew he had no other answer: "No, sir."

"Then why did you fire?"

"I heard someone else fire, sir."

"Do you *always* do what you hear other people do?"

The lad could only swallow hard and answer, "No, sir."

Hopefully all the cadets understood Pershing's message. As Hayward later observed, "In this way we soon acquired fine discipline. After that incident, I think the heavens could have fallen without a single piece being discharged until the distinct command 'Fire!'"[20]

Pershing organized a cadet record book in which he kept a list of each cadet's merits and demerits, a practice that created a sense of competition among his students. At each drill, he read the names of those who most recently received demerits. Before his first semester ended, his efforts received recognition. Again, *The Hesperian* published a glowing summary: "It is with pleasure that we are able to state that the military department is in a flourishing condition. There are 192 cadets registered. . . . Lieutenant Pershing is bound to put, and to keep, the military department on a systematic basis. Let his efforts be fruitful."[21] When Pershing arrived, the cadet battalion numbered 90 students. Before the semester's end, it had skyrocketed to 350. Chancellor Canfield could not have been happier, noting that no other department on campus had grown so quickly "or has made a deeper impression on the people of the city and of the state."[22] In time, Pershing had a campus-wide reputation and was often referred to by students and faculty alike as "the lieut," which all pronounced as "loot."[23]

Young men in his program became so committed to Pershing that they went out of their way to please him. Given his cool demeanor at inspections, they may have had little choice. In time, hundreds of cadets spent so much time trying to please Pershing—cleaning weapons, practicing their rifle skills, reading the manual of arms—that other faculty became jealous, accusing Pershing of monopolizing the students' time and energy. Some university professors suggested to the board of regents that the cadet program should be either reduced to its former insignificance or completely shut down. The board said no. Member Henry D. Estabrook recalled the controversy: "I listened to the arguments of the learned faculty and cast my vote against them. I told the faculty that there was not a study in the curriculum that in my opinion meant half so much to these young fellows ... as their military training under Pershing."[24] Canfield suggested half jokingly that some professors might improve themselves by participating in Pershing's cadet program. Pershing emphasized the values considered essential not only to a soldier but also to a well-rounded, disciplined student: obedience, service, duty, poise, temperance, a sense of deportment, and even how to carry oneself.

While his university responsibilities dominated much of Pershing's time, he found occasion to socialize off campus, just as he had managed a social life outside the confines of the three forts he had been assigned to in New Mexico. He took lodgings off campus and developed a close circle of friends. None was more important to him than a transplant from Ohio, Charles G. Dawes.

Dawes arrived in Lincoln in the spring of 1887, four years before Pershing. He grew up in Marietta, Ohio, and attended the University of Cincinnati College of Law, graduating in 1886.[25] Looking for a place to hang his shingle, young Dawes eyed the distant West and Lincoln after encouragement from a fellow law student from Nebraska. It helped that James W. Dawes, a cousin of his father's, had been elected governor of Nebraska in 1883 and remained the state's chief executive three years later. Governor Dawes also beckoned young Charles to seek his future in the Nebraska capital. But fortune and success had not yet found Charles Dawes when he and Pershing met—in Dawes's words, "Horace Greeley's advice 'Go west, young man,' was not a good short-range pecuniary counsel"—and the two became lifelong friends. Both young men had great careers and futures waiting for them.[26]

Dawes carved out a place for himself in Lincoln. He took on important cases, some directly connected to the commercial world of the Nebraska capital, including railroad cases. But even an 1888 victory against the Atchison and Nebraska Railroad in the state's supreme court did not turn him into an overnight legal success. He continued taking on an endless string of minor cases just to keep his hand in the legal profession. For several years, Dawes's father sent him fifty dollars a month to supplement his income, a sizable sum at the time.

The Nebraska transplant became more accepted by the better part of Lincoln society. Charles was invited to join one of the most prestigious and oldest social organizations in Nebraska, the Mount Pleasant Garden Club. As a member of the Irish National League, he rubbed shoulders with another recent arrival to the state from Illinois and fellow lawyer William Jennings Bryan. Bryan organized a new social club called the Round Table, whose members participated in book discussions and held friendly debates on everything from politics to religion to philosophy to the theory of evolution. Although Bryan initially restricted membership to Democrats, in Republican-dominated Lincoln, such a restriction seemed far too exclusive. Republican Dawes was soon admitted, and he and Bryan became friends, sharing membership in the Round Table as well as the legal profession; plus they were both Presbyterians.[27] (Their houses were only a block from one another as well.)

While Dawes and Bryan remained acquaintances over the years, a true friendship developed between Dawes and Pershing. They socialized regularly, taking fifteen-cent lunches at Don Cameron's Lunch Counter, then a central Lincoln landmark.[28] Both men never forgot the Lincoln eating establishment where "the food was good and, what was more to the point, the price was low."[29] Cameron's offered some of the best pancakes in town. One night, while attending an illegal boxing match in Lincoln, both young men threw themselves out of a window to avoid being nabbed during a police raid. Sometimes Bryan joined them for bean suppers at Cameron's, and the trio engaged in "debates at the Square Table."[30] (Pershing never formally joined the Round Table but did attend meetings from time to time.)

Both Pershing and Dawes struggled for several years as young professional men in Lincoln. Pershing received a second lieutenant's pay of $125 per month from the War Department, at least until November 1892, when he was promoted to first lieutenant. Dawes had a family, as he had married in 1889, and lived on an average of $100 a month. When Pershing arrived in Lincoln, he had in mind the possibility of attending the new law school at the university, and by 1893, he began attending law classes. Dawes supported his friend but cautioned him over leaving the military. "Better lawyers than either you or I could ever hope to be are starving in Nebraska," he warned his friend. "I'd try the Army for awhile yet. Your pay may be small, but it comes very regularly."[31] Pershing did receive his law degree, but the army remained his future.

Pershing found a new calling at the University of Nebraska. His cadets admired him more than he could have possibly predicted, especially given the reluctance of several to accept his leadership and the hard-edged discipline that came with it. Pershing offered the young men exciting instruction. Many felt the training was good for them and that Pershing was a professor who wanted the best for them. Pershing wanted to help them become the men he thought they could become. Cadet Hayward later recalled, "We all tried to walk like Pershing, talk like Pershing and look like Pershing. His personality and strength of character dominated us ... as I have never known in the case of any individual before or since, in or out of the Army. We loved him devotedly and yet I am sure the awe in which I stood of him during all those years was shared by every cadet."[32]

The young cadets had never met anyone like Pershing. Cadet Erwin R. Davenport said as much in an interview sixty years later: "Every inch of him was a soldier. In all my life I have never seen a man with such poise, dignity and personality. Whether in uniform or not, he attracted attention wherever he went, but he was always affable and interesting to talk with and popular with students and professors."[33]

Where professors had disregarded the cadet program before Pershing arrived, many were soon won over. Dr. Fred Morrow Fling, who taught history at UNL, noted that the second lieutenant "had a fine presence, a genial and unpretentious manner and one gained the impression that he was a man of great physical reserve coupled with unusual driving power. His speech was incisive; he was quick in action."[34] Jack Best, a UNL athletic trainer, lavished extraordinary praise on Pershing: "He was the finest man I ever worked with. It is true that he was mighty strict with his work, but the results he got were so good that everybody he worked with loved him for it. When he was here we had a regiment the University could be proud of. I just worshipped that man and everybody around the University felt the same about him."[35]

By April 1892 Pershing finagled an additional university assignment. He had barely arrived on campus the previous October when he sent a letter to Chancellor Canfield requesting an appointment as a mathematics instructor. (He did so partially out of concern that his military instructor tasks might not keep him that busy, plus he wanted the money. In his request letter to Canfield, he mentions a compensation of $750 per annum.) Faculty assignments had already been determined by then, but in the spring, he was assigned a mathematics class at the university's preparatory school, a class Canfield created to help unprepared students take on the rigors of university-level math. Once again, Pershing taught the farm boys, as he had years earlier in Laclede and Prairie Mound. But the class drew the prepared as well. In this class, Pershing also crossed paths with a pair of young Nebraska women bound for literary fame: the chancellor's daughter, Dorothy Canfield (Fisher was her married name), and her friend Willa Cather. (Pershing later also provided fencing lessons to them.) Pershing notes in his memoirs his "doubt that the study of mathematics gave either one of them a taste for literature."[36]

As for Cather, she refers directly to Pershing in her 1922 novel, *One of Ours*, for which she received the Pulitzer Prize. She wrote the novel as a tribute to her cousin Grosvenor (G. P.) Cather, who was the first Nebraska officer killed during World War I.[37] Introducing Col. Walter Scott, one of the novel's characters, she notes, "Years ago, when General Pershing, then a handsome young Lieutenant with a slender waist and yellow moustaches, was stationed as Commandant at the University of Nebraska, Walter Scott was an officer in a company of cadets the Lieutenant took about to military tournaments. The Pershing Rifles, they were called, and they won prizes wherever they went."[38]

These competitions soon became a part of Pershing's legacy at the university.

As for instructing mathematics at the university, he taught his courses in the same manner as he approached his military instruction. He simply expected his students to perform according to his instructions. If he assigned something one day, he anticipated his math students should have the material mastered when he saw them next. After taking one of his classes, Dorothy emerged largely unimpressed. "He taught a living subject like geometry as he would have taught a squad of raw recruits he was teaching to drill—that is, by telling them what to do and expecting them to do it."[39]

The famous seem to have gravitated into Pershing's sphere during his years at the university. Beyond Canfield and Cather, Alvin Johnson, who later became a famed American economist, recalled Pershing and his mathematics class. His instructor was "tall, perfectly built, handsome. All his movements, all play of expression, were rigidly controlled to a military pattern. His pedagogy was military. His questions were short, sharp orders, and he expected quick, succinct answers. . . . Never in the whole year did he give us . . . enthusiasm for mathematics."[40] During one class session, when Pershing ordered Johnson to the blackboard to work out an algebra problem, Johnson tried to beg off, claiming he should be excused because he was already behind the other students in the class. A grim Pershing responded, "You have been here a week. By next Monday be caught up."[41]

Teaching mathematics provided Pershing an opportunity to wear civilian clothing on campus rather than his uniform. On one occasion, this led to an embarrassing scene for John, who had a campus reputation for his unyielding gravitas. Scheduled to review the cadets publicly in parade formation, Pershing left his class to change into his uniform. With a large crowd gathered on the grounds, the commander appeared before his cadets, who looked smart in their uniforms, each cap festooned with a gold wreath encircling the letters NUC for "Nebraska University cadet." Everything pointed to another review featuring Pershing as stern taskmaster. He marched across the field with his usual military bearing, but soon the crowd noticed an inconsistency Pershing had overlooked. After changing clothes for the review, Pershing had failed to change hats. He was not wearing his usual military cap but an incongruous derby. Dorothy Canfield was present and wrote later that any other man would have received a burst of laughter from the crowd. But no one dared.

So the review went forward with Pershing none the wiser, as he marched the full length of the field, wheeling and facing the student adjutant who saluted him. Only when Pershing raised his arm to return the salute did he realize he was wearing the wrong hat. Without breaking military order, the cadet commander turned around and marched straight off the field, disappeared for a moment, and returned wearing the appropriate officer's headgear. Only then did the review commence, as if nothing had even happened. Canfield never forgot the event: "Did you ever in your life meet a man who would not have been laughed at in those circumstances? I have."[42]

On another occasion, during an 1892 parade along the streets of Lincoln marking the twenty-fifth anniversary of Nebraska statehood, Pershing's horse broke from formation and went into "an exhibition of bucking . . . that would have done credit to any wild west show," during which Pershing's bridle broke as one of his stirrups slipped off the saddle. But the veteran cavalry officer remained on his horse until he regained control of the animal. The alarmed crowd cheered loudly for the cadet commander's performance.[43]

Nothing Pershing did during his four years at the University of Nebraska endeared him more to the students, faculty, and administration than an 1892 rifle drill competition Pershing trained his boys to compete in. Early that year, several of

Pershing's cadets read an editorial in *The Hesperian* concerning a national drill competition scheduled for that spring in Omaha, just fifty miles east of Lincoln by train. The article read, "We have a United States officer to drill us ... something probably, of which no other company can boast."[44] The editorial reflects how much and how quickly the university had embraced Pershing and his attempts to revitalize the cadet battalion on campus. It represents a complete buy-in, one signaling a full turnaround for many who had been previously less than supportive.

When the cadets approached Pershing about possibly entering, the cadet commander immediately agreed. After all, Pershing had already competed in military competitions and performed well. Given the green light, a hundred cadets immediately volunteered for the training. Pershing soon narrowed the field to forty-five skilled competitors. The second lieutenant selected George L. Sheldon, who would one day be elected as the governor of Nebraska, as the rifle company's captain.

Pershing began putting his volunteer riflemen through their paces. The National Competitive Drills had a reputation as a serious intercollegiate event, drawing well-trained teams from universities across the country. The veteran squads included the Washington Fusiliers, the National Fencibles, Galveston's Sealy Rifles, Little Rock's McCarthy Light Guards, and the Texas Tigers. Thousands of competitors typically participated. The cadet commander drilled his cadets for two months. The handpicked cadets were expected to begin drills at 7 a.m. and engage in several hours of practice. After regular classes, they returned to the field for three additional hours of drill, often followed by evening drill. As they trained, the cadets realized their team needed a name. They chose the Varsity Rifles.[45]

By June 12, two days before the competition, the entire university campus knew of Pershing's team as the cadets boarded a train for the short ride to Omaha. They did not go alone. Chancellor Canfield and his daughter, Dorothy, just thirteen years old, went along for support, as well as a large contingent of well-wishers from the university, including professors. Nothing like this had ever been attempted by the University of Nebraska's cadet battalion, itself a testimony to Pershing's leadership. That night the UNL competitors of Pershing's Company A set up camp and got ready for an exciting tomorrow.

The next morning, they arose, finding themselves in the midst of dozens of competitive drill teams, some of which had competed previously time and again. But the young men from Lincoln were extremely prepared and revealed as much as they participated in a grand parade down the streets of Omaha in the afternoon. Their training was obvious to all who watched, as the cadets moved in precise formation, performing together like a well-oiled marching machine. But as they marched, Pershing was not pleased. He felt they were too cocksure of themselves, too certain of their chances of winning and returning as heroes to Lincoln with the $1,500 prize money and the Omaha Cup in hand. "They were too good," Pershing later observed. "They were perfect and they knew it. I couldn't let them go into a competition feeling like that."[46]

The evening before the rifle drill competition, Pershing gathered his unit of proud cadets together and turned on them. He ran them through an exacting inspection, even by Pershing's standards. He groused at them about the lack of polish on the heels of their shoes. Their brass buttons were not shiny enough. The creases in their pants were not crisp enough. He seemed disappointed, even angry with them. They had disgraced themselves and the university, not to mention him as their commander. How could they possibly think they could win against such skilled companies of cadets? They were "terrible," Pershing barked.[47] The boys' spirits crashed to the floor. They thought they had performed well that day. But Pershing was disappointed; only his opinion mattered.

Despite the browbeating from Pershing, the cadets redoubled their efforts. They spent the remainder of their evening in camp cleaning their rifles one more time, fretting over their creases and buttons, and blackening their shoes thoroughly, until some may actually have blackened their soles. No one knew what to expect the following morning, the day of the competition.

When morning came, the cadets rose to find Pershing still locked in critical mode. He lit into them again, turning his harsh tongue on every cadet. The time came to form up and march toward the competition ground. Then, just as they reached the edge of the field, Pershing completed his strategy of tearing down and building up his cadets. Stopping them short, he marched to the front of the formation. He turned toward them and announced with quiet pride, "I think you are going to win the first prize."[48] It was exactly what the cadets needed to hear. The boys drew themselves up, stood as erect as possible, and prepared to compete.

The day was important for the University of Nebraska cadet program as well as for the state of Nebraska. *The Hesperian* reported on the enthusiastic crowd: "There were about a thousand people in the amphitheatre of the M Street ballpark impatiently awaiting the appearance of the boys in blue.... At about 3 o'clock the band began to play, and the noble three hundred came marching across the field, greeted by shouts and cheers and waving handkerchiefs. It was a time when college patriotism was 50 per cent above par."[49]

The day went well for Pershing's cadets. Hundreds of university supporters, including the governor of Nebraska, watched Pershing's cadets prove themselves well trained and ready. The competition included two events: the Grand National, open to all units, and the following Maiden contest for new teams that had not previously placed above a third-place showing. The young men drew an unfortunate first place in the Grand National, meaning they were the first to perform. Since this competition was their first, they did not know what to expect from the other teams compared to their own performance. Still, they did well, even as they failed to execute "stack arms," a serious, if singular mistake.

The Maiden competition provided them with an opportunity to redeem themselves. Their skill was unparalleled. The competition provided teams with forty-five minutes to complete the assigned, precision exercises. With Pershing's training under their belts and their commander's kind words of assurance still on their minds, the team moved through its paces with machinelike accuracy. The cadets moved so well that they completed their exercises in half the time allowed. No one competing in the Maiden that day came even close to the level of performance Pershing's cadets achieved. Spectators and judges alike watched with spellbound excitement. When the tallies were revealed, the Nebraska team achieved 80.8 percent. The $1,500 prize was theirs.

Excitement spread like lightning through the large UNL crowd as the people cheered loudly, abandoning the grandstand and surging toward the field. Nothing could stop them, not even an eight-foot-tall fence, which many climbed over, including the overweight Chancellor Canfield, whose climb his daughter Dorothy described as "going like a feather."[50] Pershing and his cadets could not have been happier with the results. They relished the campus-wide support and returned to the university as triumphant and honored as a UNL football team winning a national championship.

For the cadets, their practice paid off through winning in the name of the university plus receiving the prize money, which was split among them. Nothing had a greater impact on the military program at UNL more than this competition, except for the leadership of John Pershing. The following academic year, the military program was more popular than ever. Many of the winning cadets remained on the team.[51]

By that time, Pershing was as busy at the university as ever. The law school opened its doors during the fall of 1891, just when John arrived on campus. (Since he had spent years reading through *Blackstone* and studying the law previously, he may have received some sort of advanced standing in the program.) He began taking law classes at the university's law school, the only one in the state. Pershing excelled in the study of law. Henry H. Wilson, one of his professors, described the first lieutenant as having "a keen analytical mind." He saw Pershing as "a diligent student of the law. No one intimately acquainted with the young lieutenant will doubt that he would have become an eminent lawyer had he devoted his life to the practice of that profession."[52]

That Pershing knew several Lincoln lawyers and even counted them as friends caused him to consider, as he had on many previous occasions, leaving the military. The law became a clear skill for him. One attorney friend Charles E. Magoon (who, during several years following the Spanish-American War, served as the governor of Panama and then the governor-general of Cuba) said of Pershing, "He has naturally a legal mind. . . . I doubt if he ever would have made a good jury lawyer. . . . But for grasp of legal principles, for power to discern the relation of one group of facts to another, I believe, had he followed the law, he would have stood in the fore rank of the profession."[53] Pershing and Magoon's friendship became nearly as strong as that of Pershing and Dawes. Magoon's office was on the street Pershing took from the university to home, and the military instructor often stopped by at five o'clock to talk about the law over cigars.

Whether Pershing ever really intended to leave the military to practice law remains a question with an uncertain answer. He talked about it but never concluded that he was meant for the law above the army. Chancellor Canfield suggested Pershing's plan might have been to take a law degree to use in conjunction with his military service, not in lieu of it. In a letter the university leader penned to President William McKinley after Pershing had left UNL, he observed, "He has a brilliant mind, easily grasping the salient points of any text or essay. In fact, he is made of the stuff that appears in men who on sudden opportunity become famous."[54]

Canfield could not have predicted Pershing's future more accurately. Pershing likely received certain later assignments due to his legal training. When the United States annexed the Philippines following the Spanish-American War, the need for military officers trained in the law proved crucial. Transferring territory from Spanish to U.S. control raised a mountain of issues regarding taxes, tariffs, customs operations, civil and criminal law, and property ownership. Pershing first worked on such legal issues while assigned to Washington DC under Assistant Secretary of War George D. Meiklejohn, whom John met during his years living in Lincoln.[55]

Pershing's four years of service at the University of Nebraska proved rewarding, a halcyon reprieve from desert duty in the Southwest and cold cavalry maneuvers in the Dakotas. His program even continued into the summer, between semesters. Cadets were not required to serve during the summer months, but four out of five usually did, as Pershing ran a summer camp program that had the cadets outdoors most of the time.

During the summer of 1893, Pershing left the campus for a while to enjoy a West Point class of '86 reunion. He and his classmates gathered for renewed conviviality, shared memories, and a visit to the Columbian Exposition in Chicago that "offered a rare opportunity to see the exhibits."[56] The pavilions at the World's Fair that summer dazzled Pershing, with the White City's lights blazing across its night skyline. The park presented visitors with displays paying tribute to the liberal arts and the advancement of Western civilization, as well as international exhibits that included exotic locales from Africa to the South Seas. The Midway Plaisance featured houses, peoples, and animals that delivered the world to the American heartland. Pershing had visited New York and Washington DC following his graduation from West Point, but he had not traveled outside the United States. The most exotic site he had ever visited was the Grand Canyon. The UNL cadet commandant could not have known then that he would eventually tour the world, live within foreign cultures and influences, and see prolonged service in the Philippines. Among the international exhibits that intrigued him the most during his visit to the Chicago fair were those featuring life in the Far East.

University life appealed to Pershing. He earned respect, and his efforts produced unbelievable results, more than Chancellor Canfield could have imagined. After two years of service at the university, Canfield wrote a letter to Secretary of War Daniel S. Lamont regarding Pershing's tenure. The customary practice at that time was for military instructors on college campuses to serve three years. But that policy was under review with a look to increase the time to four years. Canfield did not want to lose Pershing if he didn't have to. His letter pleads for Persh-

College, 1891–95

ing to remain longer: "He has been remarkably successful—more so than any person ever sent to us before. In all respects his work has been highly successful."[57]

Canfield's request received a positive response, and Pershing remained at UNL through another year. When his fourth and final year as the cadet commandant began in the fall of 1894, Canfield wrote another letter to the secretary of war. He knew the end of Pershing's tenure was set in stone for 1895, but he was concerned over who might replace his favorite commandant. "It is generally admitted, I believe, that we have the best cadet corps outside of West Point. I beg leave to suggest, therefore, that more than ordinary care be taken in the selection of Lieutenant Pershing's successor."[58]

Near the end of Pershing's final year at the university, the War Department dispatched Maj. E. G. Fechet to UNL to examine the cadet commandant's program. He found much to praise, observing, "The high degree of proficiency attained is due entirely to the energy, ability, and tact to organize and command, of Lieutenant Pershing." He noted how the university had not supported the program before Pershing's arrival. "Now it is just the reverse," Fechet observed.[59]

Pershing always maintained a happy balance between his professional life on campus and his personal life in the Lincoln community. During his time at UNL, his acquaintance William Jennings Bryan ran for a second congressional term, and Pershing attended a campaign debate between Bryan and his Republican opponent, Judge Allan W. Field. The debate focused on free trade, which Bryan supported, and the continuation of high tariffs, the Republican position. Bryan handily won the debate, and "the election easily went to Mr. Bryan."[60]

In some ways, the lieutenant Pershing who served the university was little different from the lieutenant Pershing who had previously served in three forts in the Southwest. While each situation called for two dramatically different skill sets, he easily adapted himself to each. Pershing was the darling of the university even as Lincoln citizens saw him in different settings—at the theater, at dances, and at social gatherings, often with a young lady on his arm. To nearly everyone who came within his sphere, "he was a thorough good fellow, fond of everything that makes for geniality."[61] Pershing's social life brought him friends and influential contacts who proved valuable in future years. Charles Dawes remained a lifelong friend, one who served Pershing well during World War I as a general assigned to the general headquarters and was responsible for procurement for the entire AEF. As noted previously, Magoon became the governor of Panama and then Cuba, and he and Pershing crossed paths often. George D. Meiklejohn was the assistant secretary of war in 1898 when Pershing desperately sought a command that would deliver him to the Cuban action during the Spanish-American War. While attending the university law school, Pershing also met Elmer Burkett. Ten years later, while serving as a U.S. congressman, Burkett encouraged President Theodore Roosevelt to promote Pershing to brigadier general. William Jennings Bryan gave Pershing access to his law library. Lorenzo Crounse, Nebraska's governor between 1893 and 1895, wrote official praise of Pershing as his aide-de-camp.[62] Historian Donald Smythe sums up Pershing's years at UNL: "The years at the University of Nebraska had been happy for Pershing. They were also formative. The Nebraska assignment brought him in contact with a more urban society, a university atmosphere, and a civilian populace."[63]

At the end of Pershing's four years of university service, he felt he had achieved singular success. His military program was one of the finest in the nation, and its popularity never waned during his tenure. Before leaving the university, he wrote a final report to the UNL Board of Regents in which he praised the members' support for his program. "In my opinion, the influence of the discipline required in the Military Department can be credited with the excellent state of affairs from a disciplinary point of view now existing in this University."[64]

For four years, he trained young, green farm boys—perhaps no different than himself at their age back in Laclede—and taught them, through discipline, to consider serving in their country's military. His leadership prepared him for future service as well. Important people noticed the work Pershing accomplished at the university. His personal discipline, his care for his cadets, his ability to socialize with practically anyone, his charisma, his no-nonsense leadership, and his capacity to remake himself and adapt to new realities—all translated into Pershing's becoming a man with a future. Pershing had spent four more years in the West—albeit the Midwest—but he had arrived in Lincoln as the town was in the midst of becoming an important city on the prairie. Both he and his community had matured together.

As the spring semester of 1895 came to an end, Pershing's cadets paid a singular tribute to their commander. On May 29 the campus drill team, the Varsity Rifles, informed Pershing the members had voted to change the name to "Pershing Rifles."[65] Pershing remained at UNL until the following fall. Just before leaving in late September, their beloved commandant was approached by a group of cadets with an odd request. They asked for a pair of his pants.

"What in the world do you want a pair of my breeches for?" Pershing asked.

The boys explained to their commander that they wanted to cut them up into blue and yellow cavalry ribbons to signify their special service to the university program under his leadership.

For a moment, Pershing was speechless, as he struggled with his emotions and his words. "I will give you the very best pair I own."[66]

The moment marked the end of Pershing's years at the University of Nebraska. Within days, he led the final corps parade. Less than a week later, he left the campus and Lincoln but not for the last time.

SEVEN

Cree, 1895–98

Prior to leaving the University of Nebraska, the thirty-five-year-old first lieutenant felt he had reached another crossroads in his military career. Since he had entered West Point being a few years older than most cadets, his biological and military clocks were out of sync. Under military regulations, he could not serve beyond the age of sixty-four, so, if he stayed in the army, he had less than thirty years remaining. Advancement in the cavalry moved at a notoriously slow pace, so he imagined the highest rank he could possibly achieve over the long haul was major, perhaps lieutenant colonel.

He had graduated West Point barely in time to take up assignments in New Mexico and catch the final mop-up actions of the Apache campaigns. With the next century only five years away, the frontier seemed headed into its twilight days, and the Indian wars belonged to the past, not the future. As for wars anywhere, they seemed unlikely. Pershing later penned his thoughts in his memoirs: "The belief was general that we were not likely to have any more war.... The future outlook for advancement for a young officer was not encouraging."[1]

Pershing's thoughts returned once again to leaving the service and hanging out his shingle as a lawyer. For him, Lincoln was always the place "where many men about my age with whom I came in contact were already successful in that or other professions, some of whom . . . then or later became national figures."² Bryan, Dawes, Magoon, and others constantly drew his attention from military service toward the legal profession.

With his UNL service winding down, Pershing cast about for possibilities. He thought he might be promoted faster if he held a staff position rather than a field or line command. He solicited support from War Eagle Carr and General Miles, among others, to write letters supporting such a lateral move. He applied for a captaincy in the quartermaster department, but his timing was off. All vacancies were already filled. He surrendered to his only other military option, to remain an active cavalry officer. He never looked back. "I was glad later that my efforts failed," he wrote in his memoirs, and Pershing took up his duties in Montana.³ Ultimately, the thought of becoming a lawyer and leaving military service remained a touchstone for Pershing until 1906, twenty years following his graduation from West Point. After that, he never talked about leaving the service again.

The fall of 1895 delivered 1st Lt. John J. Pershing back to the American West. On October 2 he reported to Fort Assinniboine in northwestern Montana, which had achieved statehood just six years earlier.⁴ The post was similar to others Pershing had served at in New Mexico; laid out around a rectangular parade ground, its four sides were framed by rows of quarters for the enlisted men and the officers' housing, plus stables, commissary, storage buildings, and a dining hall. It represented dozens of western forts designed to nail down the frontier landscape and support U.S. expansionism across the West. The fort was built following Custer's defeat at the Little Bighorn (1876) as a military deterrent to stave off future attacks both by Lakota chief Sitting Bull, who was at that time hiding out in Canada's Cypress Hills, and by the Nez Perce.

Those assigned to the Montana outpost faced hard winters of endless cold and snow. The temperatures sometimes hovered for days, even weeks, down to fifty or even sixty degrees below zero.

Fort Assinniboine was the hub of an extensive military reservation running south to the Missouri River and north to the Milk River. The Bear Paw Mountains to the south encompassed more than 1,100 square miles of territory. The fort kept tabs on several reservations—including those for the Crows, the Blackfeet, the Flatheads—all of which could be reached by a cavalry ride of no more than two days. During its heyday, Assinniboine featured more than a hundred buildings, representing the largest U.S. Army fort complex constructed during the nineteenth century.

When Pershing arrived in October, winter had not yet set in, and the first lieutenant soon discovered the region's natural charms. Just as his three fort assignments in the Southwest had featured their own unique scenery, so did Fort Assinniboine. Sharp fall weather dominated his early days in Montana, and the scenic wonders seemed to have no boundaries. Away from the fort, Mount Baldy dominated the Bear Paw Mountains, its summit commanding the landscape at nearly seven thousand feet of elevation. Local Indian legend told of a hunter encountering a bear that pinned him to the ground, prepared for a kill. Needing help, the hunter called out to the Great Spirit, which responded with thunder and lightning that killed the bear and severed the paw grasping the hunter.

Along the ridges and back trails of the Bear Paw, the last battle of the Nez Perce War (1877) transpired when Chief Joseph and his people took their final stand just forty-two miles short of the Canadian border, where they sought sanctuary from the U.S. government's long arm. When Pershing served at Fort Assinniboine, one could still follow a trail along the mountain's ridge and locate the crumbling earthen works where the Nez Perce took refuge.

In 1895 the Montana post was home to seven regiments of cavalry and infantry but with an important difference: most of the enlisted men at Assinniboine were African Americans serving under white officers. This presented Pershing with a unique opportunity, "a further test of my capacity to handle men of different race and character."[5] When he arrived at the fort, the white captain of Troop D, Tenth Cavalry was away on a recruiting assignment, so command of these Black troopers fell to Pershing. In early 1896 Pershing wrote a letter to West Point classmate Avery Andrews in which he mentioned his assignment to Fort Assinniboine: "I am getting some new experience up here, never having served with colored troops. It is not quite as pleasant as being on college duty, but I had gotten tired of that."[6]

Commanding Black soldiers posed no significant qualms for Pershing. Unlike many contemporary white Americans, he had no natural prejudice regarding African Americans. By the 1890s the era of Jim Crowism was in full form, having developed into the new social norm between the Black and white races. Segregation was the watchword following the failures of Reconstruction. Almost every element of life in the South, as well as in many parts of the North, hinged on keeping the two races apart. Black children attended Blacks-only schools in most places, as they had in Laclede during Pershing's youth. Blacks were put aside at nearly every turn, kept from public places where whites could be found, or relegated to the balconies of theaters, to the back seats of churches, and in completely separate railroad cars. Laws filled statute books that kept African Americans largely in their own world, away from whites during the age of Jim Crow. Even within the U.S. military, Black soldiers served in segregated units commanded by white officers.

Pershing was certainly aware of the U.S. norms of segregation, of the mantra of "separate but equal," but his attitudes concerning race did not fit the standard of the day. Pershing may have referred to Blacks using language common in his time, such as "darky," but his personal attitudes regarding race had been tried and tested repeatedly beginning in his youth. As noted previously, he considered Black children his friends as an adolescent, and he later taught in an African American school. In 1891 he had also commanded Indian troops.

The U.S. Army accepted African American soldiers during the Civil War, during which they distinguished themselves in combat. During the decades following the war, Black soldiers became part of the constabulary force stationed out West. They served as Indian fighters, and their enemies referred to them as "buffalo soldiers," as their hair reminded Natives of a buffalo's wiry hair.[7] Black units in the West included the Ninth and Tenth Cavalry Regiments, as well as the Twenty-Fourth and Twenty-Fifth Infantry Regiments. Through the final decades of the nineteenth century, buffalo soldiers gained positive reputations as fighting units known for their discipline, positive morale, and capacity to endure hardship. Throughout the frontier period following the Civil War, Black units composed approximately 20 percent of the cavalry troops and 8 percent of the infantry.[8] Some white officers believed Black troops had too many drawbacks, suggesting the buffalo soldiers lacked initiative and independent-minded resourcefulness. But in a fight, many conceded that African American troops could more than hold their own. Gen. William Tecumseh Sherman, although a strong advocate for white troops over Blacks, still admitted in 1874 that African American soldiers "are good troops, they make first-rate sentinels, are faithful to their trust, and are as brave as the occasion calls for."[9]

Before Pershing graduated from West Point and was assigned to his various posts in New Mexico, the buffalo soldiers of the Tenth Cavalry served in Arizona during the Apache campaign to capture Geronimo. The western artist Frederic Remington rode with them for a time and wrote in glowing terms concerning their better qualities: "As to their bravery: 'Will they fight?' That is easily answered. They have fought many, many times."[10]

Service in such units provided Black men with opportunities they often could not find in the general white population. While the army was not color-blind, and segregation was the norm, Blacks' military service often gained the respect of white officers and enlisted men. By the 1890s Black regiments often retained a high percentage of long-term veterans, men who had entered the army following the Civil War, fought during various Indian campaigns, and still called the army home. Black units were recognized for "high reenlistment and low desertion rates."[11]

Pershing did not have negative attitudes about Black troops.

He may have thought they "had their limitations and required more supervision," but his overall philosophy was that all men, Black or white, were only obligated to prove themselves capable. "My attitude toward the Negro was that of one brought up among them. Most men, of whatever race, creed or color, want to do the proper thing, and they respect the man above them whose motive is the same."[12] Through these words and the sentiments they represent, Pershing's general attitude toward race, including what he expressed concerning his Lakota scouts, reveals a man more enlightened regarding minorities than the usual retrograde views held by many white Americans during the era of Jim Crow.

Although the weather at Fort Assinniboine was seasonably mild when Pershing arrived, with local trees losing their leaves and the air crisp, this was Montana, where no one waited long for winter to set in. Soon, temperatures plummeted, and Pershing felt the sting of the season as he had never felt it before. Outdoor drills became impossible, even deadly. Remaining many weeks within the confines of the fort's buildings and grounds, the first lieutenant sought for a place among his peers. He accepted invitations to dinner with superior officers and their wives— though Assinniboine perhaps had no more than a half dozen or so women—and he mingled well with the other officers.

Pershing managed, as always, to keep himself busy. He still put his men through daily horse exercises, even if they were forced to wear "buffalo overcoats and the animals protected by heavy blankets" with temperatures dipping well below zero.[13] He and his fellow officers practiced fencing, sometimes with broad swords. Local dances and "post gaieties" always included the officers and sometimes the enlisted men. During the Christmas season, Pershing and other officers went on deer hunting excursions along the Missouri River near its confluence with the Yellowstone. One trip produced eight or ten deer for the fort's Christmas dinners.

The fort featured a group of would-be actors that enjoyed putting on plays and other performances for the entertainment of those struggling to conquer the boredom of a Montana winter. Pershing even agreed to perform with the local amateur thespians. He made a singular impression on everyone on one occasion. Acting protocol called for any and all intimacies to be avoided while on stage. If a script called for, say, a kiss between a man and woman, it was to be faked, not actually performed. During a rehearsal, Pershing either forgot or decided to take the risk, took his female counterpart in an embrace, and planted a kiss that was anything but staged. As later retold, "the leading lady forgot her lines, other actors were flustered, routine collapsed, and rehearsal was cancelled."[14]

But this indiscretion was forgotten in time, only to be replaced by a more serious breach of sexual protocol. Fort Assinniboine included a trader's post, the permanently located equivalent of the old sutler's store common during the Civil War. The trader had a young (only sixteen), vivacious, and attractive daughter who quickly caught Pershing's eye. While the first lieutenant enjoyed the trader's company and his wife's well-stocked, personal library, he became enamored of the girl, with her blonde hair, blue eyes, and womanly figure. She had an infectious laugh and enjoyed Pershing's attention. As for her parents, they appear to have had no problem with the officer's attentions. Others at the fort were critical, though, considering the daughter of a post trader as an unacceptable match for an officer and a gentleman. Assinniboine may have represented a remote frontier outpost, but the rules of sexual etiquette were as rigid there as anywhere. Fortunately, spring soon arrived, giving Pershing and Troop D of the Tenth Cavalry the opportunity to get outside the fort and away from all the gossip—at least for the moment.

His first real assignment put him once again in contact with Native Americans. A decade earlier, a mixed-blood (métis) Cree named Louis Riel led an uprising in Canada's Northwest Territory. The rebellion included a pair of battles—Duck Lake and Cut Knife, both in 1885—that the Crees and their Assiniboine allies won, resulting in dozens of Royal Canadian Mounted Police and militia casualties. Ultimately, the Cree uprising was quelled, but five hundred or six hundred of these Canadian

First Nation peoples fled across the Canadian-U.S. border to find sanctuary in Montana and North Dakota.

For years, they wandered the territory as a people without a home, unwelcome in the States, unwanted in Canada. They survived on little, having no land to call their own. They scattered in little bands, sometimes even ransacking garbage dumps outside small Montana towns for food. Several times, the U.S. State Department negotiated with Canadian officials for the return of the Crees. Finally, in 1896, they reached an agreement and designated a delivery point of Coutts Station. Congress appropriated funds for the deportation of the Crees. The first order was to locate the various bands, round them up, deliver them to the Canadian border, and transfer them to the mounted police. It fell to Pershing's Troop D of the Tenth Cavalry to carry out this complicated mission. He received his orders on June 12 to ride his men to Great Falls, Montana, and begin locating the homeless Crees. He handpicked more than forty men and 2nd Lt. L. J. Fleming, and by the following day, he and his troopers were in the saddle headed westward.

Pershing was uncertain what to expect from the Crees. Would they resist and fight? Would they scatter in a dozen different directions, a possibility that would certainly complicate his mission? He would find out in time, but his immediate focus was on reaching Great Falls within an allotted four days' march. The troop soon reached the Marias River, south of Fort Benton, with the river flowing high and fast.[15] The troopers turned their two wagons "into ferry boats by covering the sides and bottoms with canvas tent flies," then tied lariats together to provide a cable across the river. In this way, Pershing later wrote, "supplies were crossed . . . and we swam the horses and mules. It took us from daylight to dark to make this crossing, but it was a thorough test of what these black troopers could do."[16]

At least one African American trooper failed that day, so far as Pershing was concerned. The first lieutenant always expected discipline and his orders obeyed. During the crossing, he observed one trooper not pulling his weight. The entire process was complicated, chaotic, and dangerous—an all-hands-on-deck scenario. For most of the day, this shirker balked and loafed, only working hard to keep from getting his boots wet. His sergeant rode him constantly but to little avail. Finally, Pershing reached the end of his professional rope, motivating him to take a rare step as a commander. "I gave him a punch with my fist that sent him toppling full-length into the stream."[17]

Everyone learned a lesson that day. Pershing delivered a clear message to his men that he was not a commander who tolerated lazy troopers who disregarded orders. From that day forward, his African American troopers often monitored themselves and admonished malingerers: "You better git at it feller or 'Old Red' will knock you into the Marias River."[18] As for Pershing's propensity toward using his fists to force discipline, he only reverted to it a couple of times during his decades of command.

Pershing and his men reached Great Falls on June 17, as planned. There, he found the Crees split in their responses to the ordered deportation. Some had fled toward Idaho, while others were patiently waiting for soldiers to lead them to the Canadian border, where they knew they would receive much-needed food rations. On the eighteenth, Pershing's Troop D, armed and ready for action, descended on a local encampment of Crees, surprising them. Soon Pershing's men had 107 men, women, and children in their custody. He explained his purpose and made it clear to them that "the Great Mother of Canada"—a reference to Queen Victoria—had pardoned them for any involvement in Louis Riel's uprising. They soon accepted their fate.

But if the Crees did not intend to fight on the field of battle, they were soon the subjects of another kind of fight, a legal battle over their fate. A local Montana lawyer went to court, filing a writ of habeas corpus requiring the U.S. Army commander to explain in legal terms why the Crees should be detained and moved. This case gave Pershing an opportunity to change hats from that of military officer to lawyer, representing the first practical application of the law degree he had earned just a few years earlier at the University of Nebraska. For Pershing, the case was clear, and he presented the legal facts in a straightforward manner, as all good lawyers do. Before the bench, Pershing cited case law and precedents similar to his mission, basing his argument in federal authority: the state of Montana had no jurisdiction over the Canadian Crees or the federal agents who had arrived in Great Falls to help facilitate the transfer of these First Nation peoples back to Canada. Lawyer Pershing won his argument in court, but he had already hedged his bets, having placed the Crees, their belongings, and their horses on a local train headed toward Canada.

Pershing's mission was going well. Maj. J. M. J. Sanno of the Third Infantry, his commander, dispatched Pershing to round up any and all other roaming Crees. Soon, his Montana mission was reminiscent of the weeks he had spent in the Dakotas rounding up renegade Lakotas. They were scattered and to where was anyone's guess. He heard conflicting rumors and was uncertain whether he might meet with hostility. As historian Frank Vandiver notes, "Lessons taught by War Eagle and General Miles were not forgotten by Lieutenant Pershing."[19] He carefully sifted the sands of rumor before making a move and was equally diligent in keeping his men supplied. Late on June 24, he and his men caught up with eighty-four Crees, loading them on a train out of Custer toward Canada. Troop D zigzagged its way over long stretches of Montana backcountry, looking for Indians. This mission was similar to the war games Pershing had enjoyed during his early days in New Mexico, the rabbit hunts that pitted one cavalry unit in pursuit of another cavalry unit, only now it was real. Pershing rode through Great Falls and then west to Garrison, Montana, where his men discovered an abandoned Indian encampment. Then he and his men proceeded along a leg of the old Lewis and Clark Trail, headed to Fort Missoula. There, they reconnoitered with the Twenty-Fifth Infantry, an African American unit, and Troop D took a few days' rest. By this time, June had slipped into early July.

Then Pershing received intelligence placing a band of Crees near Camas Prairie, about a hundred miles north, in the midst of rugged, mountain-scarred northwestern Montana. Covering this stretch of wilderness land, one guarded by parallel mountain ranges, represented a daunting challenge. Loading his men on a train, Pershing took a short cut that covered the stretch from Perma to Horse Plains, named by Native Americans who traditionally wintered their horses on the local grasses. With his horses and mules unloaded, Pershing pointed his men toward Camas Prairie, where, on July 9, they caught up with seventy Crees before they knew the soldiers were even in the vicinity. Pershing's railroad gamble had paid off.

The combined party of troopers and Indians now numbered more than a hundred souls as Pershing faced the thorny task of delivering the Crees back east, including a difficult river crossing along the Flathead. Before heading into the western Montana wilderness to cover the hundred miles back to Missoula, he waited for supplies and rations, a sign of good planning and logistics. Pershing describes the protracted scene along the banks of the Flathead River beginning on the afternoon of July 12: "The crossing of the Flathead by that nondescript outfit made a wonderful picture—naked Indians swimming horses barebacked, yelling, handling broncos that had never been roped, the black troopers manning an old ramshackle ferry to carry the women, children, property, and vehicles across the swollen river—all added rapidly and impressively to one's experience. We were a day and a half here at the crossing, but the task was accomplished with the loss of only a few Indian ponies."[20]

The crossing resembled, for Pershing, another unique scene depicting the complicated realities of the American West: three races worked in relative tandem, providing one more vignette suggesting the end of the era of Native Americans' freedom and of the frontier generally. Pershing must have felt far removed in time and space from his days of youthful naivete growing up in Laclede. The psychic distance between Missouri and Missoula likely seemed like light years. Again, the pages of Beadle's dime novels may have flipped through his mind's eye.

As Pershing and his party moved toward Missoula, 2nd Lt. L. J. Fleming, whom Pershing had left behind with a small guard force at Missoula, captured another party of Crees. Slowly, the net around the Canadian Natives tightened. By July 22 the number of captured Crees stood at 148. The first lieutenant and his men reconnoitered and soon headed their captives along the Blackfoot River eastward "to the Marysville divide, and along the eastern slope of the Rockies to the McLeod trail, thence to the Canadian line."[21] Along the way, additional Cree men, women, and children appeared, joining ranks with their tribe, until the number reached 190. Pershing describes the trek as representing "an epic story, so filled with episodes was this strange cavalcade of typical American aborigines"; it was an "odd procession of vehicles, a few serviceable, the rest creaking old wagons, worn out buggies, often breaking down, pack ponies, and a few travois."[22] Alongside the wheeled conveyances, the Indians herded five hundred ponies. The basic task of Pershing and his men was to assist the large party when needed, help along the stragglers, repair broken vehicles when possible, and keep the convoy moving on its way to Canada.

While the Crees' exodus to Canada did not include any acts of violence or shots fired in anger, Pershing was almost killed by gunshot. During the trek, a Cree man committed suicide, shooting himself in the head. The bullet passed through him, then between Pershing, who was standing close by, and another individual.

Mishaps were bound to happen and did. Crossing the Marias was again required, if only farther upstream. Pershing made a mistake in establishing the party's camp site too close to the river, and the stream rose overnight, flooding the assemblage and resulting in absolute pandemonium. "Men were shouting, women screaming, children crying, dogs barking, and frightened horses neighing as they floundered in the flood."[23] But Pershing's African American troopers moved quickly and rescued many in the Indian party, with no loss of life. The incident represented a small lapse in Pershing's judgment—one he recognized immediately. Writing in his memoirs, he observed, "It was a practical lesson in the wisdom of an old axiom of the frontier—never camp on the near side of a river that has to be crossed if you can help it."[24] After a day's wait, the river level subsided, and the party continued.

As the group of Indians and soldiers continued their journey, the Montana scenery loomed before them, with snow-covered mountains sometimes visible in every direction, their grassy valleys dotted with copses of tall, majestic pine trees. With summer grass and endless mountain streams cutting across the trail, the migrating party easily kept its ponies fed and watered. Unfortunately, nature also interrupted its progress, with an outbreak of measles among the Indian children. One child died, even as a pregnant woman gave birth.

Once the party crossed the Continental Divide and emerged from the Rockies, the land began to flatten out, becoming much rockier, stark rather than scenic, with water less abundant. By August 6 Pershing and his men reached the Canadian border and Coutts Station. He reported to a Royal Canadian Mounted Police officer, ready to complete his mission. But when the officer learned of measles among the Crees, he refused to allow them to cross the border into his country. An exasperated Pershing informed the Mountie that "it was obligatory upon his government under the agreement to receive and hold them if necessary in quarantine upon their own soil."[25] The Mountie refused.

The commander of Troop D did not accept the situation as he found it. He sent a telegram to Gen. John R. Brooke at department headquarters, informing superiors that his party's rations were almost depleted, leaving him few options. He did not have to wait long. Canadian government officials in Ottawa responded the following day, informing the mounted police to accept the Crees across the border. Pershing was elated: "My men were glad the job was done . . . and were happy to turn our horses toward home."[26]

Troop D headed back to Fort Assinniboine; the trip took a full week. Pershing and his men returned to the fort after two months in the field, their international mission completed. They had covered more than a thousand miles of rugged Montana territory, across mountain trails and desolate passes, with women and children in tow. The march had included tense moments and perilous river crossings, challenges to humans and animals alike. It was Pershing's singular, extensive mission during his year assigned to Fort Assinniboine, and he had completed it with his usual high level of professionalism, his fist landing an African American slacker into the Marias River aside. His commander, Major Sanno, recognized Pershing's accomplishment: "Lieutenant Pershing exhibited soldierly qualities of high order and his conduct throughout is worthy of the highest commendation. He made long tedious and tiresome marches maintaining his horses in good condition."[27]

Pershing's return to Fort Assinniboine placed him back in the routine of post life and provided him time to reflect on his most recent accomplishment. Much of his earlier time in command of Troop D had focused on drill and practice. Now he had seen his men in action under his command, and they had proved themselves capable, brave, and adaptive. He emerged from the mission successfully due to the professionalism of his men and his innovative leadership. Back at the fort, he also rekindled his relationship with the post trader's daughter. Once again, tongues were wagging.

For the remainder of the Montana summer, Pershing stayed close to the fort, battling the challenges of repeated routine. But such was a military assignment in the West. Hunting proved an even greater distraction for him than the trader's daughter. Fort Assinniboine was in the midst of a hunter's paradise crowded with antelope and deer, prairie chickens and hill cranes. The fort was home to six large borzois, Russian wolfhounds, eager for a hunt.

While Pershing loved taking the borzois out on a wolf hunt, his favorite quarry was game birds. His skill at bird shooting soon produced a change in his future. Just weeks after his return from the Cree mission, the fort received an important visitor, Gen. Nelson Miles, then the commanding general of the U.S. Army. He was on an inspection tour, and his arrival was a complete surprise. Many of the fort's units were out on maneuvers, but Pershing and his Tenth Cavalry troopers greeted the visiting general. Pershing and Miles knew one another professionally, if not personally, and the first lieutenant from Missouri provided a tour of the fort and a promise of good local hunting. By September 17 Pershing had prepared a hunting expedition.

Accompanied by the Tenth, Pershing and Miles's party, including the artist Frederic Remington, headed south toward the Bear Paw Mountains, "where prairie chickens were plentiful." Fortunately, the birds appeared, and Miles proved "an excellent shot."[28] No one killed more birds on the hunt than Miles, even as Pershing also proved himself as a hunter. By evening, having shared a day of hunting and a wilderness campfire, Miles gained a new perspective on Pershing. They emerged from the experience as friends. When the hunting party returned to the fort, they brought back enough prairie chickens to provide a great feast for the entire garrison. Miles left the fort with an increased appreciation of First Lieutenant Pershing.

Following Miles's departure, Pershing remained the topic of fort gossip. His relationship with the trader's daughter reached the point that Col. J. K. Mizner, the first lieutenant's commander, could no longer watch from the sidelines. He called Pershing in for a man-to-man talk. Whatever the first lieutenant's long-term intentions were regarding the young girl, they could only spell trouble for his career. Mizner offered a comfortable way out for Pershing—a leave of absence. Perhaps things between the soldier and the trader's daughter might cool if he was gone long enough for the interest of both parties to wane. Pershing took his commander's advice and, on October 15, was on his way to Chicago by train.

He arrived just in time to catch the excitement of the 1896 presidential election. William Jennings Bryan, his lawyer acquaintance from Lincoln, carried the banner for both the Democratic and Populist Parties. While in Chicago, Pershing paid a call on another old friend from his Lincoln days, Charles Dawes, the secretary of the Republican National Committee. Through Dawes, Pershing also met Mark Hanna, the famous Republican Party chair. As a lifelong Republican, Pershing felt comfortable rubbing shoulders with such important party men. Before he left Chicago, Bryan arrived to give a series of political speeches on free silver and tariff reform, two of the hot-button topics during the campaign. One day, John stood on the corner of Michigan Avenue and Randolph Street, and watched a pro-Bryan parade that included Bryan riding along in an open carriage. Above the street corner, an anonymous "someone threw a rotten egg from a high window at Bryan's carriage."[29]

By Election Day, Pershing had returned to Lincoln, visiting family, seeking out old friends, and paying a call at the university to carry out one more inspection of the cadets. (By then, Chancellor Canfield had also moved on, having taken a position as the chief executive of Ohio State University.) John found his family well. His father operated a successful wholesale business with Pershing's younger brother Ward.[30] His mother was glad to see him, and he caught up with his siblings. May still lived in Lincoln, while Grace was stationed with her husband, Lt. Dick Paddock—one of the Three Green P's.[31] While in town, Pershing voted Republican, for sound money, even as most Nebraska voters cast ballots for their favorite son Bryan.

Pershing's leave provided him idle moments to reflect, once more, on the state of his military career. Visiting with lawyer friends such as Dawes and Charles Magoon distracted him again toward a law career. He felt he had not advanced enough in rank after more than a decade in uniform. Some of his West Point comrades, including Avery Andrews, had already opted out of the army. Pershing thought about making a lateral move while remaining in the army, which he had already promised himself he would do, and serving in the Judge Advocate General's Department. As a lawyer-officer, he could combine his military and legal training in a handy way. He wrote a letter to Canfield, seeking a recommendation for an available quartermaster position: "Chancellor, would you feel that I am asking too much to again ask you to assist me to a captaincy in the Q. M. Department. . . . There is a vacancy now existing in that department."[32] Pershing began a charm offensive, deciding he needed to make his appeals in person rather than through letters. He asked for a two months' extension to his leave and received it. Soon, he was off to Washington DC.

He visited U.S. Army Headquarters, hoping for an audience

with General Miles. A cordial meeting transpired, but the content of their conversation remains unknown. He undoubtedly appeared before Miles well recommended, and Miles's experiences hunting with Pershing were still fresh. Miles had earlier written in glowing terms of Pershing following the Pine Ridge campaign, so the first lieutenant did not approach the general as a stranger. In a letter dated January 28, 1895, to the adjutant general, Miles wrote, "In this duty as well as in all others which came under my observation, he displayed remarkable zeal, energy, and skill. In every duty which he has been called upon to perform he has displayed marked ability."[33]

But nothing came immediately from Pershing's visit to the capital, and he returned to Lincoln. After several weeks of waiting, a telegram arrived: "The Major General commanding the Army directs, as necessary for the public service, that you repair to Washington and report for temporary duty at Headquarters of the Army." Pershing soon boarded a train to Washington to serve as an acting aide to General Miles.[34]

Headed for new duties in the nation's capital, Pershing only imagined the possibilities that lay before him. At some point, the post trader's daughter faded into his past. Working for Miles proved not only professionally rewarding but socially advantageous as well. Pershing was a product of the Midwest who had cut his professional teeth in the West. Washington represented an entirely different level of social interaction, far removed from officers' dances in New Mexico or amateurish theatrical productions in Montana. Miles moved in a large social circle and could open doors for Pershing. His appointment calendar—which Pershing often oversaw—included congressmen, senators, cabinet members, even President Grover Cleveland. Miles and his wife, Mary, had family money and an earned status in the city. (Mary was the niece of Gen. William Tecumseh Sherman and former senator John Sherman [R-OH].) Pershing knew he was now swimming in a larger pond than ever before. His role included acting as a social director for Miles as well as his wife and twenty-seven-year-old, unmarried daughter, Cecilia.

Miles finished out his long and storied military career in

Washington DC as the last commanding general of the U.S. Army, a role he fulfilled between 1895 and 1903. His experiences in uniform had taught him a thousand lessons, and during his Washington years, he sought to bring significant change to the military as it transitioned from a nineteenth-century to a twentieth-century force. Pershing served Miles at a time when the old general tried to completely reorganize the army. Many U.S. military fortifications were outdated, Miles argued. Larger ships and heavy guns had already rendered coastal fortifications to the status of vulnerable targets. Pershing was acting on the inside as the leadership of the U.S. Army was considering the direction of its future.

The Washington DC Pershing experienced during the 1890s was the center of the nation's political world, but life in the city moved at a much slower pace than that of the next century. A visiting Englishman noted, "Compared with New York or Chicago, Washington, although it is full of commotion and energy, is a city of rest and peace. . . . It looks a sort of place where nobody has to work for his living, or, at any rate, not hard."[35]

The city had its usual compliment of shop clerks, common laborers, craftsmen, and the like, plus many office workers—it was home to the U.S. government, after all—but they typically went to work with a sense of leisure and an expectation of short hours. Many were still having their breakfasts at 9 a.m., and most government offices closed at 4 p.m. Lunchrooms were as ubiquitous in the city as politicians. Across from the Treasury Building, government clerks frequented a dairy lunchroom (the Starbucks of its day), where they drank coffee served in pint shaving mugs as they lounged in wicker chairs and ate the sandwiches they brought with them.

In Cather's *The Professor's House*, the Nebraska author provides a description of the nation's capital that is similar to what Pershing might have experienced:

> I got off the train, just behind the Capitol building, one cold bright January morning. I stood for a long while watching the white dome against a flashing blue sky, with a very religious

feeling. After I had walked about a little and seen the parks, so green though it was winter, and the Treasury building, and the War and Navy, I decided to put off my business for a little and give myself a week to enjoy the city.... During my days of waiting for appointments, I used to walk for hours around the fence that shuts in the White House grounds, and watch the Washington monument colour with those beautiful sunsets, until the time when all the clerks streamed out of the Treasury building and the War and Navy. Thousands of them.... I remember the city chiefly by those beautiful, hazy, sad sunsets, white columns and green shrubbery, and the monument shaft still pink while the stars were coming out.[36]

Up on Capitol Hill, the U.S. Congress, with the exception of the final days of each congressional session, ran at the same leisurely pace as the city's bureaucrats. In the House of Representatives, Democrats and Republicans maintained an informality even during sessions. They leaned back in their chairs, planting their feet on desktops, eating peanuts, and scattering shells across the floor, which was covered with strategically placed cuspidors. By the 1890s, when Pershing was in Washington, House members were encouraged to straighten up and project a more gentlemanly decorum, but the pace remained largely the same.

Congressmen engaged in as much political activity after hours as during, perhaps more. Some lived near Capitol Hill in boardinghouses, others in local hotels. They ate their meals in a variety of popular restaurants including a formal dining room located near the famed Willard Hotel's Peacock Alley, Harvey's Fish House, and, down by the Potomac River, Hall's Restaurant, where the dining room featured an immense painting depicting a nude Venus. The state of congressional salaries was such that many could barely afford to live in the city.

A variety of conveyances filled the city's streets, delivering passengers and produce to every corner. Carriages and wagons were still common, and horses dropped tons of manure from alleys to boulevards each day. Electrified streetcars seemed to cover endless miles of cityscape, even as horse-drawn omnibuses remained a Washington commonplace. On public market days, the city bustled with commercial activity, as everyone from the poorest to the local wealthy matrons delivered by carriage descended on the stalls lining Center Market in search of fresh produce, meat, eggs, and game birds hunted locally.

Sporting events were gaining in popularity, including croquet, tennis, archery, and boating on the Potomac—all signs of the extent of leisure time in Washington. By the early 1890s, a new public bathing beach opened along the river. By the late 1880s a popular country club built a new golf course, helping that sport gain traction. Rounding out the expanding base of sporting events were football and baseball, with the Senators representing Washington's contribution to the National League.

All across the city, government buildings mirrored the classical architecture of the Greeks, Romans, and Egyptians, even as the Renaissance style of the new Library of Congress, an ornate set piece completed in 1894, made the public building one of the city's most popular. The Washington Monument had been completed in 1884. The city boasted more sculpture than any other American community, with much of it on public grounds. After 1886, the Senate chamber became home to a large number of busts of vice presidents. Statues adorned the Capitol's Statuary Hall, the Corcoran Gallery of Art, and the numerous public squares and circles created by the city's early designer, Pierre Charles L'Enfant. But many of its parks, those loved today, had to wait until the turn of the century when the Senate Park Commission (the McMillan Commission) began laying out plans for the revitalization and beautification of Washington that were dedicated to the proposition that no one "be allowed to invade, to mutilate, or to mar the symmetry, simplicity, and dignity of the capital city."[37]

So many Washington landmarks did not exist during the 1890s, including the Lincoln Memorial, the Supreme Court Building, and nearly all the buildings that today are the museums of the Smithsonian that command the public spaces between the Capitol Building and the Lincoln Memorial. But for Pershing, Washington was an exciting place, where even he became part of the political scene.

As with so many lifelong military men, Pershing usually remained aloof from politics with its campaigns and party leadership. When he voted, he usually marked his ballot for Republican candidates. But on at least one occasion, while serving in Washington, Pershing did a little political dabbling of his own. In 1897, as the Cleveland presidency ended and the Republican presidency of William McKinley charted its course, an acquaintance of Pershing's, Rep. George D. Meiklejohn (R-NE), was leaving office. Meiklejohn and Pershing had crossed paths when the former was Nebraska's lieutenant governor. The two men both lodged at the old Wellington Hotel and often met for dinner, sharing views on public issues and memories of Nebraska. During one such meal, Pershing suggested to Meiklejohn that he apply for the open position of assistant secretary of war, even though Meiklejohn "said he knew nothing about military matters."[38]

Pershing explained how the position required no real military background as it was almost entirely a political role. With the retiring congressman's approval, Pershing soon set out on his new mission. Clearing the way with Miles, he approached Sen. John M. Thurston (R-NE), who had an in with the incoming McKinley administration. Soon McKinley signed off on the appointment. In a telegram sent April 14, 1897, Pershing was happy for Meiklejohn: "Congratulations on appointment. All pleased. Had never given it up. Lieut. Pershing." John found "Meiklejohn was very grateful for my interest in his appointment."[39] The first lieutenant could not have known then how much importance his friend's appointment would have for him personally the following year.

While Pershing's Washington assignment gave him the opportunity to rub shoulders with the elite and powerful, perhaps the most important contact he made during his six months back east was outside Washington. Pershing had barely arrived at Miles's headquarters when the old general sent his new aide to New York City as an observer to a month-long military tournament held in January at Madison Square Garden that was sponsored by the New York National Guard.[40] He soon met with Avery Andrews, his old classmate from West Point, who was then serving as one of three city police commissioners. (Avery was also a major and engineer officer in the First Brigade of the state's National Guard.) Pershing knew the other two commissioners by name only: Fred Grant, son of Gen. Ulysses S. Grant, and Theodore Roosevelt, whose time as the New York police commissioner became legend. Avery had a ringside box at the tournament that he shared with Pershing and Roosevelt.

Pershing and Roosevelt were still in the early stages of their eventual historical legacies. While they came from two extremely divergent backgrounds—Pershing's simple, rural Missouri roots versus Roosevelt's old-money, patrician family origins—the two men immediately hit it off. The differences between them were outweighed by what they had in common. As Andrews later observed, "They were nearly of the same age, Roosevelt being 38 and Pershing 36. Both were enthusiastic and expert horsemen and both had seen much of the West."[41]

Roosevelt's love of the American West and the history of the frontier was a lifelong passion for the native New Yorker. Pershing noted Roosevelt in his memoirs: "Having lived in the West, Roosevelt knew the life well, and having written *The Winning of the West*, he knew the valuable part the army had played in that achievement."[42] Pershing represented a part of that military legacy. Meeting Roosevelt and sharing his own experiences in the West with the future president put the two men on paths that would intersect again and again in the future. Here was Pershing in New York City, far from the West geographically, spending time with someone who was just as enamored of the West as he was. Ultimately, no one would have a greater impact on the trajectory of Pershing's military career than Theodore Roosevelt.

Pershing's Washington assignment lasted only a matter of months. By spring, General Miles received another assignment that took him away from Washington to serve as a military observer to the Greco-Turkish War that had opened in February. Pershing had no immediate plans for his next assignment. But before Miles's departure, the commandant of West Point Col. Samuel M. Mills Jr. paid a call at Miles's headquarters, where he met with Pershing and offered him an opportunity to return to West Point as an instructor in tactics. The first lieutenant from Missouri had previously been approached twice to take such a position, but "as the duty did not appeal to me I had not encouraged the appointment," he wrote in his memoirs.[43] But this time he accepted, since several of his military friends, including former West Point classmates, were then at the academy. The offer came that spring, and Miles cooperated, relieving Pershing of his Washington duties on May 1.

Pershing's few months in Washington exposed him to the kind of political gamesmanship he would find himself at the center of during World War I. It provided an opportunity for him to network in a new way, on new ground, in the midst of the nation's political capital. His social circle expanded dramatically, and he became more familiar with the highest standards of professional etiquette among the politically powerful. His Washington experience stretched him further as a military officer, one who used his position as political collateral; it resulted in his career taking new turns, leading to further success.

But Pershing did not head to West Point either immediately or even directly. His transfer was held up, necessitating his return to Fort Assinniboine. He dawdled back, stopping along the way in Chicago for another visit before arriving at his post in the West. He found the fort under a new commander, Lt. Col. Theodore Anderson Baldwin, who had replaced Mizner. For two weeks—May 15 to June 1—Pershing became acquainted with Baldwin, who seemed thrilled that his fort had an officer who had not only seen assignment in the nation's capital at U.S. Army Headquarters but also was on his way to West Point. Although their time together was short, Baldwin filed a report on his first lieutenant, rating him "an excellent and efficient officer."[44]

A fortnight after bidding farewell to Fort Assinniboine for the last time, Pershing walked through the gates at West Point.

The academy's superintendent was Col. Oswald H. Ernst, an engineer officer, and the commandant of cadets was Lt. Col. Otto Hein, an infantryman who had taken over the role from Colonel Mills. Much about West Point had not changed since Pershing's four years as a cadet more than a decade earlier. It was very much the same old place, with its hallowed buildings, rigorous training, and penchant for discipline.

Pershing immediately noticed a handful of changes that had transpired since his cadet days. Part of the training included a course in gymnastics, which Pershing thought "made decidedly for improvement in the physical development of the individual cadet."[45] There had been a makeshift gym in the academy's old academic building when Pershing served as a cadet but no official course. Physical training had largely been a matter of catch-as-catch-could. The second change was the addition of competitive football against other colleges. Nothing like it had existed during Pershing's cadet years. When he arrived, the fledgling program still had no away games scheduled, but even that restriction was soon eliminated. Pershing loved this new level of competition for the West Point cadets, calling it "especially beneficial" since "it brought the corps as a whole in contact with young men of other institutions." The third alteration was more difficult to frame. The first lieutenant perceived "a somewhat more liberal attitude in relations between officers and cadets," one he interpreted as "not so impersonal." What exactly Pershing was referring to is not clear, but it was palpable to him. This altered relationship did not mean the inmates were running the West Point asylum. Discipline was still taken seriously, and Pershing saw much in the behavior of the cadets that reminded him of his own days spent in cadet gray. He noted in his memoirs that "there was the same surreptitious violation of regulations against smoking and running lights after taps and slipping off to Highland Falls on a lark."[46]

Once Pershing took up his new role as a tactical officer at West Point, he wanted to leave his own mark on the venerable institution that meant so much to him. He thought the basic curriculum lacked an element of practicality. Many courses were theoretical, focused more on instilling discipline in the cadets than in providing them a framework and general understanding of what service as an army officer might eventually entail. On this, Pershing had strong opinions: "It seemed to me that graduates of West Point should be given a course both theoretical and practical in the kind of service they would have as commanders of platoons and companies and even higher units in battle." But when he made such a suggestion to Commandant Hein, it was summarily rejected. Pershing was at West Point to provide one service, that of an in-the-trenches tactical officer. So John Pershing, class of '86, ultimately returned to much the same West Point that had trained him with only a few tweaks made here and there.[47]

But something else proved different for Pershing at West Point. Certainly as a new tactical officer at the academy, Pershing understood that one of his primary roles was to instill discipline in the cadets. Handing out demerits simply went with the territory. It was not as if he came to West Point without having already commanded cadets; he had worked with cadets for four years at the University of Nebraska. He had expected a high level of discipline from his Nebraska farm boys, even with the expectation that the vast majority of them might never even serve in the military, much less as army officers. Clearly, much more was at stake at West Point than at UNL. The West Point cadets were in officers' training. Military service lay ahead of them. Perhaps for that reason, among others, Pershing took his role at West Point as seriously as circumstances demanded; thus, he forced a higher level of discipline on his cadets, just as had been expected of him when he stepped foot on the academy grounds more than fifteen years earlier.

Pershing expected the cadets to grumble about his disciplinary measures but ultimately to accept them and—perhaps, as his UNL boys had—even to appreciate his efforts. That did not happen. Tactical officers at West Point often met resistance, but the cadets he found at the academy were not the same as those he had encountered at UNL. While his Nebraska boys loved him and even worshiped him, at the academy, the cadets hated him. As one cadet later noted, "Of all the tacs, I would say he was the most unpopular."[48] Pershing, to several cadets, was a martinet, a wooden soldier.

This reality alone made Pershing's time as a tactical officer at West Point as miserable for him as his UNL experience had proved rewarding. As a disciplinarian, many of the academy's cadets thought he simply went too far. One example stands out. Army regulations demanded that cadets had to wear a white shirt beneath their gray jackets. In warmer weather, this made for uncomfortable wearing. Despite the regulation, many cadets habitually waived the shirt since no one could see it anyway. But it was a regulation, so Pershing went out of his way to order cadets to remove their jackets during outdoor drill to see who complied. Those who were caught received demerits.

Perhaps Pershing simply knew too much about West Point. He could recall the practices of his day, knew what cadets thought they could get away with doing or not, and recalled hiding places and long-standing cadet customs that had always been against the rules but had sometimes been tolerated, with tacs simply looking the other way. This was not Pershing's practice. He seemed relentless, uncompromising, unforgiving, a stiff shirt. As one cadet remembered him: "His offenses were inspections at unusual hours, doubling back on his tracks for second inspections, heavy punishments and what seemed to be unrealistic standards. He was gruff and unsympathetic and made a hard life harder."[49]

An examination of one of Pershing's record books reveals the various types of offenses for which he cited cadets:

Murphy, Odor of tobacco smoke in quarters at inspection, 10:20 p.m.

Hunter, Whistling loudly while going up two flights of stairs, 9:22 a.m.

McCormick, Clothing at foot of bed, 9:35 a.m.

Pope, Talking in unnecessarily loud tone of voice while going to sink at about 5:30 a.m.

Humphrey, Tent walls not properly fastened down.[50]

While nearly all the cadets disliked Pershing, one group eventually had it in for him. Pershing was assigned to ride herd over A Company, a particularly unmanageable, unruly group. If Pershing went out of his way to discipline the cadets, A Company went out of its way to challenge his authority. In February 1898 the company's cadets plotted against Pershing. William P. Wooten, one of their number, attempted the old trick of leaving a door ajar and placing a full water bucket on it to catch Pershing unawares and leave him soaked. Normally, such a ploy was played on fellow cadets, not officers. But the ranks of the conspirators proved less than ironclad, as A Company's captain Malin Craig—who later served as the army chief of staff during the late 1930s—gave Pershing a vague heads up, warning him, "Do not enter the first sergeant's room." Pershing sent a janitor to check out the situation, who was soon doused. The entire company "was placed in arrest in barracks and . . . stayed there for about three months doing all-night guard duty . . . with all privileges suspended."[51] As for Wooten's military future, he saw action in the Philippines, eventually taught at West Point, and commanded the Fourteenth Engineer Regiment in Europe during World War I as a brigadier general.

The cadets of A Company never forgot how they were punished for a failed attempt to humiliate a West Point tactical officer, one they passionately hated. In the spring, the traditional "Hundredth Night Show"—marking a hundred days before graduation—seemed almost dedicated to the bucket incident and the punishment of A Company. Since the big public production was scheduled when the company's cadets were still in lockdown, they were not allowed to participate or attend. But on the night of the show, the raised curtain revealed two large *A*s framing the arched stage. The 1898 class yearbook, *The Howitzer*, included a less than veiled reference to the incident: "An eye for an eye, a tooth for a tooth, and thirty days for a water bucket."[52]

Pershing and his cadets hardened into two immovable forces.

He seemed incapable of softening his discipline, and they refused to surrender to his iron will. Of all their attempts to slight the hated tactical officer, none hit home harder than the "silencing." Cadets at West Point rarely implemented this practice, but they made an exception with Pershing. With secretive planning, the cadets gathered one day in the cadet mess hall, taking their meal and enjoying one another's company while waiting for Pershing. When he entered the room, suddenly the place went stone cold quiet—no eating, no movement, no talking, just an eerie, symbolic, deafening silence of disapproval by hundreds of cadets in a moment of pin-drop protest. C. L. Maguire, a cadet who was present, describes the moment: "Usually after the Battalion was seated, the officer in charge that day would go into the mess hall and pass down the center aisle. Pershing made quite a feature of this passing, and one day during the passage the mess hall became very silent. He immediately called for attention and dismissed all the Companies without waiting for them to be fed."[53]

Pershing attempted to rise above the incident and treat it the same as any other challenge. Of course, additional punishments were meted out, and he even informed the cadets of A Company, "My reputation is made. There is nothing you can do to hurt me."[54] But the implications of a silencing were undeniable. By definition, for such a protest to succeed across an entire room filled with hundreds of cadets, all parties had to be complicit—not simply the frustrated cadets of A Company—including all the officers, whose actions were expected to reflect some level of maturity. But they did participate, all of them, from the most senior cadet captain to the lowliest first-year private. Doubly hurtful for Pershing was the stark juxtaposition of his reputation as a tac at West Point to the halcyon days of near deification he had enjoyed at the University of Nebraska.

A Company may also have created a nickname for Pershing, one that followed him for the remainder of his days. It was common for cadets to create such nicknames. To an extent, it was a military tradition to bestow monikers on officers, sometimes to extol a positive and, perhaps more often, to mock.

Such names typically referred to some physical trait, such as an officer's short height or baldness or abnormality. Pershing had none of these; instead, the cadets decided to hang a name on him that reflected their Jim Crow attitudes regarding race. They dubbed Pershing with "N—— Jack," a reference to his service commanding the African American Tenth Cavalry.

But as so often happens with nicknames, a negative was turned into a positive. Eventually, the name was softened into the more acceptable "Black Jack," which represented to many who were unaware of its origins a perfectly masculine nickname for a military man, one conjuring up images of a menacing billy club. In a few short years, as Pershing became a more public figure, newspaper reporters picked up the name, turning it into a sobriquet of admiration. In the end, again, A Company was beaten at its own game.

It is telling that Pershing, in later years, rarely referred to his one year of service as a West Point tactical officer. In his memoirs, he only wrote three paragraphs regarding the months he spent at the academy that year. At no point does he mention the negative cadet response, the challenges of A Company, the silencing, or anything else that might indicate any dissatisfaction or disappointment connected to his service there except for the rejection of his proposal to add a practical course in tactics. But his West Point service represented the most disagreeable experience of his military career to date and perhaps of his entire life to that point.

Through the spring term, Pershing continued his hard-line approach as a tactical officer while looking for a way out. In February 1898 he penned a letter to Meiklejohn, seeking a change without directly requesting it: "As we agreed, I have gotten out of this about all there is in it."[55] Aware of a vacancy in the Judge Advocate General's Department, Pershing applied but was turned down. His immediate escape from West Point seemed almost impossible that spring when an announcement was issued from high up the chain of command: "The Secretary of War has decided that the officers serving at the Military Academy can not be spared from their duties here and will not be relieved until close of the Academic year or until the First Class shall have graduated from the Academy."[56]

Pershing and the restless cadets of A Company seemed stuck with one another for the time being. But the approach of war soon changed everything.

EIGHT

Cuba, 1898

As the battleship USS *Maine* sailed into Havana Harbor on the morning of January 25, 1898, Charles D. Sigsbee, the ship's captain, sent a relieved telegram to his naval superiors in Washington DC informing them his ship and crew "had quietly arrived, 11 a.m. today; no demonstrations so far."[1] Captain Sigsbee was certainly aware he and his crew of 360 sailors and officers had sailed into a potentially dangerous situation. Although the U.S. Navy officially referred to the arrival of the *Maine* as a goodwill visit to the Spanish colonial island of Cuba, the very presence of the U.S. battleship at the island's largest port ignored the underlying tensions between the United States and Spain that were by then as thick as the tropical air. Colonial Cuba's thirty-year, on-again, off-again rebellion against Spain, its European master for nearly four centuries, was again coming to a head. Riots raged in the capital city, and the U.S. government was on a mission to protect its interests on the Caribbean island.

Cuba had long been an island of interest to the United States. Its location was key, situated only ninety miles south of Florida. Through the nineteenth century, some Americans had considered the island as a potential U.S. territory. Over the years, American businessmen had become entrenched in the island's lucrative sugar industry. Various U.S. presidents—James K.

Polk, Franklin Pierce, and James Buchanan—had suggested purchasing Cuba from Spain, but the Spanish government had duly rebuffed each attempt.

Then, after hundreds of years of European control, various colonies in the Caribbean began to revolt, including Cuba. In 1868 the Cuban people, rich and poor, Black and white, began demanding their independence. By 1878 Spanish officials finally crushed the revolutionaries through a show of force, augmented by promised reforms that never materialized. Then, in 1895, José Martí, a Cuban poet and revolutionary, fomented another revolt through his Cuban Revolutionary Party, and the struggle for Cuban independence was on again. To help draw attention to their revolution, these insurrectos targeted the island's sugar industry, hoping to bring the Spanish colonial power to its knees through economic chaos. This new revolt immediately drew the attention of the American public. U.S. business investments were at stake all over Cuba, but the most inspiring element of the revolution was the rebels' call for independence. For some in the United States, the Cuban fight reminded them of America's earlier struggle against British tyranny.

Despite the American public's interest in the Cuban revolution, the U.S. government was not prepared to become entangled in a fight between the Cubans and the Spanish. President Grover Cleveland announced official neutrality concerning the Cuban insurrection. Laws were enacted making it illegal for Americans to support the revolution, to arm Cubans, and to fight in the Cuban guerrilla forces. U.S. naval vessels patrolled the waters between Cuba and Florida, looking for American gunrunners. Yet congressmen on Capitol Hill soon challenged Cleveland's policy. In 1896 the Senate passed a resolution of support for the revolution that recognized the right of the Cuban people to rebel against their Spanish colonial masters. House members rewrote the bill and called for direct U.S. involvement in the revolution. By November, officers at the Naval War College had worked up a plan for U.S. action in Cuba and in other Spanish colonies, including Puerto Rico and the Philippines.

Yet, through the eighteen months that followed, the U.S. government took no overt military action against the Spanish in support of Cuba. Through those months, many sympathetic Americans read stories in their hometown newspapers about Spanish atrocities perpetrated against the Cuban people. At that time, most Americans received at least one of the country's fourteen thousand weekly or nearly two thousand daily newspapers. Sometimes small-town newspapers republished stories from some of the country's most influential papers, including the *New York Journal*, published by William Randolph Hearst, and the *New York World*, owned by newspaper tycoon Joseph Pulitzer.

Such articles included sensational details designed to solicit Americans' sympathy for Cuba. Gen. Valeriano Weyler became, for many Americans, a household name. Weyler was a Spanish military commander whose ruthless campaign against Cuban insurrectos angered many U.S. citizens. Reports told of Weyler's ferreting out alleged revolutionaries from their jungle hideouts. Those revolutionaries were then placed by the hundreds of thousands in concentration camps around Cuba, and many died of starvation and disease. Weyler's men allegedly burned Cuban homes, even whole villages, and killed thousands of innocent islanders. The U.S. press soon referred to Weyler as the "Butcher."

Laws or no laws, Americans were increasingly becoming anything but neutral toward the Cuban revolution. But as Americans' support for Cuba grew, the U.S. government remained behind the national curve. In November 1896 the country was in the midst of a presidential election, yet the candidates rarely referred to Cuba and the revolution. Republican William McKinley did not directly mention Cuba in any campaign address, and after elected, he delivered his inaugural address with only an allusion to Cuba: "War should never be entered upon until every agency of peace has failed; peace is preferable to war in almost every contingency."[2]

Despite the president's words, during his first meeting with his cabinet, McKinley received a recommendation from his consul general in Cuba, America's man in Havana, Fitzhugh

Lee. (Gen. Robert E. Lee was his uncle.) Lee suggested a warship be dispatched to Cuba as a show of force and to demonstrate to the Cubans the U.S. government's support. At that meeting, President McKinley, having just taken office, denied Lee's request. Even then, though, the Republican leader knew he and his administration might eventually have to take steps involving the United States in the Cuban revolution. The hue and cry of the American public grew louder every day.

Over the next year, the rebellion in Cuba continued as Americans watched anxiously. By October 1897, hope sprang up when a new Spanish ruler in Cuba, Práxedes Mateo Sagasta, sent General Weyler packing to Spain and promised the Cubans home rule. But the rebels wanted more. They chose to continue their struggle, unwilling to accept anything short of complete independence from Spain. "Cuba libre!" (Free Cuba!) remained the rallying cry of the island's insurrectos. In the meantime, many of the Spaniards in Cuba opposed Sagasta's policies of autonomy for their island. Military officials, government bureaucrats, and Spanish businessmen worked to block Sagasta at every turn.

Just two days after Sagasta came to power, U.S. secretary of the navy John D. Long sent orders to the captain of the USS *Maine* to sail out of Chesapeake Bay, where the ship was engaged in maneuvers, and steam south. The *Maine* was one of the U.S. Navy's newest vessels, a model for ships of the future. When Congress authorized its construction in 1886, the year John Pershing graduated from West Point, designers were handed a budget of $2.5 million to create a unique U.S. naval ship. The new vessel was designed to extend longer than a football field. It was double hulled, steel constructed, and plated with a twelve-inch-thick band of nickel-steel armor, allowing the ship to withstand direct hits from an enemy warship with minimal damage. The deck of the *Maine* bristled with armament. The *Maine* was nothing short of naval innovation on the water.

By December 15, 1897, the *Maine* arrived at Key West, less than a hundred miles from Havana. Just over a week earlier while speaking to Congress, President McKinley admonished the Spanish government to concentrate its efforts on political reform in Cuba. Soon events began to accelerate. Riots broke out in Havana on January 12. Less than a week later, McKinley took a decisive step. He ordered the *Maine* to Cuba. By January 25 Captain Sigsbee delivered his ship to the island. That morning the U.S. vessel approached the narrow channel leading into Havana Harbor and past Spanish shore batteries, where Spanish officials watched discreetly as the *Maine* sailed past. Everyone on board the *Maine* was wary, uncertain of what lay ahead. No U.S. warship had entered those waters in three years. Every man on deck had within reach a loaded gun. Gunners even took their places on the turrets of the ship's ten-inch guns, though they were out of sight to observers on shore. As a handful of sailors watched from their vantage point on the deck, one turned to his shipmates and gave an ominous prediction: "We'll never get out of here alive."[3]

As the days passed, tension on board ship remained constant. Some asked their superiors why they were there. The harbor was polluted and smelly, giving off a foul odor from raw sewage. Circulars threatening death to the Americans were tacked up along Havana streets. Rumors circulated that mines—underwater torpedoes placed by the Spanish—littered the harbor. The Cuban nights were hot and humid, and everyone on the *Maine* seemed uncomfortable, waiting for something to happen.

On the evening of February 15, history caught up with the men aboard the USS *Maine*. At 9 p.m. the ship's bell rang the hour. In his cabin, Captain Sigsbee had just finished several hours of working on the ship's correspondence with his aide, Cadet Jonas Holden. He dismissed Holden for the evening, went topside, and took a brief stroll on deck. Then he retired to his cabin to write a letter to his wife. At 9:10 the ship's bugler played "Taps," the navy's signal to "turn in and keep quiet." Sigsbee recalled later that the sound of the bugle was "singularly beautiful in the oppressive stillness of the night. The marine bugler who was rather given to fanciful effects was doing his best."[4] At 9:40 Sigsbee placed the letter he had just finished into an envelope when he heard a loud noise. Writing later to his wife, the captain described what he heard at that moment: "It was a bursting, rending, and crashing roar of immense volume, largely metallic in character. It was followed by heavy, ominous metallic sounds. There was a trembling and lurching motion of the vessel, a list to port."[5] Almost immediately, the electric lights in the quarters went out, and smoke drifted into the cabin.

Uninjured but certain his ship had experienced an explosion, the captain groped his way out of the dark cabin and followed the passageway leading to the ship's main deck. In the corridor, Sigsbee found his orderly, Pvt. William Anthony, who said urgently, "Sir, I have to inform you that the ship has been blown up and is sinking."[6]

As the USS *Maine* slowly sank into the muddy bottom of Havana Harbor, it represented the worst naval disaster in U.S. history to that point, with 260 sailors killed, nearly all of them enlisted men. No one really knew what caused the mysterious onboard explosions, but for many Americans, the details were largely insignificant. Most assumed it was the diabolical work of the Spanish, whether official or otherwise. American newspapers, short on evidence, simply fabricated facts, filled in information gaps, and whipped up Americans' lather for war. President McKinley, who had managed to divert war throughout his entire first year in office, was one of the few calling for "cool heads and cautious tongues."[7]

March saw some suggestion of hope that the United States and Spain might actually avert war. McKinley approached the Spanish with a short list of ultimatums, including ending its oppressive campaign against the Cuban rebels and offering the Cuban people their independence. By late March, the Spanish government seemed ready to agree to such stipulations, announcing it might possibly end hostilities soon. But war fever had already overtaken many Americans. That spring, U.S. flags could be seen waving in endless numbers, and patriotic songs and marches were the popular tunes at band concerts and music halls. By early April Secretary of the Navy Long, who had supported McKinley's opposition to war, penned in his diary, "The country is so clamorous for action that the president cannot delay longer."[8]

Within weeks, the United States descended into war, if only on paper. McKinley ordered a naval blockade of Cuba on April 20; four days later, he approached Congress with a request for war. Once the House and Senate voted overwhelmingly for war, McKinley then dated the declaration as the twentieth to eliminate any suggestion he had dispatched U.S. naval forces prematurely. The war most Americans had beaten drums for had finally arrived.

Pershing was part of a U.S. military that was sorely ill prepared for such an expansive international conflict. Over the previous thirty years, the U.S. population had doubled, while the army had been reduced in numbers to 2,100 officers and 25,000 enlisted men, as Pershing notes in his memoirs. McKinley soon called for volunteers, as many as 125,000 by April 23 and another 75,000 by late May. Americans could take little on faith regarding the Spanish. Officially, their army numbered more than 300,000 with nearly two of every three soldiers already stationed in Cuba.[9]

Prior to McKinley's request for war, Pershing felt the conflict was inevitable. His only question was whether he would be directly involved or be forced to remain at West Point, which represented for him a completely different set of battles. Anticipating the winds of war, Pershing wrote an application to the adjutant general on April 16 requesting active duty, which would allow him to leave West Point and rejoin his regiment, the Tenth Cavalry, and his buffalo soldiers. To hedge his bets, Pershing also broke army protocol and wrote, not one, but two letters the following day to his old friend George Meiklejohn, the acting secretary of war. In the first, Pershing included a slightly veiled panic that he might miss the conflict: "I would not miss service in the field for anything. . . . If I did not make every effort to obtain an opportunity 'for field service,' I should never forgive myself."[10]

The second letter easily represented a continuation of his thoughts regarding field service, including a twist he thought might appeal to his friend from Nebraska: "My services can easily be spared here. . . . If there is war, most of the officers will undoubtedly be ordered to their regiments, but I do not care to stay here and be pigeon-holed."[11] Pershing ends the letter suggesting a special company be formed from the Pershing Rifles at the University of Nebraska. He thought "the crack company of Nebraska" could serve as the nucleus of a new regiment of volunteers, even as he offered himself as its commanding officer with a rank of lieutenant colonel. "I'll tell you a regiment of those Nebraska boys, with some who have had military training at the University for officers . . . would make a fine outfit. . . . They all know me, too, and I think have every confidence in my ability to handle them."[12] Pershing's request reflected not only his desire to serve in the coming action but also his dissatisfaction with his situation at West Point. It is hardly ironic that even as he was attempting to distance himself from the cadets at the academy, he sought a reconnection with his former students at the University of Nebraska.

When Meiklejohn responded, he gave his old friend from their Lincoln days a yes and a no answer. As to a Nebraska regiment led by Pershing, his friend reminded him that "the Governors of the States appoint regimental officers."[13] (Accordingly, the governor of Nebraska soon appointed William Jennings Bryan, a pacifist at heart, as a colonel of a volunteer Nebraska regiment.) But John's primary request was granted. With Secretary of War Russell A. Alger, a veteran cavalryman who had fought during the Civil War, out of the office for several crucial days, Meiklejohn pulled the levers of authority for Pershing and "directed that orders be issued sending" him to his regiment.[14] Maj. Gen. Nelson Miles, Pershing's old commander during his postings in New Mexico, issued the orders on April 19 and recommended that "1st Lieut. John J. Pershing, 10th Cavalry, be relieved from duty at the Military Academy, and ordered to join his regiment in the field."[15] Pershing had been posted too late to New Mexico to participate in the capture of Geronimo and, in South Dakota, had missed (fortunately) the Wounded Knee Massacre and most of the fighting during the Ghost Shirt uprising. Now he had his opportunity to prove himself on the field of battle against a powerful international enemy. But first he had to get to his men, the buffalo soldiers of Tenth Cavalry, and then, by hook or by crook, get them all to Cuba in time to see the fight.

In the meantime, Pershing's New York acquaintance Theodore Roosevelt, who had since their time together been appointed assistant secretary of the navy—a role equivalent to Meiklejohn's army secretaryship—ordered Adm. George Dewey to sail his fleet of U.S. naval vessels from Hong Kong to Manila Bay in the Philippines and knock out Spain's Pacific Fleet. Roosevelt then resigned his post and formed his own regiment of volunteers, the First U.S. Volunteer Cavalry, one famously remembered as the Rough Riders.[16] He filled its ranks with an odd assortment of men who were all friends of one sort or another, representing two worlds—his eastern, blue-blooded roots and his western ranching days. His Rough Riders included old Harvard pals, football buddies, cowboys, Indian scouts, and frontier lawmen. All those who joined Roosevelt had experience with horses and firearms.

His regiment was one of three so-called cowboy units formed for service during the Spanish-American War, but Americans only paid attention to Roosevelt's colorful crew of volunteers that represented the genuine article, an enviable assortment of America's best young fighting men. None had more to lose than Roosevelt, who was on a trajectory of political advancement that some observers at the time thought might land him in the White House. But he, like Pershing, could not imagine missing the action. "I am going to Cuba," he announced to a friend as they walked through Washington's Lafayette Square. "I will take all the chances of meeting death by yellow fever, smallpox or by a Spanish bullet just to see the Spanish flag once on a battlefield."[17] Roosevelt would indeed find his way to Cuba, where his path would, for a second time, cross that of John J. Pershing.

Pershing received further encouragement of his reassignment on April 30 in a telegram sent by Col. Guy V. Henry of the Tenth Cavalry, which was stationed in Georgia, to the adjutant general in Washington: "I desire approval of appointment of Lieut. Pershing, now at West Point, as regimental Quartermaster and ask that he report for duty."[18] By May 2 Pershing received final orders to rejoin his regiment. He departed West Point, which had proven a less than positive experience for him and possibly the worst of his military career to date. His time at the academy did have its advantages. At West Point, Pershing had met and worked with individuals with whom he would serve during World War I, including several who would become key commanders.[19]

Pershing caught up with the Tenth Cavalry at Chickamauga National Park, where a bloody Civil War battle had been fought, and the unit was soon on its way to Tampa, Florida, the primary disembarkation port for troops headed to Cuba. When he arrived, he found the encampment in lockdown. Local citizens were none too happy about having African American soldiers entering their community, and one shop owner posted a sign in his business window: "N——s not wanted." Tensions boiled over when a Black soldier was refused a shave in a local barbershop. When racial insults were thrown at him, he snapped. From the street, he fired his pistol and killed the white barber. (The murderer was subsequently court-martialed and sentenced to death.)

When Pershing joined the Tenth, there were no actual troop vacancies for him to fill, so he was appointed to Col. Frank D. Baldwin's staff. Baldwin was the inspector general of two different corps and a veteran who had served under General Miles on various Indian campaigns. The Tenth was part of the Second Brigade, commanded by Brig. Gen. Samuel B. M. Young, who reported to Fifth Corps under the command of Maj. Gen. William R. Shafter. The latter's assignment was to deliver troops to Cuba and capture the key port of Santiago, where the Spanish Atlantic Fleet was stationed. Shafter, an old hand, was another Civil War veteran, obese, sixty-three-years-old, and struggling with gout. He represented the kind of worn-out commander Theodore Roosevelt referred to as "fat old colonels who fall off their horses or cannot stand a five-mile march."[20] But age was the best assurance of rank in the U.S. Army, a fact that rankled Pershing. He had dreamed of a lieutenant colonelcy leading a

Nebraska regiment of volunteers, but he went into the Spanish-American War as a first lieutenant.

As a regimental quartermaster, Pershing had a thankless, endless responsibility. The Tenth Cavalry was not well equipped, and the army's supply chain was fraught with snarls, tangles, great gaps, and plain old inefficiency. The United States had entered a war it was clearly unprepared to fight. When General Miles received orders to take command of an army of seventy thousand men and deliver them to capture Havana, he balked. In a meeting with President McKinley on May 8, Miles informed him of one simple problem: "There was not enough weeks' time for an army of 70,000 to fight one battle." Ammunition shortages were merely the tip of the iceberg. "Modern guns and specialized equipment, as well as ammunition, were lacking, and even uniforms could not be immediately provided."[21]

Pershing, as the quartermaster, worked day and night to equip the men of the Tenth, but even he could not manage to access everything they needed. The system was, in his words, "little short of chaotic."[22] Such confusion meant quartermasters such as Pershing were forced to open up railcars, pry open crates to identify contents, and scrounge for supplies as best they could. Despite his frustrations, Pershing's experience was crucial in preparing him for later field service. When he commanded expeditionary forces to the Philippines or into Mexico chasing after Pancho Villa or in France during the Great War, he was diligent concerning the organization of supply.

Additionally, troop encampments were a mess, especially among the volunteer units, "mainly because of the ignorance of camp sanitation among medical officers and line officers as well." Latrines contaminated water supplies, and flies carried disease. Once troops reached Cuba, such circumstances only became exaggerated. In his memoirs, Pershing notes learning an important lesson, which "was not lost on the army and every precaution was taken in our camps during the World War, both at home and abroad, with the result that our army made an exceptional record in preventing disease chargeable to unsanitary conditions."[23]

Following weeks of delay, on June 14 the U.S. Army dispatched sixteen thousand men out of Tampa on board a flotilla of thirty-two troop ships accompanied by an escort of fourteen naval vessels. The group moved in three disjointed columns that stretched out across seven miles of ocean, and the trip proved miserable. The ship carrying the Tenth was the merchant ship *Leona*, which normally plied the coast. Pershing and Lt. Col. E. J. McClernand, the adjutant general of the expeditionary force who had served as a tac officer during Pershing's cadet days, inspected the vessel and "found it in reasonably good shape. The hold had been thoroughly disinfected . . . and temporary bunks had been constructed."[24] As the flotilla prepared to depart, Pershing held his best hopes for the men's future. In a letter to Meiklejohn, he wrote, "There will never sail from our shores a finer body of men than we have right here."[25] His attitude was quite positive and insightful, despite the long days of confusion and chaos before their departure. Five months later, in a speech delivered in Chicago, Pershing described his view of the U.S. forces headed toward Cuba: "Fifty transports bearing an American army as splendid in the personnel of the officers and men of its line as ever invaded a foreign country."[26] Pershing clearly felt his time in the West, stationed in remote corners of New Mexico and Montana, had prepared him for the military task ahead.

Misery stalked the men on the *Leona*. Having already spent long days on the vessel before their departure, troopers now became seasick. Food was a problem, as the ship had no cooking galleys. Field rations became the go-to, and many men found them inedible. The men were cramped belowdecks like sardines, and their woolen uniforms were hot as the ships sailed farther south. Their blue uniforms were more suited for a Montana or South Dakota winter.[27] Mix-ups in orders between ships and a general caution—rumors of Spain's Atlantic Fleet being in close proximity previously delayed the troops' departure from Tampa on two occasions—meant the flotilla made slow progress toward its destination. (At one point, the *Leona* became separated from the flotilla for more than a day.) Pershing maintained a diary, making entries that noted mistakes, failures, improvements to be made: "More air—hammocks for men—cooking arrangements on board should be provided—travel ration unpalatable and stale—more fruit necessary—clothing too hot. Canvas washable caps better than hats. Anxious to see landing facilities—look for a lot of confusion."[28] John inventoried problems and issues, attempting to learn from the situation so that future errors might be avoided. He carried this quality through his entire military career. While obeying orders, he would take in an experience, weigh the pros and cons, and make notes of improvements for the next go-round.

After almost a week at sea, the convoy arrived off the Cuban coast at Daiquirí, a tiny coastal village fourteen miles east of Santiago, the U.S. Army's main objective. Spanish forces had been in the region but chose to abandon the location before the Americans arrived. Still, the U.S. Navy bombarded the area for over an hour to make certain. Daiquirí was hardly an ideal location for landing thousands of men and hundreds of horses and mules. The shoreline was rocky and rugged, offering no port facilities. Everything was taken ashore by small boats, including "pulling boats" and whaleboats. The troops were issued the standard field rations—three days' worth of bacon, hardtack, and coffee—which Pershing had become accustomed to during his earlier field days in New Mexico. Each blue-clad soldier carried a rifle—many were issued old Springfield muskets that fired black powder—a hundred rounds of ammunition, a blanket, a shelter tent, and a waterproof poncho.

Just loading the small boats was difficult, as the men had to scale down the sides of the ships on Jacob's ladders and drop the last fifteen feet or so into the unsteady, bobbing boats. Each had a capacity for thirty men, more or less, and were pulled by chugging steam launches. Two men drowned in the loading process. One of the thornier problems was unloading the horses and mules. With no dock platform or gangplank, the men simply pushed the animals from the decks into the warm tropical water and hoped they would gain their bearings and swim to shore. Several simply swam out to sea and drowned.

Eventually someone suggested tying several animals together and towing them in behind the boats.

Pershing had mixed feelings about the difficult landing. He put much of it off to the "inexperience of officers in transporting troops by water."[29]

Once they were onshore, the American troops met no opposition. While most of the Spanish force in the region had evacuated before the Americans landed, units of the Tenth and First Cavalry and the First Volunteer Cavalry—Roosevelt's Rough Riders—saw action the next day, engaging the Spanish in a fight at Las Guásimas and driving them from their defensive positions. Ten men were wounded, and one member of the Tenth was killed.

Pershing was not present during the fight. He remained on the *Leona*, which sailed west to Aserraderos with orders to pick up a complement of Cuban rebels under the command of Gen. Calixto García, who had spent years fighting the Spanish. The force proved worn out, even bedraggled, after fighting remotely for so long. Many of the Americans saw nothing to admire about the rebels, and a latent racism only complicated their opinions. But Pershing, as usual regarding race, saw something else: "Ragged, some half naked, wearied from hunger, laden with huge earthen water pots, heavy packs and cooking utensils slung over their backs, armed with every conceivable obsolete pattern of gun, it is no wonder that they dared not face the deadly Mauser rifle."[30] While the first lieutenant expressed sympathy toward the rebels, he could not imagine they would make any significant contribution. "A miserable lot they are, in my opinion they will prove of little service to the Americans."[31]

The following day, as he led along a pack mule carrying supplies, Pershing was back with his men, who had one fight already under their belts. He was disappointed to learn that many had abandoned any and all gear they considered unnecessary, including tent shelters and some food. Over the next five days, he remained busy, bringing up replacement supplies along jungle trails that were often invisible under heavy foliage. Conditions at the landing site were a bit better than at Tampa, with Pershing observing "at least the semblance of order."[32]

Confusion continued as the order of the day as troops gathered in jungle clearings, with supplies arriving in a pell-mell fashion and the roads turning to thick mud amid repeated bursts of rain. It was taxing on everyone, including Pershing, who managed to keep above the fray. He noted, "Everything was in the direst confusion. No one seemed to be in command and no one had any control over boats, transportation nor anything—and it was only by the individual efforts of the officers of the line that order was brought out of chaos."[33] As a long-term veteran, Pershing understood how the military sometimes worked or did not, as the case might be. He was not much for grumbling or complaining and rarely accepted it from others. When he overheard an officer grousing about General Shafter, referring to him as "a fat old slob" who wasn't giving orders in a timely fashion, Pershing exploded: "The fat Old Man you talk about is going to win this campaign. When he does, these things will be forgotten."[34] Pershing was astute enough regarding the military and field campaigns to understand that many aspects of war were simply circumstances over which few, if any, might exert any real control. War represented a form of chaos, and for soldiers to anticipate true order was nothing short of foolishness.

Shafter might have deserved criticism. Once thousands of U.S. troops were landed on Cuban soil, no one really knew what to do next, including Shafter, who admitted that "there was no strategy about it." He simply wanted to "do it quick," meaning land troops, advance them through dense jungle, occupy the known ridgelines leading to Santiago, knock out all resistance, and call for the enemy's surrender.[35] It would all be done by infantry and cavalry, he argued. Shafter even turned down the navy's offer to deliver its battleships to Santiago Harbor and blast away at shore positions. Shafter intended to approach the Spanish as if he were planning an attack on an Indian encampment out west. But grand strategy or not, he commanded and carried the weight of responsibility on his shoulders.

Cuba, 1898

The veteran first lieutenant knew how easy it was to complain about commanders. Wars require a learning curve, and Pershing knew the curve might prove lengthy in Cuba. The United States had not fought a war on foreign soil in fifty years. The challenges, to someone of his experience and insight, could easily translate into learned lessons. Such was the case. As Pershing's old friend Avery Andrews later wrote, "But out of the welter of confusion and disorder there grew, under the leadership of Theodore Roosevelt, as President, and Elihu Root, as Secretary of War, the new army which distinguished itself so greatly in the World War." It fell to Pershing to lead that new army when the time came for the next foreign war.[36]

Back in the States, with the Spanish-American War constantly in the newspaper headlines during the late spring and summer of 1898, Willa Cather was busy writing such headlines as part of her job with the *Pittsburgh Leader*. Cather also handled the incoming war dispatches from Cuba, so war-related news was always within her purview. In a letter she penned to her friend Frances Gere, dated June 23, 1898, she stated,

> It was awfully nice of you to remember me with a commencement invitation and it was a great disappointment to me not to be able to see you graduate. . . . But the horrors of war seem to be a good deal worse in newspaper offices than in the field, and I had to stay on here grilling in the heat and writing headlines about Cervera [Spanish admiral Pascual Cervera y Topete] being bottled up in Santiago harbor. I expect to start west for a two month's vacation the first of August, however, and then I will see you and hear all about the commencement festivities.[37]

During the war, Cather's cousin Grosvenor Cather was a fifteen-year-old Nebraska farm boy. Too young to volunteer, he later served in World War I. He was the first young man from Webster County to see service in Europe and the first from his county to be killed, the victim of a shell explosion while visiting his men in their trenches. As noted previously, Willa Cather would pay tribute to her cousin by fictionalizing him through the character Claude Wheeler in her novel *One of Ours*, which she published in 1922.

Even as the Americans began to gather in larger units and prepared to head straight along jungle paths to Santiago, the Spanish were also preparing, digging rifle pits along San Juan Hill. As units organized to advance, possibly cutting themselves off from supply lines, Pershing and others in the quartermaster role had to make important decisions: What foods were essential? What equipment? Ammunition was a must, but the Krag-Jorgensen rifles' .30 caliber cartridges were heavier than other ammo. Quartermaster decisions became a question of what to leave in and what to leave out.

An additional complication was the sheer size of the American units. For officers accustomed to western campaigns involving troops, companies, and regiments, the scale of the Cuban campaign did not fit. Now the U.S. military was dealing with brigades and divisions, much as it had during the Civil War more than a generation earlier. While some of the top commanders had participated in that war, the vast majority of underling officers had not. Pershing was well aware that most of the young officers who had recently graduated from West Point had little practical field training, the type of training he had just proposed but had been summarily rejected.

By June 30, American units, including Pershing's Tenth Cavalry, were on the move toward Santiago. Their primary objectives were to encounter Spanish defensive positions along a lengthy rise short of the city that included San Juan and nearby Kettle Hills, which formed the high ground comprising San Juan Heights. A fleet of Spanish warships was bottled up in Santiago Harbor with a U.S. naval fleet waiting offshore. The numerical strength of the Spanish military had been grossly overinflated, which meant the Spanish defending Santiago, Cuba's second-largest city, were themselves outnumbered.[38] The Spanish had their own advantages, including holding a well-entrenched high ground and wielding a twentieth-century weapon.

Ironically, the Spanish brought the technological advantage to the Cuban conflict. Many carried German-made Mauser rifles that fired bullets "at supersonic speeds, making a cracking sound as they flew and giving them deadly accuracy."[39] In comparison, the Americans carried the bolt-action Krag-Jorgensen rifles, which were fairly ineffective, and the out-of-date, single-shot Model 1873 Springfields that fired black-powder cartridges. When fired, the Springfields emitted a plume of white smoke from the barrel, giving away the soldier's position to the enemy. (Mausers utilized smokeless cartridges.) Even rapid-fire, breech-loading Spanish cannon were better adapted for the Cuban field than the slower-firing U.S. Hotchkiss mountain guns, the kind used during campaigns in the West, including the Wounded Knee Massacre.

On July 1 the Cuban morning dawned clear and balmy, as John J. Pershing later noted in his memoirs. He scanned the landscape directly in front of him, as several American units prepared to make an assault against a well-entrenched enemy, one hidden in the dense undergrowth of a lush tropical forest. Pershing saw nearly invisible lines of entrenchments, situated half a mile away and on the opposite side of the Aguadores River, cutting across his army's approach. Blockhouses dotted the ridgeline, protecting the crest of the hills of San Juan.

Pershing spotted a movement along the left side of the first hill. There stood a solitary Spanish sentinel, holding the reins of his horse. Behind him, to the west, Pershing could see the outer defenses of Santiago. Further distant, the young West Pointer made out the church spires, stone buildings, and towers of the city. The Cuban outpost looked like a ghost town, the civilian population having evacuated with the approach of the Americans. As Pershing continued to scan the hills before him, he saw to the northeast in the foothills the stone fortress and its ring of smaller blockhouses of El Caney commanding a rocky outcropping. There, the Spanish had taken up defensive positions. Pershing knew what every American officer and enlisted man preparing for the assault understood: these blockhouses had to be captured. The Spanish would not make that singular military goal an easy one for the newly arrived U.S. forces.

At 6:30 the quiet of the post-dawn jungle morning was suddenly shattered by rifle fire as the volunteers of the Second Infantry Division of General Shafter's Fifth Corps, under the command of Brig. Gen. H. W. Lawton, began their advance. (Lawton was a Civil War veteran and had participated in the campaigns to capture Geronimo.) From his field position, Pershing tried to determine exactly where the enemy was located, but this was warfare in the jungle. He and other cavalrymen had orders to remain in position and postpone their advance until Lawton's men had routed out Spanish resistance. The result was an anxious delay for Pershing and his comrades. Lawton had hoped his assault would complete its work within a couple of hours, but as he met stiff resistance, his right flank began to crumble.

By 8:20 a.m. General Shafter had waited as long as he could, and he ordered his artillery battery to begin firing on San Juan Hill. The barrage was pointless, however, since his guns were out of range to hit the Spanish positions, and the smoke they shot into the air gave away their own positions. The Spanish guns opened on the Americans below the hills, causing significant casualties. Some of the U.S. artillery actually hit some American cavalry troopers who were located ahead of the cannon positions. Near Pershing, American guns hit a sugar mill.

At 9:00 a.m. the cavalry began to move. Pershing mounted his horse and prepared to take part in the first serious battle of his military career. But even as his men moved forward, the Americans were bunching up on a narrow road, unable to advance significantly. This included the Tenth Cavalry, with "its men piling ahead toward the river, packing beyond the road into the bush, jamming into a solid, unsortable mass."[40] In the midst of the fight, the U.S. Army launched a great yellow balloon to provide an observation platform for spotting the enemy. But the balloon merely drew Spanish fire and informed the enemy exactly where the Americans were situated in the thick jungle.

Along a riverbank, Pershing crouched down as chaos hampered the U.S. assault up San Juan Heights. He later wrote, "Remaining there under this galling fire of exploding shrapnel and deadly mauser [sic] volleys the minutes seemed like hours."

He received orders to take his men across the Aguadores, where they would be less vulnerable to enemy fire.[41]

Without even accurate maps of the Cuban jungle that lay in front of them, Maj. Gen. Joseph Wheeler's cavalry units progressed slowly, awkwardly, blinded by the jungle. As the noise of war increased, with Mauser bullets cutting through the underbrush, several men of the Seventy-First New York Volunteers had had enough. They threw down their weapons and retreated through the jungle, creating a traffic jam of men. Finally, many of the retreating troops lay down on the jungle floor, and the Rough Riders and Pershing's troopers walked over them as they continued their advance.[42]

As the Rough Riders and the Tenth Cavalry—troops the Cubans referred to as "Smoked Yankees"[43]—moved along the narrow trail, they were met with Spanish gunfire. Pershing referred to the opening shots as a "veritable hail of shot and shell." But even as a recent grad from West Point took a hit and fell dead nearby, Pershing showed no fear.[44]

The American forces pushed forward under fire from Spanish guns situated across the hilly Cuban landscape. The thick undergrowth caused units to bunch up, slowing their movement further. With bayonets, they hacked at the "thorned vegetation, high grasses, and thickets, with bullets from the Spaniards' Mauser rifles continually hitting home."[45] Half of the Tenth's twenty-two white officers were picked off in short order. In the action, Pershing later remembered seeing the aged veteran Joe Wheeler, who had fought as a Confederate cavalry officer during the American Civil War, on his horse in the middle of a jungle stream. As Pershing approached Wheeler, an enemy artillery shot hit the water between them, sending up a dousing spray that drenched both men. Although these troops were cavalry, only a handful of officers had horses. Nearly everyone was advancing on foot, which was fortunate for many, since they would have presented a better target when mounted for the Spanish hiding above in the hills.

Pershing finally succeeded in getting his men across the river. They were in position to attack Kettle Hill, one of the two primary objectives of the assault, but they waited for their orders to advance. Spanish sniper fire continued to add to their casualties. For thirty long minutes, Pershing's Black troopers hunkered down in the lush Cuban vegetation, seeking vainly to spot the enemy above. By noon, Lawton's forces reached El Caney. Casualties were high, and the general assault that was to follow in Lawton's wake was still unorganized. Portions of regiments became separated from one another. Entire brigades had not yet been deployed forward. Shafter, overweight and ill with a fever, began to doubt the possibilities of his success in this heated jungle fight. Though the American commander was not aware at the time, the Spanish holding them back from their mountain positions numbered only six hundred men.

With shots firing all around, Pershing spotted his own captain, George Ayres, who yelled to his first lieutenant to show him the way up the hill. John Joseph Pershing pointed the way. Ayres later recalled how "the gallant Pershing ... was as cool as a bowl of cracked ice."[46] The composed lieutenant then turned to search for a second squadron he had lost in the confusion, one directly under the command of Maj. T. J. Wint, who also asked Pershing for direction. Historian Frank Vandiver describes what happened next: "Fire picked up, and the jungle shivered with alien bullets, but Pershing led the way. As the men reached a semblance of clearing they saw the river, and beyond it they glimpsed Kettle Hill."[47]

But no one ordered a direct frontal assault immediately. The blue-clad troops remained pinned down by deadly accurate enemy fire. The battle reached the point of no return. Either Shafter had to order a retreat soon or the Americans would have to take action and move forward into the face of the enemy's positions on high ground. At 1:30 p.m. the decision was made. Orders from headquarters arrived, instructing all units to advance. But the charge was already underway. Officers, angered by their own inaction, were leading individual charges with their men following close behind. One such personal charge involved 1st Lt. Jules Ord of the Sixth Infantry. He became so exasperated with the sniper fire pinning his men down that he rose up from jungle cover, stripped to the waist, brandished a bayonet in one hand and a pistol in the other, and shouted, "Follow me, we can't stay here!"[48] As Ord and his men led the way, Pershing sent his men forward as well up the southern rise of Kettle Hill.

A stream of men crossed the San Juan River, all moving forward against Spanish defensive fire. Pershing noted how his men moved "through streams, tall grass, tropical undergrowth, under barbed-wire fences and over wire entanglements" that blocked their path, momentarily slowing down their advance.[49] During the Great War, barbed wire was utilized as a defensive measure to halt the advance of the enemy, especially across the long distances between trenches, the decimated landscapes known as "No Man's Land." Here in Cuba, Pershing encountered barbed wire for the first time in combat.

Soon, some of the Black troopers of the Tenth Cavalry were moving together with the men of the Rough Riders up the hill, despite taking heavy fire from Spanish Mausers. The defensive resistance was heavier than General Wheeler had ever experienced. In all the confusion, some of the Tenth joined Ord's Sixth Infantry, while others tagged along with the Rough Riders, including Pershing. Before the day's end, Roosevelt took notice of the friend he had made at New York's Madison Square Garden. The hill itself provided little cover for the advancing Americans, but they continued up each sloping foot of exposed terrain, intent on their immediate goal, despite the never-ending hail of enemy bullets. In the midst of the action, a few American Gatling guns were delivered to the hot front and served as a rapid-fire deterrent to the Spanish. This precursor to the machine gun, the weapon of death during the Great War, provided Pershing a view of the significant contribution that such "automatic" weapons would make in future wars.

As American units rushed upward, Roosevelt's Rough Riders swung to the left and up neighboring San Juan Hill. Suddenly, Spanish resistance tapered; then it fell silent as the enemy surrendered its positions atop Kettle Hill, going back to San Juan Hill. Climbing and firing up the hill while on foot, Pershing reached the top to find the enemy entrenchments abandoned. Nearby were several men of the Tenth Cavalry. But the battle was not over. Pershing's new objective was the hill of San Juan, to his left. Having run the enemy off one hill, all units continued their advance toward the next hill. The fight was not won, but First Lieutenant Pershing had experienced his first taste of real combat. Lieutenant Ord proved himself a rallying leader during the day's assault on San Juan Heights. He was the first American combatant to breech the summit of San Juan Hill, where he was killed by enemy fire.

With multiple units gathered on Kettle Hill, now in open country and beyond the menacing jungle, American firepower could concentrate effectively against the Spanish riflemen who had plagued them for hours. For the first time that day, American Gatling guns laid down a devastating sheet of fire—3,600 rounds a minute—against the entrenched Spanish in the distance. Historian Frank Vandiver describes the shifting fortunes of the furious battle: "Now the view of the hillside changed; up out of the grass came the Yanks, in campaign hats cocked and dirty, their rifles glinting.... A last rush came after a short halt to let U.S. shells search further uphill. When the barrage lifted, the whole line stormed the crest and the enemy fled. San Juan Hill belonged to the takers."[50]

And one of those "takers" was John J. Pershing. During the November speech in Chicago, he described what he saw that day as his men moved up San Juan Hill: "Once begun it continued dauntless and unchecked in its steady, dogged, persistent advance until, like a mighty resistless torrent, it dashed triumphant over the crest of the hill and firing a parting volley at the vanishing foe, planted the silken standards on the enemy's breastworks, and the Stars and Stripes over the blockhouse on San Juan Hill to stay."[51]

Another taker that day was Theodore Roosevelt, whose fellow Rough Riders were in the thick of the action that resulted in the taking of San Juan Hill. This single military advance made him a hero back home and helped launch his career to new heights, including his election as President McKinley's second vice president in 1900 and his succession as president following McKinley's assassination just ten months later.

The day proved costly for the men of the Tenth Cavalry. In a letter handwritten in pencil to his friend George Meiklejohn—the missive opens "In Trenches, near Santiago"—Pershing extolled the virtues of the African American men under his command: "Our regiment has done valiant service—no one can say that Colored troops will not fight."[52] Approximately half of the regiment's officers and nearly 20 percent of the enlisted men were casualties. When Pershing found a wounded man of the Nineteenth lying on the field, he asked him how badly he was hurt. The trooper was gallant: "I don't know, but we whipped them, anyway, didn't we?"[53]

The adrenaline-charged first lieutenant from Missouri survived the battle and led his troops well. As the battle wound down, he looked about with concern for his comrades, helped several of the wounded, and examined the field for lingering enemy positions. Pershing was immediately proud of his Black troopers and their tenacity in the battle. "We officers of the Tenth Cavalry could have taken our black heroes in our arms," he later remembered. "Their conduct made me prouder than ever of being an officer in the American Army," Pershing wrote in his memoirs.[54] Perhaps all those years of Pershing's vacillating over whether to continue his military career or to resign to pursue the law had finally led to this moment of crystal clear clarity for him. On that hill in Cuba, Pershing likely felt he had made the right decision.

Following the capture of San Juan and Kettle Hills, as well as other advances made by U.S. forces, the fighting continued the next day. It came early when Spanish artillery split the night at 3 a.m., followed by small arms fire. Everyone on the Americans' side anticipated a Spanish counterattack, but none materialized. After a few hours, Spanish fire began to dramatically taper off. Near dawn, American units received entrenching tools and new ammunition but virtually no food. Snipers continued to menace the Americans. When a sniper wounded the regiment's adjutant, the regimental commander Col. Theodore Baldwin appointed Pershing to take his place. Pershing spent much of the day delivering messages to the front while commanding the regiment in Baldwin's absence. Not only was food in short supply, so was water. The men formed a bucket brigade to deliver water from the river to the front lines. Many men at the front became so hot during the fighting, they chose to strip off their uniforms to the waist.

Spanish resistance in Santiago did not last long. Spirited fighting continued the following day and into the next, and one of Pershing's best friends in uniform, Mal Barnum, was seriously wounded. On July 3 the Spanish fleet anchored in Santiago attempted to flee the island for open seas, but the guns of the U.S. Navy, including those of USS *Texas*, blasted away at the out-of-date, heavy Spanish ships. In the meantime, General Shafter delivered a message to the Spanish commanders in Santiago, giving them until 10 a.m. the following day to surrender. In time, the truce clock was extended several additional days before the Spanish officially surrendered.

During the days between the commencement of the truce and the surrender, Pershing and the Tenth Cavalry strengthened their defensive position. With the Americans holding the high ground outside Santiago, they began to lay down extensive trench works, the longest built by American troops since Grant's siege of Petersburg, Virginia, in 1864 that included more than fifty miles of trenches. With the truce ultimately extended to July 15, the Americans managed to dig six miles of trenches, which constantly filled with water from repeated tropical rains, turning the manmade ditches into muddy morasses. This return to trench warfare proved a dress rehearsal for the U.S. Army, whose doughboys would suffer in trenches along the western front during World War I. In Cuba, Pershing saw the trenches up close and personally.

Under Cuba's wet, tropical conditions, many men contracted diseases, including malaria and yellow fever. Pershing himself came down with malaria, which produced a high fever, but it did not stop him from seeing to his responsibilities. His main focus through the truce was to keep his men supplied. He managed to commandeer a wagon—a rare accomplishment within the ranks—and traveled back and forth from the supply depot on the coast with everything from cooking pots to medicine, food to tents. He even delivered personal baggage to officers who were on the front lines.

Pershing received two messages from the rear—one from President McKinley and the second from General Nelson Miles—that he read to his men. The popular commander promised he would soon arrive in Cuba in person along with additional forces, cheering the men. During this same lull in the fighting, displaced and desperate Cuban refugees reached the American lines, seeking relief. Pershing expressed a heart for the ragged souls caught in the midst of war: "Old and young, women, children and decrepit men of every class. . . . The suffering of the innocent is not the least of the horrors of war."[55] In these words, Pershing could have just as easily been describing the Lakotas of South Dakota and the wandering Crees of Montana.

With the surrender of the enemy, the Spanish-American War, one of America's shortest military conflicts, was over. In a report, Pershing revealed that 18 percent of the regiment was killed or wounded; half the officers were also casualties.

After the fighting, Pershing received much praise from his superiors, both for his actions during combat and for his persistence in working to keep his men supplied in the field. Supplies, including food, did not arrive regularly, and Pershing's men suffered accordingly. But their commander managed to scrounge here and take there, bypassing regulations and the proper forms, as he "appropriated mules and wagons without requisition, clothing, blanket rolls, such extra food as was available. The Tenth suffered, as did all Americans in Cuba, but less than others."[56] An admiring Colonel Baldwin later told Pershing, "You did some tall rustling and if you had not we would have starved, as none of the others were able or strong enough to do it."[57] These well-intended efforts caused Pershing to bend the rules, which he had never been able to make himself do during all his years of active military service. The war in Cuba shook loose some of Pershing's rigidity.

While Pershing remained in Cuba following the cessation of hostilities, he took another look at the lands around him and, for a fleeting moment, gave some thought to the possibilities the island might hold for him personally. In a letter to his old Nebraska friend George Meiklejohn, he wrote, "This is a beautiful country and I should like to own a ranch near here."[58] These two men from Nebraska represented "their generation of frontier-bred professional men," imagining a new American frontier in the rolling hills of Cuba.[59] In practical terms, Pershing, through his time in Cuba, had served the U.S. military in one more frontier posting.

When Pershing and his men left Cuba, the seven-day ship passage home provided him the opportunity to reflect on what lessons he learned from the experience, his first in the field of combat. He was elated at the level of patriotic spirit he saw in the men, including the volunteers. Nothing had stopped them from attaining victory, one achieved under difficult, deadly conditions. He realized that the army's weapons were woefully out of date or simply inadequate. While he was loath to criticize older commanders, he knew that a new generation of officers was needed to push the U.S. Army into the twentieth century. But more than any other problem, the issue of supply was crucial. As a quartermaster, he had seen the difficulties firsthand. He wrote, "The army of invasion [was] saddled with a lot of incompetent civilian staff officers who are simply guests. Good commissary and quartermaster sergeants or clerks would have been infinitely better and more deserving."[60] All these lessons informed Pershing when he became the commander of hundreds of thousands of doughboys during the Great War.

For his bravery under fire, Pershing gained additional praise. Capt. William Beck of Troop A noted, "The gallantry you displayed under fire and the untiring energy you evinced, were a devotion to duty exceeded by none, and equaled by few."[61] For his "gallantry in action against the Spanish forces, July 1, 1898," Pershing received the Silver Star. In Colonel Baldwin's official written report of the attack on Santiago, he named Pershing for his "untiring energy, faithfulness and gallantry."[62] In a letter written to the Missouri hero, Baldwin added to his sentiments: "I have been in many fights and through the Civil War, but on my word 'You were the coolest and bravest man I ever saw under fire in my life' and carried out your orders to the letter—no matter where it called you."[63]

The year 1898 marked the twelfth one of military service for Pershing since his graduation from West Point. Early that summer, he had become a brevet captain of volunteers. (Technically, he was still a second lieutenant in the regular army.) He had served as a cavalry officer at three frontier forts in New Mexico, his initial introduction to the wilder regions of the American West. He had seen service during the last of the Indian Wars, helped defuse the Ghost Shirt uprising, trained college cadets in Nebraska, and led a Cree exodus across Montana. The West had provided the backdrop for his time in uniform to date, and his experiences on the frontier provided him with a lengthy list of lessons learned. Additionally, for the first time, he had engaged in combat on foreign soil and emerged from those months of service with additional lessons under his belt. In a sense, Cuba represented yet another "western" experience for Pershing, "an extension of America's frontier as she moved out to make the Caribbean an American lake."[64] Over the next decade, Pershing continued to serve the military from frontier postings, but this time, the new American wilderness, and the next round of subjugating indigenous peoples, lay on the far side of the great Pacific Ocean.

NINE

Colony, 1898–1903

John Pershing entered the Spanish-American War with a new rank, that of brevet captain, and he exited the conflict with yet another—technically. Through multiple recommendations, including one from Brig. Gen. Leonard Wood, the regular army commander of the Rough Riders, Pershing was put forward for another promotion. The chain of recommendations ended at President McKinley's desk, who wrote at the bottom of a letter he received from Wood that mentioned Pershing: "Appoint to a Major, if there is a vacancy." In August 1898 he was brevetted a major of volunteers.[1]

That same month, Pershing and the Tenth Cavalry shipped out from Cuba to New York, having performed their military service well. Pershing wrote a letter to his friend and assistant secretary of the army George Meiklejohn and bragged about his African American troopers. Even though they emerged from the conflict with the highest officer casualty rate, Pershing remained exuberant about what his men had accomplished. In the speech he delivered in Chicago at Hyde Park Methodist Episcopal Church, he summarized his feelings in just three words: "It was glorious."[2]

Once he arrived back in the States, some bureaucratic cold water doused his enthusiasm. As a quartermaster, he was technically responsible for the equipment and matériel delivered to

Cuba, and the U.S. Army soon charged him as the unit quartermaster with a million dollars' worth of unaccounted for government supplies. Holding few receipts, which would have been impossible to receive in the whirlwind of supply chaos that had gripped Tampa months earlier, Pershing was in a ludicrous quandary. Fortunately, the regimental quartermaster—a young lieutenant in Huntsville, Alabama—managed to locate much of the government matériel in question, identifying his discoveries as "found in camp," and saved Pershing much trouble and culpability.[3] With the accounts settled, Pershing was off the hook, and he came out of the situation owing much to Lt. James G. Harbord. He and Pershing became well acquainted, and their paths crossed many times over the next several years, as both men served at various points in the Philippines. Their friendship led Pershing to appoint him as his AEF chief of staff during the Great War.

Next, Pershing took some time to return again to Chicago and visit with his father, mother, and James, who had moved there from Lincoln. While there, he called on the family doctor, who was alarmed at the state of John's health. He had contracted malaria in Cuba, a malady he would fight off and on over the years as the disease hit him in recurrent bouts.

By mid-August Pershing was on duty in Washington DC with the War Department. Over the next four months, he was the army's chief ordnance officer. Despite his condition, Pershing did not take a leave of absence and was soon assigned to inspect several western forts. Given the war, troop strength in these outposts was greatly reduced. Pershing examined the status of these western facilities and reported on their viability and necessity in a post–Indian wars West. Many such posts were closed or refitted for a second government purpose.

Then, by early 1899, Meiklejohn once again had a dramatic impact on Pershing's military career. Just as he had arranged for Pershing to leave his duties at West Point and rejoin the Tenth for action in Cuba, his Nebraska friend and assistant secretary of war arranged for Pershing to put his law degree to practical use with the department's Division of Customs and Insular Affairs. Once the United States signed a treaty of peace with the Spanish in October 1898, it controlled several important pieces of the old Spanish imperial real estate, including Cuba's neighbor Puerto Rico as well as Guam and the strategically significant Philippines. Suddenly, America was a colonial power over places most Americans could not locate on a map. As their administration shifted from Spanish to U.S. control, the legal questions were endless and quite complicated. Everything had to be considered: civil law, military authority, tax systems, customs issues, banking regulations, and the intricacies of administering remote colonies. Ironically, it fell to a pair of Nebraska men—Meiklejohn and Pershing—to set things straight. Pershing was soon serving as his old friend's right-hand man concerning these new frontier outposts of overseas U.S. power.[4]

Pershing was more than willing to blend his talents as a military officer and trained lawyer. He found the work intriguing. But the transfer of the Philippines to U.S. control proved the thorniest. Prior to the U.S. entry to the Spanish-American War, the Spanish had faced a native revolution that was similar in spirit to the insurrecto-led one in Cuba. Once the Americans took the place of the Spanish, they were seen as merely the next oppressors of the Filipino people. Thus, an insurrection soon broke out in defiance of U.S. control over the Philippines, piquing Pershing's interest more than mere legal matters. He began to consider how much more he could do if he were reassigned directly to the Philippines. "A battle has a fascination for a soldier," he wrote.[5] Plus he had learned a lesson from his time fighting in Cuba: nothing had provided a better jump start to his advancement in rank than active service in a foreign field.

If Pershing was certain he wanted reassignment to the Philippines, some of his closest friends were not. While Meiklejohn supported it, Charles Dawes, who had achieved much since their days in Lincoln, having become a successful lawyer and close friend to President McKinley, suggested Pershing should remain close to Washington DC. George DeShon, a former West Point classmate who was already in the Philippines, was even more discouraging: "Don't think of coming out here—You will be sick if you do—All Cuban malarial cases do very poorly here."[6] But Pershing followed his military instincts. Although his career included many assignments that placed him behind a desk, he was most at home in the field. By August 1899 his assignment came through. As he made plans to take up service halfway around the world, Laclede, Missouri, must have seemed another world away.

He did not head straight away to his Far Eastern posting but went by way of Europe, paying his own way. Save for his recent actions in Cuba and his earlier escort of the Crees to Canada, Pershing had never traveled beyond the borders of the United States. For six weeks, he indulged his dreams of traveling to England and included an official visit to the Royal Arsenal at Woolwich. (Overseas, the British were fighting their own war against the Dutch Boers in South Africa.) He took in the best London had to offer the first timer, including Trafalgar Square, the Tower of London, and Westminster Abbey. "I explored London thoroughly, crowding my days and evenings there to the full," he wrote.[7] He walked the halls of Parliament and felt England's history come alive. At the London embassy, Pershing paid a call on the American military attaché Brig. Gen. Samuel. S. Sumner, whom he had met in Washington before the war and then again in Cuba, where Sumner had commanded a cavalry division.

Then Pershing headed across the English Channel to Paris. The City of Light opened up to him as he strolled its boulevards, parks, and gardens. "Like everyone on his first visit, I was keen to see with my own eyes the Bastille, Notre Dame, the Madeleine, the Louvre, les Invalides, the Pantheon, the Opera, the Champs Elysees, the Bois de Boulogne, and Versailles."[8] He paid a special visit to the tomb of Napoleon. Pershing could not know then that he would one day return to France for a prolonged visit, one necessitated by war. He also soaked in the art of Italy, as he visited Milan, Venice, Florence, Rome, and Naples, with "smoking Vesuvius" in the distance. Pershing thought Venice was a place of "endless charm."[9]

He sailed across the Mediterranean to Egypt, where he

climbed the summit to Giza and its pyramids, and traveled through the Suez Canal and across the Indian Ocean to Sri Lanka, southeast of India. Finally, he arrived in the Filipino capital of Manila in November 1899. From there, he sailed south for six hundred miles on a "small Spanish steamer" to the expansive Philippine island of Mindanao and the city of Zamboanga, located on the tip of a far western peninsula that was home to twenty thousand Filipinos.

Pershing was stationed there for the next three years. The post was the first of his two extended stints in the Philippines that would span over fourteen years. A veteran of service in the American West, Pershing soon discovered significant similarities in his assignment in the Philippines. Once again, he was living parallel to a strange world of indigenous peoples. For Pershing, the Philippines represented a new American frontier. And the conflict that unfolded between the newly arrived Americans and the indigenous peoples of the Philippines would extend for years into the twentieth century. For the Americans, including Pershing, it was something old and something new: "It was a war of frontier, and of empire. It was a war that brought together the dominant American experience of the nineteenth century, the chaotic and defining expansion westward, with a new and at times uncomfortable imperial ambition."[10]

When the victorious Americans arrived in the Philippines to replace the Spanish, many Filipinos simply assumed they had exchanged one set of masters for another. But while the Spanish had not sought to improve the lives of their colonial subjects for so many years, the United States, new at the business of colonizing, chose to turn the Philippines into an experiment in benevolent takeover. If the Filipinos had been exploited, the Americans sought to alter their island world for good by building internal improvements, such as roads and bridges, as well as schools, hospitals, waterworks—modern advantages that could serve both the Americans and their new Filipino subjects. As a result, many of the indigenous peoples of the massive island chain began to accept a level of U.S. authority. Much of this change came at an awkward pace as the Americans themselves had to adapt to a different world. Language barriers only complicated things more. Almost all the Filipinos spoke Spanish but no English; most Americans did not speak Spanish.

In a letter Pershing wrote just three months after his arrival in the Philippines to his friend the assistant secretary of the army George Meiklejohn, John observes this very concern in a manner that reflects his past as a teacher: "Either we must learn the Spanish language or the Filipinos must learn the English language.... These people are anxious to learn our manners and our ways and the children learn rapidly. We can get closer to them and gain their confidence more completely through the medium of a common language than in any other way." Pershing then suggests the new system of education be placed under "some practical broad minded American educator, such for instance as Chancellor James S. Canfield, formerly of the University of Nebraska."[11]

Pershing was part of a large-scale U.S. occupation. During the first two years of the Americans' presence, the islands were held in the grip of a period of defiance known as the Philippine Insurrection. The counterinsurgents fought guerrilla style, hiding out in the jungles, as they had against the Spanish. By 1900 the number of U.S. forces in the Philippines reached seventy-five thousand personnel, more than the number of Americans who had fought in Cuba. They included ten special infantry regiments of veterans of the Spanish-American War.

Even as many Filipinos ultimately accepted—or simply acquiesced—to the introduction of modern American technology and the intricacies of rulers from the U.S. republic transplanted across the sea, one group of islanders did not give in to the presence of Americans any more than they had accepted the Spanish. Mindanao, where Pershing was assigned, was home to a unique group of people. While the vast majority of Filipinos were Catholics, the result of hundreds of years of Spanish influence, the people of Mindanao were practicing Muslims. Known as the Moros—which derives from the Spanish word for Moors—these people spoke Spanish, but their religion taught them to hate their fellow Christian countrymen. As nearly all the

Americans were Christian as well—even if Protestantism was dominant among them—the Moros could not reconcile themselves to accept their authority. At first the Moros were nonbelligerent and remained neutral regarding conflicts between the Americans and the Filipino people. But in time, Moro resistance took root and expanded. Pershing describes it in stark terms: "The almost infinite combination of superstitions, prejudices and suspicions blended into his character make him a difficult person to handle until finally understood. . . . He is jealous of his religion, but he knows very little of its teachings."[12]

Just as the Indians Pershing had encountered in the American West were members of a wide variety of tribes led by chiefs, so were the Moros. They generally had no organized leadership beyond tribal chiefs known as datos, who enjoyed a most favored status among their people, practiced polygamy, and often owned slaves. They were war chiefs, men born to fight, and wielded a trio of traditional and deadly weapons. The true instrument of death among the Moros was the kris, a long, wavy-edged dagger featuring a double-edged blade that was used for stabbing. Another was the kampilan, a two-handed, double-edged sword that was narrow at its base and widened to its tip and was similar to the ancient Roman gladius, only thinner. The third was the barong, which was little more than a cleaver used to lop off limbs. Wielded skillfully, such weapons could slice a man's arm off in one swing and even cut a victim completely in two. The Moros utilized these weapons to terrorize their enemies, who were most often Christians, although Moro tribes sometimes fought one another for dominance.

For Pershing, so much of the native culture he encountered in the Philippines as he studied the world of the defiant Moros reminded him of his years in the West handling American Indians. Sometimes what he wrote about them seemed more in line with the findings of an ethnographic study than that of a U.S. Army officer, but such was Pershing's tendency to try to understand those he encountered. In yet another letter to Meiklejohn, one set of observations reveals the extent of his studies: "Down here in this District [Mindanao] the vast majority of the population are Moros and they are located, as you know, in separate tribes under Dattos or chiefs, whose power is almost unlimited. Now these fellows would make splendid irregular troops and could be used against one another as we used the Indians in our own country. They are very warlike and fierce when aroused."[13]

To the newly arrived Americans, many of the Moros seemed unalterably fervent in their religion, but one group proved decidedly difficult to control since their actions were guided, or misguided, by absolute Islamic extremism. Young male Muslims sometimes dedicated themselves to kill in the name of Allah and became juramentados, which translates as "oath takers," who took a vow to murder as many Christians as they might with the anticipation that Allah would reward them with a paradise filled with young virgin women and endless food. To prepare himself for a murderous mission, a juramentado visited the local pandita (Moro priest), who absolved him of all wrong. He then dosed up on hallucinogenic drugs, bathed ceremoniously, wrapped himself in white strips of cloth—so that in case he was wounded he might not bleed to death—took up a pair of krises, and set out in search of his innocent victims. Such men took literally a passage from the Koran: "When you meet unbelievers cut off their heads until you have massacred them."[14] (By the time Pershing arrived in Mindanao, the juramentados bypassed much of the ritual to avoid detection.) Sometimes the juramentados struck against American administrators and even military personnel. Stopping a drugged Muslim fanatic proved difficult. A Krag-Jorgensen rifle shot often failed, and the army-issue .32-caliber or .38-caliber pistol was equally inadequate. Such circumstances led to the army's decision to adopt the more powerful Colt .45 revolver.

Pershing's first year or so in the Philippines saw him bounced from one assignment to another. His first role was serving as the adjutant general to the Department of Mindanao-Jolo, which was headquartered in Zamboanga. The military governor of the Philippines Brig. Gen. George Whitefield Davis and Pershing soon became well acquainted. By the early fall of 1901, John became a staff officer of the Fifteenth Cavalry and received a new assignment in October as the post commander at Iligan, located on Mindanao's northern coast. From his earliest days in the Philippines, Pershing approached the local Moros with the same combination of professional strategies he had utilized with the Native Americans he encountered in the American West. He had always considered negotiation first and force second. But before he could expect the Moros to sit down at the table of diplomacy, he first had to know whom he was facing. Pershing tried to understand them, to get inside their heads. Just as he had studied Indian dialects, he became halfway conversant in the dialects of the Moros and examined the peculiarities of their cultural norms. He learned to speak Arabic and examined the words of the Koran. He made a habit of showing up in the street bazaars and public places where he could mingle with the local people, making himself seen.

General Davis feared the Moros might not ever accept the Americans' presence on the islands and turned to Pershing to serve as a chief go-between. Most of the Moro tribes were located near Iligan and nearby Lake Lanao, which was landlocked, lying far into the interior of Mindanao. The Islamists had built up a network of fortified villages that surrounded the entire lake, representing a formidable series of strongholds and a complex that held the Spanish at bay for centuries. Never had a Spanish army even attempted marching through this beehive of Muslim warrior power.

At Iligan, Pershing commanded two companies of the Fifteenth Cavalry plus three companies of infantry. Davis expected his captain to work with the Moros, find them on good terms, and convince them that he—and, by association, the U.S. government—was their friend. But Pershing first had to make a name for himself with the troops posted at the Iligan compound. He found the place in absolute disarray: "I at once set the troops to work rebuilding the tumbledown barracks and generally preparing to make them comfortable."[15] To make it clear he was a no-nonsense commander, he inspected the mess hall, took in hand a frying pan, and gave it the white glove test. The pan failed, and an irate Pershing flung the utensil across the room at the cook. Then he repeated his ploy with several more pans until he picked up a meat cleaver, and the anxious cook shot out of the kitchen. When Pershing carried out another inspection the following week, the camp shone from top to bottom.

He soon put his charm offensive into practice. With a general knowledge and understanding of the Moro languages and culture, he met with leaders, strode through the marketplace, talked with anyone he thought important. Everywhere he went, the exotic world to which he had been assigned rose up to meet him. The marketplace represented the common ground where all were generally welcome. Pershing found the Moros eager in some respects: "They liked to talk and wanted to speak with someone in authority. In this they were given every encouragement."[16] He purchased local supplies for the post when he could and hired locals for various odd jobs, paying them a fair market wage. To a point, Pershing understood that he was selling himself, on behalf of the U.S. government, to the Moros. As much as they came to trust him, they began to put their faith in the United States and its intentions for the people of Mindanao and the greater Philippines. He had done the same in dealing with American Indians and their leaders.

Through his own efforts, local Moro leaders began to warm to the American commander. Pershing singled out Ahmai-Manibilang, a particularly influential dato who lived in the northern Lake Lanao region. He was powerful and wealthy—in the sense of a local Moro sultan—and rarely visited Iligan. The American captain ingratiated himself first with Manibilang's twenty-eight-year-old son, who delivered an invitation to his father: the American commander would like to parley. To Pershing's excitement, Manibilang agreed. The day of the visit the tall, white-bearded sultan arrived, wearing a coat of many colors, billowing white trousers, and a tilted turban; riding on a grand stallion; and flanked by slaves holding red-and-white umbrellas to shade their master. A single slave carried Manibilang's gold-mounted kris. The sultan also brought with him a variety of minor chiefs and family members. Once the two men sat down together, Manibilang peppered Pershing with questions: How long were the Americans intending to stay? What changes did they expect the Moros to make? Could they keep their slaves? Their various wives? Would Christianity be forced on them? Would they have to eat pork, or as the Moros stated it, "eat the devil"?[17]

Pershing's answers were diplomatic and firm, with two exceptions. He did not address the issues of slavery or polygamy. That could wait for another day. He assured the sultan that his people could continue to practice their religion. The captain informed Manibilang that the sultan of Constantinople and the United States already exchanged diplomats. As to the Americans' presence, Pershing said the Americans were here to stay but that the United States wanted to help the Moros and all Filipinos to improve their lives. He promised roads and other internal improvements and increased markets for local goods. Manibilang remained with Pershing for three days. The encounter ended with the two men on a seemingly strong footing of understanding. It was an added bonus when, over the following weeks, more Moro leaders came to Pershing for their own assurances.

When a return invitation eventually arrived from Manibilang for Pershing to visit his compound along Lake Lanao, the captain was excited but hesitant. Padre Tel Placido, a local Spanish priest who knew well the ways of the Moros, warned the American commander not to visit the Moros on their own turf: "The Sultans got fed up [sic] on all white men when they had the Spanish here before. These Mohammedans are waiting every day and every night to kill *you!*" To emphasize his words, the priest made a stabbing motion toward Pershing's torso. "They say up there that Americans grow nice bamboo." This was the priest's way of indicating to the army captain that he would not come back alive.[18] But Pershing was not deterred. Within days, he ordered a pair of horses readied for his departure along with an interpreter. The captain went unarmed as a gesture of good faith to Lake Lanao to meet with the powerful Moro dato.

Pershing was stepping out into a world he had only studied from a distance. He had come to know the fringes of the Moro world but not its heart. Now he was headed into the belly of the beast. As historian Frank Vandiver notes, "By the time he led his first expedition into Mindanao's interior he knew much Moro lore. Hard fighting, he understood, conferred religious virtue; those Moros who died well, especially when warring against Christians, went immediately to Mohammedan paradise—noble death, then, formed the threshold of bliss. To an old Indian fighter this warrior philosophy had chilling similarity to the Ghost Dance frenzy which drove the red men to their desperate last stands."[19]

No Spanish soldiers had ever successfully entered the region. They had attempted an incursion years earlier, taking a force of eight thousand men toward the lake. The men had slogged through the jungle for a year but failed to penetrate Moro territory. They had managed to reach the lake, build a handful of small gunboats, and fire on some villages, but they ultimately achieved nothing.

After a day's ride, Pershing reached the village of Marahui, where he noted a tumbledown Spanish barracks and fort, a church, a defensive trench, and a gunboat dock. Nothing else indicated the Spanish had ever reached the region previously. By afternoon, Pershing was sailing across the lake on a vinta, a small bamboo outrigger. Landing at the village of Madaya, the captain was escorted into the sultan's home, an expansive frame building capped with heavy timbers and a thatched roof. A meal was served with the American captain as the honored guest. The food impressed Pershing: "I have never tasted more delicious chicken, seasoned as it was with native herbs; and the rice, steaming hot, was cooked to perfection, the grains still whole, as few Americans at home ever see rice cooked."[20] Everything Pershing saw around him was more exotic than one raised in Laclede, Missouri, could have imagined, as if he were walking around in the pages of *One Thousand and One Nights*.

Manibilang took Pershing on a tour of his domain the following day, with the two men floating along the lake in the vinta along with an honor guard—or perhaps a bodyguard?—of forty warriors. Through this visit, Pershing sealed the deal with his new ally. "Manibilang was not only a warm personal friend of mine but an earnest advocate of friendly relations between Americans and Moros."[21]

Pershing regarded his mission to Lake Lanao and his meeting with one of the most powerful datos in that region as a complete success. He managed to accomplish something an eight-thousand-strong Spanish force had failed to do and singlehandedly pried open the mysterious world of the Moros. As the American journalist Rutherford Platt observed a generation later, "Barehanded and single handed Pershing captured the jungle; he captured the jungle overrun with Mohammedan devils."[22]

Manibilang's invitation to the American captain soon opened the way for additional sit-downs with other datos who were ready to follow his example. Pershing responded to each one, traveling with a small retinue usually and always unarmed. On one occasion, as he prepared to leave for another visit with yet another dato, he discovered his orderly Frank Lanckton planned to bring along a pistol. Pershing chastised him: "Lanckton, a soldier's word is more important than his gun."[23]

Pershing met with many curious Moro tribal leaders, answered endless questions, and attempted to establish friendship and understanding with nearly every one. Cultural differences sometimes complicated such visits, as when one accommodating dato brought to Pershing, as the captain was getting ready for bed, "a most attractive member of his harem who, he advised me in the most matter-of-course manner imaginable, would accompany me. . . . I managed to express my thanks and declination without giving offense, the datu sending the woman away as nonchalantly as he had brought her in."[24]

Many U.S. Army officers, as well as enlisted men, assigned to the Philippines did not agree with Pershing's approach of convincing the Filipino peoples, including the Moros, to accept American dominance over them through negotiation, diplomacy, and transplanted social hospitality. "Civilize 'em with a Krag" was a common sentiment among many of Pershing's fellow army officers. Even those serving in bureaucratic or governmental administrative roles thought of the natives as nothing more than "little brown people" who needed civilizing. But Pershing saw no problem accepting the indigenous Filipinos as human beings, worthy of respect, and the United States as in the business of elevating their lives rather than exploiting them.[25]

In the same way, while many datos eventually warmed to Pershing and the presence of the Americans, some hardcore Moro leaders did not. Several of the datos living on the southern banks of Lake Lanao continued to resist despite Pershing's best efforts. On March 9, 1902, an army private was murdered within a mile of his posting at Parang. Less than two weeks later, a gang of Moros attacked two soldiers and hacked one of them to death with a bolo. In mid-April two hundred Moros attacked a party of eighteen American troops, murdering one. It is telling that all these attacks took place outside the sector under Pershing's administrative control, where Manibilang held little sway. Such attacks led Brig. Gen. George Davis, who commanded the Department of Mindanao-Jolo, to mount an invasion into the rebellious region located on the south side of Lake Lanao. Davis contacted Pershing and asked that he inform his dato friends north of the lake of the impending retaliatory mission. The captain went to the market the following Saturday and asked the Moro leaders to remain calm and not interfere. They agreed, claiming what happened in the south had nothing to do with them. Pershing informed Davis on April 21: "If punitive expedition on South coast is limited to punishment of these [Moros] who have committed overt acts, friendly feelings [of northern Moros] will probably not be materially altered. Have lost no opportunity to reassure them that our friends will not be molested."[26]

The fight in the south did not go well for the Americans. Action took place at Pandapatan on the lake's south coast. The fight included a U.S. force storming a Moro *cotta*, a "fort" or compound with walls fifteen feet high and just as thick. The American force managed to rout the defending Moros but lost sixty soldiers.[27] This costly "victory" did not deter the rebellious Moros and actually led to a lengthy guerrilla war between the natives and the Americans. Maj. Gen. Adna R. Chaffee, the supreme commander in the Philippines, thought the attack was a mistake and that it represented poor policy. Aware of Captain Pershing's success in negotiating with the Moro leaders on the north side of the lake, Chafee ordered him to his headquarters by mid-May. When they conferred, Chaffee brought Pershing up to speed: American forces had pulled back from the location of the fight at Pandapatan and set up a firebase about a mile away at a site called Camp Vicars, after Lt. Thomas A. Vicars who had been killed in the battle. They did not want to evacuate the region completely, but they did not want another fight on their hands either. Military action had not proved effective; now they needed someone to play the diplomat.

Chaffee came to his point quickly: "You have been successful in handling the Moros on the North. I want you to go up to the Lake fort station and do what you can to pacify the Moros on this side and prevent another clash."

Captain Pershing responded to the general with his own concerns: "How can I prevent anything? Colonel Baldwin is in charge at Vicars."

"You will be in charge of Moro affairs," Chaffee informed his subordinate. "Orders will be given that no move will be made without your approval."[28]

Soon, Pershing was on his way to Camp Vicars.

The question, of course, was how much headway Captain Pershing might make in negotiating with the Moros. The situation was different in the south than in the north. Pershing negotiated from the beginning with Manibilang and the other datos without first turning to a fight. Battle had already taken place in the south, and the datos might interpret any attempt at diplomacy as a sign of weakness. Pershing had to assume the playing field he was entering was not on the same level as the one he had established in the north. Additionally, he was to serve under Colonel Baldwin, his superior officer, who was to make no overt moves without first receiving his captain's approval.

Fortunately, Baldwin and Pershing knew one another. Colonel Baldwin was a career soldier, eighteen years Pershing's senior, and a veteran of the Civil War as well as of various Indian campaigns in the West, where he had served under General Miles. He was also a two-time recipient of the Medal of Honor. Most recently, Pershing had come to know Baldwin while serving at U.S. Army Headquarters in Washington DC. Still, their friendship was tested by Pershing's new assignment. The captain came to Camp Vicars with orders to engage in diplomacy, while Baldwin still believed the answer to the Moro problem lay in the next fight. As Pershing wrote, "Colonel Baldwin was a fine soldier with a long experience in handling Indians, but he was inclined to be impetuous."[29] When Chaffee realized the two army officers were at loggerheads, he requested Baldwin's transfer by the War Department. The transfer came through, and Baldwin was promoted and sent back to the States, leaving Captain Pershing in full command at Camp Vicars. At that point, Vicars was manned by two cavalry troops, three infantry companies, and an artillery battery for a total of close to seven hundred men, or about the size of a contemporary regiment. With Pershing a mere captain, General Davis felt compelled to explain things to the War Department: "The situation in one respect has been anomalous—the assignment of a captain to so large and important command as that of Vicars—but it was in my opinion absolutely indispensable that the man to command on the spot should possess certain qualities not easy to find combined in one man."[30]

Through the intervening months, Pershing attempted to engage in more diplomacy, including sit-downs with datos and communications back and forth. He hosted meetings that sometimes dragged on for hours or even days. The Moros continued to question Pershing about possible limits placed on their religion or the forced eating of pork, which violated the guidelines of the Koran. They doubted the motives of the Americans. As Pershing observed, "They are wild and untamed and it is difficult to make them understand that you have no ulterior motive in being friendly to them.... Deception is a Malay characteristic and so deep-seated is it that they can hardly comprehend the motive for fair dealing."[31] Another problem the American captain faced was the concept of government, which the Moros only thought of on a personal level. Their datos were the government, and each Moro leader's territory was his own. Pershing had no centralized, single leader with whom he could negotiate. In turn, the Moros always thought they were simply dealing with Captain Pershing, as if there was no higher authority involved. It was, to them, all very personal; that Pershing spoke for the government of a large nation thousands of miles away was an entirely foreign concept. But he managed to make headway, just as he had with the Moros north of Lake Lanao.

For all of his enumerated skills, Pershing was not a miracle worker. He faced intractable resistance from the Moros of three cottas: Maciu, Bayan, and Bacolod. If these datos were unwilling to negotiate and accept the presence of Americans, Pershing might be forced to turn to the military option. He knew he must see success on one front or the other. To simply do nothing would lose him the support of other datos, who might see him as weak. Local Moros, meanwhile, were also harassing Camp Vicars directly through hit-and-run incursions and nighttime attacks. In late June nearly a dozen Moros surprised two American soldiers, wounded both, and took off with a rifle. Reports identified the attackers as coming from Binidayan, whose dato had promised allegiance to Pershing. When the dato failed to locate the perpetrators, Pershing took action, ordering his arrest on July 19 and delivery to Camp Vicars in irons. His message was clear: "You cannot be sultan and receive our support and recognition of your authority and at the same time deny your responsibility for acts of your people." The capture of the dato ended tragically when the Moro leader "went juramentado" and tried to kill his guards, leading to his own death. But other datos understood the lay of the land and communicated it to their people: "See here, if any of you molest the Americans in any way, off comes my head, for we do not intend to be held responsible for your foolish acts."[32]

But other datos who had not accepted American rule were

undeterred, and Camp Vicars continued to see raids. The Moros sneaked into camp, cut tent ropes, and stabbed at the trapped soldiers with their krises. They engaged in a form of psychological warfare, remaining in the jungle and beating on drums while they shouted at the soldiers. Shots were repeatedly fired into the camp. When a visiting officer noted the tents sporting bullet holes, an orderly calmly explained, "Don't mind them, sir. The Moros shoot at the tents at night, sir; but they won't hit you, sir."[33] Some attackers moved so quietly under cover of darkness they were not detected at all until the following morning when rifles were found missing. Pershing saw much in the Moros' raiding skills that reminded him of his time in the West: "In stealth of movement, these [Moro] warriors were more crafty than even American Indians."[34] Sometimes local datos took extreme action to satisfy Pershing. On one occasion, Dato Adta of Paigoay discovered a pair of perpetrators on his rancheria, dealt with them summarily, and delivered "the dead bodies . . . each lashed to a bamboo pole, and deposited them in front of [Pershing's] tent."[35]

After months of negotiating and deferred acceptance on the part of the Moros, Pershing decided to take other measures. An increase in Moro attacks on Camp Vicars during the late summer of 1902 added incentive. On August 11 twenty Moros attacked a local outpost, killing two soldiers—one had his head split open by a kampilan—and wounding two others. The following night, thirty Moros fired their rifles into the camp for nearly half an hour. Three nights later, the camp received more Moro rifle fire, this time for several hours, with the shots aimed into the camp from seemingly every direction. On September 1 the Moros attacked an American outpost seven miles southeast of Vicars, leaving one American dead and two wounded. Eventually, sentries at Camp Vicars received instructions not to bother calling out at night, "Halt. Who goes there?" They were ordered to fire on any movement in the jungle.

All this activity convinced Pershing the time for diplomacy had ended. He wrote to his superiors, "We are losing influence with our friends who continuously ask, why do you Americans not punish some of those people? ... My own conviction is that a good sound drubbing will be necessary and sufficient and it may be administered at Bacolod."[36]

General Chaffee soon gave the orders for an offensive campaign. He, like Pershing, felt the action was necessary as an example to other datos. The decision was made to launch the attack against the cotta at Maciu, since most of the recent raids originated from there. Chaffee made his intent clear to Pershing: "We are after effect—not revenge for wrongs done. So if Bacolod takes warning from our movements on Maciu, your purpose is accomplished."[37]

Pershing did not take the lead on the campaign against Maciu. That task was assigned to Brig. Gen. Samuel S. Sumner, whom the American captain had met in Washington, again in Cuba, and then in London when Pershing served as the military attaché at the embassy. Sumner ordered additional troops delivered to Camp Vicars and made certain that no officers of greater rank than Pershing's were included; that allowed Pershing to remain the commander at Vicars. Sumner sent out his troops in two columns—one under Capt. Eli Helmick and the second under Pershing—that included four infantry companies, a cavalry troop, and a platoon of artillery. In all, Pershing was in command of more than five hundred men. The Maciu cotta only contained approximately four hundred Moro warriors, most armed with the various blades common among them, a few dozen rifles, and some short-range lantakas, which were small-caliber, bronze swivel cannon that fired hundreds of slugs. The Moros also had a few small antique cannon that they had captured either from the Spanish at some distant time or from pirates. As Pershing prepared to advance against Maciu, some Moros asked to join his column, ready to bring the problematic native holdouts to account; instead, Pershing declined their offer, choosing to handpick several Moros as guides.

Pershing's forces left Camp Vicars on September 18, 1902, with his men carrying four days' rations. The column also carried a pair of Maxim-Nordenfelt 75mm mountain howitzers. After advancing ten miles to the southeast, the column set up a firebase at Pantaun; then it set out for several hostile rancherias at Guaun on Lake Butig. Here the force encountered a difficult crossfire of resistance from three cottas. Enemy fire was limited and sporadic, and Pershing ordered a methodical artillery response on each of the cottas. In a sense, the American captain fought with one hand tied behind his back. He had the firepower to absolutely level the cottas and annihilate their defenders. But he chose instead to fire his artillery from a safe distance, to provide an opportunity for the Moros to evacuate, and to hold off on sending in his infantry until the end. His mission was to convince the Moros they could not win a fight with the U.S. military while keeping casualties on both sides to an absolute minimum; in fact, the Guaun assault saw no American casualties. The Moros opted to give up and retreat. The American commander chose not to pursue his enemy. He ordered the three cottas burned—along with their storage caches of seasonal foods, including rice, cocoa, and coffee—then he and his men returned to Pantaun less than twenty-four hours after leaving.

The next day, he ordered his men to Bayabao, where he repeated his tactics. The cotta fell quickly, and Pershing headed back to his base camp. Along the way, he and his men passed the Lumbayanague Rancheria, where they were pleased to see a white flag flying. Word of the American victories spread.

On September 20 he pointed his column toward Maciu. The dato had answered Pershing's letters with a taunt: "Even though there are ten million of you, the more the better for we can then capture more rifles."[38] That morning they reached a plateau above Lake Lanao. The Americans viewed Maciu in the distance, as well as neighboring cottas at Talub and Sauir. Pershing then sent a communication to the two sultans of Maciu, suggesting a parley. They responded, "We do not want to meet you anywhere but at Maciu. We shall be waiting for you at Maciu."[39] The message was mocking, really, since there was no viable road to Maciu, and Pershing did not have vintas to use on the lake. For the moment, he accepted the situation and called off an immediate advance on Maciu. When the evacuation was ordered on September 22, the troops grimaced as the Moros across the safe inlet shouted jeers at them. Many of Pershing's men were not satisfied with what they perceived as a retreat, but he "had the officers explain that we would resume the campaign a few days later." The clock was ticking for the defenders at Maciu.[40]

A week later, Pershing returned with the same compliment of men plus an engineering detachment that was intent on opening the way to Maciu—literally—by constructing a road. The Moros had felled trees across the only trail leading to their cotta. American know-how and ingenuity became part of Pershing's strategy. Within three days, the road led straight to the defensive compound at Maciu. Several Moros waited on the ramparts, prepared, while half of their number had already abandoned the fort. Slowly, methodically, with sharpshooters providing cover, the Americans moved forward with the 75mm mountain guns. A number of peripheral defensive cottas were set on fire, and smoke filled the air as the fighting continued. Pershing did not intend, however, to burn out the remaining cotta that held most of the fighting Moros. He wanted to leave them a way out. When a reporter asked him if he intended to order his men to storm the cotta, the captain gave a surprising answer.

"No," Pershing said. "We would lose too many men."

The reporter then asked, "But aren't you afraid they'll sneak out in the long grass during the night and get away?"

"That is exactly what I expect them to do," the American captain explained.[41] Pershing literally intended on providing the Moros defending Maciu with an exit. He still did not want to see high casualties on either side.

That night, around three o'clock, the Moros slipped out of the fort and attempted a rush on the American lines, hiding under the cover of fifteen-foot-high cogon grass. But the action was merely a cover while their comrades escaped, with the cotta evacuated by morning. American soldiers set fire to the compound later that morning. The tough nut of Maciu was cracked, and Pershing led his forces back to Camp Vicars on October 3. His short campaign succeeded in leveling ten defensive cottas while killing approximately four dozen of the enemy with few American casualties. Pershing's overall strategy played out according to his rules. He wanted to make it clear to the Moros that resistance was completely futile as the Americans could reach and destroy any outpost and, in another concept that surprised the Moros, that he was willing to stop his military campaign and start negotiating. To that end, he sent out letters to many datos suggesting talks. Fighting any Moros would wait until the wheels of diplomacy had an opportunity to turn.

The majority of southern datos responded just as Pershing hoped. Two of every three were ready to talk and accept the Americans' terms. New friendships were soon forged between Pershing—the American face—and the Moro leaders. Those who did not accept Pershing's offer remained safe for the moment. He was willing to wait until they came to their senses.

In the meantime, Pershing received a welcome visitor at Camp Vicars. In mid-November Lt. Gen. Nelson Miles, Pershing's commander from his early days in New Mexico, was in the Philippines inspecting facilities. (President Roosevelt removed the older commander from Washington DC to free up Secretary of War Elihu Root to carry out some important military reforms away from Miles's prying eyes.) Miles first met with Chaffee and Davis—the three men had fought together during the Civil War—then he went out to Camp Vicars, where he saw his old comrade. Miles was gracious and spoke to the men about the days he had shared with Pershing years earlier. He spoke of having had high hopes for Pershing, all of which had proven true. The general referred to the man from Missouri as "an intelligent, judicious, and able commanding officer."[42] For John Pershing, the moment was rich.

Back in the States, twenty-nine-year-old Willa Cather had not yet published her first book (a book of her poetry was published the following year, and her first collection of short stories came in 1905), and she was teaching at a Pittsburgh high school. In 1902 she wrote the short story "The Treasure of Far Island," which features a pair of childhood friends who return to their Midwest home and visit a favorite locale of their youth— Far Island, "an oval sand bar, half a mile in length and perhaps a hundred yards wide, which lies about two miles from Empire City in a turbid little Nebraska river." The story's narrator explains, "The island is known chiefly to the children who dwell in that region, and generation after generation of them have claimed it; fished there, and pitched their tents under the great arched tree, and built camp fires on its level, sandy outskirts.... Every summer a new chief claims it and it has been called by many names."[43]

The story's island seems to provide a metaphorical link to the ongoing American action in the Philippines, action in which Pershing was playing an important role. As the two fictional adult friends reminisce, they recall a third childhood friend who "is commanding a regiment in the Philippines."[44] Even Cather's fictional Empire City is suggestive of the expanded reach of U.S. imperialism. The friends unearth an old chest they had buried long ago on the island that they contend contains a "Spaniard's heart in a bottle of alcohol."[45] While Cather rarely took serious issue with America's foreign policy of this era, in this story, she appears to be "simultaneously romanticizing and criticizing the US fight for the islands, against the Spanish colonialists and the First Philippine Republic, as an adult version of child's play."[46]

Over the following months, leading into early 1903, the Moros laid down their arms and made agreements with Pershing. In the holdout region of Bayan, where the Moros had been defeated during the Pandapatan battle in May 1902, something totally unexpected occurred. Sajiduciman, their leader, was a pandita who continually rallied his people with religious fervor, claiming the Americans were evil because they ate pork and that any Moro who cooperated with such infidels was doomed to hell. Pershing sent the holdout pandita a message in December, suggesting his patience was at an end. By early February, he organized a column to march on Bayan. When the Americans arrived, Sajiduciman emerged from his compound and greeted Pershing by kissing him on both cheeks. A nonplussed Pershing returned the gesture. But this marked only the beginning of the day's surprises. "He and Pershing squatted on their heels while attendants set down a rare copy of the Koran, the Moslem Bible. An old Mohammedan priest performed incantations under a red parasol, symbol of Moslem authority. Beautifully engraved silver boxes of betel nut were handed around and each took a chew. Then Sajiduciman leaned over, betel-nut saliva trickling down his beard. Embracing Pershing, he said with the utmost solemnity, 'You have been made a Moro datu.'"[47]

By day's end, Sajiduciman's compound flew the American flag.

The turn of events at Bayan altered the direction and pace of the immediate American neutralization of Moro power in the south as nothing had previously. Pershing was no longer simply a U.S. Army officer; he became the equivalent of a Moro chief. The Moros came to him, seeking his blessing, literally. He was asked to settle intertribal suits, and women sought his blessing on their marriages for fertility. Moro children referred to him as "my father." And the success was nearly all his. American newspapers extolled his tactics in subduing the native peoples, recognizing his diplomacy and his tendency to avoid bloodshed. "No other officer has been more frequently or more favorably mentioned," reported the *New York Sun*. "Every few days we hear of his preaching the gospel of peace to some new *datu* out in the wilds of Mindanao. Interspersed with these accounts, others come to tell of his subjugation of some rebellious *datu* whose greatest need is just such a parental spanking as Pershing bestows upon him."[48] An editorial in the *Manila Times*, dated February 17, 1903, summed up Pershing's successes: "He has won friendship where he might, fought when he had to, and has generally conducted himself in a manner to bring credit to himself and the Army."[49] Pershing's strategy won over many datos as well as many Americans.[50]

They did not include the dato of Bacolod. In Pershing's style, Sumner sent a letter to the dato asking for the opportunity to negotiate and establish friendly relations. The answer was terse: "The Sultan of Bacolod desires war at once as we wish to maintain religion of Muhamet. Cease sending us letters. What we want is war as we do not desire your friendship."[51] Pershing sent letters of his own anyway, and one came back with an equally clear message. The letter was partially burned with an explanation: "This letter goes to you burned in six places to indicate that it means war. You should not be here, for you are not like us. You eat pork. If you do not wish to leave this region, come and live in Bacolod under the sultan, who will practice circumcision on you."[52] Pershing was inclined to accept the dato's challenge of war, but he gave the sultan one more opportunity. Pershing sent another letter: "Two or three datus refuse our friendship simply because, as they say, they do not like Americans. To those datus I say that if they continue their opposition they must some day suffer the consequences of their stubborn ignorance."[53] Pershing was just as capable of throwing down the gauntlet as was the dato of Bacolod.

With no satisfactory answer forthcoming, Pershing centered his mind on another military campaign against one more dato holdout. Circumstance at the time postponed his military moves. A cholera epidemic swept through Bacolod, resulting in fifteen hundred Moro deaths. As weeks passed, Pershing hoped against hope the Bacolod dato might change his outlook; instead, Bacolod Moros began attacking Camp Vicars, just as others had previously. By March 1903 Pershing decided he had waited long enough. Any further delay might appear weak to the dato in question. He held out hope that many of the Bacolod Moros really did not want to engage the Americans in an armed conflict. He received permission to arrange a march on April 2 and three days later left Camp Vicars with six hundred men, including four infantry companies, two cavalry troops, and two artillery batteries. The artillery unit included several water-cooled Vickers machine guns.[54] This was the first time Pershing commanded a military unit carrying machine guns into the field. They would become the standard weapons of death during World War I.

Each man was to carry a hundred rounds of ammunition, his pack, his rations—including canned salmon, which the men called "goldfish"—plus two canteens. Pershing issued an order for all water to be boiled before drinking, a necessary precaution given a recent outbreak of cholera. When two of his men failed to follow the order and soon died of cholera, Pershing was unsympathetic: "Damn it, let them die! They disobeyed my orders!"[55] The advance was slow, as narrow trails proved a challenge for the transport of artillery, and mules proved less than sure-footed on hilly trails, especially going downhill. The first night's encampment was established in a style Pershing knew well from his days stationed out in the American West—a square with the men lining the perimeter and securing their horses, mules, and supplies in the center of the grounds. That beautiful night, the lake shimmered with the reflection of a silvery moon, but the night held danger. The Moros slipped past the encampment in vintas and fired shots at the Americans, wounding two soldiers.

The next day, the column resumed its march, and soon the Bacolod cotta was in sight, with red war flags flapping defiantly from the ramparts. Lantakas fired rounds of slugs toward the advancing troops. Pershing's column included a tagalong English war correspondent named A. Henry Savage Landor who wrote for the *London Mail*. He described the scene at the defended cotta fort: "We could faintly hear the distant fanatical yells of the natives, chanting their war-songs, and suddenly along the shores of the lake glittered in the sun hundreds of brandished *kris* and *campilan* blades. It was an invitation—a challenge to come on."[56]

Pershing's men advanced until they reached the vicinity of the cotta. Bacolod was situated on high ground along a ridge running to Lake Lanao. The fort measured approximately a hundred feet square with walls twelve feet high and fifteen feet thick. If an attacker approached from the trail, he would be trapped between the lake and a jungle outgrowth, and fall straight under fire from the Moros' guns. Pershing wisely chose to flank Bacolod and approach by another trail, placing his men above the Bacolod cotta. His plan was similar to previous engagements against other cottas: establish a defensive line at a safe distance, bombard the enemy fortifications, and surround the cotta on three sides while leaving an avenue of escape. The artillery fire commenced in the afternoon and continued into the evening. During the night, some Moros and their families abandoned the cotta, while those who remained inside raised a flag of truce the following morning. When the dato offered to surrender if his men could retain their weapons, Pershing refused. Before day's end, the battle was on again, and the artillery continued its deadly fire, leaving the compound little more than a pile of stone and bamboo. Many chose to leave at that point, but hard-core holdouts remained the following morning.

Pershing then ordered a direct frontal assault on the remaining defenders in the cotta. Infantrymen ran forward over a bamboo bridge spanning the protective moat that measured thirty feet across and forty feet deep. When the bridge collapsed, the Americans turned pieces into ladders on which to climb out. Frenzied Moros emerged from the fort, running toward the American soldiers "like bees from a hive, in single file, swords in hand, each man close to the man in front."[57] The Moros fought like tigers with their sharp-bladed instruments of war, inflicting several wounds on the Americans. But kampilans and krises ultimately proved no match against rifles and bayonets.

Then the powder supply in the cotta exploded, completely destroying the fort. British correspondent Landor describes the scene: "Amid hurrahs the fort was now ablaze and we retired across the trench to await events. The powder magazine blew up and with it went the solid roof of the fort, the flames shot up, and a tall, gloomy black column of smoke. That was the end of impregnable Bacolod."[58] When the smoke of battle finally cleared, the Americans found sixty enemy killed and an equal number wounded. No Americans were killed and only a few wounded. Pershing had successfully defeated one of the last of the defiant Lake Lanao cottas. In a letter to George T. Bowman, a lieutenant in the Fifteenth Cavalry who later served as a member of Pershing's staff during World War I, Pershing described the outcome of the campaign: "Bacolod is fallen, and I am gratified to say without loss of life to us. . . . Of the Moros killed there were many datus, the Panandungan in particular—all told about 120. We could have killed more but what's the use."[59]

Pershing had answered the defiant Bacolod Moros with military action but one that represented an iron fist in a velvet glove. He had not chosen to annihilate all of the opposition, an option within his power, but had given those who experienced second thoughts or who were cowed by U.S. military might the opportunity to escape and live to accept the Americans' authority. He utilized his power against the Moros with restraint and selective use of force. Pershing ultimately intended to break the Moro spirit of resistance rather than utterly destroy his enemy. Through his forbearance, he spared the lives of many Moros as well as the lives of his own men. The strategy was worthy of the soldier-diplomat Pershing, who had first fostered it during his days handling Indians in the American Southwest. Dr. Robert U. Patterson, who served as the surgeon for the Bacolod expedition and later as the surgeon general of the army, lauded Pershing's tactics against the Bacolod cotta: "Had Pershing assaulted on the first or second day, the casualties would have been terrible on our side.... How much different would have been the result had he listened to the impetuous advice of his officers."[60]

Pershing seems especially proud that his campaign had spared American and Moro lives. In fact, his ranks suffered more casualties from cholera than from the fighting. Despite his boil-water order, several men drank from the local lake. By the time Pershing's column returned to Camp Vicars, "nine enlisted men and four packers had contracted cholera, eight of whom did not recover."[61]

The American captain continued his march past Bacolod, but he found no resistance beyond the recently fallen cotta. Along the trail, he spotted "more United States flags displayed in the road and in rancherias than I supposed existed in all the country."[62] At every village, the Americans were met by "peaceful Moros, following their sultans, datus, priests, and other leaders, announcing their loyalty."[63] Many were simply in shock that Bacolod had fallen so quickly. Everywhere he went, Pershing was treated with complete respect and friendship. In the village of Oato, the locals came out to ask the American captain to settle some local legal cases. He agreed and handed out his decisions in the midst of a rice paddy. No one challenged his authority.

After several days of testing the loyalties of neighboring villages, Pershing turned his men back toward Camp Vicars. As they passed Bacolod, they saw the still-smoldering remains and newly dug mounds where the Moros had buried their dead, the ground accentuated by dozens of white umbrellas. On April 16, they were back at Camp Vicars, where they were told to quarantine before entering due to their exposure to cholera. But Pershing would not have it. He ordered the men in the camp to sleep in tents outside the encampment, while his victorious and tired men had the opportunity to sleep in their comfortable barracks.

Pershing had accomplished his military objectives during his Bacolod campaign, but he still had a nagging feeling his work was not finished. In a letter he wrote to George Meiklejohn, everything pointed to victory as the campaign represented "the largest single success that had been made in the islands. One year ago nobody but me had seen the Moro in his native Laguna.... Now we have crossed the lake and practically marched around it."[64] American forces had incurred along three sides of Lake Lanao, but twenty miles or so on the eastern side of the lake had not been opened up. On April 19, 1903, Pershing received orders to do what no one, including the Spanish, had ever done—complete a full reconnaissance around the entire lake.

The American captain left Camp Vicars on May 2 along with five hundred men, 340 horses and mules, and several Moro guides. Running parallel with the troops were six Moro vintas as "naval" support; the boats would transport any wounded or sick men back to the Vicars firebase. Much of the time, the Americans were forced to slog through swamps and marshes. Mules became stuck in the muddy morass, forcing the men to unload them and carry the supplies themselves. In some places, the troops swung machetes to cut down timbers to build makeshift bridges and causeways through the watery reaches of the eastern lake country. Friendly Moros crowded the lake's banks, waving flags and hands in friendship while offering various foods for sale, including camotes, a local sweet potato variety, to the troops. The column began passing cottas they had never encountered before, but each flew white banners instead of red flags of war. Three days out from Vicars, the Americans reached the Taraca cotta, where the Moros were bent on fighting. The encounter, a small-framed repeat of the Bacolod engagement, took less than a day and ended with Pershing forcing the local Moro warriors to swear allegiance to the United States. Word began to spread around the lake that Pershing had gone juramentado and that the Americans were killing all who resisted them.

By May 8 Pershing and his column arrived at Marahui, where the local cotta flew a defiant red battle flag with a blue border. An artillery bombardment and some infantry maneuvers by one company soon neutralized the fort. This engagement effectively represented the culmination of Pershing's encirclement of Lake Lanao, having reached all the cottas and villages. No one—Spanish or American—had ever succeeded as Pershing had. Lake Lanao was completely in the hands of the Americans. The American captain had accomplished more to subdue the Moros in three years than the Spanish had in more than three centuries. General Sumner was naturally delighted with Pershing's success and sent him a telegram on May 10, the day of the captain's return to Vicars: "Please accept for yourself and express to your command my appreciation of the soldierly manner in which they behaved during the recent expedition around Lake Lanao."[65] Praise reached Pershing from telegraph offices far beyond the Philippines. Secretary of War Elihu Root also sent a message from Washington DC: "Express to Captain John J. Pershing and the officers and men under his command the thanks of the War Department for their able and effective accomplishment of a difficult and important task."[66]

Pershing's successful march around Lake Lanao and the accompanying subjugation of the datos in the south marked the end of the American captain's first of three acts he was to perform on the Philippine stage. Over the next ten years, he saw an additional two assignments in the islands. For now, he was worn out with campaigning in the jungles and swamps of Mindanao. Malaria further racked his body. He needed time to recover from field duty. He departed his Far Eastern assignment on July 30, 1903, taking passage on a ship bound for San Francisco.

His time in the Philippines proved productive for Pershing. Through his field service fighting and negotiating with the Moros, he became well known in the American press, a near-public figure. No longer was he the young cavalry officer assigned to forts in frontier New Mexico. He had transcended those days, even as he had applied many of the lessons he had learned in dealing with the Navajos, Zunis, and Apaches of the Southwest to his handling of the Muslim Moros of Mindanao. Pershing had honed his experiences into well-crafted personal qualities that served him well in his far-flung foreign assignment. He gained new insights regarding the importance of instilling discipline in his men, especially under harsh conditions, including the threat of disease and a relentless enemy. He also carried out his campaigns against the Moros in a way that spared the lives both of his men and of his enemy, something that came to be known as "economy with life." His approach concerning the establishment of an American presence in the Philippines was based on forbearance. The Moros, for all their religious fanaticism, did not represent a highly skilled military force, and their arsenal of sharp blades could not match U.S. firepower. As with the American Indians, there was never any doubt that the U.S. military would ultimately subdue its opponents. This certainty led Pershing to reserve military action until all his other options had been exhausted. Then his use of military force was never excessive at the expense of Moro blood.

In a way, Pershing the teacher developed the winning strategies that ultimately subdued many of the datos and their people. Assimilation of the Moros was only reasonably possible "by the tedious process of education," he said. "It should not be accomplished by extermination."[67] Pershing taught lessons to others while learning important lessons of his own in the Philippines.

TEN

Courtship, 1903–9

Four-year cycles had often repeated themselves during the years of Pershing's adulthood to date. He spent four years as a cadet at West Point, four as a cavalry officer in New Mexico, four as a military instructor at the University of Nebraska, and, recently, nearly four years in the Philippines. Now he had four months to enjoy between leaving the islands and heading to his next posting. With his health compromised by malaria, he was granted three months' leave. The voyage took a month with the returning captain arriving in San Francisco on board the Pacific Mail steamer *Siberia*. Just as he had taken time to enjoy seeing part of the world on his way to the Philippines, he had done some sightseeing on the way home. He visited Hong Kong, Shanghai, Yokohama, and Nagasaki, where the United States would one day drop an atomic bomb in an effort to force the surrender of the Japanese. Pershing was variously charmed with the multicultural atmosphere of Hong Kong even as he described Shanghai as "an unholy port" where "it was said that children could be purchased for the price of a pair of shoes." He found the Chinese and the Japanese as different as "the Turks from the English." Further, he observed a significant military element among the Japanese and noted that "it is the soldier who has made Japan." He did not know then he would return to Japan in just a few short years as a military attaché and as an observer of the Russo-Japanese War. Much about his life would change during those intervening years.[1]

Crossing the Pacific, the *Siberia* reached Honolulu, then the Golden Gate. Reaching San Francisco in late July 1903, Pershing paid a call on Lt. Gen. Arthur MacArthur Jr., the commander of the Department of California, and met the general's son Douglas, a recent graduate of West Point. Although the elder MacArthur and Pershing would develop a dislike for one another over the years, Captain Pershing had a positive first impression of the son: "I was favorably impressed by the manly, efficient appearance of the second lieutenant."[2] General MacArthur, a Civil War veteran, had served in the Philippines during part of Pershing's time there but in the north, at Luzon, and followed with stints as the country's military governor and then the civilian governor. Pershing himself would one day return to the Philippines to serve as the military governor of the Moro Province, a post of four years.

During Pershing's leave of absence, he had the opportunity to visit the family from which he had been separated for so long. He took a train trip across the West, riding the rails over the Continental Divide, his first trek through the Rocky Mountains. Sadly, his mother had passed away in late November 1902 while he was the commander at Camp Vicars. He first stopped in Lincoln, Nebraska, to visit his eldest sister, Bessie, and some of his old friends, although men such as Charles Dawes, William Jennings Bryan, and George Meiklejohn had, as he had, moved on to greater and better things. He then went to Chicago to visit other family members.

Even as Pershing packed and left the Philippines, talk was already underway suggesting the man from Laclede had served the army so well in handling the Moros that he deserved an immediate advancement in rank. Some considered leapfrogging him over other officers of higher rank to an appointment as brigadier general.

Avery Andrews was among the influential supporters of Pershing's advancement to brigadier general. Not only was he a close friend of the Missouri captain and a fellow member of the

West Point class of '86 but he was also close to President Roosevelt, having served alongside him as New York City's police commissioner and, more recently, as New York governor Roosevelt's chief of staff. In November 1903, Andrews encouraged Roosevelt to promote his friend "to the rank corresponding to the service which he has already actually performed in the field," a less than veiled allusion to the role of a brigadier general. Roosevelt was straightforward in his response to Andrews: "I would have to put him over many other men.... At present it hardly seems to me that I could jump him to brigadier general."[3]

In the end, all the talk of Pershing's possible promotion to brigadier general came to nothing, leaving John at the rank of captain, even after sixteen years of active service. Pershing, at the age of forty-three, was one of the army's oldest captains. President Roosevelt, as commander in chief, had the power to advance Pershing to brigadier, and similar promotions had already taken place; but Roosevelt was not prepared to pull that particular trigger in 1903, despite Pershing's stellar service in Mindanao. To do so would have required the president to buck the army's generally hidebound seniority system.

Pershing's first assignment following the Philippines took him to Washington DC and service with the U.S. Army's General Staff. Just as his earlier service in the nation's capital had placed him in the center of its social circle, he was soon making the rounds again, with regular invitations to parties and dances. He was, after all, something of a military celebrity, given his success among the Moros. And he was quite an eligible bachelor. One dance soon changed his life. On December 9, while attending the weekly hop at Fort Myer on the Virginia side of the Potomac River, near Arlington National Cemetery, he met a girl half his age. The twenty-two-year-old Wellesley graduate only nine days earlier had broken off an engagement during her fiancé's visit to her father's estate outside Cheyenne, Wyoming.

Helen Frances Warren was the daughter of Sen. Francis Emroy Warren (R-WY), the chairman of the Senate Military Affairs Committee. A veteran of the Civil War and raised in Massachusetts, Senator Warren had received the Medal of Honor. Following the war, he migrated out west, and soon he and Wyoming became inextricably tied together. He bought an expansive cattle spread of hundreds of thousands of acres that stretched even into Nebraska and Colorado. So many cattle roamed on Warren's land that a senatorial colleague referred to him as "the greatest shepherd since Abraham."[4] Then Cheyenne was a brand-new western outpost linking the expanding railroad and the cattle industry. Warren was elected mayor and helped bring electric lights to the far western cattle town. In time, he became the governor of Wyoming Territory and the first governor when statehood arrived.

Miss Warren was well on her way to becoming one of Washington's most popular hostesses. Her mother had passed away when Helen was in high school, so the daughter served as her father's social director. She paid social visits on his behalf yet still found time for her own social life, including attendance at the Fort Myer hop. She was similar to so many other young socialites in Washington. Her father was wealthy and influential, and she had her own money, too, owning several investments that provided her an annual income of $10,000 (a considerable sum at the time and akin to $250,000 today). Still, there was something different about the young Wellesley girl whose friends called her "Frankie." She may have fit well in Washington's social circles, but she was also "a woman of the West—independent, athletic, and confident."[5] She loved to play cribbage and card games, and paid regular visits to the Library of Congress. She read what appealed to her, novels for fun and more serious fare, including books with a social conscience, such as New York City reformer Jacob A. Riis's study of the great city's immigrant poor, *How the Other Half Lives: Studies among the Tenements of New York*.

When Helen met the older captain Pershing that night, he was not a complete mystery to her. She had already heard of him. In fact, two days earlier, President Roosevelt had referred in glowing terms to the middle-aged officer in an address to Congress: "When a man renders such service as Captain Pershing rendered last spring in the Moro campaign, it ought to be possible to reward him without at once jumping him to the grade of brigadier general."[6] She recalled the speech and connected the hero of the Philippines with the man she met that evening on the dance floor. Once home, she excitedly wrote in her diary: "Went to a hop at Fr. Meyer [sic] with Papa . . . Perfectly lovely time. Met Mr. Pershing, of Moro and Presidential message fame."[7] Pershing's response was more enthusiastic, as he practically ran back to his lodgings and woke up his friend Charles Magoon, who one day would serve as the governor of Cuba and later of the Panama Canal Zone. Pershing exclaimed, "I've met the girl God made for me!"[8]

Magoon was less than sympathetic: "Look, John, maybe you're in love and can live without sleep. But I'm *not!*"[9]

Helen and John's relationship blossomed practically overnight. Over the next ten days, they saw one another repeatedly, even if the events were public. Frankie's diary tells the story:

December 11: "Had dinner with the Millards to see Capt. Pershing. . . . It was *just great.* Have lost my heart."

December 12: "Capt. Pershing told Miss Millard that I was a very 'jolly' girl—and that he thought I could keep up with the procession. Oh, joy!"

December 18: "Very elegant dinner. . . . Afterward, went to dance at the Navy Yard. . . . Danced every dance but one—and have lost my heart to Capt. Pershing irretrievably. Perfectly elegant dancer."[10]

Frankie's enthusiasm did not escape her father's eye. Senator Warren later recalled the first night at Fort Myer and reminisced, "I see now it was love at sight. They sat together, Jack and Frances, and for the most part they were oblivious of the rest of us."[11] Through December, they shared additional evenings, including a production of Shakespeare's *The Merchant of Venice*, with several of Frankie's Wellesley friends acting as chaperones. Pershing walked a straight line with Frankie, presenting himself as an officer and a gentleman. (They did not kiss for the first time until August 1904!) He sent her flowers on the twenty-seventh. The first challenge to their budding romance came soon, as Pershing was ordered to a new assignment in Oklahoma. In his absence, Frankie went to Cheyenne to stay at the Warren ranch. A slew of letters shuttled their way across the West from Oklahoma to Wyoming as the two would-be lovers kept their relationship alive. In an April 1904 missive, Pershing admitted to Frankie, on paper and for the first time, that he was in love with her. But formality remained the expectation, as he signed the letter "John J. Pershing." (First name references to one another in letters waited until that summer.)

Pershing's Oklahoma assignment involved his serving on the staff of the newly organized Southwestern Division under his previous commander in the Philippines Maj. Gen. Sam Sumner. The new division included the Departments of Texas and Colorado. It was a return to the West for Pershing, as Oklahoma was a territory, and the region "still kept some flavor of old Indian country."[12] Sumner was a perfect commander for Pershing, and the two men formed a closer relationship. The general was a hands-on leader who did not remain in the office long. During the spring of 1904, Sumner and Pershing took a tour of the forts and other installations in the Southwestern District, giving the captain from Missouri the opportunity to visit some of his old cavalry stations. Such western forts had seen their glory days, and the years of Indian fighting continued to recede into the past. Pershing was given the responsibility of creating a mobile force with connected outposts that would "consist of all the regular and national guard troops within the division."[13] Such a restructuring seemed, at the time, still unnecessary; however, when the day came for the United States to enter World War I, the restructuring had already been done.

Late in the spring of 1904, Sumner moved his headquarters from Oklahoma City to Colorado Springs, Colorado. This lateral move placed Pershing less than two hundred miles from Cheyenne. Soon, he made regular visits to help advance his relationship with Frankie. Sumner could not help but notice that "Pershing was constantly going to Cheyenne."[14] John and Helen shared their first kiss in August after a long horseback ride together across the expansive landscape of her father's ranch. Pershing wrote out his feelings in a letter that followed: "I never kissed your lips until we both said we loved each other. I should not have done so under any other circumstances. That kiss, as all others have been, was attended with feelings that to me are divinely sacred."[15]

The most lingering doubt Pershing had about their relationship and the possibility of it leading to marriage was his income. Despite her wealth, he had his pride and felt obliged to provide the necessary support should they become husband and wife. For her part, Frankie genuinely appears not to have cared about the gap between his income and hers. (As an army captain with eighteen years of service, Pershing's pay was in the range of $2,600, or about $65,000 today.) She virtually mocked his concerns, writing in a letter: "Let me tell you right here, you dear old Jack Pershing, that you might just as well stand in the middle of a field and wave a red flag at a bull as to flaunt the word 'obstacle' to me."[16] When he expressed concern over affording an engagement ring, she again brushed his doubts aside: "You are incorrigible. Next time you get on the verge of taking my view of things, stay there till I come. One can get a fine ring for one dollar ($1.00), or if worst comes to worst, one can be procured along with a stick of candy for one cent—and I'll lend you that much."[17]

She won him over through her charm offensive, and Pershing asked Senator Warren for his daughter's hand in marriage on Christmas Day 1904. They initially planned on a traditional June wedding, but, again, the army altered their plans. By late December, Pershing was summoned to Washington to meet with Secretary of War William Howard Taft. (Taft had previously served as the governor-general of the Philippines between July 1901 and December 1903.) Taft was slightly enigmatic, asking Pershing if he was a good bridge player. It was an important question, he insisted, since Lloyd Griscom, the U.S. minister to Japan, expected his military attaché to have such a skill. Pershing said he was a lackluster player but found he was being assigned to the U.S. Embassy in Japan. He immediately thought he had an out.

"There seems to be a decision by the Staff that no married officer can have a post in Tokyo," noted Pershing.

"That's right," said Taft with a smile.

"Well, Mr. Secretary, I'm engaged to be married."

"You're not married now, are you?" asked Taft through a loud laugh.

"No."

"You have the appointment, don't you?"

"Yes."

Taft assured his captain, "Then go ahead and get married. What you do after you have the appointment is your business. I know of no Army regulation which forbids a man to marry. No Army board or court will revoke an appointment because of marriage."

The secretary then asked who the lucky bride was. When Pershing informed him that it was the Wyoming senator's daughter, Taft responded, "You are a very lucky dog."[18]

June suddenly became January as Frankie and John planned their Washington wedding. Newspapers reported the engagement on January 11, 1905, and invitations soon went out across the nation's capital and all the way to Wyoming. Everyone was invited, from President Roosevelt to Supreme Court justices to congressmen, as a total of 4,500 invitations were sent. The wedding was held in Washington's Church of the Epiphany.[19] President Roosevelt, the First Lady, and their daughter Alice sat in the front row. Charles Magoon served as Pershing's best man. Senator Warren walked his daughter down the long aisle, with Frankie dressed in "white satin with elbow sleeves of lace and chiffon ruffles and a coronet of orange blossoms crowning her tulle veil."[20] The bride carried a bouquet of roses, orchids, and ferns.

At forty-four years of age, Pershing had set himself up for mocking telegrams from old army acquaintances, including some he had not seen since his West Point days of the early

1880s. One read, "You have thrown quite a bombshell into camp. You have come to the conclusion that most all of '86 arrived at long ago and are wise to desert those who are wandering around the world alone."[21] Indeed, John J. Pershing was about to wander the world again, and this time he would do so with his new bride, Frankie, at his side.

Capt. John J. Pershing's world took a decided turn with his marriage to Frankie Warren. He had found the woman he was certain was meant to share his life. For fifteen months, the man from Missouri and the Wellesley girl from Wyoming had courted, fallen in love, and finally walked the aisle. Yet despite how much she meant to him, Pershing sums up everything from their first dance at a Fort Myer hop to the day of their wedding in little more than a paragraph in his memoirs. This is not to say Frankie failed to capture his heart; instead, he reserved his literary expressions of love and emotion for the pages of his letters to her. To Pershing, none of it was for public consumption.

Despite the short planning, the wedding proved splendid, even by Washington society standards. Pershing wrote with enthusiasm in his diary entry for January 26: "Everything went off in first rate fashion. Church packed. I saw no one but Dearest Frances. Was not a bit excited but rather weak kneed.... I am the happiest man in the whole world and have the dearest, loveliest wife.–The bravest, the truest, and the best."[22]

They boarded a train to commence their honeymoon, traveling to Chicago to meet family and a few friends, including Charles Dawes, who could not attend the wedding on such short notice. Pershing's father, John Fletcher, now older than seventy, met them there, having traveled from St. Louis with John's younger brother Jim. It would prove a final reunion between father and son. By the first week of February, the happy newlywed couple was once again riding on horseback at Senator Warren's ranch near Cheyenne.

By mid-month they were on a ship bound for Tokyo, and Frankie was seasick through much of the voyage. (As luck would have it, Lt. Gen. Arthur MacArthur sailed on the same ship, bound for Japan.) Still, Pershing found an idyllic element in their onboard experiences, writing later of their departure from Hawaii: "Frances and I hung over the railing all afternoon and on into the evening—watched the twilight come and go. Oh, so sweet and how I love this dear wife of mine.... And oh! Another sweet thought came over the waters on this same evening breeze—the voices of sweet childhood, those that are coming to us—to have Frances for their mother and me for their father—so glad were they and so glad it seemed we would some day be when they come."[23]

Through such expressions of love and affection, the exacting military disciplinarian in Pershing takes a back seat to John Joseph the poet. Portions of the voyage were a repeat for Pershing as they sailed into ports he had seen two years earlier, such as Honolulu and Yokohama. Frankie and John reached Tokyo on March 5, and that evening they were guests at a dinner hosted by the Japanese war minister for General MacArthur, who had been dispatched to Japan as a military observer. Sadly, the Pershings had little time together after arriving in Japan, as Pershing and MacArthur were bound for Manchuria just four days later. Frankie saw them off at a train platform in Tokyo, a departure that Pershing referred to later as "the saddest of goodbyes." During those days between their arrival and his departure, Pershing and Frankie had repeatedly heard the word "banzai" shouted in the streets. It was similar to Americans shouting "hooray," but the word translates as a form of well-wishing, especially to the Japanese emperor. As Frankie watched and waved at her new husband's train departing for foreign fields, she shouted, "Banzai, Jack!"[24]

Through the next six months, Pershing was in the field as a U.S. military observer to the Russo-Japanese War. The use of American military observers dates back to the Crimean War (1853–56). Such military observers had become the norm, especially among the Western powers by the late nineteenth century, spurred by "the rapid advance of military technology coupled with the lack of extended general wars."[25] With America's entrance into the Philippines, giving the United States a new status as a transpacific power, the conflict between Japan and Russia related directly to America's international vital interests. Secretary of War Elihu Root saw such conflicts as being instructive for the U.S. military. By April 1904, Japan had allowed thirty-four foreign officers to accompany its troops in the field, including from Great Britain, Germany, France, Spain, Austria-Hungary, Italy, and several other nations. Among the officers from the United States were Arthur MacArthur, John Pershing, Parker West, and Edward McClernand—all of whom arrived in March 1905 during a period of stalemate.

When the war between Japan and Russia opened, it defied military logic. In its early stages, most Western military men thought the Russians would ultimately defeat the Japanese. Japan had only recently emerged from a long-standing feudal world of isolation from the West and begun to modernize, open its doors, and expand its industrial base. But one significant strength of Japan was its military, an extremely resilient force that met its Russian counterparts with skill and determination. It came as a complete surprise to Russia's czar Nicholas II, who considered his own army nearly invincible, when the Japanese took control of the city of Port Arthur, situated on an extended Manchurian peninsula in waters lying between the empires of China and Korea. During a siege of the port, the Japanese Navy destroyed most of its Russian counterpart and captured the strategically located port.

The war opened in 1904, and Japanese success came early, so Pershing had arrived almost too late to see any real action. The main battles and campaigns were practically over, and within six months or so, the Treaty of Portsmouth was signed at the Portsmouth Naval Shipyard in Maine on September 5. President Theodore Roosevelt helped broker the peace (and received the Nobel Peace Prize for his international efforts). Pershing often felt he was not allowed to see the action itself, only the aftermath. At Mukden, Manchuria, he was allowed to visit battlefields and observe many bodies and the remains of destroyed equipment, but the fight was long over. All the military observers complained of being shut out of the action, as did a hundred war correspondents who were cooped up in Tokyo. Correspondent Richard Harding Davis, who had reported from the field during the Spanish-American War, wrote in *Collier's* magazine that it was "much the same predicament as the young woman who was told that she might go out to swim but she mustn't go near the water."[26] After Pershing wrote a letter to his superiors in Washington DC complaining of his lack of direct exposure to the war—a communication he knew the Japanese would read—policies seemed to change, and within days he was on scene to witness a clash between a Japanese reconnaissance unit and a troop of Russian cavalry.

Pershing's assignment in Manchuria was certainly not a waste of his professional time. When a friend asked if he was gaining valuable insights, he was positive: "A great deal. I'm getting bits here and there, and patching them together. All invaluable if I am ever to command in the field."[27] Those bits included everything imaginable, for it seems nothing concerning the Japanese military evaded his scrutinizing eye. His reports included notes on the observation balloons, the medical corps, the military police, the gun types, the dimensions of boats, and even the Japanese military's pension program.

The experience provided him the opportunity to weigh the elements of modern warfare, some of which he had only begun to appreciate during his time in the Philippines. Since the Russians pursued generally a defensive strategy, their trench works were extensive. Both sides, however, made use of trenches and a variety of successful entrenching tools, which the United States had been slow to adopt. Pershing saw such works up close, as well as new weaponry. The Japanese used high-explosive shells and heavier-caliber artillery, which was new to the Americans. The machine gun also proved a significant weapon during the Russo-Japanese War. Introduced late in the war—almost none were in the field during the winter of 1904–5—Pershing did not see any Japanese machine guns utilized in the field, but he did have several conversations with Japanese officers of the Second Division who had seen the rapid-fire weapons at close range. Pershing included this information in his report to the War Department's General Staff: "The Japanese are averse to going against machine gun fire at anything like fair range. At 1,700 to 1,800 meters the fire from machine guns is not different from the fire of infantry. Machine guns can work with infantry and keep very close to it working behind it."[28] Pershing might have been better served if he had actually seen machine guns used in battle, as he minimized their importance: "Too much reliance in machine guns [is] dangerous. Artillery can do about all machine guns can do."[29] None of the American observers who wrote about machine gun use during the war came to any significant conclusion regarding how such weapons might be incorporated into the U.S. military structure. The ultimate lessons regarding machine guns would have to wait until World War I, as Pershing later observed in his memoirs: "Our army made no advance plans and at the beginning of [World War I] we had not even adopted a type of machine gun."[30]

Pershing found clearer lessons from his observations in the field regarding communications. He understood the importance of telegraphic communications, which dated to the U.S. Civil War, but he also saw the significance of telephone communications on the front lines. Such technologies were crucial for modern warfare. As he noted, "No longer is it possible for even Brigade commanders to observe their entire command, much less for Division and Army commanders, and the day for brigadier generals to rush forward in the firing line waving their hats and yelling 'Come on boys' is in actual warfare at least a thing of the past."[31] Wars now stretched over great expanses of territory, far beyond the eye of any one commander. This consideration proved important for the military officer who would be commanding hundreds of thousands of men placed on large-scale battlegrounds during the Great War.

But Pershing's observations regarding supply logistics were equally instructive. He had faced this issue many times over during his time in the Southwest, in the Ghost Shirt campaign, and certainly in Cuba and the Philippines on a great scale. With the Japanese, he saw up close the complications of moving supplies not simply to a battle region but also to an expansive battle space. It was important to understand the complications of moving not only military equipment and ammunition—a considerable and crucial element—to hundreds of thousands of men in the field but also supplies and provisions to maintain those troops for a prolonged period between battles. Winning future wars fought on a grand scale would require significant changes for the U.S. Army. All of these elements that Pershing studied helped prepare him for command in Europe.

Pershing also emerged from his assignment as a military observer with a stronger impression of the capacity of the average American soldier. He had served for twenty years as an officer in a variety of fields, including combat, and had been impressed with the accomplishments of his troops. To the officer from Missouri, Japanese soldiers were resilient and well disciplined. They went into battle with little thought of dying. Other military observers offered high praise to the Japanese, with some even considering the fighting men of Japan as the best anywhere. But Pershing still felt he was part of a great military fighting force: "The American is the best soldier—the best material if well trained."[32]

In the spring of 1906, John J. Pershing suffered a singular loss. On March 16, his father, John Fletcher, passed away in Lincoln, Nebraska, at the home of Pershing's sister Bessie. The guilt Pershing felt nearly crushed him. He had spent much of his adult life away from his immediate family, and for the father to die without the son at his side only doubled Pershing's grief. Memories of his father came to him like distant dreams. He recalled his father's successes and failures, his status as a leader in Laclede, his economic gains and losses, and his remaking himself during hard times to provide for his family. John Fletcher had always been one of his son's champions. The emotions that the death of Pershing's father evoked were ultimately tempered by the fact that Frankie was pregnant.

Following the Russo-Japanese War, Pershing's assignment was completed, and he returned to Tokyo and Frankie in September 1906. During his stint in Manchuria, he only returned to Tokyo once for a monthlong visit. His diary during his months of absence are littered with entries noting how much he missed his new wife and riddled with emotional expressions that he otherwise kept to himself, such as the following: "I hope this blooming war will soon end. . . . I am just about as forlorn as I can be."[33]

His return was sweet for several reasons. He was back in the arms of his beloved, who gave birth to the first of their four children, a girl named Helen Elizabeth, on September 8. The children Pershing had dreamed about were beginning to arrive. Then, great news came from Washington DC twelve days later: Pershing had been advanced in rank from captain to brigadier general. President Roosevelt had demurred at such a promotion in 1903 but had now changed his mind. He had become frustrated over the army's failure to advance Captain Pershing, but as president, he could only advance officers to a general's rank. The advancement came just days before Pershing's forty-sixth birthday, and it provoked considerable controversy. The president had jumped Pershing over hundreds of army officers of higher rank, including "257 captains, 364 majors, 131 lieutenant colonels, and 110 colonels—a total of 862 more senior officers."[34] Naturally, those 862 army officers were not particularly happy with the president's action. By itself, such an advancement did sometimes take place. In September 1906 three generals were serving who had been advanced from captain to a general's rank, including Leonard Wood, who had officially commanded the Rough Riders during the Spanish-American War. Brig. Gen. Franklin Bell had also advanced over 1,031 officers.

Complicating matters further was Pershing's father-in-law, Senator Warren, who served as the chairman of the Senate Military Affairs Committee. Roosevelt felt compelled to write a letter to the senator, one the president later made public: "The promotion was made solely on the merits, and unless I am mistaken you never spoke to me on the subject until I announced that he had been promoted. To promote a man because he marries a senator's daughter would be an infamy; and to refuse him promotion for the same reason would be an equal infamy."[35] Pershing addressed the issue years later in his memoirs, noting how he "did not meet Miss Warren until six months after the termination of the service for which I was promoted and after the President's message forecasting his action had been sent to Congress."[36]

Between disgruntled brother officers and the press, Pershing and Frankie weathered a considerable storm. Newspapers linked the senator and Pershing, implying nepotism. As the *St. Louis Post-Dispatch* conjectured, "Is not the Pershing case an excellent example of promotion by selection—selection in marriage?"[37] Such editorial innuendo completely ignored the facts of Pershing's advancement in rank, including his stellar military record of twenty years of service. Negative stories were plentiful. Some referred to Pershing as "N—— Jack" and retold tales from his unhappy days as a tactical officer at West Point. Others suggested Pershing's Tenth Cavalry had rescued Roosevelt and the Rough Riders from defeat during the charge up San Juan Hill and that the president had finally paid back that debt. The controversy may actually have led to another imbroglio, one of much greater import to Pershing and his young bride.

On December 18, the newspaper *Manila American* ran a story in which Pershing was accused of having a Filipino mistress named Joaquina Ygnacio while he served in Mindanao. A beautiful young woman, she was one of four sisters who operated a canteen for U.S. service personnel. According to the newspaper's investigation, the relationship produced two children, but one had died during a cholera epidemic in 1902. The remaining child, Petronilla, was not yet five years of age and lived with Joaquina in Zamboanga. Additionally, the newspaper report accused Pershing of sending a go-between to Joaquina to offer her fifty dollars to remain quiet about their long-term affair and the love children. She allegedly had refused the money, stating that she would never expose Pershing to scandal, as he had always treated her kindly. Several army officers had lent their versions of the story to various U.S. senators, hoping they might torpedo Pershing's advancement in rank.

The *Manila American*'s story was not the first time such an accusation was leveled at Pershing. In the spring of 1906, before the promotion was announced, an anonymous letter was sent to President Roosevelt that accused Pershing of keeping a Filipino mistress. Secretary of War William Taft had been informed, and he questioned Maj. Gen. George Davis, the former military governor of the Philippines, about the accusation. Davis was unaware of any such relationship, stating, "I heard nothing... that could justify anyone to cast a stone."[38]

Taking a native mistress was a common enough arrangement among American servicemen in the Philippines during the time Pershing was in country. Historian Gene Smith describes the commonplace practice: "Protestant morality and American ways and old barriers melted away in the heat of the tropical sun. What was called the *querida* system was quite accepted. One went to a girl's father, asked what he wanted, gave half what was mentioned, and installed her in one's quarters. When one wearied of the *querida*, the sweetheart, one's houseman or boy said, 'Time go home now, missy,' so it was recorded, and a replacement moved in."[39] But simply the existence of a system of Filipino concubines does not mean that Pershing committed the accused deeds. Without question, he had postponed marriage until his early forties, and the man from Missouri's reputation included being known as a ladies' man. But even with what exactly that term might infer at the turn of the century or even in the decades of Pershing's youth, keeping a mistress represented an extreme. The *Manila American* story claimed eyewitnesses to Pershing's indiscretion, but they were hard to come by for public statements. Three names were put forward—Col. Jasper Morrison, Capt. Sidney Cloman, and Capt. Thomas Swobe—but Morrison was already dead, and the other two denied any such knowledge. Swobe even presented a personal vouch for Pershing: "We messed at the same table, our rooms were in the same building and very close to each other.... And I stand ready to defend him against any charge his enemies may bring."[40]

Pershing's response to the charges was to categorically deny them. By early 1907, he went to the Philippines to gather evidence to refute the claims. He sent a small collection of affidavits subsequently to Secretary of War Taft along with a letter in which he stated he was "very glad to have the opportunity of . . . presenting to you proof of the falsity of these reports." Joaquina Ygnacio signed one of the most important testimonies. She denied the charges, too, and made clear that no detail of the claim was remotely accurate, especially "that the said John J. Pershing is alleged to be the father of two children by me. . . . I do hereby solemnly swear that each and every one of the above allegations is wholly untrue and false in each and every respect." She also stated that "various Americans" had attempted to pay her to testify that Pershing was the father of her children. Her husband, Zellar H. Shinn, swore to the same.[41]

The drama and resulting scandal involved an international cast, but the one person's opinion of Pershing's alleged sexual indiscretions that mattered most was that of his wife, Frankie. Although he met her after the years in question, he was still concerned how she might respond. Newspaper reports suggested she intended to divorce him. Nothing proved further from the truth. Her immediate response on hearing the news was to pen a supportive, reassuring letter to her husband, one that might prove the envy of any man who found himself in such a delicate state of scandal: "I love you wholly, devotedly, with all my strength, for always and always and always. You will know that my love is the same whether it is true or not."[42]

For the immediate moment, the accusations and their concomitant notoriety swirled menacingly for several months; then they finally died out for lack of traction. Pershing weathered the storm, in part, due to his own dogged efforts. But such rumors do not die natural deaths. They continued to stalk him for much of the remainder of his life, a Filipino enemy that even he could not subdue.

Ironically, perhaps, Pershing's next assignment took him back to the Philippines to command Fort William McKinley outside Manila. The fort was home to a pair of infantry regiments (effectively a brigade), an artillery battery, a company of engineers, and a medical outfit. It was the only "reinforced brigade" the army had in operation at that time, along with the largest number of American army personnel outside the United States. When he arrived in Manila, he soon faced officers who had only recently outranked him, including some he had served under previously. Frankie and their baby went with him, and soon she was carrying out all the social duties expected of a brigadier general's wife.

When Pershing arrived at the fort, the commander was Col. Henry P. Kingsbury, who was several years Pershing's senior. He had been a part of the Sixth Cavalry when Pershing first arrived in New Mexico. The command at Fort McKinley provided Pershing an opportunity to implement some of the changes he had been considering after his observations of the Russo-Japanese War, especially those involving large-scale field maneuvers. It was the kind of activity he engaged in while stationed in New Mexico, including the war games centered on the rabbit hunts between competing cavalry troops. "It was amazing to find how many officers and non-commissioned officers there were with little conception of their duties and responsibilities in the conduct of actual operations," Pershing wrote.[43]

His early days at the fort were awkward. Pershing had been a junior officer for so many years, and he had to accustom himself to commanding men who had previously been his superiors. But he hit the ground running. The man from Missouri established a training program to help officers work together in coordinating various brigades. "Fort McKinley was an ideal place for training," Pershing later wrote. "There was an area nearby of about a hundred square miles available for all kinds of field training and maneuvers. . . . The artillery could fire every day in the year over a different range, and other arms could find an infinite variety of ground for separate or combined exercises."[44] His training program involved the skill set he had acquired years earlier in Laclede as a teacher, a role he had repeated several times over the years. He requested that all troops stationed in the Philippines be exposed to his program at the fort, but his superior, General Wood, said no, as it would be too inconvenient. Wood, a medical doctor by training, simply did not see its value. If Pershing had been given the

Courtship, 1903–9

opportunity to train the hundreds of officers, it would have well served the U.S. effort in the Great War.

Pershing was stationed at Fort William McKinley from January 1907 until July 1908, and it proved an enjoyable post. He rubbed shoulders with many officers, including those who would one day serve under him in France. His men appreciated their commander, and Pershing, once again, ingratiated himself among his fellow officers and the enlisted men. One of them commented, "There was absolutely no high hatting in or about General Pershing. He was not comfortably settled in his quarters before he began lightening our duties, such as reducing the number of sentries for guard duty . . . and improving our food."[45] Unlike his early posts that were sometimes far off the beaten path, Fort McKinley was an important outpost. Secretary of War William Howard Taft came for a visit in October 1907. A minor difficulty arose when Pershing organized a banquet in the secretary's honor. Taft came to the general all in a dither.

"My valet forgot to pack my waistcoat," he informed Pershing. "Do you have one here I can borrow?"[46]

The request was not an easy one to fulfill, since Taft weighed more than three hundred pounds. But Pershing punted and located a spare waistcoat, splitting the back open to provide the required room and using adequate underpinning to hold the ensemble in place, at least temporarily.

Throughout Pershing's year and a half at McKinley, he was only absent once for an extended period when an assignment sent him back to Japan as a military observer. He found the Japanese military was similar to the one he had witnessed a couple of years earlier, but he did note increases in its use of machine guns. His report stated as much, but the U.S. Army made no moves to adopt the weapon prior to World War I. Pershing did note, as he had earlier, the expansive ambitions of the Japanese and left Japan certain that one day the American Philippines would become its target.

Pershing never accepted lengthy absences from his beloved Frankie. The Japanese assignment was a challenge for him, and even his regular duties sometimes distracted him from his family more than he liked. In March 1908 a second child arrived, a daughter named Anne after Pershing's mother and Miss Anne Orr, one of Frankie's closest friends at Wellesley and her bridesmaid. (Anne Orr subsequently married Lt. W. O. Boswell, who became an aide to Pershing in 1909–11, when the general was assigned a third time to the Philippines.) Pershing, however, missed the event. His loneliness while in Japan prompted desperate letters expressing professional and personal frustration: "I am not going to stay in the service away from you. Damn the service."[47]

Pershing's doubts about remaining in the army had plagued him repeatedly during his younger days in the service, especially when advancement in rank did not come when he expected. Yet, even as a general, he sometimes found army life distracting, even unfulfilling. In 1907 he considered resigning and moving his family either to Europe or to the distant wiles of the Klondike. But as with every previous doubt concerning his commitment to the army, he remained committed to the service.

At the end of July 1908, Pershing's Fort McKinley assignment—his second tour in the Philippines—was over, and he packed up his family for their return to the United States. On a Saturday evening, four hundred well-wishers gathered at Fort McKinley to bid the Pershings farewell. The tour "marked a happy time in Pershing's life, eighteen months of accomplishment. . . . And he knew, too, that in the warmth and affection of his good brothers came his fullest achievement—friendship."[48]

As he had done in his previous travels, John and Frankie took the long way back home, choosing to sightsee through Russia and then Europe. Hong Kong and Nagasaki were again on the itinerary. He planned the trip as if he were launching a campaign, setting timetables and estimating the cost of the extended journey home. Along the way, he discovered prices outpaced his plans. He and his family had only reached Vladivostok, with more than three thousand miles remaining, when his funds were nearly depleted. (One burdensome cost was their enormous amount of luggage, which included more than a dozen pieces, plus baskets of books, Asian rugs, wine bottles, and, naturally, souvenirs.) He experienced some problems cashing a bank draft drawn on a bank in Washington DC. Once he did cash the draft, he received the equivalent of $600 in rubles. After purchasing the family's train tickets, plus all the tips to baggage handlers and for additional services rendered, he was down to three rubles, which were worth little more than $1.50. Ahead of them lay ten days' travel to Moscow on a Russian train with no money for food. Their options seemed limited. The normally stalwart Frankie began to cry, along with the children. Pershing thought fast. The nearly penniless American general recalled spotting a Danish naval officer on the train. He dug out a box of fine Filipino cigars, swallowed his pride, and went in search of the officer. In the fellow's compartment, Pershing spilled out his story and offered the cigars. The unknown Dane was amused and delighted to help, and loaned him money to complete his trip. Pershing later admitted, "Anything was pardonable to save those we love."[49]

Otherwise, the trip was a glorious adventure for the Pershing family. They toured Russia, where they visited St. Petersburg and Moscow, and took in the sights, including the grand churches with their unique onion domes and the revues of Russian soldiers. While in Germany, Pershing called on the German War Office and made some quick observations that revealed the extent of the German military machine, which greatly impressed him. In Berlin they dawdled as tourists, taking in "parks, palaces, and museums by day, and in the evenings to theaters and operas or dinners with friends."[50] Pershing met with Henry P. Fletcher, one of Roosevelt's Rough Riders, who had become a U.S. diplomat. They went on to Belgium, and John took Frankie on a tour of the Waterloo battlefield, where Napoleon Bonaparte finally met his end as a grand field strategist. In France, Pershing visited the Metz battlefield, the site of a German victory during the Franco-Prussian War of 1871. The visit reminded the man from Laclede of his days in northern Missouri. Pershing recalled, "The sight of the battlefield brought back to mind how the wiseacres of Laclede, my old hometown, used to gather in front of father's store and Dick Mitchell's drugstore next door and, whittling in Missouri fashion, hold forth on the strategy of the campaign."[51] The novelist Thomas Wolfe would one day suggest "you can't go home again," but the well-traveled Pershing, after decades away, found it as easy as if his old hometown were just around the corner.

Once back in the United States, Pershing saw to his health. He was on his way to fifty years old, and while he had generally been in good health his entire life, some problems were nagging at him. He had recurring bouts of fever from the malaria he had contracted in Cuba. He also manifested sprue, a disease that caused his small intestines to become inflamed, which led to anemia. Pershing was also dealing with heart palpitations. (All these ailments had played a crucial role in Pershing's decision to ask for a transfer out of the Philippines.) His years in the tropics were finally catching up with him.

He met with the army's surgeon general, whose immediate advice was for Pershing to quit smoking. An inveterate smoker most of his adult life, he had in more recent years nursed a twelve-cigar-a-day habit. He quit nearly cold turkey and rarely smoked for the remainder of his life. But other issues proved challenging. Historian Frank Vandiver describes the extent of Pershing's downward health spiral: "Fear inspired despair, and Jack felt his first twinge of mortality. He was forty-eight; would he ever again return to duty?"[52]

Pershing needed immediate answers. He took decisive action, which was his military way, and checked himself into a sanitarium in New York for three months, followed by another month of recuperation at the Army-Navy Hospital in Hot Springs, Arkansas. His doctor was an old classmate from the class of '86, Maj. George DeShon. After thoroughly examining his comrade, DeShon delivered his diagnosis: "John, we have subjected you to every known test, and in my opinion and in that of my associates there isn't a damn thing the matter with you. Tomorrow morning two saddle horses will be ready at seven o'clock and we shall take a ride."[53]

Pershing continued to ride over the next two weeks. The outdoor therapy revived him. "I was galloping over the hills as I had when a lieutenant of cavalry" until the "fear had vanished entirely and I knew that once more, thanks to the army medical man, I was ready for active duty."[54]

Pershing soon established a continuing health regimen for himself, one that included "two hours on a horse each day, lots of sleep, a good diet, forty minutes of calisthenic exercises followed by a salt rub, [and] a daily hour nap."[55] He also prepared to return to the Philippines for a third tour, which turned into another four-year stint as events transpired. During his months of illness, his family grew when Frankie gave birth to Pershing's only boy, Francis Warren Pershing. Named for his maternal grandfather, he was always known as "Warren" and came into the world at a noticeable twelve pounds.

ELEVEN

Conquest, 1909–13

The Pershing family arrived in the Philippines on November 11, 1909, just a few months shy of John's fiftieth birthday. This time he was to serve as the military governor of the Moro Province, a position he held until 1913. Technically, the governorship was a civilian position; however, dating back to 1903, the practice was to appoint U.S. Army generals to the role, given the presence of so many troops in the Philippines. Pershing was the last of the military governors of the island chain. From his headquarters in Zamboanga, a city of twenty thousand people, Pershing carried out his duties as a civil governor and army commander from two offices in two separate buildings that operated independently of one another, spending mornings in one and afternoons in the other. He even changed clothes between offices from civilian dress to a uniform.

Moro Province included the islands of Mindanao, Pershing's earlier stomping ground, plus Jolo and was divided into five, American-created districts: Zamboanga, Sulu, Davao, Cotabato, and Lanao. In 1909 the population was larger than half a million souls, with over 60 percent Moros (Muslims) plus eighty-five thousand Filipinos (usually Catholics) and 105,000 native tribal peoples (considered little more than pagans). The district represented ground on which Pershing had already trod. This time, though, he was not stuck in some remote jungle firebase such as Camp Vicars; instead, he and his family lived in a beachfront villa outside Zamboanga with a vast array of servants, including maids, cooks, housekeepers, drivers, and aides. The grounds were lush with palm trees and the scent of orchids in season. The villa was roomy, including a dining room to accommodate sixty guests. While the family often enjoyed their time together in Zamboanga, Frankie took the children to Japan to avoid the hot season and even made trips to Wyoming. So, once again, Pershing was sometimes separated from his family and missed them all, especially the woman he loved. Letters were always their fallback when separated, and their pages were typically filled with emotional expressions of love. In one letter, Pershing wrote, "To the sweetest, dearest woman in all the world . . . I am mighty lonesome for you. Last night, I simply gave way and couldn't keep back the tears. My Heavens, I simply worship you." The letter reached Frankie during a Cheyenne visit, and her fervency outdid his: "My own darling, darling Heart—my great lover—oh, Jack, I just go mad for love of you—I adore you. I love you from the top of your dear curly head to the very end of your toes."[1]

Pershing was disappointed with the state of things in his district. He had spent earlier years in Mindanao negotiating and subduing the various Moro datos, achieving grand success at the time, but a new leadership had failed to follow up or even maintain Pershing's initial inroads. Successive leaders had not done the heavy lifting of coming to terms with the multitude of Moro cultures that Pershing had, an effort that had always served as the bedrock foundation of his dealings with one dato or another. Maj. Gen. Leonard Wood, the senior commander in the Philippines, was much more prone to simply wearing down the Moros with military action, wielding an iron fist in a glove of steel.

Pershing and Wood had their differences, dating back to the Spanish-American War, but Pershing found a friend in the governor-general Cameron Forbes. The two men established a strong affinity for one another. Sometimes their joint strategies proved extremely unique, such as the time a boundary dispute was settled by playing a baseball game. When one tribe refused the Americans' arbitration offer regarding its quarrel with a neighboring tribe over boundaries, the tribal leaders suggested a baseball matchup between themselves and the Americans, including Pershing and Forbes. As the American general described the situation, "The Governor General covered one base, the Secretary of the Interior another and I the last. Aides and secretaries took other positions in the nine. The natives, although new at the game, played well and were surprised that they did not win, as they had been practicing." The challenging tribe accepted the Americans' settlement of the boundary line.[2] The baseball skills Pershing honed during his days at Fort Stanton as a young trooper served him well in the Philippines twenty years later.

Soon, General Pershing was up to his old ways in the Philippines. When possible, he rekindled earlier ties with familiar datos and sultans, and negotiated with new ones. The intervening six years since his Camp Vicars service represented lost ground. Pershing wrote, "Though force has to be used to a certain extent, and to the utmost limits when dealing with criminal elements, it was clear that there had been too much haste in using arms to enforce laws and regulations that ran counter to age-old customs."[3] He was greatly disappointed to discover many of the datos in the Lanao District, where he had worked so diligently at both diplomacy and military action, had become completely alienated toward the Americans' presence.

The general went from village to village, speaking and listening, as he had earlier. He was remembered as a great leader, one who spared Moro blood more often than spilled it. He played fair with the Moros, and his reputation had not died. Pershing again began to eliminate points of friction. He pulled many American troops out of a string of forts around the district to separate them from regular contact with the native populations. Then, he began to encourage relations in a different way, by building up the infrastructure more dramatically than he had accomplished years earlier. He utilized troops, not as a local constabulary force keeping an oppressively close watch on the

Moros, but as engineers and builders. Everything from roads to bridges to schools to medical clinics, even electric plants, sprang up across the Philippine landscape. Pershing employed many Moros as common laborers—some even volunteered, knowing the changes would improve the lives of their people—and guaranteed a fair wage.

Pershing discovered how much he had been missed. As one sultan told him, "Since you left we have been like orphans, with no hope except in God, but now that you are returning we are very happy and glad."[4] The general continuously smoothed over problems, worked closely with datos old and new, and established once again his unique brand of leadership. He was likely better with age. Pershing had long ago developed the skill to speak with nearly anyone and make him or her feel as if he or she was being heard. One of his chief qualities in dealing with the Moros had always been patience. And he often went out of his way to be courteous. His longtime orderly Frank Lanckton once observed of his commander, "It never made much difference whether he was talking to a half-naked semi-civilized Moro chieftain or to the King of England. He was always courteous and polite. He has a way of making anyone certain of his good will. It is not so much what he says, because he does not talk very much, but his ability to say the right thing at the right time and in the right way."[5]

Even though several years had passed since Pershing called Mindanao home, many of the same concerns that had previously troubled the datos still remained. The American leader had usually been understanding and reassured them that the Americans were not in the Philippines to convert the Moros from their Islamic faith. They also had been allowed to keep their multiple wives, and even slavery was allowed to continue. This time around, Pershing was still intent on cooperating with the Moros by largely leaving their cultural norms in place. As he said to them, "Again I wish to state that this is not the country of the Americans, but is the country of you Moros, and we are not going to bring here Americans to push you out."[6] The Americans had supported the practice of Islam among the Moros, and Pershing intended to continue the policy.

Pershing set an important goal of bringing the various peoples of Mindanao together. In February 1911 he hosted a special event and invited all the Moros in his district to attend. It was a grand trade fair, the largest ever held in the Philippines. Large buildings were fashioned from bamboo and illuminated with electric lights, a great curiosity among the natives. It was a dazzling display of cultural and industrial progress, a type of world's fair but with only one foreign nation's goods and services on display—those of the United States. Pershing had his personal staff automobile at the fair. A U.S. battleship was open for native tours in the Zamboanga harbor. There were machines and recent inventions and a noisy merry-go-round. One of the most curious moments of the fair was a wedding hosted by Pershing. The groom was a Jolo dwarf named Diki Diki who stood only three feet tall. He married a nine-year-old local native girl. After the ceremony, Pershing gave them a ride in his touring car.

The event also gave the Moro tribes an opportunity to shine. Everyone came in flashy, colorful native costumes decorated with everything from seashells to tinkling bells. Some natives came out of the jungle wearing little but their jewelry and strategically placed feathers. To many Americans, the event was reminiscent of county fairs back home, only with more skin. The days of the fair included lots of friendly competitions, including foot races, horse races, diving events, cattle shows, and even tugs-of-war. With forty tribes in attendance, the one common denominator they shared was General Pershing himself. At least twenty thousand came to enjoy the fair, a number equivalent to the entire population of Zamboanga. So many tribes attended the event, and some had not even been previously aware of the other's existence. The culmination of the special event was when Pershing drove his automobile in front of the reviewing stand where dozens of datos cheered him, waving their turbans in the air. It was a grand triumph the likes of which Pershing would not see again until World War I.

As Pershing reestablished his place in the world of the Mindanao Moros, this particular assignment to the Philippines proved the most rewarding of the three tours between 1900 and 1913. In later years, he looked back with great fondness on his time spent with Frankie and the children in their tropical paradise and considered them the best days of his life. Their house was one of the nicest they ever lived in, "a spacious place, set close to the beach, facing the small parade ground or plaza, around which the barracks and quarters of the garrison and department staff were grouped."[7] It was expansive, with large rooms and windows of sliding panels. A great veranda ran along the length of the second story. The grounds were lush with plants, including rare orchids. Cool breezes wafted in from the sea. The household servants represented a multiracial gathering that included an African American coachman, a Filipino houseboy, a Japanese nursemaid, a Chinese cook, and a white American trooper, Private Lanckton, as Pershing's orderly.

So much of Pershing's family life was idyllic, with days spent in the leisure afforded to American officials in this island paradise. He describes them in his memoirs: "At Zamboanga we led a life in the open air.... When at home hardly a morning went by that we did not take a dip in the sea, which was but twenty paces away.... Usually in the afternoons we went horseback riding, and here again Mrs. Pershing, having been raised in Wyoming and accustomed to horses, was very much at home."[8]

Children held the center of the Pershings' domestic life, and they kept coming. A fourth child, a girl named Mary Margaret, arrived on May 19, 1912. Even when Pershing was away from his family from time to time, he wrote letters to Frankie and often mentioned them: "Kiss those dear Kiddies for me—their papa."[9]

There was plenty to keep the Pershings' social calendars filled, including parties, dances, luncheons, and official dinners. The U.S. military community with its officers and their wives was a tight one, and the wives often leaned on one another for support, especially when their men were on assignment in the field. Pershing ordered the construction of a golf course and a polo field to encourage friendly sports rivalries. He went deep-sea fishing, and hunting forays were common diversions.

Pershing, although rarely an overtly religious man, found

time to attend worship services. He had already converted to the Episcopal Church during his first assignment in the Philippines. When Charles Brent, a local bishop, suggested to Pershing that his children needed baptizing, the general agreed, stating, "We must do all we can to start children on the right road." In January, the children were baptized, and Bishop Brent confirmed John and Frankie into the church.[10]

But all was not perfect in paradise. Pershing still had to deal with significant issues. One of the more recent problems the Moros were contending with when the general returned to Mindanao was pressure exerted on them, not by the Americans, but by Catholic Filipinos. In the greater Philippines, Catholics counted for the vast majority of the indigenous population. But in the Moro Province, the tables were turned, with Catholics numbering only about 10 percent of the population. Some datos complained that their greatest concern was the encroachment of Filipino Catholics, and they were willing to fight for their Islamic way of life if needed. As Pershing observed in a 1913 report, "The Filipino regards the Moro as a barbarian or a savage. They are in no sense brothers, but are irreconcilable strangers and enemies in every sense."[11]

The comparisons he makes are similar to his experiences among the American Indian tribes in the West. Pershing did not condone the Filipinos' efforts to encroach on the Moros; instead, he believed the Americans provided a positive influence on both groups. "Peace in the Moro Province," he argued, "can be maintained only by continuance of American control."[12]

Because of this perceived problem between Muslims and Catholics, plus the ongoing presence of the Americans, the years between Pershing's commands in the Mindanao District had witnessed a significant rise in the number of juramentados, the blade-wielding extremists who sought to kill as many non-Muslims as possible. Pershing had worked hard during his first stint in the Moro District to alleviate the threat of the juramentados, and he was troubled to find the practice still active. Not only were Catholic Filipinos attacked but Americans were sometimes targeted as well. One example hit Pershing especially hard. "A particularly cruel case was that of the killing of Lieutenant W. H. Rodney of the Second Cavalry, one Sunday afternoon in Jolo, close to the barracks. The Lieutenant was out walking with his little daughter, about five years old, when a Moro who passed him on the road suddenly drew his barong, turned and killed him with several quick and vicious slashes from behind."[13]

What made it difficult for Westerners such as Pershing to make inroads against the juramentados was the theological element that motivated them to carry out such acts of terrorism. These religiously inspired zealots believed they were doing the will of Allah and that if they were killed while assassinating infidels, they would gain a ticket to paradise. Pershing took unprecedented steps to deal with the threat, one based in a singular fear held by nearly every Muslim on the islands—exposure to swine. The American general describes the tactic in his own words: "These *juramentado* attacks were materially reduced in number by a practice the army had already adopted, one that the Mohammedans held in abhorrence. The bodies were publicly buried in the same grave with a dead pig. It was not pleasant to have to take such measures but the prospect of going to hell instead of heaven sometimes deterred the would-be assassins."[14]

In a way, such a tactic—purposefully exposing Muslim extremists to pigs—was not one Pershing enjoyed, as his own words indicate. The tactic was already in use by the time he returned to Mindanao in 1909. While he did not condemn the practice, there is a question of how often it was relied upon under his watch. To the cultural purist, such actions do not represent an acceptable policy. But for Pershing, it was a matter of maintaining law and order and stemming the actions of those he considered little more than assassins motivated by their religious zeal. It was a repulsive business but likely one he never lost any sleep over.[15]

Pershing actually turned to a variant solution for the juramentado problem and that of the continuing violence among the Moro tribes. While it represented an extreme measure in its own right—many doubted it was even feasible—he decided to disarm the entire Moro population in his district. The Moro way of life always included the element of warrior culture. To anticipate all Moros willingly surrendering their weapons, whether blades or bullets, required a fully cooperative population. Pershing could not imagine an alternative. When he put the solution to General Wood, the senior commander thought it patently absurd. As for Forbes, he offered his support.

Pershing made the official announcement on September 8, 1911, with the issuance of Executive Order No. 24. He proclaimed the mere possession of any weapon, including the traditional kris and kampilan, illegal. He set the clock for December 1, giving the Moros only three months to comply. What Pershing offered was equivalent to a weapons buyback program: when a weapon was turned in to U.S. authorities, the owner was promised a reasonable compensation. It came as no surprise that many who cooperated by turning in weapons were already friendly toward the Americans and that those who were still hostile held on to theirs. Some even challenged the American general with the equivalent of the old Texan rallying cry: "Come and Take It."

Hot-spot resistance centered in two of Pershing's five districts—Jolo and Lanao. Just as in earlier days, negotiations alone did not deliver the sought-after results. Pershing believed his plan would serve the Moro people as well as the Americans: "For years the good people of these areas had been harassed by outlaw bands whose disarmament could be accomplished only by the energetic use of force."[16] To the American general, the time had come for such force. After an American soldier was killed and three others wounded in an attack, Pershing set his sights on those he held responsible. To clear the way for a military campaign, the general wrote letters to all the datos he believed were leading the resistance against his proclamation. In a final attempt to negotiate before marching, he wrote, "All Moros are the same to me as my children and no father wants to kill his own children. . . . Give up the guns and save your own lives and the lives of your people."[17]

Despite his best efforts, holdout Moros waved their weapons in defiance and fortified the cottas on a mountaintop called Bud Dajo. A fight had taken place at that fortress in 1906, before Pershing's return, when General Wood surrounded the cotta and unleashed an artillery barrage that left no escape for those holed up inside. Twenty-one Americans were killed, and more than six hundred Moro men, women, and children were annihilated.[18] Pershing did not intend to approach Bud Dajo with the same bull-in-a-china-shop approach. He stated in a letter to Frankie: "I would not have . . . [that] on my conscience for the fame of Napoleon."[19] But a showdown seemed inevitable.

Bud Dajo represented a difficult target for the U.S. Army. Situated on a high mountain, the Jolo cotta was considered sacred to the Muslims. Inside an extinct volcano, the fort was manned by as many as eight hundred warriors armed with approximately two hundred rifles. Practically every defender carried a blade or blades for defense. Hugh L. Scott, the former American commander of Jolo Island, had approached the fortress in 1905 and found its position formidable: "Bud Daho [sic] was a very difficult nut to crack, and I did not want to be obliged to assault it. . . . It was plain that many good Americans would have to die before it could be taken."[20]

Early on the morning of December 16, 1911, Pershing dispatched a squadron of cavalry to examine the perimeter of the Bud Dajo compound. In addition to the troopers, Pershing commanded three infantry companies, three Philippine scout companies, and a machine-gun platoon—more than a thousand men total. The cavalry reconnaissance revealed three trails leading to the cotta, and Pershing established encampments at the base of each, cutting supplies and escape routes so completely, as the general wrote home to Frankie, "a cat could not sneak out."[21] With intelligence indicating the defenders had not adequately stockpiled supplies, he chose to surround the site and lay down a siege. He would rather wait out the Moros than storm the cotta and lose many lives. In time, the Moros began to surrender until only the absolute diehards remained. The final assault resulted in the collapse of the fort and the deaths of a dozen defenders with only three Americans wounded.

Through the six months following the Bud Dajo operation, American personnel collected weapons from nearly every corner of the Moro District with one large-scale exception. Dato Amil, who occupied the cotta at Bud Bagsak in a twenty-mile area called Lati Ward on Jolo Island, led a most "stubborn, defiant, and difficult" cadre of Moros still holding out against the Americans.[22] Rumors told of thousands of Moro insurgents taking up defensive positions at the cotta along with their wives and children. Pershing, as usual, did not intend to attack first and negotiate later. He spent months attempting some form of reconciliation with Dato Amil but to no avail. The Moros under his leadership did not intend to surrender themselves or their weapons.

In the midst of the disarmament campaign in February 1912, Pershing received an offer to leave the Philippines and take command of the Mounted Service School at Fort Riley, Kansas. While the offer was enticing—the cavalry always held a soft spot in his heart—he reminded himself he had agreed to remain in the islands for at least three years. He let the offer pass. Later that same year, the old scandal over Pershing's alleged affair with a Filipino woman resurfaced. (At that time, rumor had it the brigadier was up for another posting, this time as superintendent at West Point.) Once again, jealous officers intended to discredit Pershing. He wrote to his father-in-law: "That crowd of sneaks. I have always regretted that I did not shoot the editor [of the *Manila American*] and sue the paper for slander."[23] When the story was reprinted in American newspapers, including the *New York World*, Pershing did sue for libel and won, forcing the *World* to retract the story.

In the meantime, Amil became more belligerent with each passing month in 1912. His men went about collecting their own weapons stockpile until they had accumulated an arsenal of between five thousand and eight thousand guns and blades. Amil even sent a taunting message to the local American governor Lt. William W. Gordon: "Tell the soldiers to come on and fight."[24]

Pershing initially delivered troops to Bud Bagsak by early

1913 but did not order an attack. By mid-February the Moros seemed willing to negotiate, possibly because they were running short on supplies. On March 7 Dato Amil emerged from the cotta, leading 1,500 Moro warriors, who followed him to Taglibi to parley with the Americans. The Moros agreed to return to their homes if the Americans pulled back to Jolo City. For the moment, the warriors were allowed to retain their weapons and promised they would cooperate fully with Pershing in the future, no matter what he demanded of them.

It was largely a ploy. A few months later, the Moros announced they had no intention of laying down their weapons, and many returned to Bud Bagsak. With the Moros in complete defiance—they even began menacing the capital of Jolo City—Pershing declined to negotiate any further. But he did not want to attack the cotta if it held many women and children. Soon, he devised a clever ploy, including a surprise attack, that was launched before the Moro warriors had the opportunity to call their wives and children back into the cotta. (Many were not in the fortress but lived at the base of the mountain, where they worked the local fields.)

The deception soon began. Pershing ordered the troops surrounding the Bud Bagsak fortress area to withdraw in early June and return to Fort McKinley, leaving the impression the Americans were giving up even before a fight. Four days later, he announced that he was leaving his headquarters at Zamboanga to visit his family; then he would spend the hot summer months at Camp Overton, Mindanao. He even boarded the transport steamer *Wright* and sailed toward Overton, but once the ship was away from Zamboanga, he ordered it to alter course straight toward Jolo. Along the way, two companies of troops joined Pershing, all sailing for Jolo City. Additional troops headed to Bud Bagsak by land. Even Pershing's field commanders were kept in the dark concerning his plan until his arrival. American troops converged on the area of Bud Bagsak, completely surprising the enemy. The fight soon commenced in the early morning hours of June 11 with an artillery barrage.

The main American force included six infantry companies,

two mountain gun detachments, and a demolition unit. A fifty-man detachment of the Eighth U.S. Cavalry brought up the mountain guns. In all, Pershing delivered 1,200 men to the base of Bud Bagsak before the defending Moros knew what was happening. The fighting proved intense. The cotta represented the final, significant holdout of Moros in the region. Even Pershing was surprised at the enemy's resilience, as he wrote to Frankie: "The fighting was the fiercest I have ever seen."[25] Artillery blasted away as American soldiers bundled four sticks of dynamite together and tossed them toward the Moro fortress walls. Slowly but defiantly, the Americans inched closer to the compound until they were a hundred yards from the main fort. Rifle fire split the air as the Moros' shouts signaled their intent to die to the last man. Waves of Moro warriors emerged from the fortress, leading to hand-to-hand combat.

The fight stretched on to June 15, and the final day involved long hours of encircling the enemy and destroying bamboo fence lines. Pershing did not command from the rear; instead, just as he had during the assaults up Kettle and San Juan Hills in Cuba, he directed the engagement at the front, with arrows and spears and bullets whizzing past him. One man later observed, "I think it was largely due to his coolness and courage that the soldiers did such effective work. General Pershing stood so close to the trench, directing operations, that his life was endangered by flying barongs and spears which were being continually hurled from the Moro stronghold."[26] Philippine scouts stormed through the gaps in the lines and met the Moros in their trenches. The fight was finally over by 4:30 p.m., with the surrender of the cotta. The battle resulted in fifteen Americans killed and twenty-five wounded. The number of Moros killed was never definitively established, but Pershing estimated between two hundred and three hundred people.[27]

Pershing's long game of disarming the Moros finally succeeded. The Battle of Bud Bagsak marked the end of Moro resistance in the district, allowing Pershing to return to the work he thought was much more important for the future of the Moro District—improving the lives of the indigenous peoples.

During the fight at Bud Bagsak, Pershing went above and beyond to place himself in the thick of battle, sometimes barking orders outside cotta walls as Moro fighters flung spears in his direction from as close as fifteen yards. Remaining cool under fire, his presence in the swirl of combat led his superiors to write multiple recommendations for him to receive the Medal of Honor. In one letter, Capt. George C. Charlton described how the brigadier general "personally assumed command of the firing line when matters looked desperate for our side and by his personal presence, encouragement, and example in the firing line" led his men to success on the field of battle.[28] Once the nomination was made, Pershing weighed in and opposed it, stating in humble terms, "I do not consider that my action on that occasion was such as to entitle me to be decorated with a Medal of Honor. I went to that part of the line because my presence there was needed."[29] His letter of protest ultimately did not matter, for the War Department's Decorations Board decided against issuing the medal before his missive was received.

In 1922, following World War I, after Pershing had distinguished himself as the leader of the Allied Expeditionary Forces, Congress created a new military medal, the Distinguished Service Cross. At that time, the Decorations Board took another look at Pershing's actions during the Bud Bagsak engagement and recommended that he receive the honor. Again, Pershing demurred. His decision was final, since he was his own chief of staff at the time, with the power to veto the board's decisions. In the end, President Franklin Roosevelt had the final say-so. In 1940, years after Pershing had retired from the military, Roosevelt invited the old general to the White House on his eightieth birthday, and the president awarded him the Distinguished Service Cross. The citation represented a nation's response, not merely to Pershing's fearless diligence as a commander during the Bud Bagsak battle, but also to his years of service in the Philippines, one of America's first imperialist experiments.

With the action at Bud Bagsak completed, Pershing's military efforts turned again to his work as a civilian governor.

For all Pershing's negotiations with the Moros, his actions may have spoken louder. Not only did he engage in limited military missions to further subdue recalcitrant datos and their followers, but he also worked hard to improve the lives of the average Moro. During his four years (1909–13) as the governor of the Moro Province, Pershing oversaw the building of two hundred miles of telephone lines and five hundred miles of much-needed roads. Many communities in his district were isolated and only accessible by narrow jungle trails. The new roads opened up these areas, and the appreciative Moros found they made it easier to transport their goods to sell in local markets and beyond.[30] The Moros wanted roads so badly that they did not simply applaud the American effort but also pitched in, with hundreds of Moros volunteering to work for free on road construction. Little improved the lives of the average Moro more than this extensive system of interconnecting roads.

Another Pershing improvement was the establishment of U.S.-built medical clinics and small hospitals. By the general's last year in the country, thirty-seven dispensaries were in operation, handing out medicines at cost to many of the Moro poor. Even the most hardened Moro opponent of the Americans gained an appreciation for the improved medical care they provided.

Education was always an important value to Pershing, having been a teacher in several schools before going to West Point and later attending university. He knew the best way to bring the Moros into the twentieth century was to provide them with a Western education. Nearly one of every six dollars that Pershing spent on the Moros went to building and providing schools for the local peoples. By 1913 twice as many Moro children (and some adults) attended U.S.-built schools as had attended in 1909. A shortage of teachers was sometimes a problem, but the education system was much improved over earlier models. Teaching English to the natives was an important aspect of the new education system, helping facilitate better communication.

Pershing even put his skills as a lawyer to work in the Philippines, something he had done through the Division of Insular Affairs a decade earlier when the island chain became a U.S. territory. One problem with the U.S. legal system in the district was the length of time that often elapsed between the arrest of an accused criminal, the trial, and the punishment in the case of conviction. The old system was based on the Moros' being tried in a Court of First Instance, an insular court that only met every six months. And before a case appeared before the Court of First Instance, an investigation was held in the local ward courts. The Moros did not understand why a "second" court was necessary and why it took so long for the whole process to transpire. Often the time between an alleged criminal action and a conviction was well over a year. Pershing changed the system, pushing a new law into effect that gave greater power to the local ward courts, allowing them to effectively deal definitively with most criminal and civil cases, except those involving capital punishment.

This was a system the Moros understood. The trials were closer to home, cases were handled swiftly, and local datos were often involved, since many were designated as local governors. The change was based on a combination of U.S. and Moro practices, further appealing to the Moros' sense of justice.

Connected to legal reform was the issue of prison reform. Pershing's administration opened a prison/work farm at San Ramon, situated thirteen miles outside Zamboanga. The 2,500-acre facility provided incarceration for convicted felons while operating a work program that supported much of the cost of the facility. In 1911 alone, the seventy inmates at San Ramon constructed a new building on the grounds, cleared land, and planted a grove of seventy-five thousand coconut trees. In just over a decade, the grove was so productive it supported the cost of the prison facility. By that time, the prison was home to nearly seven thousand inmates. The labor opportunities required of the prisoners also gave them valuable training and work experience.

Another reform established during the Pershing years was land redistribution. The Americans controlled a significant number of acres of workable land in Mindanao, so they took efforts to transfer ownership portions of land to peasants who did not own property. The concept was similar to the Homestead Act that the U.S. Congress passed in 1862 to encourage American and immigrant pioneers to settle the Great Plains. Moro settlers were prompted to claim a stake of land and to farm or otherwise improve it, and in time the property rights reverted to them. Pershing's ultimate goal through such programs was to float as many Moro boats as high as possible economically. In an interview he gave in 1911 to the *Sulu News*, a local newspaper, he said, "The [American] government does not desire riches for itself, but it desires the people to be rich. And I am sure that when the Moros understand this, they will heartily cooperate with the government. Indeed, they can hardly do otherwise, since when they help themselves in the proper way, they are carrying out the wishes of the government."[31]

All such efforts—the establishment of schools, the building of roads and bridges, the opening of hospitals, the revamping of the legal system—further improved the lives of the Moros, and Pershing was viewed as the American leader who provided these developments.

Not everyone in the Philippines, including some well-placed American officials and officers, appreciated all of Pershing's efforts. General Wood was often not supportive. Relations between the two were typically strained, as Wood was not a leader who liked being eclipsed. The American schools were criticized as inadequate. Pershing also was accused of spending too much money, as with his grand trade fair in February 1911 that cost the American taxpayers 50,000 pesos and did not manage a profit. The brigadier general was faulted for his weapons confiscation program as well, largely because he did not consult with anyone first, including Maj. Gen. J. Franklin Bell, the supreme commander of U.S. Army forces in the Philippines. But the praise he received outweighed the criticism by far. In fact, in November 1913, near the end of Pershing's tenure over the Moro District, Bell commended the brigadier: "I know of nothing connected with the service of General Pershing and the Army in Mindanao during the past three years which merits anything but praise."[32]

Pershing very nearly and neatly wound up his final military assignment in the Philippines with the complete subjugation of the Moros, including their requisite disarmament. By the end of the summer of 1913, however, he was struggling with health issues once again. August saw him in a Manila hospital with indigestion, a sore mouth, and chronic diarrhea. Once doctors were through with him, the army gave him his marching orders: he was to leave the Philippines as soon as possible. He packed up Frankie and the four children, and they prepared to return to the States. In a repeat of four years earlier, when the Pershings had departed Manila for America, a large crowd of well-wishers saw them off.

TWELVE

Calamity, 1913–16

The Pershings took passage on the transport *Sherman*. The ship was a wonderland to the children, and the family spent many days together on deck, watching sunsets and allowing the kids to run off excess energy. They celebrated Christmas Day at sea, and their holiday dinner included turkey and plum pudding for dessert. John and Frankie handed out Christmas gifts they had purchased before leaving Manila. Along the way, the family stopped in Hawaii and enjoyed some shore leave, taking in the tropical paradise that must have reminded them of the Philippines. Pershing's new posting was to San Francisco's Presidio, the most prestigious army post on the West Coast, and command of the Eighth Brigade. When the ship arrived, the children's grandfather Senator Warren was there to greet them home. He was so excited to see his grandchildren, he paid a tugboat captain to deliver him to the ship, where he climbed up a Jacob's ladder to hug them before the *Sherman* even docked.

The children had never known life in America, and Frankie was especially excited to be back after several years at foreign postings. Senator Warren had previously scouted out the available housing at the Presidio and suggested a large house with an expansive yard for the children. They moved in and started settling in at their new American home. They began taking in the local sights and otherwise enjoying the Bay Area. Not long after their arrival, Pershing took his children to see *Buffalo Bill's Wild West*, which was then touring with Sells Floto Circus. Buffalo Bill and Pershing had crossed paths years earlier in Nebraska, and the showman sent the general complimentary tickets. The show proved more than simple entertainment for Pershing, who was surprised to see some of the old Lakota scouts he had briefly commanded following the Ghost Shirt uprising in South Dakota had become performers in the *Wild West*. Several circled the arena as bareback stunt riders. Pershing reminisced, "It reminded me of old times to see those Redskins on the mock warpath again, and the children sat in wonder at this and other thrilling performances. The kiddies were in ecstasy."[1] Pershing's orderly, Frank Lanckton, who witnessed the brigadier as he spent time with his children, observed later, "What gave the Old Man his happiest moments ... was the presence of his family."[2]

But Pershing had barely made his mark as the commander at the Presidio before he received orders to move 3,500 members of the Eighth Brigade to El Paso, Texas. There was trouble on the border.

Once again, the American West provided the backdrop for Pershing's military career. Problems with America's neighbor to the south had been brewing for several years. Dating to 1876, Mexico was led by a harsh ruler named Porfirio Díaz, who maintained power through intimidation, utilizing his federal police troops (*federales*) and rural police forces to crush any opposition. He maintained control based on a policy he called *pan y palo* (bread and bludgeon). Díaz remained on his self-made throne until 1911. By that time, Mexico was home to fifteen million people, who were as racially mixed as the indigenous populations of the Philippines. Most were mestizos, persons of mixed blood, often including Indian and European stock. Approximately one out of three, though, were full-blooded Indians who identified with long-standing tribal groups.

In her novel *O Pioneers!*, Willa Cather paints a picture of Mexico City through the eyes of her character Emil, the younger brother of the novel's heroine, Alexandra. In a letter, Emil describes "the gay life in the old Mexican capital in the days when the strong hand of Porfirio Diaz was still strong. He told about bull-fights and cock-fights, churches and fiestas, the flower-markets and the fountains, the music and dancing, the people of all nations he met in the Italian restaurants on San Francisco Street." The novel was published in 1913, by which time the Mexican Revolution had forced an end to the long, dark days of the Díaz's regime.[3]

As Díaz's reign stretched into the twentieth century, he opened Mexico to foreign investment, especially to large-scale U.S. companies, which were often led by some of the wealthiest families, including the Hearsts, Rockefellers, Guggenheims, and others. American investors built Mexican railroads, opened mines, drilled oil wells, and bought cattle ranches and large farm spreads. The U.S. investment in the northern states of Chihuahua and Sonora brought increased power and wealth to Díaz without providing much economic gain to the Mexican poor, peasants who numbered in the millions.

In 1911 Mexican revolutionaries—including Francisco Indalecio Madero, an educated, wealthy landowner from Coahuila; Francisco "Pancho" Villa, a former cattle rustler who fought with an army of followers called Villistas in Chihuahua; and Pascual Orozco Jr., who led forces in the southern state of Morelos—overthrew Díaz. The popular Madero came to power, promising democracy and economic reform for millions of Mexican peasants—a light at the end of a long tunnel. Díaz was sent by train to Veracruz on the Gulf Coast, where he boarded a ship bound for Europe. On the train, the guard commander was Gen. Victoriano Huerta, a "bullet-headed [mestizo] Indian with weak eyes and a rumbling bass voice."[4] Díaz assured Huerta, "Now they will be convinced, by hard experience, that the only way to govern the country well is the way I did it." Although Díaz did not realize it at the time, he was offering political advice to a man who would one day be president of Mexico.[5]

Madero remained in office for sixteen months, from October 1911 until February 1913. Although the U.S. businesses invested in Mexico were uncertain how Madero's presidency might affect them, Woodrow Wilson supported Madero, whom he believed was a champion of democracy. (Wilson, of course, was only campaigning for the presidency during the time Madero was president.) But just before Wilson took office, Madero was assassinated through a conspiracy including Díaz's nephew Gen. Félix Díaz and others with support from U.S. ambassador Henry Lane Wilson. During the overthrow, Huerta switched to the rebels' side. (Madero had never gained full control of Mexico during his months in office, and he had relied on Huerta, who commanded the federales, to fight those who were disappointed in his leadership.) Huerta soon came to power.

While other world powers, such as Great Britain and Japan, recognized the new Huerta government, Wilson did not. Huerta's supporters had murdered Madero, and the new U.S. president could not sanction a government that came to power outside the rule of law. Meanwhile, in Mexico, the Constitutionalists, an opposition group led by Venustiano Carranza, took up arms against Huerta. President Wilson then tried to put himself in the middle of the revolution by offering to broker a compromise between the two warring sides, but neither group was interested. By 1914 Carranza was able to buy guns from the United States, as Wilson attempted to isolate Huerta by persuading the British to drop their support of the Mexican dictator in exchange for U.S. promises to protect British business interests in Mexico.

But Huerta stubbornly remained as president. Then, in the spring of 1914, the U.S. government took advantage of a trifling incident in the Mexican port of Tampico—a smelly industrial town riddled with U.S. oil refineries—where, on the morning of April 9, a small group of American sailors on the warship USS *Dolphin* rowed a supply boat to shore, received supplies at a local warehouse, and began loading them into their small vessel. A squad of Huerta's federales suddenly appeared and arrested the sailors, claiming they had illegally entered a military zone. Although they were soon released, the encounter became an international flash point, with President Wilson suddenly requesting congressional approval to use military force to "obtain from General Huerta and his adherents the fullest recognition of the rights and dignity of the United States."[6]

Soon, Wilson dispatched U.S. gunboats to the port city of Veracruz, blockading the harbor and cutting off Mexico's customs duties, a key source of income for the Huerta government. The Americans' presence also blocked the delivery of two hundred machine guns and fifteen million rounds of ammunition from a German vessel. U.S. forces bombed and then occupied the port of Veracruz. Nineteen Americans and 126 Mexicans were killed, plus sixty-three Americans and 195 Mexicans wounded, setting off a series of protests throughout Latin America. Argentina, Brazil, and Chile intervened to mediate a solution. Wilson agreed to the request from the "ABC Powers," but Carranza and his followers, the Carrancistas, soon managed to overthrow Huerta. As for the U.S. invasion at Veracruz, nothing could have consolidated anti-American sentiments across Mexico more. The German government agreed to provide Huerta passage out of Mexico on the German battle cruiser *Dresden*, and he left Mexico in July bound for Spain. By then he was dying of cirrhosis of the liver. He was later allowed to return to the Americas and died among relatives living in El Paso, Texas.

Once in power, Carranza did not consider Wilson to be a friend to Mexico; rather, he spoke out against the U.S. president's show of military power on his country's soil. Wilson was uncertain in which direction he should turn. For a while, he gave support to Pancho Villa, a former ally of Carranza's who had helped remove Huerta. Villa, dissatisfied with Carranza's leadership, turned on his former revolutionary comrade in September 1914 and continued to fight the Mexican government under Carranza's leadership.

Just as had happened under Madero's leadership, Carranza was constantly swatting at rebellious wasps. Much of Mexico devolved into violence and anti-government anarchy. The border region between the United States and Mexico became a lawless landscape where bandits and pistoleros—some may have actually been politically motivated—took advantage of the lack of government control and carried out raids on small villages, stopped and robbed trains, and killed isolated ranchers and miners, sometimes Americans. Rumors flew from Chihuahua to Sonora concerning such attacks and raids, and who was responsible. Pancho Villa was often blamed for the border violence. With rumors of planned raids by Villa supporters mounting, the U.S. government responded preemptively, summoning large numbers of troops to occupy the northern side of the border.

Pershing had the opportunity to meet the enigmatic Villa without even leaving El Paso. Since stories of his threats to the United States seemed more fancy than fact, Villa was able to cross the wooden International Bridge over the Rio Grande at his leisure and walk the streets of the U.S. border town. His greatest lure was the Elite Confectionery, where he indulged in some of the best ice cream on the border. In August 1914, Villa and Pershing crossed paths in the street as the Mexican pistolero was on his way to a conference in Nogales. Wanting to size up his potential foe, the brigadier invited him to Fort Bliss to witness a review of the troops, perhaps hoping to impress Villa with the scope of the U.S. presence on the Texas side. Villa accepted, and afterward the two men spent time in Pershing's quarters over drinks. The Mexican leader had entered the town wearing civilian clothes, not his field khakis, and Pershing could not help but notice how his guest's pockets bulged with several pistols. But Villa seemed the one ill at ease, perhaps uncomfortable in the presence of the American general. When his bodyguard, Rodolfo "the Butcher" Fierro, failed to take off his hat indoors, Villa dressed him down in front of Pershing: "Take off your hat, you brute, you animal!"[7] Before the two commanders parted, they posed for a photograph together on August 26, with Pershing smiling widely and Villa dressed in his Sunday best, a nervous smile barely visible beneath his well-trimmed black mustache. At Villa's right stands the uniformed Mexican general Alvaro Obregón. Posing to Pershing's left and just behind him is a young George S. Patton.

Pershing judged Villa variously. When his friend Carlo Husk

said something positive about Villa in Pershing's presence, the general agreed with him: "My impression of the general corresponds to your own. I think he will yet do great things for his beloved Mexico."[8] But Pershing also had a certain amount of skepticism concerning Villa. He likely thought in terms of his old strategies toward the Moro datos: make friends as you can, put your best foot forward, be ready for anything, deal from a position of strength. Without question, when Pershing engaged with Mexicans in El Paso, they were pleased that the general "spoke Spanish and had a personality that the Mexicans liked, being what they called 'simpatico.'"[9]

The threat that had delivered Pershing and the Eighth Brigade seemed to have evaporated, so the brigadier and his men settled into their station at Fort Bliss. As Pershing's Texas exile extended into months with no end in sight, Frankie took the children to Cheyenne and enrolled the two oldest girls, Helen and Anne, in school. While she and John were in the Philippines, Frankie's father had remarried. His new wife, Clara, was nearly as young as Frankie, but the two got along well. Pershing took the train to Wyoming as often as he could.

Time moved slowly in El Paso, and Pershing kept his men busy with drills and field practices and inspections. Pershing developed a regular routine, taking tea every afternoon at four thirty at the Hotel Sheldon, where newspaper reporters knew they could find him. He received constant letters from Frankie and even from his children. Frankie had become a bowling enthusiast, playing well, and sent Pershing her bowling scores. Pershing spent time reading newspapers describing the early action in a completely different theater of conflict. Europe had descended into war by late summer of 1914, and despite President Wilson's insistence that the Unites States remain neutral, Pershing, though his roots were German, was decidedly supportive of the Allies. In May 1915 the sinking of the British passenger liner *Lusitania* by U-20, a German submarine, galled him. He could not help expressing his outrage in a private letter to Frankie: "What do you suppose a weak, chicken-hearted, white-livered lot as we have in Washington are going to do? ... Good God, deliver us from the disgrace of the present administration. It makes me ashamed to be in its service.... We need strong and courageous men at the head of affairs and not meek sops."[10] Pershing was speaking not just of President Wilson but also of his secretary of state, Pershing's old acquaintance from his days at the University of Nebraska, William Jennings Bryan. A few days following the liner's sinking, Wilson spoke to a crowd in Philadelphia and seemed as appeasing as ever to the brigadier general. In another letter to Frankie written three days later, Pershing was beside himself: "I suppose he is trying to outdo Bryan in idiocy.... Deliver us from theorists and sophists and psalm singers. I had rather die on the field of battle supporting the right than live a thousand years in dishonorable peace.... Oh, Lord, all this makes my blood boil."[11]

Wilson was Pershing's commander in chief, so the brigadier had to remain cautious of any public criticism of the president. He could not then know what future relationship the two American leaders would share once the expanding war in Europe finally drew in the United States as a combatant.

Within a few weeks of the *Lusitania*'s sinking, Pershing decided he had been apart from his family long enough. "I'm tired of living alone," he informed a friend. "I'm having my quarters fixed up so that my wife and children can join me."[12] Taking a period of leave, he boarded a train to Cheyenne, scooped up his family, and returned with them to the Presidio. Frankie was to pack up their belongings, as Pershing no longer felt that his service in Texas required him to remain apart from his loved ones. While John returned to Fort Bliss, Frankie and the children stayed behind so Mrs. Pershing could fulfill a few obligations before leaving for the American Southwest. She had agreed to work as a volunteer at the Montessori education booth at the Panama-Pacific International Exposition.[13] She also attended the Wellesley West Coast alumnae meeting held on August 25 at the exposition's Massachusetts Building.

Frankie was a featured speaker. On the night of the event, she spoke of how her days at Wellesley had prepared her for her life's experiences, which had certainly been full, since her marriage to General Pershing. She gave great credit to her alma mater, saying it "has helped me in every kind of crisis, great or small, from the time they brought me and laid in my arms my first baby, to the time I backed out of an audience with the emperor of Japan in a train twelve yards long."[14] The evening represented a personal triumph for Frankie Pershing, the last of a life soon cut short.

The Pershings' house at the Presidio was full on the night of August 26–27. Frankie, fresh from her Wellesley speech, had several guests, including her Wellesley roommate and maid of honor, Anne Orr Boswell; her two children; and Mrs. Margaretta Gray Church, an old friend of Frankie's late mother, who had worked the Montessori booth with Frankie. That evening, the six children were tucked into bed early while the three friends stayed up and talked in the parlor, putting off their bedtime until nearly midnight.

At some time between two and three o'clock in the morning, Anne Boswell woke to a glimmer of light beneath her bedroom door. She rose to investigate and found the hallway filled with smoke and the staircase engulfed in flames to the second floor. She called out, "Frank! Frank!" but received no answer. The smoke was so thick in the hall she retreated into her room. Her children were in a different room, so she hurriedly climbed out a window, walked along the roofline to the adjacent bedroom, and struck the glass, shattering the pane onto the floor. Her maid awoke; roused the two boys, ages six and three; and joined their mother on the roof. Meanwhile, Mrs. Church awakened, was alarmed by the smoke and fire, and managed to escape through a bathroom window. Soldiers were already gathering outside, having spotted the flames and heard the alarm bell. They soon rescued everyone on the roof. Anne tossed her boys down to the soldiers, while her maid leaped into a flowerbed. They were taken to the officers' club to recover.

For a moment, those gathered outside the house believed everyone was safely out, assuming the women and children included Mrs. Pershing and her little ones. Precious minutes were lost while firemen shot great streams of water at the house and made no attempt to ensure no one was still inside.

"Thank God there's nobody left in there," a witness observed. "The damned old firetrap might as well burn right down."[15]

Then, someone from the officers' club arrived to tell the firemen the Pershing family was still inside the blazing house. Panic soon spread as the men realized the Pershing family had not made it out of the dwelling. Soldier-firefighters rushed in. Three climbed up on the roof and entered through a bedroom window. Inside, they felt their way through the smoke. Pvt. Fred Newscome stumbled over a child lying on the hallway floor—Warren, Pershing's only son. He was unconscious. The firefighters picked him up and handed him off to others waiting on the roof. The men then returned to the hallway, which was teeming with smoke, and tried other bedroom doors. All were locked, and no one responded to the men's shouts. The smoke finally drove them from the hallway to the outside and fresh air.

Meanwhile, hope still lingered. Other firemen had reached the porch roof and opened a front bedroom window. Inside, the men found two girls, Helen and Mary, in one bedroom, and Frankie and Anne were in the adjacent one. They were all still in their beds and gave the appearance of restful sleep. The flames had not reached their rooms, but they were filled with heavy smoke. None had awakened before succumbing to smoke inhalation.

Once Frankie and the girls were taken outside, attempts were made to revive them. But their lives were over. The only saving grace was that their bodies had not been charred beyond recognition. At least Pershing would have the opportunity to see his girls one more time, even if the opportunity represented the greatest tragedy.

In the days following the unfortunate and deadly fire at the Presidio, the *San Francisco Chronicle* ran a front-page editorial, signed by the publisher, condemning the state of housing at the military compound. The house the Pershing family occupied had an appalling reputation as a firetrap, "a flimsy shack built forty years ago, destitute of modern safety appliances and sanitary improvements."[16] Changes should have already been made, given that previous house fires at the Presidio also had proven fatal, with two women and three children dying. These earlier tragedies "should have aroused the government to the necessity of guarding against the horror which the last accident has brought it face to face with."[17]

How the fire started was answered upon an examination of the burned-out remains of the house. Live coals had rolled out of a corner grate in the family's dining room and had landed on the newly waxed floor. The same thing had happened a few days earlier but during daylight hours, and someone had noticed before any real danger had happened. While much of the house had burned in the next instance, the real problem for Frankie and the children had been the smoke.

Then a second tragedy followed the first. A house fire at the Presidio was considered news, and local sources reported on the fire, with early reports going out on the wire services. In the offices of the *El Paso Herald*, a pair of reporters—Norman Walker, an Associated Press correspondent, and Hubert S. Hunter, the news editor at the *Herald*—read the story when it arrived on the newspaper's teletype. The original story told of a fire at the Presidio that had destroyed the home of the Pershings. A later wrap-up included the deaths of the Pershing family with the exception of young Warren. By that time, Walker thought General Pershing, whom he knew, must surely have received the news officially. He called Fort Bliss, was patched through to Pershing's quarters, and heard a voice on the line. Thinking it was Lt. James L. Collins, the general's aide, Walker said, "Lieutenant Collins, I have some more news of the Presidio fire."

The voice replied, "What fire? What has happened?"

Only then did Collins realize he was speaking directly to the one person he did not want to have on the telephone—General Pershing, who was obviously not aware of the fire.

Pershing repeated himself: "What fire?"

Having no other options, Walker then informed the general of the details. He read aloud to him the wrap-up, which included the deaths of all his family save for Warren.

Instinctively, unthinkingly, Pershing said, "Oh, God! My God! What's that? Read it again!"

Once more, Walker read the news to the general, who was only then beginning to absorb the true meaning of what he was hearing.

"My God! My God! Can it be true?" asked Pershing.

All Walker could manage was to tell the general he was sorry for confusing him with Lieutenant Collins and offered his personal condolences. Pershing then spoke.

"Wait a minute. Who is this? Who am I speaking to?"

Walker said who he was. Then Pershing spoke his last words during the tragic phone call: "Thank you, Walker. It was very considerate of you to phone."[18]

Soon, Pershing and Lieutenant Collins were on a train bound westward for San Francisco. In Bakersfield, John's friend Frank A. Helm joined him and accompanied the grieving general to the Presidio. They reached the city at eight thirty on the morning of August 29. During the trip, Pershing broke down repeatedly, wailing in tears, struggling to absorb the full implications of his loss. Helm later said of his friend, "I really believe that if Warren had also been lost, Pershing would have lost his mind."[19]

Once in the city, Pershing went straight to the funeral parlor to view the bodies of his wife and girls. After a few moments, he asked to be left alone in the room. Friends went out but kept an eye on him, uncertain of his mental state. They watched as he fell to his knees and prayed at the foot of each casket, taking several minutes at each one. The man from Laclede, whose mother raised him with the Gospel in her voice, who grew up seated with his family in a Methodist pew, and who, as an adult, maintained a faith more formulaic than fervent, bowed his head in the most agonizing moment of his entire life and sought God's peace. He and Frankie had worshiped together as Episcopalians and had made certain their children were baptized. Of all the decisions he had made throughout his long life, he was likely most comforted by that single expression of hope in Jesus.

From the funeral parlor, he went immediately to the site of the tragedy. The night of the fire, Frankie and baby Mary Margaret were sleeping in the front, second-floor bedroom, with sisters Helen and Anne in the adjoining bedroom. Warren was in a room separated from the others by a bathroom. Since Mary had been sick with a cold, Frankie had closed the windows in both adjoining rooms, but to provide some airflow, she had opened the doors to both rooms, including those leading to the back staircase. When the fire broke out downstairs, the airflow through the rooms pulled in the billowing smoke, asphyxiating Frankie and her daughters. In Mrs. Boswell's room and in Warren's room, the windows had been left open. Anne and her boys had escaped, as had Warren, but he had fallen unconscious in the hall trying to get out.

As Pershing walked through the smoke-blackened hall, he saw the full scope of events that tragically transpired that night. "I am now satisfied that nothing could have been done. They had no chance. I wanted to see that for myself."[20]

Pershing's third stop was at Letterman Army Hospital, where he was reunited with his six-year-old son. During the car ride to the Hotel Stewart, the father held the son tightly on his knee. Warren was still not informed of the full tragedy and the fate of his mother and siblings. As the car drove past the International Exposition, Pershing asked Warren if he had been to the fair.

"Oh, yes," he replied. "Mama takes us a lot."[21]

Once again, Pershing broke down, sobbing uncontrollably. Frank Helm took the boy in his arms.

Episcopalian funeral services were held late that day, a Sunday, and Pershing dressed in a black suit. Senator and Mrs. Warren were in attendance. The bodies of John's wife and children were then transferred by train on the Overland Limited to Cheyenne for burial in the Warren family plot.

The weeks that followed represented a shadowy valley for Pershing. There were endless letters and telegrams offering condolences from friends, family, and comrades, as well as some unlikely others. One such telegram read, "With enormous sorrow I heard that your estimable family had the misfortune to perish in a house fire and for this unfortunate accident permit me to send my sincerest condolences. Yours faithfully." The message was signed "Pancho Villa."[22] Pershing went through the family's belongings and wept over the personal effects shipped to him at Fort Bliss. His sister May, who never married, moved to be with him through this sad time. He kept Warren close by, but as it was impossible for his young son to live with him at the fort, Pershing then asked May and their sister Bess, a widow by that time, to take the boy to live with them in Lincoln, Nebraska.

Just two weeks before her tragic death, Frankie had written a letter to her beloved Jack. Its lines were filled with the same sweet sentiments as always but with a pall of irony since she and the girls were gone from Jack's life forever: "The world is so clean in the morning—there is the sound of meadow larks everywhere. And God be thanked for the sunshine and the blue sky! . . . Do you think there can be many people in the world as happy as we are? I would like to live to be a thousand years old if I could spend all of that time with you." It was the last letter he received from her.[23] She was only thirty-five years old.

For a decade, Frankie had served as the light in John's eye, his tender tether to a world of love and children. He had become a man who loved, singularly, a woman who was every bit his equal, who had domesticated his spirit, and who had joined him at posts from the Presidio to Tokyo to Zamboanga. No one would ever touch the better angels of his nature than had his beloved Wellesley girl from Wyoming.

THIRTEEN

Chase, 1916–17

By 1915 the Carrancistas defeated Pancho Villa, and President Wilson chose to recognize Venustiano Carranza as the legitimate leader, the "first chief" of Mexico. With a relatively stable base of political power, Carranza's troops managed to gradually gain limited control over northern Mexico at the expense of Villa's men. Soon, the Mexican pistolero realized he was losing both the political and the military fight in his own backyard. But Villa was not yet a completely spent cartridge. He remained in the north, in Chihuahua, where he served as a thorn in Carranza's side. In need of revenue and in response to Wilson's support of the Carranza regime, Villa sometimes targeted U.S. interests, which were often unpopular among the region's peasants. In January 1916 Villa stopped a train in Chihuahua, pulled sixteen American miners off, ordered them to strip off their clothes, and shot them in cold blood. While such moves seemed reckless to politicians on both sides of the border, Villa likely had a plan in mind. If he could embarrass Carranza by killing Americans in the north, he could accomplish two goals at once: to make Carranza appear as a weak leader unable to control his own territory and to encourage U.S. intervention into Mexico, a move that would likely be extremely unpopular with the people of Mexico. Such military action might provide

Villa an opportunity to further assert his presence at Carranza's expense. To that end, he planned a bold gambit.

Through the cool, desert darkness of a spring night, Pancho Villa and nearly five hundred of his men crossed the lonely border between Chihuahua and the United States. It was just after 1 a.m. on Thursday, March 9. The men were well armed and ready to surprise their victims. They rode as quietly across the inky landscape as two thousand horse hooves could carry them and saw only a few moving lights in the far-off distance, eerie train lamps snaking their way in opposite directions from one another across the flatlands. Villa's men split into three columns, with two flanking groups to support the main column, as they prepared to descend on a small, sleepy New Mexican town.

Columbus was a dust-covered, desert outcropping and a remote border town whose permanent inhabitants numbered in the hundreds. Col. Andrew O. Bailey, who lost an arm during the Civil War, named the community Columbus during the early 1890s in recognition of the four hundredth anniversary of Columbus's discovery of America. The town could not boast a single tree along its streets, which were little more than dusty lanes dividing a handful of storefronts and weather-beaten houses from one another. Adobe was a favorite building material, and the sun-dried bricks were fashioned from mud, small stones, and hay. Out from those streets and in every direction, the landscape ran monotonously brown, punctuated here and there by broken-backed cacti and scrawny clusters of mesquite. The only significant interruption in the land was a trio of cone-shaped mountains to the northwest known as the Tres Hermanas, the "Three Sisters." The community's lifeline was the El Paso and Southwestern Railroad, which bisected the town and ran east for seventy-five miles to El Paso, Texas, where John Pershing had been assigned to Fort Bliss.

Life was possible—if not preferable for most—in Columbus, and the arrival of the U.S. Army a few years earlier provided the remote community with a significant shot in the arm. South of the railroad line was Camp Furlong, home to several hundred enlisted men. Their presence increased the local population in 1916 to close to 1,300 souls, enough to justify the existence of "three hotels, a bank, drugstore, livery stable, two restaurants, and several general stores."[1] Columbus also had several churches, schools, and even a newspaper office. The town had a few automobiles, even if the outlying territory was short on roads. Owners sometimes rented out their autos for twenty-five cents a mile, plus one dollar for every hour of "standing time," the tourist equivalent of leaving the auto and sightseeing on foot.

Just outside the town, Villa's main column hid in a long, deep arroyo close to a railroad bridge. "We were finally so close to the tracks that when the train passed, we were able to see the passengers in the coaches," recalled Maud Wright, an American woman who had been captured and kidnapped by the Villistas several days earlier from her ranch in northern Mexico.[2] Around 4 a.m., as Villa ordered the attack on Columbus, his men rode in hard, shouting, "Viva Villa! Viva Mexico! Matemos a los gringos!" (Let's kill the gringos!) Announcing the attack, Mexican bugles blared across the arroyo.

The Mexican buglers were soon competing with lower-pitched U.S. Cavalry bugles, signaling troopers to take up arms. Out in the darkness, up on a nearby hill, someone played the song "La Cucaracha," one of Villa's favorites.

For the next three or so hours, the Mexican attackers rampaged through the short streets and alleyways of Columbus, looting as many stores and businesses as they could and killing civilians, including a few soldiers. The looting was an important part of the raid. Mexican fighters moved on the bank, while others hit the train station. They broke through the doors of the Commercial Hotel and took everything they could. In the dry goods stores, the raiders threw off their dusty clothing and put on new pants and shirts. Everything on store shelves was fair game. From the local jeweler, they lifted rings, watches, lockets, cuff links, small bags of jewels, nine boxes of chocolates, and a jar filled with chewing gum. They raided stores, taking those items representing their stock in trade: saddles, blankets, pistols, gun scabbards, and ammunition. From another, they stole clothing, bed sheets, ladies' shoes, handkerchiefs, and men's underwear. One special target was Sam Ravel, a local gun dealer whom Villa thought had cheated him on a previous weapons buy. Ravel had taken about $2,500 from Villa for weapons he had never produced. As attacker Juan Muñoz explained years later in an interview, "We did not go to Columbus to kill women and children as it has been said. We went to Columbus to take Sam Ravel and burn his properties for the robbery and treason which he committed. *Esa es la verdad* [That's the truth]." As for Ravel, the Villistas had no opportunity to exact revenge on the person of the Columbus merchant, as he was out of town for a dentist appointment in El Paso.

Camp Furlong was home to the Thirteenth U.S. Cavalry regiment, and the garrison included 345 soldiers and civilians. Villa had managed to surprise the community completely, but the response from the residents of Columbus, including the troopers, was quick and relentless. Not only was the town hit, but Camp Furlong was targeted as well. A soldier ran out into the street early during the attack, shouting at the Villistas. He took a shot to the stomach but fired off several shots, killing three pistoleros before dying. Over at the cook's shack at the fort, army cooks emerged in the predawn light, firing shotguns at the Mexicans. As the attack continued, the cooks slung boiling water at the assailants; then, swinging axes, they engaged in hand-to-hand street fighting. Elsewhere at the fort, troopers converged on the supply shack and retrieved their thirty-pound, French-made Benét-Mercié machine guns, which they set up near the railroad tracks. One machine gun was placed atop the town's water tower and another on a nearby rise called Cootes Hill. This type of machine gun was a finicky model that required expert hands, which were not present at Camp Furlong. Instead of using belts of ammunition, they were loaded with long, stiff stripper clips. In the early morning darkness, it was too easy to accidentally insert the clips into the guns upside down. Jamming proved a problem, but the Benét-Mercié operators managed to fire off at least twenty thousand rounds, which dramatically elevated the number of Villa's pistoleros killed.

Other soldiers shot from cover around the fort and, along with some civilians, in the town. The wife of Col. Herbert Slocum, the commander at the fort, remembered, "The bullets were falling like rain."[3]

Pancho Villa remained in the eye of the storm. Maud Wright later wrote how Villa "had been in the thick of the fight, for many times I heard his stallion squeal from some particularly noisy section of town."[4] At some point, his horse was shot out from under him, and one of his men soon provided him with another horse. Some of Villa's energy was spent forcing his men to remain in the fight, as he rode down streets, slashing his sword at them.

After two hours of wild gunfire, the Villistas rode or ran off into the desert toward the Mexican border that lay only a few miles away. A detachment of cavalry numbering approximately sixty men gave chase, pursuing the enemy for several miles. They managed to kill several dozen before returning to the fort, having run out of food and water.

As they returned, the troopers saw a pall of smoke hanging over Columbus before they could see even a single house or business. The Mexican raiders had torched much of the village. The fires spread quickly, destroying many buildings. The Commercial Hotel burned rapidly due to the combustion of kerosene and gasoline stored close by in a Ravel-owned warehouse. A few hours of fighting ended with casualties on both sides. The people of Columbus mourned the loss of nine civilians and eight soldiers. The invaders paid dearly, with their dead numbering between two hundred and three hundred men. Some of the smoke hanging in the warm desert air wasn't from burning wood and hay but from human flesh; dead Villistas were collected, piled into a nearby arroyo, doused with kerosene, and set afire, just as the raiders had burned the lonely American outpost.

No one in Columbus had any doubts who was responsible for the Mexican raid on their community. After all, Maud Wright, whom Villa set free before the raid, had spoken to Villa himself. If irrefutable proof was required, American troopers, while collecting items among the dead pistoleros after the battle, found a pair of saddlebags in which they discovered a letter from Francisco Villa addressed to Emilio Zapata, a revolutionary leader in southern Mexico. In the text, Villa encouraged Zapata "to march north and join in the attack on the U.S."[5]

Pancho Villa and his ragtag force of hundreds of pistoleros had pulled off a surprise attack on the town of Columbus and the troopers stationed at nearby Camp Furlong. The soldiers at the fort might have been better prepared for the attack if their commander, Colonel Slocum, had taken Juan Favela, a local Hispanic cowboy, more seriously. The day before the attack, Favela, who worked for the local ranch Palomas Land & Cattle Company, had been out in the afternoon sun, riding the line and looking for stray cattle. (The American ranch stretched across the Mexican border.) Cresting a hill, Favela spotted a large force of Villa's pistoleros in the distance, heading north. He spurred his horse and headed toward Columbus. At the Mexican customs station, he warned local Carrancista soldiers of the presence of Villa's men; then he headed to Fort Furlong to inform Colonel Slocum. He told the American officer that "they were heading for the border; they were just south of Palomas; they would raid Columbus before dawn."[6] Slocum sent Favela on his way, encouraging him to go and get a drink to calm his hysteria. Even without Favela's warning, the army commander should have put his men on alert. Between July 1915 and June 1916, Mexican bandits, including Villa's men, engaged in thirty-eight raids on U.S. targets. Signs had been in the wind of the Villistas' moving closer to the U.S. border back in February. To an extent, the Americans were at the mercy of the local Carrancista garrison for information about Villa and other potential raiders, but its information was spotty and often spurious. As for any long-term blame falling on Colonel Slocum, given his failure to prepare for such an attack, an army investigation cleared him later that year.

As the smoke of the Columbus raid dissipated, one question soon circulated: why had Pancho Villa crossed the international border and carried out a raid against an American community, knowing his actions would be condemned by U.S. officials as well as the American people? To Villa, it was a matter of desperate expediency. He had lost out in assuming any real leadership of the Mexican revolution to Carranza. He felt betrayed, left behind, and Balkanized to a status so inconsequential he chose to lash out in a way that would place him at the center of already-strained relations between Mexico and the United States. Wilson had abandoned him for his rival, Carranza. In Villa's mind, through the Columbus raid, he delivered dual blows at the expense of both the U.S. and Mexican presidents. They, he believed, had much more to lose than he.[7]

The Americans' attention fell upon Pancho Villa within hours of the Columbus attack. Electricity delivered the news to telegraph keys across the country. Within less than twenty-four hours, the Wilson White House issued a press release that included his name: "An adequate force will be sent at once in pursuit of Villa and with the single object of capturing him and putting a stop to his forays. This can and will be done in entirely friendly aid of the constituted authorities in Mexico and with scrupulous respect for the sovereignty of that Republic." Within two days of the attack, the press picked up the story, running headlines that mirrored the *New York American*'s banner: "FUNSTON TOLD TO GET VILLA DEAD OR ALIVE!"[8]

"Funston" was Maj. Gen. Frederick R. Funston, the commanding general of the Southern Division headquartered at San Antonio, Texas. The day following the attack, he received orders from the War Department in response to Villa's raid: "You will promptly organize an adequate military force under the command of General J. J. Pershing and will direct him to proceed promptly across the border in pursuit of the Mexican band which attacked the town of Columbus."[9]

Pershing was the immediate and unquestioned choice of his superiors for the mission to chase down Villa and his men. Chief of Staff of the Army Gen. Hugh Scott and Assistant Chief of Staff Tasker Bliss both thought he was their man. Pershing later claimed he was selected to command the expedition into Mexico because he "was simply on the ground and more available than anyone else," but few men previously assigned to the Southwest had as much experience as Pershing.[10] Although Funston held higher rank, he was younger than Pershing, and rumors of his personal drinking problems pointed Pershing's superiors in John's direction.

Such a campaign of intervention into Mexico caught the War Department a bit off guard. Most contingency plans focused more on a landing at coastal sites such as Veracruz, not on a border crossing along a lonely stretch of desert between old and New Mexico.[11] There was even some confusion between the men who spoke for President Wilson and the top military men. Funston had announced a campaign to destroy Villa's roving bands of pistoleros, while Secretary of War Newton D. Baker, who took over the role the day following the Villa raid, cast the mission with an important difference: "The President has directed that an armed force be sent into Mexico with the sole object of capturing Villa and preventing any further raids by his band, and with scrupulous regard to the sovereignty of Mexico." The difference is more than slight. It would be one thing for Pershing to accomplish the breakup of Villista bands across northern Mexico, but engaging in a mission to capture one man (similar to the modern military's former objective of neutralizing Osama bin Laden) would prove a much more difficult task. The difference would also frame later interpretations of Pershing's mission to Mexico regarding his ultimate success or lack there of.[12]

Pershing arrived in Columbus late in the day on March 13, just four days following the Villa raid. He had already selected the units he intended to utilize for the Mexican campaign, including the Seventh Cavalry (Custer's old unit), the Tenth (Pershing's former command of African American troopers), the Eleventh Cavalry, and the Thirteenth Cavalry. Infantry units included the Sixth and Sixteenth, and a pair of batteries of the Sixth Field Artillery. (The Sixth and Sixteenth had formed the Eighth Brigade, which Pershing had taken to El Paso from the Presidio.) Following this Punitive Expedition, with America's entrance into World War I, the general would take the Eighth Brigade and the Sixth Field Artillery to France as half of the First Division, which was one of his favorite units. Without realizing such at the time, Pershing began to shape in Mexico the units that he would lead in the Great War.[13]

One young lieutenant who may have reminded Pershing of himself in earlier days practically stalked the brigadier, looking for an assignment with the expedition. At Fort Bliss, Pershing could hardly enter his office without the eager junior officer begging for a command.

"Everyone wants to go," Pershing reminded him one day. "Why should I favor you?"

The response was immediate and fervent: "Because I want to go more than anyone else."[14]

Pershing finally relented. He called the relentless lieutenant and asked when he could report for his duty assignment. The young man told the brigadier he was already packed and ready. Just as Pershing had harassed superiors and influential friends for his inclusion in the Cuban campaign nearly twenty years earlier, so a young George Patton had done the same. Pershing made him a personal aide.[15] Patton was only one of several young officers who came under Pershing's direct guidance during the expedition, and some would play significant roles in World War I or World War II or—as in Patton's case—both.

Even as Pershing selected and organized his various units of infantry, artillery, and cavalry, when the time came for him and his men to move across the border into hostile territory, they were accompanied, as armies have throughout history, by a varied collection of hangers-on; others attached themselves to the military columns intent on chasing down Villa. Historian Gene Smith notes, "The Old West gathered for its final moment in the sun, old-time trappers and prospectors hiring out to the army as guides through uncharted Chihuahua, Apaches who knew the area, gunfighters looking to sign on, muleteers and college boys and taxi drivers, assorted hands who wanted to exchange a seat on a cow pony for one behind a steering wheel on one of thirty trucks swiftly purchased."[16]

Pershing cut his military teeth through assignments on the

frontier of the American Southwest, and now, as he returned, his career had come full circle. The desert recognizes no political borders. For Pershing, the expedition represented his final cavalry ride through the same deserts where he had discovered excitement and fulfillment as a young trooper. His return placed him at the head of four thousand American men, leading a mission that, while it resembled much that signified his past, would help prepare him for his future on another foreign field.

Any military officer worth his salt assigned to organize such a complicated military expedition across the border into hostile Mexican territory knew that the challenges would prove extraordinary. Just the problems of transportation and supply represented a logistics hydra. The land of northern Mexico was barely different since the Spanish explorer Coronado had passed through during the early 1540s. The state of Chihuahua stretched across desert and mountain country, covering a total of ninety-four thousand square miles. In the east, a great plateau occupied 80 percent of the state, its barren alkaline flats and sandy plains cut occasionally by short barren hills. On the western side, the Sierra Madre chain rose to an elevation of ten thousand feet, a great interior barrier that was only passable through a series of jagged, disconnected canyons. "The country itself was an enemy," observes historian Richard O'Connor, "wrinkled and tawny as the skin of a dead lion."[17] James L. Collins, one of Pershing's aides, even suggested a subterranean passageway to the Sahara Desert must connect the desert lands of Chihuahua. The desert was filled with inhospitable creatures, including scorpions and deadly snakes. Lieutenant Patton killed a pair of rattlesnakes in a single morning, dispatching them with his pistol rather than his saber, as that weapon, he claimed, was only to be used when on horseback.

In her novel *Death Comes for the Archbishop*, Willa Cather describes the landscape Pershing and his men would soon enter to track down Pancho Villa. Although Cather's description is set in mid-nineteenth-century Mexico, little had seemingly changed in the intervening seventy years, except for a couple of railroads crisscrossing the landscape: "There are no wagon roads, no canals, no navigable rivers. Trade is carried on by means of pack-mules, over treacherous trails. The desert down there has a peculiar horror; I do not mean thirst, nor Indian massacres, which are frequent. The very floor of the world is cracked open into countless canyons and arroyos, fissures in the earth which are sometimes ten feet deep, sometimes a thousand. Up and down these stony chasms the traveler and his mules clamber as best they can. It is impossible to go far in any direction without crossing them."[18]

Even though Pershing's expedition included automobiles and trucks, the landscape proved as formidable to negotiate as it had in the days of Father Jean Marie Latour, the novel's priestly protagonist. Plus, the railroads were off limits to the Americans.

The weather represented a daily variable, with anything from dust storms to sudden snow squalls possible, depending on the season. Springtime in northern Mexico presented daily weather extremes of relentlessly burning sun followed by freezing nights. Trails barely scratched the ancient landscape, and the few roads were often unpassable by horse, much less by unreliable automobiles and trucks. These primitive land routes were all unpaved, leaving Mother Nature to determine whether a traveler struggled over hard, sun-baked ruts or wallowed in mud following sudden rainstorms that turned every dry cut in the ground into its own waterway. Even if a man could find forage for his horses or mules, the environment pushed hard against livestock. The state of Chihuahua was known as grass country, but the land had not seen rain for ten months. When Pershing's men set out into this barren country, things were drier than normal, and summer grass seemed a lifetime away. Everything on the path of the Americans was parched, dry as sun-struck bone. A further complication was a lack of adequate maps of the region. As Funston reported, "There is no part of Mexico which is more poorly mapped than the northwest section of Chihuahua."[19]

Thirty years earlier, when Pershing had served as a green West Point grad in a trio of New Mexican forts, railroads had minimized the relative remoteness of the region. Chihuahua featured two lengthy railroads. The Mexico North-Western Railway ran out of El Paso, cut diagonally southwestward across Chihuahua to Casas Grandes, and then curved back to the east to the city of Chihuahua, forming a reverse capital D. The Mexican International Railroad also ran out of El Paso and headed nearly straight south to Chihuahua and then farther southward. These rail lines could have saved Pershing's columns much difficulty in maintaining supply, troop movement, and logistical support if they had been available to him. But Carranza denied Pershing and his forces the use of both. Without rail service to facilitate the movement of his men and matériel, the brigadier moved through northern Mexico with one hand tied behind his back.

Columbus became the primary supply depot for the Punitive Expedition. Supplies poured in by wagon and by rail—Pershing had complete access to the line running out of El Paso—and soon the little hamlet, already nearly burned out and struggling, was inundated with freight cars filled with supplies. Since the trains arrived ahead of the bills of lading, Pershing faced the chaotic supply situation of Tampa all over again, if only on a smaller scale. Transport of equipment, food, and supplies was sometimes accomplished with the durable vehicle synonymous with the American West—the covered wagon. Otherwise, the army moved supplies by a new mode of transportation.

The U.S. Army already began to transition from wagons to motor vehicles by 1900 and trucks by 1902. When Pershing prepared to mount his expedition across the border, he had access to trucks and a few automobiles, as well as motorcycles and a handful of airplanes. The planes were practically experimental, and the handful that were assigned to the Punitive Expedition were used for communications and reconnaissance, not as combat planes.[20] Given the number of his troops, the general knew he must rely on trucks, not the pack mules he had employed in an earlier era in the Southwest. On March 25 he reported he would need approximately 118 trucks to deliver seventy-five thousand pounds of rations and grain *daily* to a U.S. depot he established at Casas Grandes. (Also known as

Paquimé, the site was home to the ancient Mogollon culture and is today renowned for its skilled potters, those who produce delicate Mata Ortiz works reminiscent of their ancestors' ceramics.) By mid-April he had 160 trucks operating in theater, but they were too few to meet his daily needs. By late June more than 200 additional trucks—including models from Packard, Locomobile, Peerless, Four-Wheel Drive, and others—were in desert service.[21] A truck company during Pershing's expedition into Mexico typically included thirty-three trucks and only one automobile. Drivers proved scarce. One driver assigned from an artillery unit had never driven previously. He read up on it, took a couple of hands-on lessons, and spoke of his truck and fuel as one would a horse and hay.

In this first time the U.S. Army utilized large numbers of trucks in a full-fledged field operation, they proved extremely valuable to Pershing. They faced many problems, both technical and logistical, however. In a sense, their use in the field was largely experimental. Mexican roads were a constant challenge. As Pershing later reported, "The wheels of heavily loaded trucks sank deep into the friable alkali soil and cut great furrows that filled to the level with dust ground as fine as powder."[22] With the roads in such poor condition, several engineer units spent the lion's share of their time rebuilding them. Still, overall, the Punitive Expedition provided Pershing and other American officers with extensive and practical insights into the possibilities of motor transport through its use in the field under a variety of weather and topographical conditions. With the entrance of the United States into World War I following closely on the heels of the Mexican campaign, these memories and experiences were fresh and not yet forgotten.

Pershing dispatched three parallel columns of troops across the border on March 15. Within a few days, the columns converged at Colonia Dublán. Then, beginning at 3 a.m. on March 18, Col. James B. Erwin and 675 men of the Seventh Cavalry rode southward in search of Villa.[23] Pershing's plan called for two columns to leave from Columbus: one moved southward toward Culberson's Ranch, while the other left east of the town and headed into Mexican territory. It was a fairly simple plan, one fitting the terrain and the lack of substantive intelligence on Villa's location. The two running columns reminded the brigadier commander of his earlier days in New Mexico when one cavalry troop chased after another in the raid-and-pursuit games he had enjoyed so much as a young lieutenant. Pershing instructed all his officers to remember they were moving on foreign soil as virtual guests of the Carranza government: "Make the utmost endeavor to convince all Mexicans that the only purpose of this expedition is to assist in apprehending and capturing Villa and his bandits. Citizens as well as soldiers of the de facto government will be treated with every consideration."[24]

Pershing relied on sweeping movements by his cavalry. The east-most column included the Thirteenth Cavalry, which had taken the brunt of Villa's Columbus raid, plus the Sixth and Sixteenth Infantries and Battery C of the Sixth Field Artillery. Pershing moved with the western column, including the Seventh and Tenth Cavalries and the Sixth Field Artillery's Battery B. As the days and weeks unfolded, the infantry always brought up the rear as the cavalry scouted out the terrain, searching for possible Villa strongholds.

The expedition included modern military innovations—planes, trucks, radio units—but essentially Pershing's military columns represented old-school army movements, which were much the same as that of General Miles's cavalry troopers when in search of Geronimo thirty years earlier. Pershing's men wore khaki rather than blue woolen uniforms, even as machine guns and .45 pistols had taken the place of Sharps carbines and gleaming sabers, but there was much about it all that he recognized from his days stationed at Fort Bayard or Stanton in the 1880s. Pershing may have relied more on a Dodge automobile to take him through the desert, but everywhere he looked he saw the reminders of his past. As one of the brigadier's officers, Col. H. A. Toulmin Jr., noted, "The Pershing Expedition placed its reliance on guides, cowmen of the ranges, half-breeds, ranch bosses, adventurers who had fought either against or with Villa, gunfighters, gamblers—the remnants of the old Indian frontier. This expedition revived old ghosts—life came to the border once more. Once again the great southwest was alive with the United States army in pursuit of ruffian bands."[25]

The basic elements played as they had for tracking Geronimo: ride hard and fast, think like your enemy, and never forget how hostile the land can treat those who fail to respect its dangers.

In fact, among the modern elements included in the Punitive Expedition, most proved quite unreliable. The First Aero Squadron's eight Jenny planes did not function well in the dusty, sandy environment. Six of the old biplanes broke up within the first month, and the remaining two soon became irreparable. The Signal Corps brought along a handful of field radios—a new technology, indeed—but they only operated within a twenty-five-mile radius. Trucks and automobiles broke down. Even telegraphic communications, which had been utilized effectively during the U.S. Civil War, proved unreliable, as the enemy, as well as civilians who were sympathetic to the Villistas, frequently cut the lines.

General Pershing had relied on Indian scouts during earlier action in the West, and the Punitive Campaign was no different. He took along a handful of Apache scouts, some of whom had participated in the Geronimo campaign, including Corporals Big Sharley and B-25, whose face had been badly scarred by a Mexican bullet. Chief among the scouts was First Sergeant Chicken, who worked alongside Hell Yet-Suey, an older Apache warrior belonging to the White Mountain band. The scouts also included a pair of brothers, Sergeant Chow Big and Corporal Monotolth. Although most of the Apache scouts had never even been to Mexico previously, they had a strong hatred for Mexicans. Captured Mexicans quaked in fear at the sight of the Apache scouts, especially Hell Yet-Suey, who enjoyed interrogating prisoners.[26]

While Pershing was always a stickler for spit-and-polish proficiency among his men, on the Punitive Expedition, neatness was practically impossible to maintain—even for him. He dressed in a khaki shirt with the requisite tie, britches, black leather field boots, and a four-dented campaign hat. He always carried a .45 pistol on his hip, a practice he had taken up in the Philippines. Pershing was in his midfifties in 1916 and still trim. He also sported a mustache, as he had for decades. He slept under the stars in a bedroll, as his men did, often without a protective tent. He rode a horse occasionally—one of the most frequently copied photographs of Pershing depicts him on horseback crossing the Santa Maria River in the early days of his campaign—but a Dodge touring car was his most consistent transportation.

He maintained a light, mobile headquarters, never setting up camp for long before pulling up stakes and determining a new center of gravity. He did not even maintain an inner circle of staff officers. His entourage included Patton, his aide; an African American cook named Booker—who only had the army basics of corn meal, canned beef, hardtack, bacon, and coffee for cooking meals—and four enlisted men who served as a guard unit. Pershing's entire headquarters, including personnel and equipment, could all fit into four Dodge touring automobiles. The brigadier ordered all his officers, including himself, to travel with no more than fifty pounds of personal baggage. Behind these vehicles followed a Model T Ford and a Hudson touring car carrying the designated journalists—including Robert Dunn (*New York Tribune*), Floyd Gibbons (*Chicago Tribune*), and the boys of the Associated Press—although the Hudson broke down with a busted axle only eight miles into Mexico.

With cavalry units sometimes ranging over hundreds of square miles of territory in a few short days, Pershing sometimes did not know where all his forces were located. It was simply part of moving thousands of men in multiple directions at once in an effort to locate and box in one man. The brigadier, in his undermanned, mobile headquarters, was often vulnerable to attack himself. Conditions were constantly poor, with field positions scattered and remote. The simplest activities put Pershing at risk. Supplies sometimes reached him; sometimes they did not. Colonel Toulmin observed, "With a canvas bucket for a washtub or a Mexican creek for a bath tub, sleeping in his clothes from day to day in the open, acting as press censor for newspaper correspondents by correcting their copy on his knee, evading ambush and capture while travelling detached from his troops—these were some of the qualifications of a headquarters commander with the Mexican Expedition."[27]

No one could fault Pershing's men for not covering enough ground. Within the first thirty-six hours of leaving Columbus for the border, Pershing moved his columns across 140 miles of Mexican territory. Cavalry troops rode as hard as their horses could gallop under the harsh desert conditions, sometimes covering fifty or sixty miles a day, searching for any sign of Villa and his men. As the horsemen crisscrossed great swathes of territory, the trucks and automobiles wheezed across the trackless desert, covering a few miles each day, if a breakdown didn't bring them to a halt. Truck drivers wore goggles and tied bandanas over their mouths against the otherwise blinding, dust-bearing winds. But if the Americans expected local citizens to help them in their search for Villa, they were mistaken. Locals kept quiet or provided false information of Villa's hiding out in this mountain or that one.

Just identifying the enemy was problematic. The deserts of Chihuahua harbored a variety of unaffiliated denizens wearing an array of uniforms and uniform remnants; some fired at the Americans, including at the First Aero Squadron planes flying low overhead, taking photographs of the landscape. The Mexicans might be Villa's men or Carrancistas or even Díaz loyalists or just independent gangs of free agents accustomed to firing their rifles at any and all targets. Pershing's men in time realized that the Villistas often wore hatbands woven from human hair held together with a small silver buckle, a form of identification close up and personal. In the meantime, the Americans were expected to treat all Mexicans with restraint. An exception was made for those who fired on Pershing's men; then the troops had permission to fire back in defense.

Early rumors of Villa's being within close proximity to the swiftly moving American columns evaporated. On the eighteenth, Pershing entered Colonia Dublán, without knowing Villa was nearly a hundred miles south at Namiquipa. When Villa moved on, four days elapsed before a squadron of the Tenth Cavalry arrived. In the meantime, Pershing reorganized his men and sent out four new columns, staggering their departures on March 20, 21, 24, and 30. All four columns comprised cavalry squads drawn from the Thirteenth and Eleventh Cavalries. Some of these squads roamed for many days over vast stretches of desert land. One provisional squad of the Eleventh Cavalry, numbering 265 men under the command of Maj. Robert Howze, ranged for twenty-two straight days, faced a snowstorm with no available tents, and rode nearly seven hundred miles. By the time he returned, he had his men and horses down to half rations, and all his troops' leather stirrup hoods had been stripped and utilized as replacements for the men's shoe soles.

By March 27, less than ten days out from Columbus, Pershing and his men reached Casas Grandes and established an advance base. Rumors put Villa in the area, and Pershing wanted to be close to the action. But the brigadier remained cautious regarding Villa's capture. One of Pershing's scouts, a red-shirted horse wrangler from Arizona named Tracy, approached him and reported on the situation at hand. "As I figure it General," he said with a touch of irony, "we've got Villa entirely surrounded—on one side."[28] Pershing, along with the reporters who were standing by taking notes, could only laugh.

Three days later, after experiencing mountain snowstorms, Pershing arrived farther south at San Geronimo, where a dispatch rider informed him of a field fight outside Guerrero in the mountains to the southwest. Four hundred troopers of the Seventh Cavalry under Col. George A. Dodd had performed well, killing thirty of Villa's men and capturing two machine guns. Villa, seriously wounded, escaped in a buggy. At least that was the rumor. Dodd believed the Mexican leader would soon be boxed in on all four directions. Villa proved elusive, however, and ultimately escaped.

On April 1 Pershing and his headquarters entourage caught up with the Thirteenth Cavalry under Maj. Frank Tompkins at Bachiniva near the Santa Clara River. At this point, the Punitive Expedition had penetrated 350 miles into Mexico, and Villa was nowhere to be found. Sitting around an evening campfire, Pershing asked the commander of the Thirteenth, "Tompkins, where is Villa?"

Major Tompkins could only answer, "General, I don't know, but I would mighty well like to find out where he is."

"Where would you go?" asked the brigadier.

Tompkins gave his best guess: "I would head for Parral and would expect to cut his trail before reaching there." The major was referring to a small town more than 150 miles to the southwest, near the southern border of Chihuahua.

"Why?"

The major's guess was a studied one: "The history of Villa's bandit days shows that when hard pressed he invariably holes up in the mountains in the vicinity of Parral. He has friends in that region."

Pershing remained silent for a short interval. Then he asked Tompkins, "How many mules would you want?"

"Twelve," Tompkins said.

By the next morning, Pershing gave orders to the major: "Go find Villa wherever you think he is." The brigadier issued him twelve mules from the Eleventh Cavalry, five days' rations, and 500 silver pesos. Within a couple of hours, Tompkins and his men were on the trail to Parral.[29]

For the next ten days, Pershing remained at Bachiniva, waiting to hear from Tompkins, his only commander who had even expressed an educated guess regarding Villa's whereabouts. Then discouraging news arrived. Tompkins's ride across southern Chihuahua had proceeded without major incident. On April 10 his column entered Valle de Zaragoza and caught twenty-five Villistas raiding a local factory. The men of the Thirteenth chased the pistoleros away, recovered the stolen merchandise, and returned the items to their owner. Goodwill allowed him to purchase much-needed supplies including clothing and boots for his men. Tompkins purchased additional food as well, with welcomed replacements for hardtack and bacon including salmon, eggs, bread, frijoles, beef, and tomatoes. Capt. Antonio Mesa, a local Carrancista officer, met with Tompkins and informed him he could enter Parral with no expectation of incident.

On the morning of the twelfth, Tompkins and the Thirteenth Cavalry set out across their last eighteen miles to Parral. At noon, the Mexican town was in view, and Tompkins went ahead with an advance guard to confer with the local Carrancista commander Gen. Ismael Lozano. When they arrived, Lozano blustered in protest, informing the American commander he had no right to be there. In the meantime, local townspeople, aware of the presence of the Americans, began to gather in the streets, where they shouted, "Viva Villa! Viva Mexico!" They angrily threw rocks and garbage, and some fired random shots. Lozano attempted to intervene, ordering his men to disperse the crowd.

The Americans began to retreat. Then Tompkins realized the local Carrancista garrison was moving parallel to his force, threatening to flank his position. He dispatched a squad to force the Carrancistas back. The Mexican troops opened fire, and the major ordered his men to fire back in self-defense. Tompkins organized a retreat, as the Carrancistas, now numbering more than three hundred, continued to flank him. Tompkins led his men to a small fortress at Santa Cruz de Villegas to take up a defensive position. Tompkins was desperate to avoid a full-on battle, knowing the consequences might jeopardize the Punitive Expedition altogether.

At the fortress, the fight continued, as Tompkins placed his best sharpshooters on several select rooftops. As the Carrancistas approached, a shot rang out from the American defenders, fired by Capt. Aubrey Lippincott. From a distance of approximately eight hundred yards, the captain hit a mounted Carrancista officer. The Mexicans pulled back. Lozano soon sent a courier under a white flag to the American-held fortress, requesting the removal of Tompkins's men back to the north. The major said he would do so if assured safe passage for his men. In the meantime, Tompkins sent three troopers in search of Col. W. C. Brown's Tenth Cavalry, knowing he was only a few miles away. When Brown showed up to reinforce Tompkins, along with Maj. Charles Young's squad of buffalo soldiers, the Carrancistas in the vicinity of Santa Cruz de Villegas evaporated and returned to Parral.

When Pershing received word of the treatment of his troops—including one Carrancista officer's assuring Tompkins he could enter Parral only to be attacked by another unit of Carrancistas—the brigadier was beside himself. He felt his men had been lured into a trap, or "an ambuscade," as he described it.[30] The incident served as one more reminder to the commander of the expedition that he was fighting more than one enemy and that his mission was little more than a fool's errand. Finding one man in the vast desert wastelands of Chihuahua would prove a challenge even if he had support from the local civilians. The incident represented a serious encounter, and Pershing became certain that he did not have enough men in country. If Mexican forces were gathered en masse against him, they would have dramatically superior numbers, leaving his situation quite precarious. He wanted to increase all his regiments to full capacity, plus add another regiment of both infantry and cavalry. Pershing even favored capturing Chihuahua City and commandeering the railroads for his use.

From a military and strategic standpoint, Pershing's thoughts made sense. But President Wilson, who was already concerned over the tense international situation—he was also focusing on the war in Europe—was not interested in escalation. When U.S. Army chief of staff Hugh L. Scott recommended calling up the Organized Militia to patrol the border, Wilson vetoed the proposal.[31] Wilson, in fact, began to redefine the mission entirely. Instead of Pershing's mission being the capture of Villa and the destruction of his supporters, Wilson wanted the U.S. Army's presence in Mexico to be used as leverage to compel the Carranza government to take up the mission itself. Capturing or killing Villa would remain the objective, but the Mexican government would be more directly involved. Wilson saw the possibility of both the Americans and the Carrancistas working together toward a goal mutually beneficial to both nations. If Carranza neutralized Villa, the Americans would have no reason to remain in Mexico any longer. By redefining the purpose of the Punitive Expedition, Pershing and his men had become political pawns in a much larger and new Wilsonian gambit.

The running skirmish at Parral immediately altered the direction of the Punitive Expedition. Pershing's campaign was different after the Parral fight. Previously the Carrancistas had played a dual game, but now they revealed their true hand: they had no intention of cooperating with the Americans, Villa or no Villa. Within days, the brigadier moved his headquarters northward, even if only to make a point. He would never establish another headquarters farther south. From the back seat of his Dodge, he watched the land fade behind him. By the morning of the sixteenth, his headquarters had moved 115 miles to the north.

The embedded journalists saw what was happening. One brought him a dispatch to read—Pershing had full power to censor any newspaper's reporting—and its theme was blunt: "The United States Punitive Expedition directed against Pancho Villa and his followers has apparently come to a standstill. Whether the halt is to be permanent depends largely on circumstances beyond the control of General Pershing. From a military standpoint he has for the time being come to the end of his line."[32]

Pershing perused the copy and signed off on its message. Pershing himself espoused that viewpoint over the following weeks. In a June interview with journalist James Hopper, he said as much: "With the Parral incident, the expedition came practically to a stop. The pursuit of Villa ceased for fear of a clash."[33]

On June 15, in a communication with Brig. Gen. Enoch H. Crowder, whom he considered a friend in Washington, Pershing sounded as though he had completely lost his drive. Perhaps he was just being realistic: "I . . . feel just a little bit like a man looking for a needle in a hay stack with an armed guard standing over the stack forbidding you to look in the hay."[34] What Pershing felt was the incapacitating pressure of limited war. Commanders in Vietnam a half-century later could have easily identified with his sentiments.

Meanwhile, as the days slipped into weeks, and Pershing's

search took him deeper and deeper into Mexico, the appearance of his mission seemed not only to the Mexican people but even to many Americans to represent a full-fledged invasion rather than a long version of his old rabbit hunts in New Mexico. He usually kept the embedded journalists on a short leash, but he could not control editorials about his expedition written back in the States. The *New York Tribune* published one stating how "our fast and loose diplomacy with the Carranza government sent an undersized American force into Mexico without clear guarantees of friendly assistance."[35]

The farther Pershing's forces moved into Mexican territory, the greater their problems. With hundreds of miles between the expedition's position and the supply depot at Columbus, the greater the logistical issues became. Abundant supplies were found outside the town where Villa's attack had taken place, but without the use of Mexican railroads, getting them to the troops who were constantly on the move was nearly impossible. Wagon roads were impassable, and mountain trails required mules that were not always available. In time, Pershing did manage to organize a workable truck convoy system. (He would do the same in France within a few short years.) In an effort to guarantee his trucks reached their various destinations, Pershing ordered his engineers to build roads, as he had done in Mindanao. By the summer's end in 1916, his engineers had constructed nearly 160 miles of roads and improved another 224 miles of preexisting ones.

After the Parral incident, Pershing's forces engaged in other fights but with Villa's men. On April 20 the Seventh Cavalry fought at the Verde River and outside the town of Tomachie, where several Villistas were killed. On the same day, Colonel Dodd heard a rumor of the Villistas being in Yoquivo. He rushed his 155 men to the village to surprise Villa's men, only to find they were already gone. One of Villa's strategies complicated Pershing's operations even further, as the Mexican leader allowed various bands of his men to operate independently of one another. Finding one group of Villistas did not ensure finding Villa himself. Pershing met this organizational strategy with one of his own, taking his cues from the British, who had divided their forces in India during the nineteenth century into different district commands. The districts allowed several of Pershing's troops to remain within a given region, where they became a known entity to the local citizens. Sometimes this paid off, with some citizens cooperating with the Americans.

On May 4 a pair of local officials from the village of Cusi appeared at Pershing's headquarters and informed him of the presence of two of Villa's lieutenants, Julio Acosta and Cruz Dominiques, near their town. They were in command of approximately 120 men. The people of Cusi did not want trouble from the Villistas, and they sought help from the Americans. The brigadier ordered a squad of six mounted troops and a machine gun unit to the village. They arrived after midnight and received a report that the Villistas had fought local Carrancistas and then moved on to the Ojos Azules Ranch, where they encamped. By 6 a.m. on May 5, the American troops caught up with the pistoleros at the ranch. First Sergeant Chicken led his men in a flanking maneuver ahead of the main column and soon spotted dozens of Villistas. The American troops then emerged from the darkness, the sounds of their automatic pistols splitting the dawn. The engagement ended with forty-four Villistas dead and no American casualties, despite several troopers of the Eleventh Cavalry taking bullets through their uniforms. First Sergeant Chicken was excited: "Damn fine fight!"[36]

Other successful engagements with the Villistas were equally important, even if smaller framed. A few of Villa's top commanders, including Col. Julio Cárdenas, who was known to serve as the commander of Villa's bodyguard, became notorious among the Americans. Intelligence reached Pershing by mid-May that Cárdenas was seen at a nearby village. On the fourteenth, Pershing dispatched Lieutenant Patton, along with ten troopers and five civilians; the entire group traveled in three Dodge automobiles. They drove toward the village of Las Ciénegas, where an uncle of Cárdenas's owned a hacienda at the local San Miguelito Ranch. Patton halted the autos a mile from the ranch, and he and his squad approached on foot. They first spotted four cowboys skinning a steer but saw no one else. As they closed in on the hacienda, three men on horseback suddenly appeared, firing their guns at the Americans. Patton sprang into action, drawing his pistol. An excellent shot, the young lieutenant killed one man and shot the second rider's horse, which caused the animal to collapse on top of the Villista. As Patton dispatched two men, Patton's comrades took out the third. Cárdenas was killed by E. L. Holmdahl, a former Villista who was then cooperating with the Americans. The automobiles were retrieved, and Patton ordered the bodies of the three Villistas tied to the hoods of the cars so they could be delivered to Pershing himself as proof of their kill. In this manner, the Americans were successful in isolating portions of Villa's men and successfully engaging them in random firefights. But Villa was rarely present during such battles.

As spring rolled into summer, Pershing and his men faced a more serious challenge. The patience of the Carranza government was growing thin. Wilson's secretary of war Newton Baker, who had been in that office as long as Pershing had been in Mexico, called for a meeting between Chief of Staff Scott and General Obregón, Carranza's minister of war. Carranza agreed to the meeting. On April 30 the generals—along with General Funston, commander of the Southern Department—met at the Hotel Aguana in Juárez. The conference went quite badly. Speaking for Carranza, Obregón insisted the Punitive Expedition leave Mexico immediately. He claimed Villa had been killed, so the Americans could go back home. The international exchange became red hot, with Funston boiling over in anger and banging on a table until he stormed out of the session. Scott adjourned the meeting, stating he needed more information from Washington. Three days later, he met with Obregón again, this time in El Paso at the Hotel Paso del Norte. The tête-à-tête stretched on for twelve hours. Although they came to a limited agreement, Carranza later refused to cooperate with the Americans.

Further complicating these delicate negotiations was a new attack across the border into the United States: Mexican raiders splashed across the Rio Grande on May 5 and struck the tiny Texas towns of Glenn Springs and Boquillas. Near Glenn Springs, the pistoleros attacked a small garrison (eight men plus a sergeant) of the Fourteenth Cavalry that fought from the shelter of an adobe house, which the assailants set on fire. The defenders scattered into the underbrush and continued the fight, and three were killed. The Mexicans then attacked a local general store and killed the owner's four-year-old son. At Boquillas, they raided another store and kidnapped the proprietor and an employee, as well as seven office personnel at the International Mining Company. Two days passed before General Funston in El Paso learned of the attack. He dispatched two troops of the Eighth Cavalry by train to Marathon, Texas, with orders to chase down the raiders in another punitive expedition.

By the time the troopers reached Boquillas, the mining company employees, having escaped, met them with three Mexican pistoleros in tow. They provided intelligence to the commander of the expedition, Maj. George T. Langhorne, and several escapees offered to act as guides for the soldiers. On the morning of May 12, a party of a hundred cavalrymen crossed the border with twenty horses, a truck, and a Ford automobile. Tagging along were a pair of journalists and a second Ford carrying a motion picture film crew. Langhorne rode in a chauffeur-driven Cadillac.

The chase went on through the next several days, resulting in the return of the store owner and his employee. Near Rosita, the troopers sped along in the automobiles, chasing pistoleros on horseback across the Mexican desert. No one was killed on either side, but one of the Fords suffered a broken axle. A running fight later opened near the Castillon Ranch, where the Americans surprised their quarry. They killed several, captured two, and took seventeen horses and mules, plus a wagon. After a week, the cavalry unit gave up on any further chase and returned to Texas. Carranza naturally condemned the raid. (He may actually have been complicit in organizing such provocative raids to provide himself with further ammunition regarding the Americans and their lack of respect for Mexican sovereignty.) Wilson did not sit on his hands, however; by May 10 he called out the Organized Militia. Soon referred to as the National Guard, troops from Arizona, Texas, and New Mexico were federalized and sent to protect the border. In time, more than 150,000 Americans troops were assigned there.[37]

The Pershing mission became untenable to both nations. Wilson and Baker feared Pershing's presence threatened more harm than good and that no matter how carefully the brigadier and his forces moved through Mexico, the Carranza government would constantly be looking for an opportunity to turn on the unwanted Americans and force a confrontation. Funston and Scott reported to Wilson on May 8 and suggested the Carranza government was operating "with bad faith, that [the] Mexicans are convinced that they are not able to carry out the agreement . . . and they desire to keep the United States troops quiet until Mexican troops are in position to drive them out of Mexico by force."[38]

As for Villa, he remained at large, despite the assurances of the Carranza government to the contrary. Rumors were always plentiful, and such contradictory information only managed to complicate Pershing's mission. Depending on which version one heard, Villa had died in a cave from a serious wound, had been assassinated by his own men, was killed in a brawl at a remote ranch, or was shot and his body cremated. By early summer, Carrancistas became more aggressive, taking up positions at river fords, at road intersections, and along railroad lines. Pershing even received a telegram from Carrancista leader Gen. Jacinto Treviño, informing him of his new orders from the Mexican government: he was to "prevent, by the use of arms, new invasions of my country by American forces and also to prevent the American forces that are in this State from moving to the south, east or west of the places they now occupy. . . . Your forces will be attacked by the Mexican forces if these indications are not heeded."[39]

Despite the awkwardness of his assignment as the commander of all forces in the operational area of Mexico, Pershing pushed back: "In reply you are informed that my government has placed no such restrictions upon the movements of American forces."[40] Pershing signed his communication "respectfully," and Treviño signed his "courteously."

Rumors continued suggesting Carranza's military was organizing a large-scale assault on Pershing's troops. But the attack did not materialize. The Mexicans likely found the Americans' presence on their soil represented a significant challenge. By the end of the first week in June, Pershing was in command of more than ten thousand men supported by twenty pieces of artillery and an equal number of machine guns. While the force represented a significant massing of U.S. troops and firepower, Pershing and his men were, being on foreign soil, constantly surrounded by opponents. The Carrancistas in Chihuahua City alone numbered twenty-two thousand men, with four times Pershing's artillery and five times more machine guns. "They are all about us," the brigadier observed. "Our patrols are in constant contact; we cannot go anywhere without running into Mexican troops; the pursuit is brought to an absolute standstill. And from all sides we are hearing threats."[41]

Every day, the threatening winds of escalation swirled around Pershing and his men until they formed a whirlwind at a place called Carrizal. On June 18 General Pershing sent a reconnaissance force into the Ahumada District to determine the veracity of a rumor that claimed the Mexican military was massing between eight thousand to ten thousand men in the area. With his airplanes all out of commission, a cavalry unit was Pershing's only reliable eyes and ears. Pershing tapped Capt. Charles T. Boyd, who had served as the brigadier's adjutant at Fort William McKinley in the Philippines. Boyd was an officer of experience and a graduate of West Point's class of '96 and, more recently, of the U.S. Army Staff College. Pershing trusted him with the delicate and potentially dangerous mission. Boyd led Troops C and K of the Tenth Cavalry, Pershing's old unit from his Montana days. In giving his orders to Boyd, Pershing suggested he proceed no farther east than the Santo Domingo Ranch, eighteen miles short of Ahumada. He told Boyd in a memo, "This is a reconnaissance only, and you will not be expected to fight. In fact, I want you to avoid a fight if possible. Do not allow yourself to be surprised by superior numbers."[42]

By the evening of June 20, Boyd and his men reached the Santo Domingo Ranch with Troop C and met up with Capt. Lewis S. Morey, the commander of K Troop. Between them, they had close to eighty men. The ranch's American foreman provided them with the information they were looking for: Carrancistas numbering in the hundreds were at Carrizal, west of Ahumada. The American officers talked things over, and Lt. Henry Adair of Troop C suggested the Mexican soldiers would not fight in the face of American troops. Lem Spilsbury, a Mormon scout, disagreed. Captain Boyd chose to advance farther east. After a short ride in the early morning hours of June 21, the Americans were a mile west of Carrizal. Boyd sent ahead his Mormon scout, who spoke Spanish, to meet with the town commandant Gen. Felix Gomez and ask permission to continue eastward to Ahumada. The first Carrancista officer Spilsbury met, Maj. Genovevo Rivas Guillén, told him, "There are no Villistas in this part of the country, and if there are any enemies of yours over here, we're them!"[43]

General Gomez was summoned, and he and Boyd met outside Carrizal on a roadside. Gomez was polite, but he demurred, "I have orders to stop any movement of American troops through this town and am therefore duty bound to oppose you. Whether you were one or a thousand, we should try to stop you."[44] Even as Gomez spoke his warning, the American captain observed Mexican troops taking up defensive positions. Boyd ended the conference, angry at what he interpreted as threatening maneuvers on the part of the Mexicans. He railed at his Mormon scout, the spit flying from his mouth along with his words: "Tell the son-of-a-bitch that I'm going through." He shot a sharp look at Gomez as he shook his fist at him. "God damn you! I've never disobeyed an order yet, and I'm not going to now. I'm going through your goddamned town!"[45]

Gomez responded even before Boyd's words were translated into Spanish: "You might pass through the town, but you'll have to walk over my dead body."[46]

As for the orders Boyd was intent on obeying, he had already taken steps beyond those laid down by Pershing. But Boyd was angry and ready to teach the Mexicans a lesson. When Boyd returned to his men, he told his sergeant, "We're going to have a fight."[47]

Weeks of rumors of war finally converged outside Carrizal. Boyd prepared his men for an assault even as Captain Morey protested, reminding Boyd he was exceeding his orders from Pershing. But Boyd ignored him, telling the men of Troops C and K, "My orders are to go east to Villa Ahumada on the other side of this town, and I'm going through and take all of you men with me." His words drew a cheer from the men, who numbered approximately eighty when including the horse holders.

Boyd excited his men further: "I value each of you as ten Mexicans. Do not let it be said that the American troops fired the first shot. If they fire on us, we will answer them, shot for shot. The only thing I will not forgive is showing your back to the enemy."[48]

The American captain ordered his men to dismount and had the horses taken to the rear. With the horse holders moving the mounts, approximately sixty troopers were left to advance toward approximately three hundred Carrancistas, who were entrenched and supported by four machine guns. Boyd's men were completely exposed as they moved over the bare plain. Once the Americans moved to within 250 yards of their opponents, the Mexicans opened fire. Their first volley overshot the skirmishers and hit the horses, which stampeded in a chaotic panic.

The Americans returned fire. General Gomez was killed instantly with a shot to the head. Then Boyd was killed, and Henry Adair, who had earlier argued the Mexicans would not fight the Americans, was seriously wounded. With their officers killed and wounded, the troopers were uncertain of their orders, and that only added to the confusion. Mexican machine-gun fire created a deadly cross fire on the field, delivering swift death. The battle dragged on for nearly ninety minutes, but the Americans ultimately pulled back as the Mexican defenders shouted, "Rendirse, rendirse!" (Surrender, surrender!) Two dozen or so troopers were unable to escape the fight and surrendered, along with Lem Spilsbury, the Mormon scout. The exact number of American casualties at Carrizal varies, depending on the source. Col. Frank Tompkins's report cited a dozen killed, eleven wounded, and twenty-three captured. The official army inquiry listed nine killed, twelve wounded, four missing, and twenty-four captured. In general, the American troopers suffered an approximate casualty rate of 40 percent. The prisoners were later released and delivered by train to El Paso.

When Pershing learned of the deadly encounter at Carrizal, he was surprised at Boyd's actions. Writing in his memoirs years later, he treated the question of why Boyd had pressed an attack as a still-unanswered question. "To this day Boyd's course at Carrizal has puzzled me.... No one could have been more surprised than I was to learn that he had become so seriously involved. Even had such instructions not been given Boyd it is difficult to comprehend why."[49]

In an undated memorandum regarding the Carrizal affair, Pershing was just as blunt: "As to the conduct of the fight, there is little that can be said in approval." Even after years of considering and reconsidering Boyd's actions at Carrizal, they remained inexplicable to Pershing, only signifying a bridge too far.[50]

News of the Carrizal battle spread quickly along Mexican telegraph wires and was announced as a great victory against the Americans. Pershing found out about it in a roundabout way from General Bell in El Paso, who learned of the incident through the Mexican consul; he, in turn, had received word from Mexico City. Pershing dispatched troops to pick up those who had survived the battle. After the brigadier questioned several participants to learn what exactly had happened, he requested permission to launch a counterstrike against the Mexicans, but the War Department said no. In the meantime, Pershing intercepted a message from Carranza seeking to rally the Villistas and the Carrancistas together to drive out the Americans. Pershing lacked adequate manpower if a broader war opened, and no one in Washington was prepared for that. General Funston sent a message to Pershing that was semi critical: "It is so difficult to understand why 75 men were sent 80 to 90 miles from your lines in the face of [an] unknown large organized force ... undertake no move that is not thoroughly safe. One more such incident as that of June 21 will raise the morale of the others to such an extent that it will be costly to reduce it again."[51]

Although Pershing defended himself and his actions, he admitted to Funston that Captain Boyd had not acted logically or prudently leading up to the Carrizal encounter. He was also certain that his mission was forever compromised. "Our presence here almost certain to bring on clash. Consider it miraculous we have not already had several clashes in view of necessity of protective patrolling."[52]

The Carrizal fight was the last one of any significance for the remainder of Pershing's mission in Mexico. In a sense, the enemy had shifted completely from those Villistas who had raided Columbus, New Mexico, in the early hours of March 9 to the Mexican Army itself. The last fight involving the Villistas on June 9–10 was at Santa Clara Canyon, where a small squad of the Thirteenth Cavalry skirmished with pistoleros, killing two and scattering a couple dozen. Throughout the first hundred days of the Punitive Expedition, Pershing's men engaged in ten fights directly with the Villistas, starting with the encounter at Guerrero on March 29 and culminating with the limited action at Santa Clara Canyon in June. During these engagements, U.S. Army troopers killed 169 Villistas and wounded 65, compared to six Americans killed and nineteen wounded. Adding the number of the Villistas killed and wounded during the Columbus raid, total casualties, including killed and wounded, for Villa numbered more than four hundred. The fights with the Carrancistas at Parral and Carrizal caused eleven American deaths, nineteen wounded, and three missing. This placed American casualties during the months of campaigning in Mexico at seventeen killed, thirty-eight wounded, three missing, and two dozen captured.

The Pershing expedition, following the Carrizal fight, slipped into an extended period of doldrums. Even the Carrancistas seemed less aggressive after the encounter. Mexican pistoleros—

Villistas or otherwise—led no more raids across the U.S. border. With more than one hundred thousand National Guard troops on the border, such an attack might have proven suicidal. During the last six months of 1916, the Carranza administration faced other domestic problems at hand, including fighting twenty thousand revolutionaries under Zapata's leadership in southern Mexico.

Pershing always believed his mission in Mexico was compromised and hampered by three circumstances generally out of his control: First, the region of northern Mexico was vast and largely unmapped, making coverage for his men and their search for Villa and his pistoleros difficult. Second, the Americans had difficulty gaining any significant support, cooperation, and information from local citizens regarding Villa's whereabouts, as the locals knew they might face Villa's wrath if their cooperation were known. Finally, the troops completely lacked any cooperation from the Carrancistas, a problem that only became worse as the Punitive Expedition dragged on and farther into Mexico.

Meanwhile, Villa and his men were free to move at will; to separate into smaller bands, making it more difficult for the Americans to find any larger numbers in one place; and to receive intelligence regarding the presence of Pershing's men from either sympathetic or intimidated citizens. The Villistas could steal from the local people what they needed, whether supplies or horses. Once they wore out their animals through hard riding, they could simply replace them by stealing more horses. The situation in Mexico never represented a level playing field for the Americans. It was part of the high cost of intervening across the border into a hostile foreign country.

While Pershing's efforts to capture Villa always represented an uphill battle, he did manage some success with some local citizens. Typically, when the Americans rode into a remote Mexican village in search of Villa and his followers, the peasants naturally looked at them with trepidation. But as Pershing had done in the Philippines, he tried to ingratiate himself with the citizens and make them understand he and his men were not there to exploit or harass them. Whereas Villa and his men simply took what they wanted, the Americans paid good silver pesos for food, firewood, horses. This practice sometimes caused the people of a given town or pueblo to feel comfortable with the Americans' presence, because it was profitable, plus they could be protected from future attacks by the Villistas. This part of Pershing's "hearts and minds" strategy, reflecting what he learned in the Philippines, did have limited payoffs. But it was never enough to turn popular Mexican sentiment away from Pancho Villa, who still retained, in the minds of many Mexican peasants, a status equivalent to that of Robin Hood.

As for Pershing, the campaign took a toll on him. The loss of his wife and daughters was still a fresh wound, and his sense of loss never left him. As a man in his midfifties, he still could enjoy field command, but he had his limits. He told Junius B. Wood, an embedded journalist, that it "added ten years to my life."[53] Pershing also suffered from chronic indigestion and other ailments, but he took up smoking cigars again after several years. He was always on, working constantly. As another reporter for the *Chicago Daily News* observed, "A light may burn in his tent until early morning, while he sits alone reading over reports and planning moves for future days. He may be up at daylight, walking through the sleeping camp and observing with his own eyes. He believes in keeping men busy—officers and privates. 'Don't let them stagnate,' he says. 'If they get out of the habit of working they won't be in condition when they are needed. Idleness has ruined more armies than battles have.'"[54] Through the final months of 1916, most of the duties performed by Pershing's troopers centered on reconnaissance and continuous training.

To that end, during the last six months of the Punitive Expedition's time in Mexico, he introduced a training course for companies and brigades to provide better experience and exposure to tactics and the use of machine guns in combat. He maintained his supply lines as best he could and kept the U.S. military machine in Mexico running under constant difficulties. The military historian Col. William A. Ganoe later summed up the challenges Pershing faced on foreign soil: "He was allowed to attack one party but not the other, while both were equally antagonistic. He was in the position of the man who had to walk into a hungry leopard's cage with orders to beat Mr. Leopard, but under no conditions resist Mrs. Leopard with her cubs. With such a mission, who could have done better?"[55]

Even as the Mexican mission devolved into a motionless, seemingly pointless exercise on foreign soil, Pershing's professional reputation did not seem to suffer. He was promoted to major general in September, with no accompanying protest. The *New York Sun* reported, "If there is any officer in the army who deserves the honor as much as Pershing, we don't know who it is."[56]

With the men, Pershing was the same as he had often been—a strict disciplinarian and an exacting leader who expected the best from his troops at all times, under all conditions. They respected him as their commander and took him seriously. It was not as though they had any real choice. But they saw him as a fair man, one who did not expect more of others than he expected of himself. One trooper might have spoken for many when he described Pershing years later as an "S.O.B." and said that he "hated his guts." That same veteran also added, "But as a soldier, the ones then and the ones now couldn't polish his boots."[57]

During those final months of the expedition, Pershing's men faced a different sort of problem—how to keep up their morale when the mission seemed largely abandoned even though they were still in country. They made the best of what they had on hand. While the doughboys who stationed in Europe during the Great War would receive distractions and entertainments provided by various U.S. civic and religious organizations—such as the Young Men's Christian Association, the Knights of Columbus, the Salvation Army, and the like—the troopers encamped in Mexico did not have the advantage of their support.[58] So they did as other American armies had before them: gambled, played sports, including baseball, and enjoyed other games of chance and distraction. "Each camp had its baseball league during warm weather," observed Pershing, "and in the winter each regiment organized its football team." With so many horses available, the men even laid out a polo field. Relying on safety in numbers, men went on hunting forays, with the Apache scouts as guides. Given the semipermanent nature of the encampments, many abandoned their tents and began to build houses, fashioning them from local adobe bricks, which the Americans made themselves. Pershing noted, "Their first efforts were rather primitive. . . . But with practice they became quite expert in making the 'dobe' bricks. . . . The adobe shacks not only withstood the rain and dust storms but were cool in summer and warm in winter."[59]

With the Americans based somewhat permanently, the presence of prostitutes became an added distraction. Operating out of barrios, such as Colonia Dublán and Nueva Casas Grandes, women plied their trade and took the troopers' silver while all too often infecting the men with venereal diseases. Realizing the relative impossibility of keeping the men away from such brothels, Pershing, working with a local Mormon bishop at Colonia Dublán, allowed a special red-light district to operate under the direction of army guards, out of sight of the encampments, and the women could receive regular examinations to detect the presence of disease. As Pershing later wrote, "Soon we had the traffic under perfect control with a resulting low rate of venereal disease. Everybody was satisfied, as the towns have been kept absolutely clear of that sort of thing. . . . The establishment was necessary and has proved the best way to handle a difficult problem."[60]

By September, Pershing was exchanging opinions with General Scott regarding the timing of the removal of U.S. troops from Mexico. Pershing suggested capturing or killing the revolutionary leader "would accomplish little or nothing so far as Mexico is concerned."[61] General Scott did not want Pershing and his men to leave Mexico prematurely. He was afraid that if after the Americans left and troops were compelled to go back in to address another crisis, the Carranza government would prove antagonistic and refuse completely. The general stated that President Wilson "prefers to keep you where you are for the time being. How long this is going to continue, none of us know."[62] In fact, Wilson had long given up on capturing Villa. Secretary of War Baker even stated years later in a U.S. Army War College lecture that he never wanted Villa captured: "I was in hopes they would not catch him. I would not know what to do with him if they did, and Villa captured was much less use to us than Villa at large."[63]

That same month, U.S. officials met with representatives of the Carranza government in New London, Connecticut, to negotiate the withdrawal process for U.S. troops. The Americans wanted assurances from Mexico regarding safety on the border, while Mexico insisted it was already safe. (The Mexicans were not prepared to admit the presence of Pershing and his troopers had anything to do with their assertion.) The claim was unfounded, of course. Villa was no longer crossing the border, but he was still an active entity. In August, he raided Chihuahua City and broke open the local penitentiary, letting the prisoners scatter to the winds—all at Carranza's expense. When General Treviño gave chase, his own bodyguard turned on him and joined the Villistas. Most of Carranza's artillerymen did the same. By late November Villa and his men had captured Chihuahua City. When an anxious Pershing requested permission to renew the chase against Villa, Washington denied him the opportunity.

The order for withdrawal came in early January 1917. By the twenty-eighth, Pershing scheduled a slow march, taking a full week to move from Colonia Dublán and back across the border to Columbus. Once at Columbus, Pershing stood at attention on a grandstand as his men marched past him. It was hardly a spit-and-polish affair, and even Pershing wore his field uniform and four-dent campaign hat, a .45 pistol still hanging at his side. The accompanying military bands played the popular tune "When Johnny Comes Marching Home."

After nearly eleven months in Mexico, Pershing, as well as government and military officials, considered the gains and losses of the Punitive Expedition. Certainly, U.S. forces never caught Villa, but the controversy still persists over whether the goal of the expedition was to eliminate Villa or merely to hamper and scatter his troops, representing two different outcomes. Pershing felt a sense of failure, but he could easily put his finger on why he failed, if failure was, in fact, the considered result. He did not receive support from the Carranza government—just the opposite—and Mexican citizens either blocked his actions or only cooperated in small numbers. It was a variation of the old adage "The enemy of my enemy is my friend." The Carrancistas and the Villistas shared no love for one another, but they dually hated the Americans. Moreover, the landscape constantly provided too many places for one man to hide. "From the very first," mused Pershing, "from the time we crossed the line, we were met by nothing but misinformation and subtle maneuvers to lead us off on wrong trails. And throughout the pursuit we never received a bit of correct information till it was too late."[64]

Admittedly, the Punitive Expedition did manage to make Villa's world a much more difficult place. With thousands of U.S. troops riding in every direction across Chihuahua, the Villistas always remained watchful for a lengthy dust cloud in the distance signaling the approach of a U.S. cavalry troop. Failing to capture Villa was not equivalent to completely failing the mission. As Pershing wrote, "We had not captured Villa, to be sure, as we had hoped to do, but when active pursuit stopped we had broken up and scattered his band, which was our original mission." The general knew the human ledger all too well, noting that "one hundred and thirty-five of the bandits had answered to us with their lives, eighty-five were known to have been wounded, and nineteen captured."[65] Many of Villa's pistoleros did not remain in the field with their much-sought-after commander and chose instead to abandon him for safer circumstances. As historian James Hurst observes, "The naked truth is that Pershing harried Villa closely, killed his chief officers as well as most of his men, and kept him on the run."[66]

The Punitive Expedition had delivered John Joseph Pershing back into the bleak desert country of the American Southwest. But just as his early assignments in New Mexico as one of the Green P's had proved formative for him as a young cavalry officer, the Punitive Expedition also provided important experiences for Pershing, some of which served him well for the command he soon gained to lead the AEF in Europe. The expedition was not a learning opportunity for him alone, of course. In all, he led over eleven thousand men in country during the campaign, with all gaining important combat experience that later served many of them well in Europe. The Mexico campaign also gave significant command opportunities to several key officers who eventually made their way to Europe, including Patton, Lesley J. McNair, U. S. Grant III, Courtney Hodges, and others. The Punitive Expedition also helped Pershing identify weak colonels and other officers, several of whom he would not rely on for service in World War I. Border issues with Mexico led the U.S. Army to create the modern National Guard as well. Placing more than 100,000 troops on the border helped provide an experienced core of troops that made up the first American divisions sent overseas. In effect, the American frontier, once again, helped prepare Pershing's American troops for war.

Pershing learned a host of additional lessons from his eleven months in Mexico. He understood how deficient the U.S. military was and the issues it would face in fighting a large-scale war in the immediate future. Supplies, including ammunition, were often short. The campaign revealed early on that "the total amount of U.S. artillery ammunition was estimated to be enough for just three minutes of shooting."[67] The general realized during the expedition the military's shortfall in manpower within the ranks and that conscription was probably going to be necessary.

Little things in Mexico translated into important changes later. The shoes issued to regular infantry did not hold up well under constant campaigning, and a replacement was subsequently introduced to the men of the AEF. The types of trucks, automobiles, and airplanes that worked best in the field also became clearer during the Punitive Expedition.

As for Pershing, the lessons proved incalculable. He had commanded more men than any American general had since the

Civil War. His service added to his reputation as a field commander, one who pushed his men hard even as he tried to provide for them as best he could.

Despite failing to capture Villa, Pershing emerged from the Punitive Expedition, in the minds of many Americans, as an extraordinary military commander. On that day in Columbus, as the troops filed past, Pershing was reminiscent of Nelson Miles, whose thirty years of field service in the U.S. Army ended in a review of his troops on a wind-swept prairie in South Dakota. If John's military career had ended in 1916, no one would have faulted him. He had served the U.S. Army for his thirty years through assignments that took him from New Mexico to the Dakotas to Montana to the Far East to California and back again, and at the cost of his family. What Pershing could not know with certainty in January 1917 as he stood on the grandstand at Columbus was what the future held for him as a man wearing two stars on his shoulders. Ahead of him loomed the greatest command of his days in uniform, with even more stars yet to come.

Conclusion

Civilian, 1917–48

After nearly a year of chasing Pancho Villa, General Pershing and his men returned to Columbus, New Mexico. Within two months, President Wilson addressed a joint session of Congress and requested a declaration of war against Germany. The war in Europe had been underway for almost three years. During that period, Germany had engaged in unrestricted submarine warfare, raising the ire and patriotic fervor of many Americans to a final breaking point. The United States also received information from British Naval Intelligence revealing a secret proposal between the German foreign secretary in Berlin and the German minister in Mexico City, suggesting negotiations with the Carranza government toward a military alliance against the United States. In this, events regarding Mexico did indeed finally lead to war. By May 1917, Pershing received a telegram from Senator Warren, Frankie's father, asking Pershing how well he spoke French.

Two months earlier, while still stationed at Fort Sam Houston, Texas, Pershing received a telegram from Chancellor Samuel Avery of the University of Nebraska. It contained a request and an invitation: "The senior class invites you to give commencement address June 13. . . . Hope you can accept. Colonel Roosevelt and several of the governors will be in the city on occasion of the semi-centennial statehood celebration. Hope to

Conclusion

make it a great patriotic occasion. Will be glad to receive acceptance subject to approval by the federal department of war."[1]

Although Pershing accepted the invitation immediately, other commitments soon intervened. In the years that followed, the city of Lincoln and the university he loved honored their favorite son over and over. Today, one can find his name across the city: Pershing Auditorium, Pershing School, Pershing Armory, Pershing Road.[2] John returned several times to Lincoln following the Great War. Just as Lincoln adopted him, so he held a fond place for the Nebraska prairie capital. As he once noted, "I have always considered Nebraska at least one of my homes, but today I confess that is the most important of them all."[3]

Pershing exchanged Nebraska for Europe. Soon, he was secretly whisked on board the White Star ocean liner RMS *Baltic*, with an escort of several navy destroyers, bound for Europe. During the next two years, his historical legacy became fixed.[4]

The Americans' presence on the western front managed to tip the scales of the conflict in favor of the Allies. By November 1918 Pershing and his men clearly had helped lead the United States and the Allies to ultimate victory. Throughout weeks of fighting, the tenacious American Expeditionary Forces, with support from artillery, planes, tanks, and the capable, stern leadership of Gen. John J. Pershing, had fought the Germans and their allies to a standstill. Concerning the last great battle of the war, the Meuse-Argonne Offensive, where thousands of Pershing's men fought against strong resistance and counterattack, the American commander wrote: "Between September 26th and November 11th, 22 American and 6 French divisions, with an approximate fighting strength of 500,000 men ... had engaged and decisively beaten 43 different German divisions, with an estimated fighting strength of 470,000. Of the 22 American divisions, four had at different times during this period been in action on fronts other than our own. The enemy suffered an estimated loss of over 100,000 casualties in this battle and the First Army about 117,000. It captured 26,000 prisoners, 874 cannon, 3,000 machine guns and large quantities of material."[5]

Conclusion

With the end of the Great War, Pershing never saw combat again.

Following World War I, Pershing was lionized on multiple continents. As America's hero, the possibilities of political office seemed likely. Previous American generals—Washington, Jackson, Grant—had all been elected president. In 1919 British king George V expressed his opinion: "You, of course, will be the next American president."[6] Supportive steps came early, with the formation of the Pershing Republican League by Ohio Republicans just weeks following the signing of the armistice. A Democratic congressman from Pennsylvania spoke on the House floor and even suggested that both parties nominate their hero. In December, during a visit to Lincoln, Nebraska, Pershing seemed noncommittal about it all. Not until April 1920 did Pershing make his candidacy official. But by that time, other possible candidates had already gained traction, with a *Literary Digest* poll placing Pershing ninth in a field of fourteen potential Republican candidates. Pershing stepped back, waiting to see if popular acclaim might support his candidacy. But such support did not materialize.

His military career continued in peacetime until 1924, the year he turned sixty-four, the mandatory retirement age for U.S. Army officers. He became the most respected living general in America and was promoted to general of the armies. In this role, he became the only active-duty, six-star general in U.S. history.[7] On September 12 he ended a career that had begun with his graduation from West Point nearly forty years earlier. Once again, after decades in uniform, Pershing was a civilian. As a retired American general—actually, *the* retired American general—he lived as fully as he could manage, traveling to Europe and visiting old battlefields. In a *New York Times* interview given the day following his retirement, Pershing reflected on his time as an American soldier: "There's no 'glory' in killing. There's no 'glory' in maiming men. There are the glorious dead, but they would be more glorious living. The most glorious thing is life. And we who are alive must cling to it, each of us helping."[8]

Conclusion

One of Pershing's most important roles following his retirement was as the appointed head of the American Battle Monuments Commission. In this role, he was responsible for selecting designs for war monuments to commemorate the contributions of U.S. forces during the war and to maintain the memory of their sacrifices.[9] As the head of the monuments commission, Pershing spent months at a time in France, giving him the opportunity to continue a relationship that began during the war. At a Paris reception in mid-June 1917, Pershing met Micheline Resco, a petite, twenty-three-year-old Romanian artist who was soon commissioned to paint his portrait. She charmed the older Pershing, and within a few weeks, he was writing her letters. By the fall, they began a long-term romantic relationship. Pershing visited her in Paris as often as he could during the war, with John coveting such opportunities for respite and female companionship. Once the war was over, Pershing returned to the States but did not offer to take Resco with him. When in Europe, he returned to her, spending many evenings at her side. Pershing sent Micheline a check every month and, as early as 1926, made her the beneficiary of his life insurance policy. They secretly married in 1946 and remained companions until his passing in 1948. After his death, Warren delivered a final letter from his father to Micheline that expressed emotions reminiscent of John's earlier letters to his first wife, Frankie: "How happy have been the days we have spent together. . . . In all the future the lingering fragrance of your kisses shall be fresh on my lips."[10]

John also spent several years writing his memoirs, which were published in 1931 in the two-volume book, *My Experiences in the World War*. For his efforts, he received the Pulitzer Prize in history in 1932. Willa Cather was present at the Pulitzer Prize ceremony, which was held at the Plaza Hotel in New York. During his acceptance speech, John mentioned Cather's having been a student of his at the University of Nebraska.

Through the decades, Pershing and Cather rarely met, but their fame overlapped each other's on occasion. Both received an honorary doctorate from UNL in 1917. Cather accepted hers

Conclusion

in person, but Pershing received his in absentia, since he was serving in Europe with the war. They each received the Pulitzer Prize, although nine years apart. Both Pershing and Cather became members of the International Mark Twain Society, and each served a term as the vice president of the literary organization.[11]

The years slipped by, with Pershing often remaining in Washington DC, where he was recognized on the streets as he took long walks in various parks. Although officially retired, America's leaders occasionally called on Pershing, as when President Franklin Roosevelt asked him to attend the coronation of the new British monarch King George VI. But such occasions were rare, for Pershing begged off most of them. Reaching his seventies, he struggled with chronic conditions and suffered frequent colds that spurred him to spend his winters in Arizona, placing him back in the Southwest, where his military career had begun. In 1937 Pershing attended Warren's wedding, even though two months earlier John had fallen seriously ill with heart and kidney issues. Despite newspaper headlines suggesting the former general was declining quickly, he had managed to recover.

During the 1930s, Pershing watched with dismay the expansionist dictatorships in Europe and Asia. As did many Americans during the years of the Great Depression, Pershing feared another "great war," one that might pull the United States into a second international vortex of death and destruction. At the 1937 dedication of the World War I chapel at Flanders Field, Pershing, the American Battle Monuments Commission's first chairman, warned: "If amidst the difficult problems that confront all nations today, there exists a profound aversion to all violent solutions, it is because so many millions of men are alive who know the horrors of war. The last conflict profited no one and left so many problems unsettled." He observed the fragility of the existing peace and the dramatic build-up of extensive stockpiles of weapons at "ruinous cost." He also opined how "distrust and hatred still reign." If another war came, Pershing cautioned, it could easily mean "the end of western civilization."[12]

Conclusion

He advocated continually for greater U.S. preparedness. No one knew better than he how unprepared the U.S. military had been as it delivered its young men to the killing fields along the western front. He also campaigned on behalf of Brig. Gen. George C. Marshall, who had served as the operations officer for the First Army during World War I and afterward as Pershing's right-hand man. During a White House meeting with Franklin Roosevelt in the summer of 1939, Pershing informed the president, "There is a young general over in the Army Plans Division who you need to have over here for a talk before you make your decision as to who will be the next chief of staff."[13] Ultimately, Marshall was appointed to the important role. Even in retirement, John Pershing's was still a respected voice.

By 1941 the United States did enter World War II, as Pershing's health began to fail. He was suffering from heart trouble by this time. He moved his permanent residence to an apartment in Walter Reed Army Hospital, Washington DC, so he could be near his favorite physician, Dr. Shelley Marietta. There he led a quiet life. Micheline Resco moved to Washington and visited him almost daily. He played cards, read, and saw frequent visitors, including old friends from Nebraska and from his long service in the military. A 1943 *Time* magazine feature presented Pershing as living a Spartan existence. "Every day he rose at 8, draped a bathrobe over his pajamas and watched his breakfast roll in—grapefruit, cereal, soft-boiled egg, toast, coffee. There were few things an old man could enjoy, but he damn well did like and insist on grapefruit, and for lunch a chop and spinach. He liked spinach. No cigars. Gave up cigars 35 years ago on the advice of his doctor. A touch of whiskey now and then."[14]

On July 15, 1948, at 3:50 a.m., Gen. John Joseph "Black Jack" Pershing died of coronary artery disease and congestive heart failure at Walter Reed Army Hospital. He was eighty-seven years old. General Marshall planned the details of his memorial services. He was given a state funeral, and 300,000 people observed the procession on the streets of Washington even as a heavy rain fell. Sixteen generals led the procession, including Gen. Dwight D. Eisenhower, the supreme Allied commander

Conclusion

during World War II. Pershing is buried in Arlington National Cemetery with a common soldier's grave marker. According to his wishes, his gravesite is near the graves of the doughboys he commanded.[15]

His military career had spanned decades and taken him far from his Laclede, Missouri, roots. During Pershing's halcyon days as the commandant of the cadet program at the University of Nebraska, undergraduate Willa Cather won first prize for a short story titled "The Fear That Walks by Noonday." The story unfolds during a college football game, a plot suggested by her friend Dorothy Canfield. Cather describes Horton, one of the college players, with words that might be fitting as a eulogy for John Joseph Pershing, who was "one of those men who, by the very practicality of their intellects, astonish the world. He was a glorious man for a college. He was brilliant, adaptable, and successful; yet all his brains he managed to cover up by a pate of tow hair, parted very carefully in the middle, and his iron strength was generally very successfully disguised.... In short he possessed the one thing which is greater than genius, the faculty of clothing genius in such boundless good nature that it is offensive to nobody."[16]

John Pershing's nature, although sometimes rough around the edges and stern by practice, constantly revealed a man who was inherently good, the product of an honest upbringing on a farm in the Midwest. He remained true to himself through the years, maintaining a strong sense of duty and responsibility to those entrusted to him, whether family or troop. He was recognized then and even now as a man driven by purpose, brave to a fault, fair dealing, strict regarding rules and regulations. A stickler to detail who was often seen as cold and removed, he was not loved but certainly respected by his troops. Pershing himself was capable of expressing great emotion and passion, especially toward his family and those women he held closest. He was a lifelong student and teacher. The man from Missouri was also capable of seeing the humanity in all who crossed his path regardless of race.

In Willa Cather's novel *One of Ours*, her doughboy protagonist,

Conclusion

Claude—molded in the likeness of her cousin G. P. Cather—dies in action under the command of General Pershing. Prior to his death, Claude and his comrade in arms David Gerhardt enjoyed the company of a French farm couple, Papa and Madame Joubert, who provided Claude with his first billet in France. It was an evening of reunion, with a supper featuring a dozen-egg omelet, warm baths, clean pajamas, and sheets infused with lavender.

As Pershing lay in a warm hospital bed at Walter Reed, near death, one may only wonder where his mind turned—perhaps to his exciting days as a young cavalryman in the sagebrush southwestern frontier, or the ivy-covered halls of the University of Nebraska, or the pine-studded hills of Montana, or the lush jungles of the Philippines, or his sun-parched days in Mexico, or heroic moments along the western front. Perhaps he spent his final moments reaching across psychic distance back to the arms of his beloved Frankie. John's memories may have even stretched to Laclede, the home of his American origins. Perhaps Cather's words eulogize Pershing's final moments of mortality, reflecting Claude's golden night, one wrapped in a French rurality and a natural simplicity reminiscent of his old Missouri home, a place of streams, wheat fields, orchards, and family:

> All along the river valleys the poplars and cottonwoods had changed from green to yellow—evenly colored, looking like candle-flames in the mist and rain. Across the fields, along the horizon they ran, like torches passed from hand to hand, and all the willows by the little streams had become silver. The vineyards were green still, thickly spotted with curly, blood-red branches. It all flashed back beside his pillow in the dark: this beautiful land, this beautiful people . . . gold poplars, blue-green vineyards, wet, scarlet vine-leaves, rain dripping into the court, fragrant darkness . . . sleep, stronger than all.[17]

Acknowledgments

As with any writer, I could not have written this book without help from others. I relied on a wide variety of secondary and primary sources, as well as more than four dozen articles to develop this biography. Others made contributions to my work in unique ways. But some contributions were quite singular.

Among the sources I reference in this book, the most significant is a product of Pershing's own pen. Following his retirement from the U.S. Army in 1924, at the mandatory age of sixty-four, Pershing set out to write about his service during the Great War and, in 1931, saw the publication of his book, *My Experiences in the World War*, a work that won the Pulitzer Prize in history the following year. His lengthy, excruciatingly detailed—and well-written—account provides readers with a unique perspective into the conflict itself and the decisions he and others made in its pursuit, as well as the political back-and-forth that went on between the American commander and the various Allied generals and the political leaders they served.

Once Pershing completed his book, he took up another personal writing project, the story of his life prior to the Great War, a full biography of a man many Americans wanted to know better. Pershing worked on it for several years, relying often on assistance from the U.S. Army and others for details and fact

Acknowledgments

checking. But his timing was off. By the mid-1930s, Pershing was in his midseventies. He had lost an element of personal drive and sometimes found it difficult to express himself regarding extremely personal experiences, including the deaths of his wife and three daughters in the Presidio fire of 1915. As a result, he completely omitted that tragedy from the final draft of his manuscript. Ultimately, Pershing did not complete the manuscript to his satisfaction before his death in 1948.

Through the intervening decades, the Library of Congress Manuscript Division held the lengthy manuscript as an unpublished resource and made it available to historians and other researchers. One historian would finally distill the various chapters Pershing had written and partially edited and remove them from academic obscurity. John T. Greenwood, the former chief of the Office of Medical History, Office of the Surgeon General, U.S. Army, produced a well-formed, definitive version of Pershing's personal story that the University of Kentucky Press published in 2013, nearly a century following the campaign described in the book's final chapter—Pershing's Punitive Expedition. In an appendix to his version of Pershing's life, Greenwood provided mini biographies of close to 250 individuals Pershing referenced, many of whom no longer ring bells with even the most rabid of history buffs.

Greenwood's efforts made my own so much simpler and, hopefully, helped me produce a better book than I might have been able to write otherwise. Pershing's own voice is infused throughout my own narrative, giving the reader a clearer sense of the man in question. For Greenwood's work, I am extremely grateful.

Other works proved crucial in writing *Time in the Wilderness*. Historian Frank Vandiver, who served as the president of Texas A&M University, the University of North Texas, and Rice University during various tenures, was a Civil War historian who embarked on a study of John Pershing by the late 1950s. After nearly twenty years of research, Vandiver published in 1977 *Black Jack: The Life and Times of John J. Pershing*, which became a runner-up for a National Book Award. His study is

Acknowledgments

full and his words poetic. Father Donald Smythe, a Jesuit priest, was a professor of history at John Carroll University and lectured at the U.S. Army War College and the National War College. In 1973 his book *Guerrilla Warrior: The Early Life of John J. Pershing* represented the first scholarly biography of Pershing, spanning the general's life and career to 1917. Few scholars have studied the life of Pershing to a greater extent than Smythe. No study of Pershing should begin without Smythe's book within easy reach.

In a different but crucial way, Barney McCoy, a professor at the College of Journalism and Mass Communications, University of Nebraska–Lincoln, must be recognized for his influence on this book. In 2004 I wrote a short book for younger readers on the life of General Pershing. Ten years later, Barney—a recipient of six Emmy Awards—contacted me about a film documentary he was working on based on Pershing's life. My wife and I first met him at a restaurant in Lincoln, and he filled me in on the project. I was intrigued. In the spring of 2015, he included me as an on-camera consulting historian for his film *Black Jack Pershing: Love and War*, which was released in 2017 and went on to win various prestigious recognitions, including an Eric Sevareid Award from the Midwest Broadcast Journalists Association. McCoy's project rekindled a flame for me regarding Pershing. The result is this book. Barney also graciously agreed to read my manuscript and critique it with the eye of a journalist-turned-historian. His critique was kind, complimentary, keen, and straight to the point. The changes he encouraged helped make this a better book.

Thanks also go to Dr. Mitchell Yockelson, an investigative archivist at the National Archives and Records Administration in Washington DC, who read my manuscript and provided wonderful insights as a historian entirely familiar with John J. Pershing. He, too, provided advice wrapped in tremendous support for this book, and further improvements bear his fingerprints.

Thanks to Matt Piersol, a reference librarian at the Nebraska State Historical Society, and his staff for providing assistance

Acknowledgments

in accessing boxes of John J. Pershing's papers as well as the George DeRue Meiklejohn papers.

My appreciation to Ryan Brubacher, reference librarian in the Library of Congress's Prints and Photographs Division, for guidance in locating photographs.

Thanks to Pete Brink, assistant archivist for the University of Nebraska–Lincoln Libraries, whose assistance in locating and securing permissions for several photographs was crucial.

I'm grateful and thankful to several of the fine folks who work at Potomac Books, including Tom Swanson, Taylor Rothgeb, and Sara Springsteen, as well as copy editor Vicki Chamlee. Each made his or her contribution to making this book as solid a work as possible.

Finally, I must acknowledge the support of my wife, Beverly. A retired English professor, she read the entire manuscript and provided crucial suggestions and insights. In addition, she was the one who suggested the University of Nebraska as a possible publisher for my manuscript. For her support on this project, I will always be grateful, even though I will never be able to repay her for all the evenings I spent time researching and writing in one part of the family room, while she entertained herself in another.

Notes

Introduction

1. The modern equivalent of this route is a section of the old Route 66 (today's Interstate 40) running from the New Mexico–Arizona border through the Navajo Reservation to U.S. Highway 89 outside Cameron, Arizona, and then to Arizona's State Highway 64, which reaches the Grand Canyon. But none of those paved highways marked Pershing's path in 1889.

2. Smythe, "'Black Jack,'" 11–23.

3. Wallace, "Lieutenants Pershing and Stotsenburg," 265–84. Wallace actually misidentifies the year of the Pershing-Stotsenburg Grand Canyon adventure even as he misspells Stotsenburg's name. The crux of the Wallace article is actually a diary written by Stotsenburg, who described the misbegotten trip, and was previously unpublished.

4. Wallace, "Lieutenants Pershing and Stotsenburg," 269.

5. In Pershing's published memoirs, he refers to Tom Keams as Tom Kearns. Pershing, *My Life*, 65.

6. Cather, *Song of the Lark*, 295.

7. Fourteen years later, famed photographer Edward Sheriff Curtis took his first photographs of Walpi, a place he returned to many times over a twenty-year span.

8. Smythe, "'Black Jack,'" 15.

9. Wallace, "Lieutenants Pershing and Stotsenburg," 268.

10. Wallace, "Lieutenants Pershing and Stotsenburg," 274.

11. Smythe, "'Black Jack,'" 16. The 1887 "Railroad and County Map of Arizona," created by George F. Cram, spells "Moenkopi" as "Moen Kapi." Whether Pershing and Stotsenburg had access to this map is not known, but the map does mark such sites as Walpi, Oraibi, Tuba City, and other mile markers

along their route. The map is also misleading. It does not indicate a lack of water sources or other difficulties along the route the two army officers followed. This is the difficulty of working with a two-dimensional map in a three-dimensional environment.

12. Wallace, "Lieutenants Pershing and Stotsenberg," 275.
13. Smythe, "'Black Jack,'" 18.
14. Wallace, "Lieutenants Pershing and Stotsenberg," 276.
15. McGee, "Desert Thirst as Disease," 295. Historian Nathaniel Philbrick refers to this landmark study and provides additional details regarding the effects of dehydration on those crewmen who were left as survivors in whaleboats following the sinking of their whaling ship by a rogue whale. One additional circumstance these ocean-bound survivors also contended with was the effects of consuming seawater. See Philbrick, *In the Heart*, 126–28.
16. McGee, "Desert Thirst as Disease," 283.
17. Kemper, *Splendid Savage*, 79.
18. Sides, *Blood and Thunder*, 77.
19. Wallace, "Lieutenants Pershing and Stotsenberg," 276.
20. Smythe, "'Black Jack,'" 19.
21. Wallace, "Lieutenants Pershing and Stotsenberg," 277.
22. Wallace, "Lieutenants Pershing and Stotsenberg," 277.
23. Wallace, "Lieutenants Pershing and Stotsenberg," 277.
24. Wallace, "Lieutenants Pershing and Stotsenberg," 278.
25. Smythe, "'Black Jack,'" 20.
26. Pershing, *My Life*, 66. According to Stotsenburg's account, Pershing made himself a toddy with the remaining whiskey and tried to make coffee for his comrade, which turned out disappointing because "he did not let the water boil at all." Still, Stotsenburg states he did not complain. Wallace, "Lieutenants Pershing and Stotsenberg," 278.
27. Wallace, "Lieutenants Pershing and Stotsenberg," 278.
28. Wallace, "Lieutenants Pershing and Stotsenberg," 278–79.
29. Pershing, *My Life*, 67.
30. Cheek, *Arizona*, 68.
31. McNamee, *Grand Canyon Place Names*, 59.
32. Wallace, "Lieutenants Pershing and Stotsenberg," 280. The original Hance cabin was located near where the modern-day Grand Canyon Village stands, the most popular destination for visitors to the canyon. Today's New Hance Trail is used by intrepid hikers, since it is a difficult circuit, rugged, and engineered along multiple switchbacks. Hance was a fixture at the canyon for nearly forty years, having arrived perhaps as early as 1883. The former Confederate built a tent encampment on his property to house tourists. Even when the famed western hotelier Fred Harvey bought property along the South Rim after the turn of the century, Hance was hired as a storyteller and official tourist greeter. He died

in the spring of 1919, a mere matter of weeks before the Grand Canyon was declared a national park.

33. Pershing, *My Life*, 67.
34. Wallace, "Lieutenants Pershing and Stotsenberg," 281.
35. Cather, *Song of the Lark*, 313.
36. Wallace, "Lieutenants Pershing and Stotsenberg," 281.
37. Smythe, "'Black Jack,'" 22.
38. Wallace, "Lieutenants Pershing and Stotsenberg," 283.
39. Wallace, "Lieutenants Pershing and Stotsenberg," 283.
40. Wallace, "Lieutenants Pershing and Stotsenberg," 283.
41. Wallace, "Lieutenants Pershing and Stotsenberg," 283.
42. Stotsenburg and Pershing crossed paths several times through the years following their Grand Canyon adventure. Both men served in the Pine Ridge Expedition to quell the Ghost Shirt uprising and in the Philippines. Stotsenburg was killed in action on April 23, 1899, at Quinqua, Bulacan, as he led a charge against entrenched Filipino positions. Fort Stotsenburg in Luzon was named for him in 1903. Eventually it included Clark Field and became Clark Air Base.
43. Smythe, *Guerrilla Warrior*, 280, 282.

1. Childhood, 1860–73

1. MacAdam, "His Boyhood," 46.
2. Pershing, *My Life*, 11.
3. Pershing, *My Life*, 11.
4. Pershing, *Pershing Family*, cited in Pershing, *My Life*, 1n2.
5. MacAdam, "His Boyhood," 46.
6. MacAdam, "His Boyhood," 46.
7. MacAdam, "His Boyhood," 46.
8. Pershing, *My Life*, 13–14.
9. Pershing, *My Life*, 15.
10. As with so many other writers of fiction, Cather relied on her life's experiences with people and places to frame her novels and short stories. Nebraska provided extensive fodder for her works, to the point, as Cather biographer James Woodress notes, "it is hard sometimes to tell where the reality leaves off and the fiction begins." Woodress, *Willa Cather*, xiv.
11. Cather, *My Ántonia*, ix–x.
12. McAdam, "His Boyhood," 52.
13. Smythe, *Guerrilla Warrior*, 1.
14. Smythe, *Guerrilla Warrior*, 2.
15. Beilein, *Bushwhackers*, 136.
16. Beilein, "Guerrilla Shirt," 183.
17. O'Bryan, "Red Legs." For additional background on Buffalo Bill's days with the Red Legs, see Warren, *Buffalo Bill's America*, 33–37.

18. Pershing, *My Life*, 17.
19. Davis, Perry, and Kirkley, *War of the Rebellion*, 1031.
20. Beilein, *Bushwhackers*, 137. By contrast, Holtzclaw's men, facing shotguns and rifles, probably carried pistols exclusively. This did not automatically translate into a distinct advantage for the soldiers, however. Bushwhackers in Missouri typically relied on revolvers rather than long guns. They could carry several six-shot revolvers at a time, adding to their firepower. The Missouri guerrilla leader Bloody Bill Anderson was known to have often carried a brace of six pistols at a time. The favorite pistol of guerrillas during the Civil War was the Colt Navy 1851 model .36 caliber. The weapon sometimes did not inflict a fatal wound, so guerrillas would have to execute their victims with a head shot after the battle. When former guerrillas turned to train and bank robbing after the Civil War, they adopted new weapons. Jesse James's new favorite was the Colt 1873 Peacemaker. Later when the James boys ran with the Younger Gang, they often relied on Remingtons and the Smith and Wesson Scofield .45 caliber. See Trimble, "Did Jesse James?"
21. Vandiver, *Black Jack*, 1:4–5.
22. Smythe, "'Black Jack,'" 3.
23. Smith, *Until the Last Trumpet*, 6.
24. Pershing, *My Life*, 17.
25. Pershing, *My Life*, 19.
26. Pershing, *My Life*, 18.

2. Community, 1873–82

1. MacAdam, "His Boyhood," 53.
2. MacAdam, "His Boyhood," 53.
3. MacAdam, "His Boyhood," 53.
4. Pershing, *My Life*, 20.
5. Pershing, *My Life*, 22.
6. Pershing, *My Life*, 20.
7. Pershing, *My Life*, 20.
8. Cather, *My Ántonia*, 198–99.
9. Pershing, *My Life*, 20.
10. Vandiver, *Black Jack*, 7; and Pershing, *My Life*, 19.
11. Smith, *Until the Last Trumpet*, 8.
12. Pershing, *My Life*, 24.
13. Pershing, *My Life*, 24.
14. Pershing, *My Life*, 25.
15. Pershing, *My Life*, 25.
16. Pershing, *My Life*, 26.
17. Pershing, *My Life*, 26.

18. Pershing, *My Life*, 26.
19. Vandiver, *Black Jack*, 7.
20. Tomlinson, *Story of General Pershing*, 14–15.
21. O'Connor, *Black Jack Pershing*, 21.
22. Perry, *Pershing*, 4.
23. "Heartland."
24. Pershing, *My Life*, 31.
25. Cather, "Enchanted Bluff," 780.
26. MacAdam, "His Boyhood," 55.
27. Vandiver, *Black Jack*, 14.
28. MacAdam, "His Boyhood," 55.
29. Smith, *Until the Last Trumpet*, 13.
30. O'Connor, *Black Jack Pershing*, 20.
31. Pershing, *My Life*, 23. Before Pershing's memoirs were published, his original manuscript copy read: "I was always able to hold my own." At some later date, he altered his words, scratching out the word "always" and replacing it with the more accurate "usually."
32. Pershing, *My Life*, 33.
33. Vandiver, *Black Jack*, 15; and Pershing, *My Life*, 33–34.
34. Today, the former normal school is Truman State University, part of the University of Missouri system.
35. Smith, *Until the Last Trumpet*, 13.
36. Vandiver, *Black Jack*, 11.
37. Charlie Spurgeon, quoted in "Pershing's 'Jinx' Birthday," 58–61.
38. O'Connor, *Black Jack Pershing*, 23–24.
39. MacAdam, "His Boyhood," 55.
40. O'Connor, *Black Jack Pershing*, 23; and Smythe, "Early Years," 19.
41. In his memoirs, Pershing states that when he arrived for the exam in Trenton, he "found sixteen other applicants," making a total of seventeen including himself. See Pershing, *My Life*, 36. Other sources identify numbers between fifteen and eighteen. Twenty-five years after his graduation from West Point, Pershing wrote a "Greeting to the Class" in which he suggested the number was eighteen. Andrews, *1886–1911*, 6.
42. Frederick Palmer, "Pershing: Master of Million Men; Kindly of Heart, but an Iron Ruler," *Los Angeles Times*, January 11, 1931, 1, newspaper clipping, John J. Pershing Papers, ca. 1861–1963, box 1, Nebraska State Historical Society Archives, Lincoln.
43. Pershing, *My Life*, 38.
44. Tomlinson, *Story of General Pershing*, 33.
45. Tomlinson, *Story of General Pershing*, 38.
46. Tomlinson, *Story of General Pershing*, 30.
47. Tomlinson, *Story of General Pershing*, 33–34.

Notes to Pages 61–72

3. Cadets, 1882–87

1. That summer, 144 young men reported to West Point to take the entrance examination. When the test smoke cleared, 40 had not passed. The date of Pershing's birth is at the center of a small-framed controversy. While officially his birth date is September 13, 1860, some sources identify a different date in January 1860. At least one Laclede neighbor, interviewed when Pershing was an adult, recalled a January birth date. A boyhood friend stated that he and Pershing were born on the exact same day, January 13, 1860. Pershing's normal school records at Kirksville show him at age twenty when he enrolled in the spring of 1880. If his birthday was in September, he would have been nineteen, instead. One possibility for the discrepancy might have to do with West Point and its entrance qualifications. Twenty-two was the official cutoff. If Pershing was born in January, then he was too old to apply to West Point in the spring of 1882. A falsified birth date in September placed him at an age three or four months younger, thus qualifying him to become a cadet.

2. Vandiver, *Black Jack*, 23.

3. Following the Civil War, Howard served as the head of the Freedman's Bureau, a federal program designed to help freed slaves assimilate into society. By 1867 he became one of the founders of an African American college later named Howard University in his honor. In 1872 Howard was dispatched into the West to parley with the Apache leader Cochise. When he was brought into the chief's presence, Howard, known as "the Christian General," fell to his knees and began to fervently pray out loud for God to convince Cochise to surrender to him and sign a peace agreement. The Apache leader agreed to do so. Cochise would later return to resistance, however.

4. Pershing, *My Life*, 39.
5. Smith, *Until the Last Trumpet*, 21.
6. Smith, *Until the Last Trumpet*, 39.
7. MacAdam, "West Point Days," 164.
8. Perry, *Pershing*, 11.
9. Pershing, *My Life*, 45.
10. Perry, *Pershing*, 11.
11. Mead, *Doughboys*, 110.
12. Pershing, *My Life*, 46.
13. Smith, *Until the Last Trumpet*, 23.
14. Smythe, *Guerrilla Warrior*, 12.
15. Smythe, *Guerrilla Warrior*, 13.
16. U.S. Military Academy, *Official Register*, 10.
17. Smythe, *Guerrilla Warrior*, 14.
18. Pershing, *My Life*, 51.
19. Vandiver, *Black Jack*, 49
20. Vandiver, *Black Jack*, 49.

21. Yockelson, *Forty-Seven Days*, 20.
22. Cather, *Death Comes*, 64.
23. Cather, *Death Comes*, 64.
24. Myers, *New Mexico Military Installations*, 11.
25. University of Nebraska–Lincoln, *History of the Military Department*, 3. Italics in original.
26. Utley, *Frontier Regulars*, 82.
27. King, *War Eagle*, 232.
28. Utley, *Frontier Regulars*, xi. For a detailed study of the changing purposes of the U.S. Cavalry during the nineteenth century, see Showalter, "U.S. Cavalry," 6–23.
29. Lane, *Chasing Geronimo*, 5.
30. Crook, "Apache Problem," 597–98.
31. Bourke, *On the Border*, 329.
32. Yockelson, *Forty-Seven Days*, 20.
33. Pershing, *My Life*, 56.
34. MacAdam, "Indian Campaigns," 289–90.
35. Pershing, *My Life*, 57.
36. The spring was not named for the Mangus whom Pershing and his men were pursuing but for his father, Mangus Coloradas, the father-in-law of Cochise.
37. Pershing, *My Life*, 58; and Vandiver, *Black Jack*, 57.
38. The capture of Mangus proved a bit anticlimactic. After a large-scale "manhunt" by the U.S. Army, when he was finally captured, his followers numbered a pair of warriors, three women, a couple of young boys who may have been old enough to fight, and five younger children. Vandiver, *Black Jack*, 59.
39. Vandiver, *Black Jack*, 59.
40. MacAdam, "Indian Campaigns," 290.
41. Lacey, *Pershing*, 13.
42. O'Connor, *Black Jack Pershing*, 31.

4. Cavalry, 1887–90

1. Macadam, "Indian Campaigns," 290.
2. Pershing, *My Life*, 58.
3. Vandiver, *Black Jack*, 62.
4. Pershing remained an ardent supporter of the value of the rifle and the field combatants who carried them throughout much of his lengthy military career. He was slow to accept the view that the machine gun was becoming the key weapon of combat by World War I, but his exposure to the value of machine guns while serving as a military observer during the Russo-Japanese War (1904–5) and the Great War itself finally convinced him of the weapon's essentiality. That learning curve from rifle to machine gun, for Pershing, proved lengthy.

5. Vandiver, *Black Jack*, 61.
6. Pershing, *My Life*, 59.
7. Pershing, *My Life*, 67. Pershing witnessed this during his harrowing trip to the Grand Canyon with Stotsenburg.
8. Swartley, *Old Forts*, 56–57.
9. When Pershing arrived at Fort Stanton in August 1887, the fort was entering its twilight years. The Apaches were finally subdued, so the main purpose for which Stanton existed was eliminated. A revolving door of cavalry and infantry units manned the fort until October 1894, when Troop A, First Cavalry was the last posted. Come January 1896, the First Cavalry was removed for duty in Arizona. By 1899 Fort Stanton passed into the hands of the U.S. Marine Hospital, largely as a facility to treat tuberculosis patients, a role that continued under various auspices well into the twentieth century. See Myers, *Fort Stanton*, 40–42.
10. Smythe, *Guerrilla Warrior*, 16.
11. Utley, *Billy the Kid*, 18.
12. Utley, *Billy the Kid*, 19.
13. Pershing, *My Life*, 62.
14. Perry, *Pershing*, 19; and Smith, *Until the Last Trumpet*, 30. Pershing's original letter to Penn contains a blank today. Penn, decades after the fact, donated the Pershing letter to the Library of Congress. Before doing so, he engaged in a bit of editing and used a sharp blade literally to cut out the end of the cited sentence. What the passage may have referred to may only be surmised, but Pershing might have alluded to a shortage of female companionship at Fort Stanton. The letter is dated October 10, 1887.
15. O'Connor, *Black Jack Pershing*, 32.
16. MacAdam, "Indian Campaigns," 291.
17. Cather, *Death Comes*, 92.
18. Pershing, *My Life*, 62.
19. Vandiver, *Black Jack*, 69.
20. Vandiver, *Black Jack*, 70; and Pershing, *My Life*, 63.
21. O'Connor, *Black Jack Pershing*, 31.
22. O'Connor, *Black Jack Pershing*, 31.
23. Pershing, *My Life*, 60.
24. Pershing, *My Life*, 60.
25. Pershing, *My Life*, 63.
26. Buffalo Bill's *Wild West* grand-scale productions were preceded by a couple of original programs involving William Cody. In 1872 Cody went to Chicago to appear in a stage production titled *The Scouts of the Prairie*, which also featured his friend Texas Jack Omohundro. While Cody's acting left much to be desired, the play proved a hit with audiences. The following year, Wild Bill Hickok joined the cast. Then, in 1874, Cody established the *Buffalo Bill Combination*, which toured for ten years and included Cody reenacting

the 1876 Indian fight at Warbonnet Creek, where he claimed he killed and scalped a Cheyenne warrior. By 1883 in North Platte, he premiered his *Wild West* production. For more on Buffalo Bill, see Warren's *Buffalo Bill's America*.

27. Ingraham, "Adventures of Buffalo Bill."
28. Vandiver, *Black Jack*, 73.
29. Pershing, *My Life*, 63. Cody had served under Carr during the late 1860s as his personal scout and as the chief of scouts for the Fifth Cavalry. Following the Republican River Expedition—launched in the early summer of 1869 to protect settlers on the Southern Great Plains from Cheyenne raids—Carr wrote glowingly about the contributions of Buffalo Bill: "Our Scout William Cody . . . displayed great skill in following [the trail], and also deserves great credit for his fighting . . . his marksmanship being very conspicuous. . . . I hope to retain [Cody] as long as I am engaged in this duty." See King, *War Eagle*, 99. For details regarding the expedition, see King, "Republican River Expedition," 165–99.
30. Miller, *Soldiers and Settlers*, 234. For further details regarding Carson's forced "Long Walk" of the Navajos, see Sides, *Blood and Thunder*.
31. Giese, *Echoes of the Bugle*, 3. Gen. Douglas MacArthur lived at Fort Wingate as a child in 1881 and 1882, several years before Pershing's arrival. There, MacArthur's father, Capt. Arthur MacArthur, commanded Company K, Thirteenth U.S. Infantry.
32. Pershing, *My Life*, 64.
33. Birchell, *Frontier Forts*, 124.
34. Vandiver, *Black Jack*, 74.
35. Pershing, *My Life*, 64.
36. Pershing, *My Life*, 64.
37. Smythe, "Frontier Cavalryman," 232–33; and MacAdam, "Indian Campaigns," 292. The dialogue presented in this scene is provided by MacAdam. In Pershing's memoirs, he downplays his part in the encounter. As he speaks of his role, he does not mention approaching the cabin, kicking in the door, and facing the three men with guns, thus avoiding the kind of braggadocio for which William F. Cody was famous.
38. Unfortunately, one of the three horse thieves escaped a few days later. The other two were handed over to local authorities but were subsequently released, presumably, mused Pershing in his memoirs, "for lack of evidence against them." Pershing, *My Life*, 65.
39. Howard Bryan, "A Close Call," *Albuquerque Tribune*, November 15, 1969, 1. The article is based on the recollections of Russell C. Charlton, who had interviewed Pershing.
40. Bryan, "Close Call," 1.
41. Pershing, *My Life*, 67.
42. Pershing, *My Life*, 68.
43. Pershing, *My Life*, 68.
44. Smythe, "Frontier Cavalryman," 236–37.

5. Cloak, 1890–91

1. Pershing, *My Life*, 69.
2. Wilson, "Bison in Alberta," 5.
3. Pershing, *My Life*, 69–70.
4. Vandiver, *Black Jack*, 82.
5. Richardson, *Wounded Knee*, 122.
6. Richardson, *Wounded Knee*, 118.
7. Wovoka's new Ghost Dance religion was not an entirely unique Indian movement. Indian mystics occasionally rose up to preach a new messianic message, which usually included defying the advancement of whites against the Indians. In 1680 a Tewa holy man named Pope led the Pueblos to rebel against the Spanish. Following the French and Indian War, the Ottawa chief Pontiac used such language to encourage a coalition of tribes to drive out the English from their lands. During the early nineteenth century, the Shawnee leader Tecumseh and his holy man brother, Tenskatawa, otherwise known as the Prophet, convinced several tribes of the Old Northwest to rally against whites and their corrupting influences. Even as Wovoka began preaching his message during the late 1880s, other Native leaders, including an Apache medicine man named Nakaidoklini and the Crow prophet Sword Bearer, preached their own enticing messages of a new Indian millennialism. See Brown, *Bury My Heart*, 510.
8. Matteoni, *Prairie Man*, 233. For Wovoka's preaching, see Brown, *Bury My Heart*, 478.
9. Brown, *Bury My Heart*, 511.
10. MacAdam, "Sioux Campaign," 453.
11. MacAdam, "Sioux Campaign," 453.
12. King, *War Eagle*, 239.
13. Pershing, *My Life*, 74.
14. MacAdam, "Sioux Campaign," 454.
15. Remington, "Galloping Sixth," 57–58.
16. Brown, *Bury My Heart*, 513.
17. Brown, *Bury My Heart*, 513.
18. King, *War Eagle*, 243.
19. The Badlands Wall is located six miles west of the modern-day headquarters of Badlands National Monument. The area where the Native men worked to repair the washed-out trail is still known today as Big Foot Pass.
20. Pershing, *My Life*, 74.
21. Pershing, *My Life*, 74.
22. Pershing, *My Life*, 74.
23. Brown, *Bury My Heart*, 516.
24. Armitage and Mercier, *Speaking History*, 19.
25. Brown, *Bury My Heart*, 521.

Notes to Pages 122–135

26. Brown, *Bury My Heart*, 521.
27. Utley, *Last Days*, 212.
28. Remington, "Sioux Outbreak," 61.
29. Utley, *Sioux Nation*, 213.
30. Utley, *Sioux Nation*, 213.
31. Neihardt, *Black Elk Speaks*, 98.
32. Neihardt, *Black Elk Speaks*, 218.
33. Pershing, *My Life*, 76.
34. MacAdam, "Sioux Campaign," 458–59.
35. Pershing, *My Life*, 76.
36. Vandiver, *Black Jack*, 97.
37. MacAdam, "Sioux Campaign," 459.
38. Pershing, *My Life*, 78.
39. Pershing, *My Life*, 78.
40. Vandiver, *Black Jack*, 99; and Pershing, *My Life*, 78.
41. By 1891 the Oglala Lakota chief Red Cloud was nearly seventy years old. He had engaged in years of combat against both Native enemies, including the Pawnee, and Anglo-Americans. Through his lengthy career as a warrior, he accumulated more than eighty coups. In December 1866 he participated in the famous Fetterman Massacre during which eighty-one cavalry troopers were killed. By the early 1870s, he became convinced that Indian resistance was futile, and he accepted reservation life.
42. Pershing, *My Life*, 78–79.
43. Pershing, *My Life*, 79.
44. Pershing, *My Life*, 79.
45. Just weeks before Pershing was assigned to police the Wounded Knee battlefield with his Lakota scouts, Lt. E. W. Casey of the Twenty-Second Infantry, another white commander of such scouts, had been killed at Pine Ridge. Casey and his Indians had entered an encampment of Lakotas. He greeted them as friends, and they responded similarly. But while Casey was talking with a group of Lakota men, a warrior named Plenty Horses approached him from behind and shot Casey in the head, killing him instantly. MacAdam, "Sioux Campaign," 460.
46. MacAdam, "Sioux Campaign," 460.
47. Pershing, *My Life*, 80.
48. Vandiver, *Black Jack*, 101.
49. Vandiver, *Black Jack*, 101.
50. Vandiver, *Black Jack*, 102.
51. Efficiency Report on JJP by Carr, May 1, 1890, in 3849 Appointment Commission and Personal Branch 1886, cited in Vandiver, *Black Jack*, 102.
52. Vandiver, *Black Jack*, 103. Pershing's full, official title at the university was "Professor of Military Science and Tactics; Commandant Univer-

sity Battalion; Teacher in Fencing." See also Smythe, "John J. Pershing at the University," 170.

6. College, 1891–95

1. Dick, "Problems of the Frontier," 133.
2. Slote, *Kingdom of Art*, 7.
3. The Lansing Theatre was located on the southwest corner of Thirteenth and P Streets and was built by the Lincoln real estate investor J. F. Lansing. The venue was renamed the Oliver Theater in 1898. The Funke opened in 1882 and was located at the corner of Twelfth and O Streets. The first moving pictures in Lincoln were screened at the Funke. Both theaters were located south of the university campus. See "Funke Opera House."
4. Wimberly, "Oscar Wilde Meets Woodberry," 108. Wilde toured Nebraska in the spring of 1882 and gave short lectures in Omaha, where he spoke at Boyd's Opera House, and in Lincoln at the University of Nebraska's University Hall. At the latter, he criticized the dilapidated condition of University Hall and encouraged the students to call for the construction of a new gymnasium where, the poet opined, "might be seen models of the old Greek athletes, such splendid examples of physical beauty." See "Oscar at the University," *Nebraska State Journal* (Lincoln), April 25, 1882, 4.
5. The university struggled with constant repairs and reconstruction on University Hall through the first half of the twentieth century. Steel rods were added in 1916 to hold the building together. In 1925 the mansard roof and upper stories were removed. Its stunted remains were finally razed in 1948. The hall's bell remains as a part of the garden at Wick Alumni Center. See University of Nebraska–Lincoln, "University Hall."
6. Cather, *Professor's House*, 143.
7. Cather, *My Ántonia*, 292.
8. Smythe, "John J. Pershing at the University," 171.
9. MacAdam, "Experiences at the University," 539.
10. MacAdam, "Experiences at the University," 539.
11. MacAdam, "Experiences at the University," 539.
12. *The Hesperian*, October 1, 1891, 10.
13. MacAdam, "Experiences at the University," 539.
14. Pershing, *My Life*, 82.
15. Smythe, "John J. Pershing at the University," 177.
16. Smythe, "John J. Pershing at the University," 172.
17. Pershing, *My Life*, 82.
18. Johnson, *Pioneer's Progress*, 77–78.
19. The .45-70 Springfield fired a .45 caliber ball powered by seventy grains of black powder.
20. MacAdam, "Experiences at the University," 542; and Smythe, "John J. Pershing at the University," 173.

21. MacAdam, "Experiences at the University," 540.

22. Smith, *Until the Last Trumpet*, 41.

23. Smith, *Until the Last Trumpet*, 41.

24. Smith, *Until the Last Trumpet*, 41.

25. While Dawes was destined to leave his mark on American history as an American banker, a general who served directly under Pershing during the Great War, a diplomat, the nation's thirtieth vice president of the United States, and a corecipient of the Nobel Peace Prize, he also had a famous ancestor. His great-great-grandfather William Dawes rode as an alarm rider on the same night (April 18, 1775) Paul Revere made famous. Revere took the road from Charlestown to Lexington, while Dawes covered the route from Boston to Concord. Dawes avoided British Redcoats by cutting across meadows and marshlands, while Revere was captured and later released.

26. Timmons, *Portrait of an American*, 17.

27. Through the years that followed, Charles Dawes and William Jennings Bryan moved in political circles that seemed to intersect repeatedly. Bryan became the Democratic-Populist presidential candidate facing Republican William McKinley in 1896 and 1900, while Dawes actively campaigned within the McKinley organization, leading to his appointment as McKinley's comptroller of currency, a key role in an era of monetary politics regarding the gold standard, free silver, and controversies over greenbacks. In 1924 Charles Dawes ran for vice president along with Republican president Calvin Coolidge, while Bryan's brother Charles was the Democratic nominee for veep.

28. Don Cameron's Lunch Counter was located at 114–118 South Eleventh Street in downtown Lincoln, close to the university. Cameron was the stuff of Lincoln legend. Some suggested he was a Spanish grandee who found his way to the Midwest, where he introduced Spanish cooking. More likely is the suggestion that he had been a cook to Minnesota and Wisconsin lumberjacks and later for miners out in Colorado and Wyoming. Eventually he settled down in Lincoln, "halfway between the lumber and mining camps." Timmons, *Portrait of an American*, 25.

29. Pershing, *My Life*, 86.

30. Timmons, *Portrait of an American*, 25.

31. Dunlap, *Charles Gates Dawes*, 25–26.

32. William Hayward, "Cut up Pershing's Breeches," *Boston Sunday Globe*, August 5, 1917; and Smythe, "John J. Pershing at the University," 174.

33. Smythe, "John J. Pershing at the University," 174.

34. Smythe, "John J. Pershing at the University," 175.

35. Smythe, "John J. Pershing at the University," 175; *Joplin (MO) Globe*, February 24, 1918; and Tomlinson, *Story of General Pershing*, 58.

36. Pershing, *My Life*, 85.

37. Cather's cousin was a member of the Fifth Nebraska National Guard. He was an expert marksman. The Fifth was sent to Mexico during Persh-

ing's Punitive Expedition to capture the pistolero Pancho Villa. In 1917 G.P. earned an officer's commission at the first Officer's Candidate School. Commissioned a second lieutenant, he joined the American Expeditionary Forces (AEF); his commanding officer in the First Division (the Big Red One) was Maj. Theodore Roosevelt Jr., President Roosevelt's eldest son. Cather was killed in action during the fighting at Cantigny, France, on May 28, 1918.

38. Cather, *One of Ours*, 345.
39. Smythe, *Guerrilla Warrior*, 35.
40. Johnson, *Pioneer's Progress*, 77–78.
41. Bjork, *Prairie Imperialists*, 104.
42. Smith, *Until the Last Trumpet*, 43.
43. Vandiver, *Black Jack*, 128.
44. "Editorial Notes," *The Hesperian*, March 1, 1892, 2–3. The editors of *The Hesperian* wrote in further detail concerning which cadets should compete at the drill competition and who should not: "If it is possible, the company should be made of large men. We believe it would be a good plan to take no one below five feet eight inches, or over six feet. This would make a fine looking company. However, if it should be impossible to get enough good men between these two extremes, the rule might be slightly relaxed. Better to have a greater variety in size than to take poorly drilled men" (2).
45. Perhaps ironically, while the UNL newspaper, *The Hesperian*, originally had supported the university cadet program's involvement in the Omaha drill competition in a March editorial, by June the newspaper was complaining that the drill practices were taking up too much of the students' time. "Does it pay? Does what pay? This twenty-one hours a week that company A has been undergoing. Even the most enthusiastic have become weary of the business during the last week. . . . Some of them were unable to finish their required work for graduation until a week after the regular time. Many who were on class day program, and class committees, were unable to do credit to themselves or to the university. The last ten days were hurry and worry. Not a few were denied the privilege of enjoying but a small part of the commencement exercises. But they may win a prize? Oh yes, and again they may not." "Editorial Notes," *The Hesperian*, June 15, 1892, 2–3.
46. Department of Military Science and Tactics, *History of the Military Department*, 17; and Smythe, *Guerrilla Warrior*, 33.
47. Smythe, "John J. Pershing at the University," 181.
48. Smythe, "John J. Pershing at the University," 182.
49. MacAdam, "Experiences at the University," 540.
50. Smith, *Until the Last Trumpet*, 44.
51. The following fall, the boys on the winning team paid Pershing a special tribute by presenting him with a gold-mounted cavalry saber, and Chancellor Canfield hosted a special dinner, which included oysters, at a Lincoln restaurant. The saber was engraved: "The Nebraska University Cadets /

Winners of Maiden Prize / National Competitive Drill / To Lieutenant John J. Pershing / Sixth U.S. Cavalry / Commandant / Cadet Battalion." Smythe, "John J. Pershing at the University," 182.

52. Smythe, *Guerrilla Warrior*, 34.

53. MacAdam, "Experiences at the University," 543.

54. MacAdam, "Experiences at the University," 543.

55. Smith, *Until the Last Trumpet*, 55. In 1897 Pershing played a key role in supporting Meiklejohn's appointment as the assistant secretary of war.

56. Pershing, *My Life*, 85.

57. MacAdam, "Experiences at the University," 541.

58. MacAdam, "Experiences at the University," 541. Although not Pershing's immediate successor at the university, his old Grand Canyon trek comrade John Stotsenburg became the commander at UNL in December 1897.

59. MacAdam, "Experiences at the University," 541.

60. Pershing, *My Life*, 86–87. Bryan's election to the U.S. House of Representatives was not as easy as Pershing recalled in his memoirs. The margin between Bryan and Judge Field was actually only 140 votes. Sawyer, *Lincoln*, 2:19.

61. MacAdam, "Pershing at the University," 543.

62. As governor, Crounse was the state's commander in chief. Pershing, as an officer serving at the university, was technically part of the Nebraska National Guard; thus, he had the role as Crounse's aide-de-camp from Lincoln.

63. Smythe, *Guerrilla Warrior*, 38.

64. Smythe, *Guerrilla Warrior*, 38.

65. Today, the Pershing Rifles represent the oldest continuously operating U.S. college organization dedicated to the instruction of military drill. Universities and colleges across the country boast scores of chapters.

66. Vandiver, *Black Jack*, 135; and Smythe, "Pershing at the University," 195.

7. Cree, 1895–98

1. Pershing, *My Life*, 85.

2. Pershing, *My Life*, 86.

3. Pershing, *My Life*, 85.

4. Fort Assinniboine, named for a local Indian nation, is spelled differently than the tribal name, Assiniboine with only two *n*'s.

5. Pershing, *My Life*, 88.

6. Andrews, *My Friend and Classmate*, 51.

7. For additional details regarding the origins of the Indian reference "buffalo soldiers" as applied to African American soldiers, see Schubert, *Voices of the Buffalo Soldier*, 47–49.

8. Schubert, "Buffalo Soldiers," 15. See also Parker, "Evolution of the Colored Soldier," 223–28.

9. Utley, *Frontier Regulars*, 26.

10. Remington, *Frederic Remington's Own West*, 69.
11. Utley, *Frontier Regulars*, 26–27.
12. Pershing, *My Life*, 88.
13. Bjork, *Prairie Imperialists*, 111.
14. Vandiver, *Black Jack*, 140.
15. Meriwether Lewis named the Marias River after his cousin Maria Wood during the expedition of the Corps of Discovery in 1806. Near the Marias, Lewis killed a Blackfeet warrior in 1806 during an attack on a small contingent of the Lewis and Clark expedition. This encounter witnessed the only violent deaths that the exploring party experienced in its twenty-eight-month odyssey.
16. Pershing, *My Life*, 91.
17. Pershing, *My Life*, 91.
18. Vandiver, *Black Jack*, 143; and Pershing, *My Life*, 91. Why Pershing's men referred to him as "Old Red" is not clear. He did not have red hair. It was common for Black troopers to nickname their white commanders, and the moniker they placed on Pershing may have been a reference to Pershing's complexion, with his face turning red when angry.
19. Vandiver, *Black Jack*, 146.
20. Pershing, *My Life*, 92.
21. Pershing, *My Life*, 92.
22. Pershing, *My Life*, 93.
23. Pershing, *My Life*, 93.
24. Pershing, *My Life*, 93.
25. Vandiver, *Black Jack*, 149.
26. Pershing, *My Life*, 93.
27. Vandiver, *Black Jack*, 149–50.
28. Pershing, *My Life*, 94.
29. Pershing, *My Life*, 94.
30. Ward Pershing also became a soldier. He graduated from the University of Chicago in 1898, joined the Illinois National Guard, and was commissioned a second lieutenant of the Sixth Artillery on July 9. Like his brother, he transferred to the cavalry the following year (Fourth Cavalry, Troop C) and saw considerable combat in Northern Luzon, Philippines, in 1899 until he became seriously ill late that same year. Although he saw more action in early 1900, he took medical leave home that spring. Through the following years, he was promoted to first lieutenant and rejoined the Fourth Cavalry at the Presidio in San Francisco, where his brother would one day serve. Ward attended the Infantry and Cavalry School in Leavenworth and was promoted to captain, serving with the Tenth Cavalry at Fort Robinson, Nebraska, repeating his brother's service alongside African American troopers. Ward developed tuberculosis and died in a Denver sanitarium on August 28, 1909. Pershing, *My Life*, 570–71.

31. Paddock served out west in New Mexico, where he met Pershing's sister. He was part of the Pine Ridge campaign during the Ghost Shirt uprising and served in Cuba during the Santiago campaign, including the charge up San Juan Hill. Like his comrade John Pershing, Paddock contracted malaria but served in the Philippines with the Sixth Cavalry. By late 1900 his unit was dispatched to China to help put down the Boxer Rebellion. His malaria worsened, and he died in Tientsin on March 9, 1901. Grace Pershing Paddock passed away three years later on April 24, 1904. Pershing, *My Life*, 563.

32. Vandiver, *Black Jack*, 155.

33. Andrews, *My Friend and Classmate*, 50–51.

34. Vandiver, *Black Jack*, 157.

35. Green, *Washington*, 77.

36. Cather, "Professor's House," in *Novels and Stories*, 222.

37. Gillette, *Between Justice and Beauty*, 102.

38. Pershing, *My Life*, 95.

39. Pershing to Meiklejohn (telegram), April 14, 1897, box 28, file 176, George DeRue Meiklejohn Papers, Nebraska State Historical Society Archives, Lincoln.

40. Four venues have gone by the name of Madison Square Garden in New York City, with the first being from 1879 to 1890. The venue Pershing visited in 1897 was the second, which covered the years 1890 to 1925. The famed New York architect Stanford White designed the building, and a syndicate that included J. Pierpont Morgan, Andrew Carnegie, P. T. Barnum, W. W. Astor, and others built it. The third version was in use between 1925 and 1968. The fourth version, built in 1969, serves as the home for the New York Knicks and the Rangers.

41. Andrews, *My Friend and Classmate*, 54. For more on Roosevelt's personal time in the American West during the 1880s when he was ranching out in the Dakota Territory, see Blake, *Cowboy President*.

42. Pershing, *My Life*, 94.

43. Pershing, *My Life*, 96.

44. Vandiver, *Black Jack*, 169.

45. Pershing, *My Life*, 96.

46. Pershing, *My Life*, 96–97.

47. Pershing, *My Life*, 97. One additional change Pershing discovered in his return to West Point was Commandant Hein's call for an end to hazing. This was likely part of Pershing's noting a "more liberal attitude between officers and cadets." Hazing was a significant part of the West Point tradition during Pershing's cadet days, and he did not like seeing it eliminated. He expressed his opinion to a West Point cadet who had previously met Pershing at UNL. Cadet Ernest D. Scott asked Pershing point-blank: "I hope you have not changed your views about hazing." "No, I haven't. And I never will," Pershing responded. Smythe, "Pershing at West Point," 42–43.

48. Smythe, *Guerrilla Warrior*, 40.

49. Smythe, *Guerrilla Warrior*, 41.
50. Pershing, *John J. Pershing Papers*.
51. Smythe, *Guerrilla Warrior*, 42.
52. MacAdam, "Experiences at the University," 546.
53. Smythe, *Guerrilla Warrior*, 43.
54. Smythe, *Guerrilla Warrior*, 44.
55. Vandiver, *Black Jack*, 172.
56. MacAdam, "Experiences at the University," 546.

8. Cuba, 1898

1. McNeese, *Discovering U.S. History*, 7.
2. Phillips, *William McKinley*, 92.
3. McNeese, *Remember the* Maine, 48.
4. Samuels and Samuels, *Remembering the* Maine, 93.
5. Kinzer, *True Flag*, 32.
6. Young, *History of Our War*, 61.
7. Hagedorn, *Leonard Wood*, 141.
8. Long, *America of Yesterday*, 176.
9. Pershing, *My Life*, 100.
10. MacAdam, "Pershing's Own Account," 683.
11. MacAdam, "Pershing's Own Account," 683.
12. MacAdam, "Pershing's Own Account," 684.
13. MacAdam, "Pershing's Own Account," 684.
14. Pershing, *My Life*, 102.
15. MacAdam, "Pershing's Own Account," 684.
16. The name "Rough Riders" was not Roosevelt's idea. It was taken from one of the touring troupes of Buffalo Bill's *Wild West*. Roosevelt specifically asked reporters, who were prone to creating shorthand nicknames for such units, not to use it. "Please do not call us Rough Riders," he begged. "The name evokes a hippodrome." In the end, he became accustomed to the name and used it to title his war memoir. Risen, *Crowded Hour*, 62.
17. Risen, *Crowded Hour*, 59. For Roosevelt's own version of his time with the Rough Riders, see Roosevelt, *Rough Riders*.
18. Vandiver, *Black Jack*, 174.
19. A list of those significant contacts would easily include Fox Conner, Malin Craig, Robert C. Davis, Leon B. Kromer, George S. Simonds, George Van Horn Mosely, Stuart Heintzelman, Wilson B. Burtt, and Upton Birnie Jr.
20. O'Connor, *Black Jack Pershing*, 44.
21. Margaret Leech, *Days of McKinley*, 216.
22. Smythe, *Guerrilla Warrior*, 47.
23. Pershing, *My Life*, 106.
24. Vandiver, *Black Jack*, 186.
25. Vandiver, *Black Jack*, 191.

26. Cashin, *Under Fire*, 197–98. The quotation is taken from a lecture delivered by John J. Pershing at the Hyde Park Methodist Episcopal Church in Chicago during a patriotic thanksgiving service on Sunday, November 27, 1898.

27. Nearly every American soldier who made his way to Cuba during the summer of 1898 wore woolen uniforms. Only Theodore Roosevelt's volunteer Rough Riders wore lighter khaki uniforms, which were more suited for tropical environs, and canvas leggings. Their broad-brimmed campaign hats, which turned fashionably up on one side, were also a better choice for fighting in Cuba. Roosevelt outfitted his men at his own expense. As for himself, he had his uniform tailor-made at Brooks Brothers. Officers at that time were required to provide their own uniforms and commonly utilized the New York tailoring house. Despite the logic of having his men wear khaki uniforms, Roosevelt and Leonard Wood may have chosen the fabric based on the assumption that since everyone else would be outfitted in blue wool, the buff-colored khaki would be less in demand and might be delivered to the Rough Riders sooner. See Risen, *Crowded Hour*, 93.

28. Smythe, *Guerrilla Warrior*, 48.

29. O'Connor, *Black Jack Pershing*, 46.

30. Cashin, *Under Fire*, 203.

31. Smythe, *Guerrilla Warrior*, 50.

32. Hymel, "Black Jack in Cuba," 1–6.

33. Smythe, *Guerrilla Warrior*, 50.

34. Harbord, *American Army in France*, 43–44.

35. Hassler, *With Shield and Sword*, 229.

36. Andrews, *My Friend and Classmate*, 58.

37. Jewell and Stout, *Selected Letters*, 50.

38. Later statistics indicate the Spanish had gathered approximately thirteen thousand soldiers and sailors in the vicinity of Santiago prior to the American assault. This translates into less than 1 percent of the nearly two hundred thousand Spanish troops on the island of Cuba. See Sargent, *Campaign of Santiago de Cuba*, 134–35.

39. Perry, *Pershing*, 40.

40. Vandiver, *Black Jack*, 201.

41. Tomlinson, *Story of General Pershing*, 72.

42. Sargent, *Campaign of Santiago de Cuba*, 115. Sargent was a captain in the Second Cavalry who served as a colonel of the Fifth U.S. Volunteer Infantry during the Spanish-American War. His firsthand accounts are quite detailed.

43. Bjork, *Prairie Imperialists*, 127.

44. Pershing, *My Life*, 114.

45. Smith, *Until the Last Trumpet*, 54.

46. Cashin, *Under Fire*, 226.

47. Vandiver, *Black Jack*, 203.

48. Hymel, "Black Jack in Cuba," 4.

49. Cashin, *Under Fire*, 208.

50. Vandiver, *Black Jack*, 206.

51. Cashin, *Under Fire*, 208.

52. John J. Pershing to George Meiklejohn, July 11, 1898, box 28, file 177, George DeRue Meiklejohn Papers, Nebraska State Historical Society Archives, Lincoln.

53. Cashin, *Under Fire*, 209.

54. Buckley, *American Patriots*, 147.

55. Cashin, *Under Fire*, 213.

56. Smith, *Until the Last Trumpet*, 55.

57. Lacey, *Pershing*, 31.

58. Bjork, *Prairie Imperialists*, 128–29.

59. Bjork, *Prairie Imperialists*, 128. For more details regarding the Nebraskans George Meiklejohn and John J. Pershing and their contributions to the expansion of U.S. colonial power overseas following the Spanish-American War, as well as American activity in the Philippines, see Bjork, "Prairie Imperialists," 216–19.

60. Vandiver, *Black Jack*, 213; and Hymel, "Black Jack in Cuba," 5.

61. Vandiver, *Black Jack*, 211.

62. Vandiver, *Black Jack*, 211.

63. Smythe, *Guerrilla Warrior*, 52.

64. Smythe, *Guerrilla Warrior*, 280.

9. Colony, 1898–1903

1. Smythe, *Guerrilla Warrior*, 58. The U.S. military began brevetting during the Revolutionary War and continued the practice through the nineteenth century. Such promotions became quite common at that time given the army's many frontier forts, such as those Pershing served at in New Mexico. With its many forts and other stations, the army was not always able to appoint officers of appropriate rank to these posts. As Congress allowed for a limited number of such officers of each rank, an officer of lower rank could receive a brevet commission to a rank requisite for a particular assignment. Also, newly commissioned officers sometimes received a brevet rank until a fully authorized posting became available. If West Point graduated too many cadets to post as second lieutenants, for example, some graduates might be appointed as brevet second lieutenants until an opening in rank occurred. In Pershing's case, he was granted a brevet rank of major in recognition for his gallant service during the Cuban campaign. By June 1899 Pershing's brevet rank reverted to the permanent regular army rank of captain in 1901. Brevetting ranks were actually on their way out at the end of the nineteenth century, with such honor being given through medals instead. All brevet ranking ended in 1922.

2. Cashin, *Under Fire*, 209.

3. Smythe, *Guerrilla Warrior*, 60.

4. For details regarding Pershing and his work as a lawyer, see American Bar Association, "General John J. Pershing—Lawyer," 131.

5. Smythe, *Guerrilla Warrior*, 60.

6. Smythe, *Guerrilla Warrior*, 60.

7. Pershing, *My Life*, 131.

8. Vandiver, *Black Jack*, 236.

9. Vandiver, *Black Jack*, 237.

10. Silbey, *War of Frontier*, xi.

11. John J. Pershing to George Meiklejohn, March 1, 1900, box 28, file 178, George DeRue Meiklejohn Papers, Nebraska State Historical Society Archives, Lincoln.

12. Goldhurst, *Pipe Clay and Drill*, 105.

13. Pershing to Meiklejohn, February 12, 1900, box 28, folder 179, George DeRue Meiklejohn Papers, Nebraska State Historical Society Archives, Lincoln.

14. Pershing, *My Life*, 147.

15. Pershing, *My Life*, 150.

16. Pershing, *My Life*, 150.

17. Arnold, *Moro War*, 31.

18. Platt, "There Was a Captain," 181–85.

19. Vandiver, *John J. Pershing*, 12–13.

20. Pershing, *My Life*, 152.

21. Pershing, *My Life*, 153–54.

22. Platt, "There Was a Captain," 185.

23. Smith, *Until the Last Trumpet*, 60.

24. Smith, *Until the Last Trumpet*, 62. Manibilang made the same offer to Pershing when he visited, but Pershing also turned it down. Pershing's primary concern was not offending his host by rejecting an offer of female comfort. In his memoirs, he writes of such concern, as he asked his interpreter "to put the rejection in the finest Moro phraseology at his command. Whereupon Manibilang sent the lady away in the same matter-of-course manner as he had brought her in." Pershing, *My Life*, 153.

25. The Americans' effort to "civilize" the Moros and otherwise assimilate them into the new U.S. colony would produce mixed results. Pershing became a model for others through relentless negotiations, councils, and letters in an effort to ingratiate himself with the various dato leaders on behalf of the U.S. government. One problem he faced repeatedly was the Moros' concern that the Americans were intending to force them to eat pork, to halt the common practice of polygamy, and to end slavery. These issues became the subject of a satirical play back home in America. Titled "The Sultan of Sulu, an Original Satire in Two Acts," the musical was written by composer Alfred G. Wathall and George Ade, an American humorist and playwright. Premiering in Chicago on March 11, 1902, at the Studebaker Theatre, the play mocked

some of the American efforts to change the Moros without interfering with polygamy or slavery. As Ade observed, there was a certain irony since "the Americans were trying to 'assimilate' him [the sultan] without incurring his opposition: and it was a real problem because Sulu was committed to polygamy and slavery and these two institutions were known in the United States as the 'twin relics of barbarism.'" See Fulton, *Moroland*, 141.

26. Smythe, *Guerrilla Warrior*, 74.

27. The details of the fight at Pandapatan are described in detail in Fulton, *Moroland*, 99–120.

28. Smythe, *Guerrilla Warrior*, 78.

29. Pershing, *My Life*, 161.

30. Smythe, *Guerrilla Warrior*, 80–81.

31. Smythe, *Guerrilla Warrior*, 82.

32. Pershing, *My Life*, 641. Both quotes are taken from a letter from Pershing to his longtime Nebraska friend Charles Magoon. Pershing to Magoon, January 28, 1903, Pershing Papers, Philippines: 1901–3, box 369, Library of Congress.

33. Evans, *Admiral's Log*, 233.

34. Pershing, *My Life*, 170–71.

35. Pershing, *My Life*, 163.

36. Smythe, *Guerrilla Warrior*, 86.

37. Fulton, *Moroland, 1899–1906*, 148.

38. Smith, *Until the Last Trumpet*, 67.

39. Smythe, *Guerrilla Warrior*, 89.

40. Pershing, *My Life*, 177.

41. Thomas, "Pershing—United States Soldier," 8181; and Edgerton, *American Datu*, 63.

42. Arnold, *Moro War*, 57.

43. Cather, "Treasure of Far Island," in *Collected Short Fiction*, 265.

44. Cather, "Treasure of Far Island," in *Collected Short Fiction*, 277.

45. Cather, "Treasure of Far Island," 280.

46. Roberts, "Archipelagic American Studies," 69.

47. Smythe, *Guerrilla Warrior*, 92; and Pershing, *My Life*, 192–93.

48. Smith, *Until the Last Trumpet*, 66.

49. Editorial, *Manila Times*, February 17, 1903; and Fulton, *Moroland*, 149.

50. Pershing's strategy in handling the resistant Moros in south Mindanao was extremely modern in its details. In 2006 during the Iraq War, Gen. David Petraeus and Gen. James Amos wrote a counterinsurgency manual known as FM 3-24 that laid out viable U.S. strategies relating to Islamic extremists in Iraq. The manual and its policy emphasized that commanders should keep open minds regarding their opponents, show respect for local cultural norms, work with people of other cultures, and maintain a high level of patience, moral and physical courage, and authority in working with indigenous pop-

ulations. Much of the emphasis found in FM 3-24 is reflected in Pershing's approach to the Moros, including the following: (1) keeping military violence to a minimum, (2) relying on locals to carry out law enforcement, (3) providing government land for mosques, (4) taking a slow path toward changing problematic tribal customs, and (5) providing economic and social advantages to locals at government expense. Taking in the overall strategy Pershing pursued during 1901–3, even from a modern perspective, the American captain appears enlightened. See Greenberg, "Pershing in Mindanao"; and Perry, "What Black Jack Pershing."

51. Steinbach, *Long March*, 184.
52. Smith, *Until the Last Trumpet*, 67.
53. Perry, *Pershing*, 59.
54. The Vickers machine gun was a relatively new model. It was based on the Maxim gun that was invented during the late nineteenth century and used in various colonial conflicts against native rebels. In 1896 British-owned Vickers purchased the Maxim Nordenfelt Guns and Ammunition Company, which became Vickers, Sons & Maxim, and retooled the gun into a new, more efficient model. The Vickers machine gun was commonly used during the Great War.
55. Smythe, *Guerrilla Warrior*, 94.
56. Landor, *Gems of the East*, 289.
57. Smythe, *Guerrilla Warrior*, 100.
58. Landor, *Gems of the East*, 296.
59. Smythe, *Guerrilla Warrior*, 101.
60. Lacey, *Pershing*, 45.
61. Pershing, *My Life*, 199.
62. Smythe, *Guerrilla Warrior*, 101.
63. Pershing, *My Life*, 198.
64. Smythe, *Guerrilla Warrior*, 102.
65. Brig. Gen. Charles Sumner to J. J. Pershing, May 10, 1903, in U.S. War Department, "Occupation of the Lake Lanao Region," *Annual Report*, 3:321.
66. Pershing, *My Life*, 202.
67. John Joseph Pershing, "Moro Band at Bay," *Augusta (KS) Journal*, March 26, 1909, 6.

10. Courtship, 1903–9

1. Pershing, *My Life*, 208–9.
2. Pershing, *My Life*, 212.
3. Smythe, *Guerrilla Warrior*, 212.
4. Smith, *Until the Last Trumpet*, 75.
5. Perry, *Pershing*, 69.
6. "Pershing, Our Leader in France," 342.
7. Smith, *Until the Last Trumpet*, 77.

8. Lacey, *Pershing*, 51.

9. Harold F. Wheeler, "Pershing's Beautiful Marriage Romance," *Boston Sunday Post*, January 19, 1919, 39–40; and Smythe, *Guerrilla Warrior*, 113.

10. Smythe, *Guerrilla Warrior*, 113.

11. Wheeler, "Romance of General Pershing," 7.

12. Vandiver, *Black Jack*, 341.

13. Vandiver, *Black Jack*, 342.

14. Wheeler, "Romance of General Pershing," 8.

15. Lacey, *Pershing*, 51.

16. Smith, *Until the Last Trumpet*, 80; and Perry, *Pershing*, 71.

17. Smith, *Until the Last Trumpet*, 80.

18. The dialogue is presented in Smythe, *Guerrilla Warrior*, 118; and Smith, *Until the Last Trumpet*, 80.

19. The Episcopalian Church, located at 1713 G Street Northwest, dates back to 1844. Jefferson Davis had rented Pew 14 before becoming president of the Confederacy, only to have Secretary of War Edwin Stanton take over the pew in his absence. Pershing had converted to the Episcopalian Church when he was serving in the Philippines. See Church of the Epiphany, "July 16."

20. Smith, *Until the Last Trumpet*, 83.

21. Smith, *Until the Last Trumpet*, 82.

22. Smythe, *Guerrilla Warrior*, 118.

23. Smythe, *Guerrilla Warrior*, 120.

24. Perry, *Pershing*, 74.

25. Greenwood, "U.S. Army," 1–14.

26. Davis et al., *Russo-Japanese War*, 89.

27. Frederick Palmer, "Pershing, the Master of a Million Men Found Glory Enough in Army's Victory," *Kansas City Star*, January 11, 1931.

28. Greenwood, "U.S. Army," 8.

29. Smythe, *Guerrilla Warrior*, 123.

30. Pershing, *My Life*, 255.

31. Smythe, *Guerrilla Warrior*, 123. Pershing is referring to the Confederate general Lewis Armistead, who led a brigade during Pickett's Charge on July 3, 1863. During the assault, he fixed his hat on the tip of his sword and encouraged his men forward. Armistead was mortally wounded. See McPherson, *Battle Cry of Freedom*, 662.

32. Palmer, *John J. Pershing*, 61.

33. Smythe, *Guerrilla Warrior*, 125.

34. Lacey, *Pershing*, 54. The exact number of officers that Pershing leapfrogged over is not exactly clear. A commonly stated number is 862, as shown previously, but others have claimed different numbers. Historians James R. Arnold and Frank E. Vandiver both place the number at 909, but the number 835 has also been stated. Arnold, *Moro War*, 218; and Vandiver, *Black Jack*, 390.

35. Pershing provides the full letter in his memoirs. But Roosevelt wrote the letter in November 1910 and not at the time of the initial controversy. Pershing, *My Life*, 244.

36. Pershing, *My Life*, 244.

37. Editorial, *St. Louis Post-Dispatch*, October 3, 1906. In the end, despite such newspaper editorials, Pershing received his new rank. The Senate confirmed the appointment on December 10, 1906. Senator Warren suggested, before the vote, that he recuse himself from voting, but his colleagues did not think it necessary. No significant concern was expressed within the Senate over Pershing's advancement in rank. Smythe, *Guerrilla Warrior*, 126–27.

38. Smythe, *Guerrilla Warrior*, 128.

39. Smith, *Until the Last Trumpet*, 62.

40. Smythe, *Guerrilla Warrior*, 130.

41. Smythe, *Guerrilla Warrior*, 130–31.

42. Smythe, *Guerrilla Warrior*, 131.

43. Pershing, *My Life*, 249.

44. Pershing, *My Life*, 250.

45. Smythe, *Guerrilla Warrior*, 136.

46. Smythe, *Guerrilla Warrior*, 137.

47. Smythe, "John J. Pershing," 66–72.

48. Smith, *Until the Last Trumpet*, 100.

49. Smith, *Until the Last Trumpet*, 102.

50. Pershing, *My Life*, 265.

51. Pershing, *My Life*, 267.

52. Vandiver, *Black Jack*, 458.

53. Pershing, *My Life*, 269.

54. Pershing, *My Life*, 269.

55. Vandiver, *Black Jack*, 458.

11. Conquest, 1909–13

1. Perry, *Pershing*, 86.

2. Lacey, *Pershing*, 62–63.

3. Lacey, *Pershing*, 63.

4. Lacey, *Pershing*, 63.

5. Ginsburgh, "Pershing," 11.

6. Smythe, *Guerrilla Warrior*, 147.

7. Pershing, *My Life*, 271–72.

8. Pershing, *My Life*, 275–76.

9. Smythe, *Guerrilla Warrior*, 175.

10. MacAdam, "Story of His Activities" (May 1919), 102.

11. Smythe, *Guerrilla Warrior*, 154–55.

12. Letter from Pershing to General Leonard Wood, November 20, 1913, quoted in Smythe, *Guerrilla Warrior*, 155.

13. Pershing, *My Life*, 284. Lieutenant Rodney was the son of Brig. Gen. George H. Rodney, who had only recently retired from army service. The younger Rodney was newly assigned to a post at Jolo when he was killed. Soon after the attack, General Rodney, as well as other American officers, placed much of the blame for the attack on Pershing, insisting his policies toward the Moros were too lenient. As a result of this attack, General Pershing began to implement his program of disarming the Moros. See "Biographical Appendix: Walter H. Rodney," in Pershing, *My Life*, 577–78.

14. Lacey, *Pershing*, 66.

15. The historical record seems relatively clear that Pershing, while serving in the Philippines and battling the fanatical Islamic Moro juramentados, was at a minimum aware that condemned Muslim fanatics were buried along with the carcass of a pig or that their bodies were exposed to pig blood. He may well have ordered such actions himself. But another version of Pershing's alleged exposing juramentados to pigs' blood has circulated through the decades and continues to make the rounds even today. In February 2016 Republican presidential candidate Donald Trump, during a campaign speech event in South Carolina, referred to modern-day Islamic terrorism by telling an oft-repeated story of John Pershing gathering fifty Moro juramentados together and ordering all, save one, to be shot with bullets dipped in pigs' blood. By allowing the remaining one to escape and inform other Moros of their comrades' fates, Pershing was using their deaths to deter other juramentados from killing Americans or Catholic Filipinos. In Trump's first telling of this story, Pershing's tactic brought an immediate end to the Moro rebellions, ushering in twenty-five years of stability and peace throughout Mindanao. Candidate Trump repeated the story in April, only this time he jacked up the period of Moro peace to forty-two years. Once elected president and following a terrorist attack in Barcelona, Spain, Trump sent out a tweet in August 2017 encouraging his followers to "study what General Pershing of the United States did to terrorists when caught." Despite Trump's multiple references, there appears to be no truth to the story of Pershing's ordering juramentados executed with bullets dipped in pigs' blood. See Hasian, *President Trump*, 2, 9, 98–99, 117. See also Alex Horton, "Trump Said to Study General Pershing: Here's What the President Got Wrong," *Washington Post*, August 18, 2017; and Katz, "What General Pershing Was Really Doing."

16. Lacey, *Pershing*, 67.

17. Perry, *Pershing*, 91–92.

18. For details of the 1906 battle of Bud Dajo, see Hawkins, "Managing a Massacre," 83–105.

19. Gems, *Sport and the American Occupation*, 344.

20. Scott, *Some Memories*, 379–80.

21. Smith, *Until the Last Trumpet*, 116.

22. Lacey, *Pershing*, 70.

23. Letter from Pershing to Francis E. Warren, February 9, 1912, quoted in Smythe, *Guerrilla Warrior*, 179.

24. Smythe, "Pershing and Counterinsurgency," 85–92.

25. Perry, *Pershing*, 93.

26. Smythe, "Pershing and the Mount Bagsak," 3–31.

27. Arnold, *Moro War*, 240.

28. Smythe, *Guerrilla Warrior*, 204.

29. Gowing, *Mandate in Moroland*, 241.

30. Finley, "Commercial Awakening," 325–34.

31. John J. Pershing, "A Few Words of Advice," *Sulu News*, June 30, 1911.

32. "Pershing, Our Leader in France," 344.

12. Calamity, 1913–16

1. Smith, *Until the Last Trumpet*, 120.

2. Ginsburg, "Pershing," 64.

3. Cather, *O Pioneers!*, 199.

4. Johnson, *Heroic Mexico*, 13.

5. Johnson, *Heroic Mexico*, 69.

6. Welsome, *General and the Jaguar*, 43.

7. Turner, *Bullets, Bottles, and Gardenias*, 203.

8. Teitelbaum, *Woodrow Wilson*, 322.

9. O'Connor, *Black Jack Pershing*, 108.

10. Letter from John J. Pershing to Francis Pershing, May 11, 1915, quoted in Neiburg, *Path to War*, 74.

11. Letter from John J. Pershing to Francis Pershing, May 14, 1915, quoted in Smythe, *Guerrilla Warrior*, 207.

12. MacAdam, "Story of His Activities" (June 1919), 148.

13. San Francisco hosted this world's fair between February 20 and December 4, 1915. The international event was ostensibly intended to celebrate the opening of the Panama Canal, which had been completed in 1914. But it was also viewed as San Francisco's opportunity to show the world how it had recovered and rebuilt following the devastating earthquake of 1906. The fairgrounds covered more than six hundred acres between the Presidio and Fort Mason, which is today known as the Marina District.

14. Smith, *Until the Last Trumpet*, 126; and Perry, *Pershing*, 100.

15. Smythe, *Guerrilla Warrior*, 209.

16. O'Connor, *Black Jack Pershing*, 111.

17. "Senator Chamberlain Takes a Hand," 28.

18. Interview with S. L. A. Marshall in the *Detroit News*, January 8, 1931. Marshall was also in the *El Paso Herald* office when Walker and Hunter picked up the story of the fire on the teletype.

19. "Senator Pershing Takes Bodies to Wyoming," *San Francisco Chronicle*, August 30, 1915.

Notes to Pages 307–317

20. *San Francisco Chronicle*, August 30, 1915.
21. Smythe, *Guerrilla Warrior*, 213.
22. Carroll, *My Fellow Soldiers*, 10.
23. Carroll, *My Fellow Soldiers*, 11. Pershing did not see the letter until he had been summoned to the Presidio after the fire. When he returned to Fort Bliss, the letter was waiting for him.

13. Chase, 1916–17

1. Welsome, *General and the Jaguar*, 83.
2. Welsome, *General and the Jaguar*, 111.
3. Welsome, *General and the Jaguar*, 114.
4. Welsome, *General and the Jaguar*, 127.
5. White, "Muddied Waters," 83.
6. De Quesada, "March 9, 1916."
7. Boghardt, "Chasing Ghosts in Mexico," 9–10.
8. *New York American*, March 11, 1916, quoted in Palmer, *Newton D. Baker*, 1:13.
9. Bruscino, "Troubled Past," 39.
10. Smythe, *Guerrilla Warrior*, 220.
11. Cross-border raids did not begin with Pancho Villa. The U.S. military engaged in previous punitive expeditions extending back well into the nineteenth century. As often as not, those U.S. military incursions into Mexico were to track down Indians who had raided across the border. Sometimes such actions were carried out with the cooperation of the Mexican government. Rippy, "Some Precedents," 292–316.
12. Smythe, *Guerrilla Warrior*, 220.
13. Several National Guard units were also eventually deployed including the Nebraska Fifth Infantry, which was dispatched to Texas in July 1916. Willa Cather's cousin G. P. Cather was a member of the Fifth and a noted expert marksman who, like Pershing in his younger days, won sharpshooting contests all across the United States. Cather's Company M returned to Nebraska in February 1917, and he earned an officer's commission at the first Officer's Candidate School. Second Lieutenant Cather was soon sent to France to join Pershing's AEF. Pershing handpicked Cather for duty, and G.P.'s commanding officer in the First Division was Maj. Theodore Roosevelt Jr., former president Roosevelt's eldest son. See Lukesh, "G. P. Cather."
14. Daniel, *Patton*, 38.
15. Patton also introduced Pershing to his sister, Anne, whom everyone called "Nita." She was twenty-nine years old and was on a protracted visit to Fort Bliss from California to see her brother and his wife. Pershing began a relationship with Nita that continued until Pershing was assigned a command in France in 1917. Rumors eventually flew that the two were planning to marry. However, Pershing was not yet ready for such a commitment and, in time, broke off their affair. See Smith, *Until the Last Trumpet*, 141.

Notes to Pages 317–335

16. Smith, *Until the Last Trumpet*, 140.
17. O'Connor, *Black Jack Pershing*, 126.
18. Cather, *Death Comes*, 7.
19. Millard, "Army Logistics in Mexico," 393.
20. Miller, *Preliminary to War*, 1.
21. Miller, "Wings and Wheels," 14–29. Four Wheel Drive (FWD) Auto Company developed and manufactured all-wheel drive vehicles. The company was founded in 1909 in Clintonville, Wisconsin, as the Badger Four-Wheel Drive Auto Company. The army ordered nearly 150 FWD trucks, Model B, for use on the Punitive Expedition.
22. Thomas and Allen, *Mexican Punitive Expedition*, appendix D, A-14. This work represents the official history of the Punitive Expedition.
23. Erwin carried with him into Mexico a copy of the proclamation by Mexican secretary of war and navy Alvaro Obregón that served as permission from the Carranza government for U.S. troops to enter Mexico. Pershing believed the proclamation gave him complete authorization for his campaign, but Mexican officials at the time did not see things as the Americans did. The Carranza government interpreted the proclamation as authorizing such a U.S. military presence if any cross-border raids took place in the future. The U.S. government interpreted the proclamation to refer to past raids, such as the Villa raid against Columbus. By the time U.S. government officials admitted they had interpreted the proclamation at their convenience, Pershing's mission in Mexico had accomplished about as much as it was going to do. See Smythe, *Guerrilla Warrior*, 224.
24. Mason, *Great Pursuit*, 245.
25. Toulmin, *With Pershing in Mexico*, 20–21; and O'Connor, *Black Jack Pershing*, 124.
26. Jastrzembski, "Folklore," 302.
27. O'Connor, *Black Jack Pershing*, 126.
28. Eisenhower, *Intervention!*, 258.
29. Eisenhower, *Intervention!*, 265.
30. O'Connor, *Black Jack Pershing*, 130.
31. The Organized Militia predated the National Guard. Before the passage of the National Defense Act of June 3, 1916, the states operated their own organized militias. Under the new act, the National Guard was established under federal control to operate during times of war and national emergency. See Hurst, *Pancho Villa*, 106.
32. Elser, "General Pershing's Mexican Campaign," 447.
33. Smythe, *Guerrilla Warrior*, 245–46.
34. Smythe, *Guerrilla Warrior*, 246.
35. Dunn, *World Alive*, 238.
36. Hurst, *Pancho Villa*, 85.
37. For details regarding National Guard numbers delivered to the international border, see Cunningham, "Shaking the Iron Fist," 2.

38. Haley, *Revolution and Intervention*, 208.
39. MacAdam, "Punitive Expedition into Mexico," 153.
40. MacAdam, "Punitive Expedition into Mexico," 153; and Pershing, *My Life*, 356–57.
41. Smythe, *Guerrilla Warrior*, 255.
42. Smythe, *Guerrilla Warrior*, 256.
43. Young, *Ordeal in Mexico*, 223.
44. Wharfield, "Affair at Carrizal," 36; and Young, "Fight," 20–21.
45. Smythe, *Guerrilla Warrior*, 257.
46. Carroll, *My Fellow Soldiers*, 70.
47. Clendenen, *Blood on the Border*, 307; and Young, "Fight," 21.
48. Clendenen, *Blood on the Border*, 307.
49. Pershing, *My Life*, 358–59.
50. Pershing, *My Life*, appendix J, 463.
51. Smythe, *Guerrilla Warrior*, 260.
52. Smythe, *Guerrilla Warrior*, 260.
53. O'Connor, *Black Jack Pershing*, 137.
54. As quoted in Army Times Publishing Company, *Yanks Are Coming*, 53.
55. Ganoe, *History*, 460.
56. O'Connor, *Black Jack Pershing*, 137. With Pershing's new rank of major general, he became a two-star general. Just a year later, with U.S. involvement in the Great War underway, Pershing was advanced to full general on October 6, 1917. To distinguish himself from other generals (the accepted insignia was four silver stars), Pershing chose four gold stars as he was recognized as the general of the armies. During World War II, Congress officially created the rank of general of the army, and that allowed for five stars. Since Pershing had already achieved that rank, the change allowed him unofficially to have six stars, but he died before Congress approved that level of insignia.
57. Frazer, *Send the Alabamians*, 18.
58. The Red Cross did provide support to the Pershing Expedition. Most memorable were Christmas packages the organization provided to each man in the field. The packages were handed out during Christmas Day celebrations despite a "terrific storm which was a combination Montana blizzard and Sahara dust storm." Christmas included roast turkey, a great star of Bethlehem on display, carol singing, and even Santa Claus, "accompanied by a blare of trumpets amid a shower of fireworks." Pershing, *My Life*, 361.
59. Pershing, *My Life*, 360.
60. Lim, *Porous Borders*, 135.
61. Smythe, *Guerrilla Warrior*, 266.
62. Smythe, *Guerrilla Warrior*, 266.
63. Baker, "Secretary of War," 5.
64. Smythe, *Guerrilla Warrior*, 269.

65. Pershing, *My Life*, 362. Historian Donald Smythe observes that of the 485 Villistas who attacked Columbus in March 1916, 273 were killed, including 2 of Villa's top generals, and another 108 men were wounded. The Carranza government granted amnesty to 60. By June 30, only 25 of those who raided Columbus were still alive. Smythe, *Guerrilla Warrior*, 272.

66. Hurst, "Pershing Punitive Expedition," 14.

67. Smythe, *Guerrilla Warrior*, 274.

Conclusion

1. Samuel Avery, "Avery to Pershing, 1917 Mar. 27," Archives & Special Collections, University of Nebraska–Lincoln Libraries.

2. Pershing Auditorium, built during the 1950s, is a 4,500-seat venue with a doubtful future. The auditorium is too small to accommodate large-scale concerts and other performances and events. No major programs have been held in the facility since 2014 (when it hosted an August concert of the Goo Goo Dolls). Its last usage was a roller derby match in August 2014 between the No Coast Derby Girls and the Kansas City Roller Warriors.

3. Pahlke and Baker, "General Pershing's Legacy."

4. Part of that legacy includes a continuation of the military tradition through his son and grandsons. Col. Frances Warren Pershing served in World War II as an adviser to U.S. Army chief of staff Gen. George C. Marshall. Pershing's two sons (John's grandsons) also served. Richard W. Pershing was a second lieutenant (Company A, 502nd Infantry, 101st Airborne Division) and killed in Vietnam in 1968. According to the official telegram of notification, he died of "wounds received while on a combat mission when his unit came under hostile small-arms and rocket attack while searching for remains of a missing member of his unit." See "Richard Warren Pershing," Arlington National Cemetery Website. Col. John Pershing III served as special assistant to former army chief of staff Gen. Gordon R. Sullivan. Through his service, John helped expand the army's Reserve Officer Training Corps. He died of cardiovascular disease in 1999.

5. Pershing, *My Experiences*, 2:411.

6. Daugherty, "General Pershing's Run."

7. Pershing's six-star general status is more complicated than it might appear. Following World War I, Pershing was deemed general of the armies of the United States, making him the first military officer in U.S. history so honored. Pershing was already a four-star general, the highest rank at that time, and distinguished his rank with four gold stars rather than the traditional silver. In 1944 the five-star rank was created and would include the likes of George Marshall, Douglas MacArthur, Dwight D. Eisenhower, "Hap" Arnold, and Omar Bradley. But the War Department specified that Pershing was to be considered the highest-ranking military official, even though, technically, the rank of six-star general was never actually created. Then, in

1976, during America's bicentennial, Congress passed a law posthumously promoting George Washington to general of the armies of the United States. (Washington had served as a two-star major general, but President John Adams advanced him to lieutenant general, which carries three stars.) The law specified that Washington was to be considered the highest-ranking officer in U.S. military history. Conradt, "George Washington."

8. "General Pershing on Peace or War."

9. Today, the American Battle Monuments Commission maintains twenty-six U.S. cemeteries and twenty-nine memorials, monuments, and markers in sixteen countries.

10. Smythe, *Pershing*, 322. During the mid-1920s, rumors in Washington DC linked Pershing with another young woman, an attractive twenty-six-year-old heiress named Louise Cromwell Brooks. She claimed Pershing asked her to marry him, but the older general denied it, stating, "If I were married to all of the ladies to whom the gossips have engaged me I would be a regular Brigham Young." Instead, Miss Brooks married Douglas MacArthur. Lacey, *Pershing*, 186.

11. Olin-Ammentorp, *Edith Wharton*, 218. Cather and Pershing died just fifteen months apart, she in April 1947 and he in July 1948. In 1961 the Nebraska Hall of Fame was established to provide recognition to prominent "Nebraskans" (which includes not only those born in Nebraska but also those significants who gained prominence while living in Nebraska). Cather was inducted in 1962 and Pershing the following year. Buffalo Bill Cody was inducted in 1967. All three are represented by bronze busts in the Nebraska State Capitol Building in Lincoln.

12. Conner, *War and Remembrance*, 131.

13. Lacey, *Pershing*, 190.

14. "ARMY & NAVY: Old Soldier," 60.

15. Pershing's son, Warren, died in 1980 at the age of seventy-one. His body was cremated.

16. University of Nebraska–Lincoln, *The Sombrero*, 224–31.

17. Cather, *One of Ours*, 403–4.

Bibliography

Archives

Avery, Samuel. Archives & Special Collections, University of Nebraska–Lincoln Libraries.

Meiklejohn, George DeRue. Papers. Nebraska State Historical Society Archives, Lincoln.

Pershing, John J. Papers, ca. 1861–1963. Nebraska State Historical Society Archives, Lincoln.

Pershing, John J. Papers, Philippines: 1901–3. Library of Congress, Washington DC.

Published Works

American Bar Association. "General John J. Pershing—Lawyer." *American Bar Association Journal* 32, no. 3 (March 1945): 131.

Andrews, Avery D., ed. *1886–1911: In Commemoration of the 25th Anniversary of Graduation of the Class of '86, U.S.M.A., West Point, June, 1911*. Philadelphia: Holmes Press, 1911.

──── . *My Friend and Classmate, John J. Pershing, with Notes from My War Diary*. Harrisburg PA: Military Service Publishing, 1939.

Armitage, Sue, and Laurie Mercier. *Speaking History: Oral Histories of the American Past, 1865–Present*. New York: Palgrave Macmillan, 2009.

"ARMY & NAVY: Heroes: Old Soldier." *Time* 42, no. 20 (November 15, 1943): 55–60.

Army Times Publishing. *The Yanks Are Coming: The Story of General John J. Pershing*. New York: Putnam, 1960.

Arnold, James R. *The Moro War: How America Battled a Muslim Insurgency in the Philippine Jungle, 1902–1913*. New York: Bloomsbury Press, 2011.

Bibliography

Baker, Newton D. "The Secretary of War during the War." Army War College Lecture, Carlisle PA, May 11, 1929.

Beilein, Joseph M., Jr. *Bushwhackers: Guerrilla Warfare, Manhood, and the Household in Civil War Missouri*. Kent OH: Kent State University Press, 2016.

——— . "The Guerrilla Shirt: A Labor of Love and the Style of Rebellion in Civil War Missouri." In *Bleeding Kansas, Bleeding Missouri: The Long Civil War on the Border*, edited by Jonathan Earle and Diane Mutti Burke, 169–86. Lawrence: University Press of Kansas, 2013.

Birchell, Donna Blake. *Frontier Forts and Outposts of New Mexico*. Charleston SC: History Press, 2019.

Bjork, Katharine. "Prairie Imperialists: The Bureau of Insular Affairs and Continuities in Colonial Expansion from Nebraska to Cuba and the Philippines." *Nebraska History* 95 (Winter 2014): 217–29.

——— . *Prairie Imperialists: The Indian Country Origins of American Empire*. Philadelphia: University of Pennsylvania Press, 2019.

Blake, Michael F. *The Cowboy President: The American West and the Making of Theodore Roosevelt*. Guilford CT: TwoDot, 2018.

Boghardt, Thomas. "Chasing Ghosts in Mexico: The Columbus Raid of 1916 and the Politicization of U.S. Intelligence during World War I." *Army History* 89 (Fall 2013): 11–15.

Bourke, John G. *On the Border with Crook*. New York: Charles Scribner's Sons, 1891.

Boyd, John A. "America's Army of Democracy: The National Army, 1917–1919." *Army History* 109 (Fall 2018): 6–27.

Brown, Dee. *Bury My Heart at Wounded Knee: An Indian History of the American West, the Illustrated Edition*. New York: Fall River Press, 2009.

Bruscino, Thomas A. "A Troubled Past: The Army and Security on the Mexican Border, 1915–17." *Military Review* 4 (July–August 2008): 31–44.

Buckley, Gayle. *American Patriots: The Story of Blacks in the Military from the Revolution to Desert Storm*. New York: Random House, 2002.

Carroll, Andrew. *My Fellow Soldiers: General John Pershing and the Americans Who Helped Win the Great War*. New York: Penguin Press, 2017.

Cashin, Herschel V. *Under Fire with the Tenth U.S. Cavalry*. Niwot CO: University Press of Colorado, 1993.

Cather, Willa. *Death Comes for the Archbishop*. New York: Vintage Classics, 1990.

——— . "The Enchanted Bluff." *Harper's Monthly Magazine* 118 (April 1909): 774–81.

——— . *My Ántonia*. New York: Houghton Mifflin, 1918.

——— . *The Novels and Stories of Willa Cather*. Boston: Houghton Mifflin, 1938.

——— . *One of Ours*. New York: Knopf, 1922.

——— . *O Pioneers!* Boston: Houghton Mifflin, 1913.

——— . *The Professor's House*. New York: Knopf, 1925.

Bibliography

——— . *The Song of the Lark*. Boston: Houghton Mifflin, 1915.

——— . "The Treasure of Far Island." In *Willa Cather's Collected Short Fiction, 1892–1912*, edited by Virginia Faulkner, 265–82. Lincoln: University of Nebraska Press, 1970.

Cheek, Lawrence W. *Arizona*. New York: Compass American Guides, 2004.

Church of the Epiphany. "July 16: John Joseph Pershing (1948)." July 14, 2017. http://epiphanydc.org/2017/07/14/july-16-john-joseph-pershing-1948/.

Clavin, Tom. *Tombstone: The Earp Brothers, Doc Holliday, and the Vendetta Ride from Hell*. New York: St. Martin's Press, 2020.

Clendenen, Clarence C. *Blood on the Border: The United States Army and the Mexican Irregulars*. New York: Macmillan, 1969.

Conner, Thomas H. *War and Remembrance: The Story of the American Battle Monuments Commission*. Lexington: University Press of Kentucky, 2018.

Conradt, Stacy. "George Washington, History's Only Six-Star General (. . . Sort Of)." *Mental Floss*, July 3, 2015. https://www.mentalfloss.com/article/65227/George-washington-historys-only-six-star-general-sort.

Crook, George. "The Apache Problem" (1886). In *The Struggle for Apacheria*. Vol. 1, *Eyewitnesses to the Indian Wars, 1865–1890*, edited by Peter Cozzens, 593–603. Mechanicsburg PA: Stackpole Books, 2001.

Cunningham, Roger D. "Shaking the Iron Fist: The Mexican Punitive Expedition of 1919." *Army History: The Professional Bulletin of Army History* 54 (Winter 2002): 1–16.

Daniel, J. Furman, III. *Patton: Battling with History*. Columbia: University of Missouri Press, 2020.

Daugherty, Gregg. "General Pershing's Run for President Was a Sure Thing—until His Troops Spoke Up." *History*, May 23, 2018. https://www.history.com/news/john-j-pershing-presidential-campaign-world-war-i.

Davis, Britton. *The Truth about Geronimo*. Lincoln: University of Nebraska Press, 1976.

Davis, George B., Leslie J. Perry, and Joseph W. Kirkley. *The War of the Rebellion: A Compilation of the Official Records of the Union and Confederate Armies*. Series 1, vol. 34, part 1—*Reports*. Washington DC: Government Printing Office, 1891.

Davis, Richard Harding, Frederick Palmer, James F. J. Archibald, Robert L. Dunn, Ellis Ashmead Bartlett, James H. Hare, Henry James Whigham, and Victor K. Bulla. *The Russo-Japanese War: A Photographic and Descriptive Review of the Great Conflict in the Far East*. New York: P. F. Collier and Son, 1905.

Department of Military Science and Tactics, University of Nebraska. *History of the Military Department, University of Nebraska, 1876–1941*. Lincoln: University of Nebraska, 1942.

De Quesada, Alejandro. *The Hunt for Pancho Villa: The Columbus Raid and Pershing's Punitive Expedition, 1916–17*. Oxford, UK: Osprey, 2012.

Bibliography

———. "March 9, 1916: Pancho Villa and the Villista Raid on Columbus." *The History Reader*, March 8, 2013. https://www.thehistoryreader.com/modern-history/march-91916-pancho-villa-villista-raid-columbus/.

Dick, Everett. "Problems of the Frontier Prairie City as Portrayed by Lincoln, Nebraska, 1880–1890." *Nebraska History* 27 (June 1947): 132–43.

Dunlap, Annette B. *Charles Gates Dawes: A Life*. Evanston IL: Northwestern University Press and the Evanston History Center, 2016.

Dunn, Robert. *World Alive: A Personal Story*. New York: Crown Publishers, 1956.

Edgerton, Ronald K. *American Datu: John J. Pershing and Counterinsurgency Warfare in the Muslim Philippines, 1899–1913*. Lexington: University Press of Kentucky, 2020.

Eisenhower, John S. D. *Intervention! The United States and the Mexican Revolution, 1913–1917*. New York: W. W. Norton, 1993.

Elser, Frank B. "General Pershing's Mexican Campaign." *Century Magazine* 99 (February 1920): 433–47.

Evans, Robley Dunglison. *An Admiral's Log: Being Continued Recollections of Naval Life*. New York: D. Appleton, 1910.

Finley, John P. "The Commercial Awakening of the Moro and Pagan." *The North American Review* 688 (March 1913): 325–34.

Frazer, Nimrod T. *Send the Alabamians: World War I Fighters in the Rainbow Division*. Tuscaloosa: University of Alabama Press, 2014.

Fulton, Robert A. *Moroland, 1899–1906: America's First Attempt to Transform an Islamic Society*. Bend OR: Tumalo Creek Press, 2007.

———. *Moroland: The History of Uncle Sam and the Moros, 1899–1920*. Bend OR: Tumalo Creek Press, 2007.

"Funke Opera House." *History Nebraska*. Accessed February 17, 2020. https://history.nebraska.gov/publications/funke-opera-house.

Ganoe, William A. *The History of the United States Army*. New York: D. Appleton, 1924.

Gems, Gerald R. *Sport and the American Occupation of the Philippines: Bats, Balls, and Bayonets*. Lanham MD: Lexington Books, 2016.

"General Pershing on Peace or War." *The Homiletic Review* 88 (November 1924): 383.

Giese, Dale F. *Echoes of the Bugle*. Tyrone NM: Phelps Dodge, 1976.

Gillette, Howard, Jr. *Between Justice and Beauty: Race, Planning, and the Failure of Urban Policy*. Philadelphia: University of Pennsylvania Press, 2006.

Ginsburgh, Robert. "Pershing as His Orderlies Knew Him." *The American Legion Monthly* 5 (October 1928): 9–11, 64–68.

Goldhurst, Richard. *Pipe Clay and Drill: John J. Pershing, the Classic American Soldier*. New York: Reader's Digest Press, 1977.

Gowing, Peter G. *Mandate in Moroland: The American Government of Muslim Filipinos, 1899–1920*. Quezon City: Philippine Center for Advanced Studies, University of the Philippines System, 1977.

Bibliography

Green, Constance McLaughlin. *Washington, Capital City, 1879–1950*. Princeton NJ: Princeton University Press, 1963.

Greenberg, Lt. Col. William L., (Ret.). "Pershing in Mindanao: Leadership in Counterinsurgency." *Small Wars Journal*, September 26, 2012. https://smallwarsjournal.com/jrnl/art/pershing-in-mindanao-leadership-in-counterinsurgency.

Greenwood, John T. "The U.S. Army Military Observers with the Japanese Army during the Russo-Japanese War (1904–1905)." *Army History* 36 (Winter 1996): 1–14.

Hagedorn, Hermann. *Leonard Wood: A Biography*. New York: Harper & Brothers, 1931.

Haley, P. Edward. *Revolution and Intervention: The Diplomacy of Taft and Wilson with Mexico, 1910–1917*. Cambridge MA: MIT Press, 1970.

Harbord, James G. *The American Army in France, 1917–1919*. Boston: Little, Brown, 1936.

Hasian, Marouf A., Jr. *President Trump and General Pershing: Remembrances of the "Moro" Insurrection in the Age of Post-Truths*. New York: Palgrave Macmillan, 2019.

Hassler, Warren W., Jr. *With Shield and Sword: American Military Affairs, Colonial Times to the Present*. Ames: Iowa State University Press, 1982.

Hawkins, Michael C. "Managing a Massacre: Savagery, Civility, and Gender in Moro Province in the Wake of Bud Dajo." *Philippine Studies* 59 (March 2015): 83–105.

"Heartland." *America: The Story of US*. Produced by Nutopia. Video, episode 6. Santa Monica CA: Lionsgate, 2010.

Hurst, James W. *Pancho Villa and Black Jack Pershing: The Punitive Expedition in Mexico*. Westport CT: Praeger, 2008.

———. "The Pershing Punitive Expedition of 1916–17: Mission Misunderstood." *Southern New Mexico Historical Review* 11 (February 2004): 9–18.

Hymel, Kevin. "Black Jack in Cuba: General John J. Pershing's Service in the Spanish-American War." *Army History* 45 (Summer 1998): 1–6.

Ingraham, Col. Prentiss. "Adventures of Buffalo Bill from Boyhood to Manhood." *Dime Novels and Penny Dreadfuls*, 78_1_1, 1998. From *Beadle's Boy's Library of Sport, Story and Adventure* 1, no. 1 (1882?). http://www.gutenberg.org/ebooks/15583.

Jastrzembski, Joseph C. "Folklore, Personal Narratives, and Ethno-Ethnohistory." In *New Perspectives on Native North America: Cultures, Histories, and Representations*, edited by Sergei A. Kan and Pauline Turner Strong, 285–309. Lincoln: University of Nebraska Press, 2006.

Jewell, Andrew, and Janis Stout, eds. *The Selected Letters of Willa Cather*. New York: Vintage Books, 2013.

Johnson, Alvin. *Pioneer's Progress: An Autobiography*. New York: Viking Press, 1952.

Johnson, William Weber. *Heroic Mexico: The Violent Emergence of a Modern Nation*. Garden City NY: Doubleday, 1968.

Bibliography

Katz, Jonathan. "What General Pershing Was Really Doing in the Philippines." *The Atlantic*, August 18, 2017.

Kemper, Steve. *A Splendid Savage: The Restless Life of Frederick Russell Burnham*. New York: W. W. Norton, 2016.

King, James T. "The Republican River Expedition, June–July, 1869: I. On the March." *Nebraska History* 41 (1960): 165–99.

———. *War Eagle: A Life of General Eugene A. Carr*. Lincoln: University of Nebraska Press, 1963.

Kinzer, Stephen. *The True Flag: Theodore Roosevelt, Mark Twain, and the Birth of American Empire*. New York: Henry Holt, 2017.

Lacey, Jim. *Pershing: Lessons in Leadership*. New York: Palgrave Macmillan, 2008.

Landor, A. Henry Savage. *The Gems of the East: Sixteen Thousand Miles of Research Travel among Wild and Tame Tribes of Enchanting Islands*. New York: Harper & Brothers, 1904.

Lane, Jack C., ed. *Chasing Geronimo: The Journal of Leonard Wood, May–September 1886*. Lincoln: University of Nebraska Press, 1970.

Leckie, William H. *The Buffalo Soldiers: A Narrative of the Negro Cavalry in the West*. Norman: University of Oklahoma Press, 1967.

Leech, Margaret. *In the Days of McKinley*. New York: Harper & Brothers, 1959.

Lim, Julian. *Porous Borders: Multiracial Migrations and the Law in the U.S.-Mexico Borderlands*. Chapel Hill: University of North Carolina Press, 2017.

Long, John D. *America of Yesterday: The Diary of John D. Long*. Edited by Lawrence Shaw Mayo. Boston: Atlantic Monthly Press, 1923.

Lukesh, Jean. "G. P. Cather Made the Supreme Sacrifice as 'One of Ours' in WW I." *Grand Island Independent*, July 4, 2000. Updated December 16, 2011. https:www.theindependent.com/life/g-p-cather-made-the-supreme-sacrifice-as-one-of-ours-in-wwi/article_a6808977-f3c2-5f1e-a421-5780424ab239.html.

MacAdam, George. "The Life of General Pershing: Experiences at the University of Nebraska." In *The World's Work*, edited by French Strother and Burton J. Hendrick, 539–46. Garden City NY: Doubleday, Page, March 1919.

———. "The Life of General Pershing: His Boyhood and Entrance at West Point." In *The World's Work*, edited by French Strother and Burton J. Hendrick, 45–56. Garden City NY: Doubleday, Page, November 1918.

———. "The Life of General Pershing: Indian Campaigns in Arizona." In *The World's Work*, edited by French Strother and Burton J. Hendrick, 281–94. Garden City NY: Doubleday, Page, January 1919.

———. "The Life of General Pershing: Pershing's Own Account of His Spanish-American War Experiences." In *The World's Work*, edited by French Strother and Burton J. Hendrick, 681–97. Garden City NY: Doubleday, Page, April 1919.

Bibliography

———. "The Life of General Pershing: The Punitive Expedition into Mexico." In *The World's Work*, edited by French Strother and Burton J. Hendrick, 148–58. Garden City NY: Doubleday, Page, July 1919.

———. "The Life of General Pershing: The Sioux Campaign." In *The World's Work*, edited by French Strother and Burton J. Hendrick, 449–61. Garden City NY: Doubleday, Page, February 1919.

———. "The Life of General Pershing: The Story of His Activities in the Philippines." In *The World's Work*, edited by Arthur W. Page, French Strother, and Burton J. Hendrick, 86–103. Garden City NY: Doubleday, Page, May 1919.

———. "The Life of General Pershing: The Story of His Activities in the Philippines." In *The World's Work*, edited by Arthur W. Page, French Strother, and Burton J. Hendrick, 148–58. Garden City NY: Doubleday, Page, June 1919.

———. "The Life of General Pershing: West Point Days." In *The World's Work*, edited by French Strother and Burton J. Hendrick, 161–73. Garden City NY: Doubleday, Page, December 1918.

Mason, Herbert Molloy, Jr. *The Great Pursuit: Pershing's Expedition to Destroy Pancho Villa*. Old Saybrook CT: Konecky and Konecky, 1970.

Matteoni, Norman E. *Prairie Man: The Struggle between Sitting Bull and Indian Agent James McLaughlin*. Guilford CT: TwoDot, 2015.

McGee, W. J. "Desert Thirst as Disease." *Interstate Medical Journal* 13 (March 1906): 1–23.

McNamee, Gregory. *Grand Canyon Place Names*. Boulder: Johnson Books, 1997.

McNeese, Tim. *Discovering U.S. History: The Gilded Age and Progressivism, 1891–1913*. New York: Chelsea House Publishers, 2010.

———. *Remember the Maine: The Spanish-American War Begins*. Greensboro NC: Morgan Reynolds, 2002.

McPherson, James. *The Battle Cry of Freedom*. New York: Oxford University Press, 1988.

Mead, Gary. *The Doughboys: America and the First World War*. New York: Penguin Books, 2001.

Miles, Nelson Appleton. *Personal Recollections and Observations of General Nelson A. Miles*. Chicago: Werner, 1896.

Millard, Maj. George A. "Army Logistics in Mexico, 1916." In *United States Army Logistics, 1775–1992*, edited by Charles R. Schrader, 389–99. Washington DC: U.S. Army Center of Military History, 1997.

Miller, Darlis A. *Soldiers and Settlers: Military Supply in the Southwest, 1861–1885*. Albuquerque: University of New Mexico Press, 1989.

Miller, Roger G. *A Preliminary to War: The 1st Aero Squadron and the Mexican Punitive Expedition of 1916*. Washington DC: Air Force History and Museums Program, 2003.

Bibliography

———. "Wings and Wheels: The 1st Aero Squadron, Truck Transport, and the Punitive Expedition of 1916." *Air Power History* 42 (Winter 1995): 14–29.

Myers, Lee. *Fort Stanton, New Mexico: The Military Years, 1855–1896*. Lincoln NM: Lincoln County Historical Society Publications, 1988.

———. *New Mexico Military Installations*. Globe AZ: Southwest Parks and Monuments Association, 1966.

Neiburg, Michael S. *The Path to War: How the First World War Created Modern America*. New York: Oxford University Press, 2016.

Neihardt, John G. *Black Elk Speaks: Being the Life Story of a Holy Man of the Oglala Sioux*. Albany: State University of New York Press, 2008.

O'Bryan, Tony. "Red Legs." *Civil War on the Western Border: The Missouri-Kansas Conflict, 1854–1865*. Accessed January 21, 2020. https://civilwaronthewesternborder.org/encyclopedia/red-legs.

O'Connor, Richard. *Black Jack Pershing*. Garden City NY: Doubleday, 1961.

Olin-Ammentorp, Julie. *Edith Wharton, Willa Cather, and the Place of Culture*. Lincoln: University of Nebraska Press, 2019.

Pahlke, Jackson, and Nathan Baker, eds. "General Pershing's Legacy." Gen. John J. Pershing: Contributions and Commemoration at UNL, 1891–1985. Nebraska U: A Collaborative History, from the Archives of the University of Nebraska–Lincoln. Fall 2010. https://unlhistory.unl.edu/exhibits/show/generalpershing/general-pershing-s-legacy.

Palmer, Frederick. *John J. Pershing, General of the Armies*. Harrisburg PA: Military Service Publishing, 1948.

———. *Newton D. Baker: America at War*. 2 vols. New York: Dodd, Mead, 1931.

Parker, W. Thornton. "The Evolution of the Colored Soldier." *North American Review* 507 (February 1899): 223–28.

Perry, John. *Pershing: Commander of the Great War*. Nashville: Thomas Nelson, 2011.

Perry, Mark. "What Black Jack Pershing Can Teach Us about Fighting Terrorists." *Politico Magazine*, August 20, 2017. https://www.politico.com/magazine/story/2017/08/20/what-black-jack-pershing-can-teach-us-about-fighting-terrorists-215509.

Pershing, Edgar J. *The Pershing Family in America: A Collection of Historical and Genealogical Data, Family Portraits, Traditions, Legends and Military Records*. Philadelphia: George S. Ferguson, 1924.

Pershing, John J. *John J. Pershing Papers: Diaries, Notebooks, and Address Books, January 13–September 3, 1897*. Manuscript/Mixed Material. Library of Congress. Accessed April 22, 2020. https://www.loc.gov/item/mss35949042/.

———. *My Experiences in the World War*. Vols. 1 and 2. Franklin Park IL: Arcadia Press, 2019.

———. *My Life before the World War, 1860–1917: A Memoir of General of the Armies John J. Pershing*. Edited by John T. Greenwood. Lexington: University Press of Kentucky, 2013.

Bibliography

"Pershing, Our Leader in France." In *The World's Work*, edited by Arthur W. Page, 340–44. Garden City NY: Doubleday, Page, July 1917.

"Pershing's 'Jinx' Birthday, and Something about His Boyhood." *Literary Digest*, September 7, 1918, 58–61.

Philbrick, Nathaniel. *In the Heart of the Sea: The Tragedy of the Whaleship Essex*. New York: Penguin Books, 2000.

Phillips, Kevin. *William McKinley: The 25th President, 1897–1901*. The American Presidents Series. New York: Times Books, 2003.

Platt, Rutherford. "There Was a Captain by the Name of Pershing." In *The World's Work*, edited by French Strother and Burton J. Hendrick, 181–85. Garden City NY: Doubleday, Page, December 1923.

Remington, Frederic. *Frederic Remington's Own West*. Edited by Harold McCracken. New York: Dial Press, 1960.

———. "The Galloping Sixth." *Harper's Weekly*, January 16, 1892, 57–64.

———. "The Sioux Outbreak in South Dakota." *Harper's Weekly*, January 24, 1891, 57–62.

Richardson, Heather Cox. *Wounded Knee: Party Politics and the Road to an American Massacre*. New York: Basic Books, 2010.

"Richard Warren Pershing, Second Lieutenant, United States Army." Arlington National Cemetery Website. Updated November 12, 2007. Accessed June 2, 2020. www.arlingtoncemetery.net/richardw.htm.

Rippy, J. Fred. "Some Precedents of the Pershing Expedition into Mexico." *Southwestern Historical Quarterly* 4 (April 1921): 292–316.

Risen, Clay. *The Crowded Hour: Theodore Roosevelt, the Rough Riders, and the Dawn of the American Century*. New York: Scribner, 2019.

Roberts, Brian Russell. "Archipelagic American Studies: An Open and Comparative Insularity." In *The Routledge Companion to Transnational American Studies*, edited by Nina Morgan, Alfred Hornung, and Takayuki Tatsumi, 51–60. New York: Routledge, 2019.

Roosevelt, Theodore. *The Rough Riders*. New York: Fall River Press, 2014. Originally published in 1899.

———. *The Winning of the West*. Vol. 1, *The Spread of English-Speaking Peoples*. New York: G. P. Putnam's Sons, 1889.

Samuels, Peggy, and Harold Samuels. *Remembering the* Maine. Washington DC: Smithsonian Institution Press, 1995.

Sargent, Herbert H. *The Campaign of Santiago de Cuba*. Chicago: A. C. McClurg, 1907.

Sawyer, Andrew J., ed. *Lincoln, the Capital City, and Lancaster County, Nebraska*. 2 vols. Chicago: S. J. Clarke, 1916.

Schubert, Frank N. "Buffalo Soldiers: Myths and Realities." *Army History* 52 (Spring 2001): 13–18.

———. *Voices of the Buffalo Soldier: Records, Reports, and Recollections of Military Life and Service in the West*. Albuquerque: University of New Mexico Press, 2003.

Bibliography

Scott, Hugh L. *Some Memories of a Soldier*. New York: Century Company, 1928.

"Senator Chamberlain Takes a Hand." *Lumber World Review* 36 (January 10, 1919).

Showalter, Dennis. "The U.S. Cavalry: Soldiers of a Nation, Policemen of an Empire." *Army History* 81 (Fall 2011): 6–23.

Sides, Hampton. *Blood and Thunder: The Epic Story of Kit Carson and the Conquest of the American West*. New York: Anchor Books, 2007.

Silbey, David J. *A War of Frontier and Empire: The Philippine-American War, 1899–1902*. New York: Hill and Wang, 2007.

Slote, Bernice, ed. *The Kingdom of Art: Willa Cather's First Principles and Critical Statements, 1893–1896*. Lincoln: University of Nebraska Press, 1966.

Smith, Gene. *Until the Last Trumpet Sounds: The Life of General of the Armies John J. Pershing*. New York: John Wiley & Sons, 1998.

Smythe, Donald. "'Black Jack' Pershing's Brilliant Career Almost Ended in an Attempt to View Arizona's Awesome Grand Canyon in 1889." *Montana: The Magazine of Western History* 13 (Spring 1963): 11–23.

———. "The Early Years of John J. Pershing, 1860–1882." *Missouri Historical Review* 58 (October 1963): 1–20.

———. *Guerrilla Warrior: The Early Life of John J. Pershing*. New York: Charles Scribner's Sons, 1973.

———. "John J. Pershing: A Study in Paradox." *Military Review* 49 (September 1969): 66–72.

———. "John J. Pershing at the University of Nebraska, 1891–1895." *Nebraska History* 43 (1962): 169–96.

———. "John J. Pershing: Frontier Cavalryman." *New Mexico Historical Review* 38, no. 3 (1963): 220–43.

———. "Pershing and Counterinsurgency." *Military Review* 46 (September 1966): 85–92.

———. "Pershing and the Disarmament of the Moros." *Pacific Historical Review* 3 (August 162): 241–56.

———. "Pershing and the Mount Bagsak Campaign of 1913." *Philippine Studies* (Ateneo de Manila University Press) 12 (January 1964): 3–31.

———. "Pershing at West Point, 1897–1898." *New York History* 48 (January 1967): 42–43.

———. *Pershing: General of the Armies*. Bloomington: Indiana University Press, 1986.

Steinbach, Robert H. *A Long March: The Lives of Frank and Alice Baldwin*. Austin: University of Texas Press, 1989.

Swartley, Ron. *Old Forts of the Apache Wars: A Travel Guide to 17 Old Forts in Arizona, New Mexico, and West Texas*. Silver City NM: Frontier Image Press, 1999.

Tate, James P., ed. *The American Military on the Frontier*. Washington DC: The Office of Air Force History Headquarters and United States Air Force

Bibliography

Academy, 1978. Presented at the Proceedings of the 7th Military History Symposium, U.S. Air Force Academy, September 30–October 1, 1976.

Teitelbaum, Louis M. *Woodrow Wilson and the Mexican Revolution, 1913–1916*. New York: Exposition Press, 1967.

Thomas, Robert S., and Inez V. Allen. *The Mexican Punitive Expedition under Brigadier General John J. Pershing, United States Army, 1916–1917*. Washington DC: Office of the Chief of Military History, May 1, 1954, appendix D.

Thomas, Rowland. "Pershing—United States Soldier." In *The World's Work*, edited by Walter H. Page, 8179–81. Chicago: Doubleday, Page, November 1906.

Timmons, Bascom N. *Portrait of an American: Charles G. Dawes*. New York: Henry Holt, 1953.

Tomlinson, Everett T. *The Story of General Pershing*. New York: D. Appleton, 1919.

Toulmin, Col. H. A., Jr. *With Pershing in Mexico*. Harrisburg PA: Military Service Publishing, 1935.

Trimble, Marshall. "Did Jesse James Really Pack Eighteen Handguns? Setting the Record Straight." *True West*, September 14, 2019. https://truewestmagazine.com/jesse-james-handguns/.

Turner, Frederick Jackson. "The Significance of the Frontier in American History." In *Major Problems in the History of the American West*, edited by Clyde A. Milner II, 1–21. Lexington MA: D. C. Heath, 1989.

Turner, Timothy G. *Bullets, Bottles, and Gardenias*. Dallas: Southwest Press, 1935.

University of Nebraska–Lincoln. *The Sombrero*. Lincoln: Press of Jacob North & Company, 1895.

———. "University Hall." An Architectural Tour of Historic UNL. 2005. https://historicbuildings.unl.edu/building.php?b=43.

U.S. Military Academy. *Official Register of the Officers and Cadets*. West Point NY: USMA A. G. Printing Office, 1950.

U.S. War Department. *Annual Report of the Secretary of War*. Vol. 3. Washington DC: Government Printing Office, 1903.

Utley, Robert M. *Billy the Kid: A Short and Violent Life*. Lincoln: University of Nebraska Press, 1989.

———. *Frontier Regulars: The United States Army and the Indian, 1866–1891*. Lincoln: University of Nebraska Press, 1973.

———. *The Last Days of the Sioux Nation*. New Haven CT: Yale University Press, 1963.

Vandiver, Frank E. *Black Jack: The Life and Times of John J. Pershing*. Vol. 1. College Station: Texas A&M University Press, 1977.

———. *John J. Pershing and the Anatomy of Leadership*. The Harmon Memorial Lectures in Military History, #5. Colorado Springs: U.S. Air Force Academy, 1963.

Wallace, William Swilling, ed. "Lieutenants Pershing and Stotsenberg [sic] Visit the Grand Canyon: 1887." *Arizona and the West* 3 (Autumn 1961): 265–84.

Warren, Louis S. *Buffalo Bill's America: William Cody and the Wild West Show.* New York: Alfred A. Knopf, 2005.

Welsome, Eileen. *The General and the Jaguar: Pershing's Hunt for Pancho Villa, a True Story of Revolution and Revenge.* New York: Little, Brown, 2006.

Wharfield, H. B. "The Affair at Carrizal." *Montana* 18 (Autumn 1968): 24–39, 45.

Wheeler, Harold F. "The Romance of General Pershing." *Ladies' Home Journal* 36 (July 1919): 7–8, 44.

White, Bruce. "The Muddied Waters of Columbus, New Mexico." *The Americas* 32 (July 1975): 72–98.

Wilson, Michael Clayton. "Bison in Alberta: Paleontology, Evolution, and Relations with Humans." In *Buffalo*, edited by John Foster, Dick Harrison, and I. S. MacLaren, 1–17. Edmonton: University of Alberta Press, 1992.

Wimberly, Lowry Charles. "Oscar Wilde Meets Woodberry." *Prairie Schooner*, Spring 1947, 108.

Woodress, James. *Willa Cather: A Literary Life.* Lincoln: University of Nebraska Press, 1987.

Yockelson, Mitchell. *Forty-Seven Days: How Pershing's Warriors Came of Age to Defeat the German Army in World War I.* New York: New American Library, 2016.

Young, James Rankin. *History of Our War with Spain, including Battles on Sea and Land.* Washington DC: Office of the Librarian of Congress, 1898.

Young, Karl. "A Fight That Could Have Meant War." *American West* 3 (Spring 1966): 17–23, 90.

———. *Ordeal in Mexico: Tales of Danger and Hardship Collected from Mormon Colonists.* Salt Lake City: Deseret Book, 1968.

Index

ABC Powers, 299
Acosta, Julio, 332
Adair, Henry, 337–38
Adam, Emil, 121, 124
Adta, Dato of Paigoay, 238
"Adventures of Buffalo Bill from Boyhood to Manhood," 99
Aero Squadron, First, 323, 325
Ahumada District, Mexico, 336–37
Alger, Russell A., 200
Allen, John C., 134
American Battle Monuments Commission, 352, 353, 392n9
American Expeditionary Forces (AEF), 70, 290, 347, 350
Amil, Dato, 287, 288
Anasazis, 5
Anderson, William "Bloody Bill," 31, 364n20
Andrews, Avery, 166, 178, 184, 208, 254
Anthony, William, 198
Apaches, 74, 75, 76, 87, 92, 95, 163, 167, 251, 317
Arapahos, 111
Arlington National Cemetery, 355
Armistead, Lewis, 384n31
Army-Navy Hospital (Hot Springs AR), 275
Army Plans Division, 354

Aserraderos, Cuba, 206
Atchison, Topeka and Santa Fe Railroad (AT&SF), 72, 114, 148
Avery, Samuel, 349
Ayres, George, 213

B-25 (Apache scout), 323
Bachiniva, 326
Bacolod, Philippines, 237, 244, 247, 249
Badlands (SD), 118, 119, 370n19
Bailey, Andrew O., 310
Baker, Chauncey B., 106, 107
Baker, Newton D., 316, 333, 345
Baldwin, Frank D., 202
Baldwin, Theodore Anderson, 185, 216–17, 218, 219, 235–36
Baltic, RMS, 350
Barnum, Mal, 217
barong, 227, 284
Baruch, Bernard, 144–45
Bayabao, Philippines, 240
Bayan, Philippines, 237, 243–44
Bayard, George D., 74
Beadle's dime novels, 42, 71, 87, 90, 99, 136, 173
Bean, Wiley, 72
Beard, Dewey, 122
Bear Paw Mountains (MT), 165, 177
Beast Barracks, 62

405

Index

Beck, William, 219
Bell, Franklin, 267, 293, 339
Bellevue Rifle Range (NE), 135
Benét-Mercié machine guns, 312
Best, Jack, 150
Big Foot, 119, 121, 123
Big Sharley (Apache scout), 323
Billy the Kid. *See* McCarty, Henry (Billy the Kid)
Binidayan, Philippines, 237
Black Coyote, 122, 123
Black Elk, 124
Black Hills (SD), 114
Black Mountains, 94
Blackstone's Commentaries on the Laws of England, 55, 156
"Bleeding Kansas," 29, 99
Bliss, P. P., 4, 13
Bliss, Tasker, 315
Bonney, William. *See* McCarty, Henry (Billy the Kid)
Boquillas, 334
Border Ruffians, 29
Bosque Redondo Reservation, 100
Boswell, Anne Orr, 273, 303
Bowman, George T., 247
Boxer Rebellion, 97
Boyd, Charles T., 336, 338, 340
brevet ranks, explanation of, 380n1
Brewster, Andre W., 88
Brooke, John R., 175
Brooks, Louise Cromwell, 392n10
Brooks Brothers, 379n27
Brown, John, 29
Brown, W. C., 328
Bryan, William Jennings, 142, 148, 159, 160, 164, 177, 200, 302
Buckskin Mountains, 9
Buckskin Scouts, 34
Bud Bagsak, Philippines, 287, 288–89
Bud Dajo, Philippines, 286
Buffalo Bill. *See* Cody, William (Buffalo Bill)
Buffalo Bill Combination, 368n26
Buffalo Bill's Wild West, 98, 103, 118, 124, 296
buffalo hunting, professional, 110–11

"buffalo soldiers," 167
Bullard, Robert, 96
Bull Head, Henry, 117–18
Burden, Jim (fictional character), 28
Bureau of Indian Affairs, 113
Burkett, Elmer, 160
Burro (Havasupi Indian), 15

Cameron, Don, 373n28
Camp Furlong, 310, 312
Camp Overton, Philippines, 288
Camp Vicars, Philippines, 235, 237–38, 241, 245, 249, 278
Canfield, Dorothy (Fisher), 141, 146, 150, 153, 156, 355
Canfield, James H., 141, 147, 150, 153, 156, 157, 158, 178, 226
Capitan Mountains, 81, 89
Cárdenas, Julio, 332
Carleton, James, 100
Carlisle Indian School (PA), 2
Carr, Eugene A. "War Eagle," 75, 95, 100, 101, 103, 104, 106, 114, 115, 116, 117, 120, 127, 135, 164, 172, 369n29
Carranza, Venustiano, 298, 309, 315, 320, 333, 339, 341, 345, 349
Carrizal, battle at, 336–40
Carson, Kit, 11, 88, 99, 101
Casas Grandes (Paquimé), 320, 326
Casey, E. W., 371n45
Castillon Ranch, 334
Catch-the-Bear, 118
Cather, Grosvenor (G.P.), 150, 208, 356, 373n37, 388n13
Cather, Willa, 4, 16, 28–29, 42, 50, 73, 92, 139, 140, 150, 180, 208, 242, 296, 318, 352–53, 355, 392n11
Chaffee, Adna R., 235, 239, 242
Charlton, George C., 290
Cheyenne River Agency, 112, 119
Cheyenne WY, 256
Chicago, Burlington and Quincy Railroad, 26
Chicago Daily News, 342
Chicken, First Sergeant (Apache scout), 323, 332
Chief Joseph, 165

Index

Chihuahua, 297, 309, 318, 319
Chihuahua City, capture of, 345
Chisholm Trail, 37
Chisum, John Simpson, 90
Chow Big (Apache scout), 323
Church of the Epiphany (Washington DC), 260
Cleveland, Grover, 179, 194
Cloman, Sidney, 269
Cochise, 77
Cody, William (Buffalo Bill), 114, 115, 296, 392n11; and *Buffalo Bill Combination*, 368n26; meets JP, 98–99; as Red Legs member, 34; and *The Scouts of the Prairie*, 368n26
cogon grass, 241
Collins, James L., 305–6, 318
Colonia Dublán, 321, 325, 344, 345
Colorado River, 1
Colorado Springs CO, 258
Columbian Exposition (Chicago), 158
Columbus NM, 310–13, 320, 345, 349
Constitutionalists, 298
Cootes Hill, 312
Corps of Cadets (UNL), 98, 141, 143–44
Court of First Instance, 292
Coutts Station, 170, 175
Craig, Malin, 189
Crazy Horse, 111, 124
Crees, 169–70, 172, 173–75, 176, 218
Crook, George, 76–77, 88, 111, 121
Crounse, Lorenzo, 160
Crowder, David, 32
Crowder, Enoch H., 330
Crowder, Sally, 41
Cuban Revolutionary Party, 194
Culberson's Ranch, 321
Culebra Range, 73
Curtis, Edward Sheriff, 361n7
Cusi, Chihuahua, 332
Custer, George Armstrong, 62, 76, 111

Daiquirí, Cuba, 205
datos, 227
Davenport, Erwin R., 149
Davis, George Whitefield, 228, 229, 234, 236, 242, 269

Davis, Richard Harding, 264
Dawes, Charles G., 147, 148, 160, 164, 177, 178, 223, 261, 373n25
Dawes, James W., 147
Death Comes for the Archbishop (Cather), 73, 318
DeGrew House, 30
Delmonico's, 71
Department of Arizona, 76, 91, 100
Department of California, 254
Department of Colorado, 258
Department of New Mexico, 100
Department of Texas, 258
Department of the Platte, 76, 77
DeShon, George, 223, 275
Dewey, George, 201
Diamond S Ranch (NM), 103
Díaz, Félix, 298
Díaz, Porfirio, 296–97
Diki Diki, 281
Distinguished Service Cross, 290
Division of Customs and Insular Affairs, 222–23, 291
Dodd, George A., 326, 331
Dodge, Richard, 110
Dominiques, Cruz, 332
Don Cameron's Lunch Counter, 148, 373n28
Drexel Mission (SD), 125
Drum, William, 117
Dunn, Robert, 324

Eden Musée, 71
Eighteenth Missouri Volunteer Infantry, 30
Eighth Cavalry, 121
Eisenhower, Dwight D., 354
El Caney, Cuba, 210, 213
Elite Confectionery, 300
El Paso and Southwestern Railroad, 310
El Paso Herald, 85, 305
El Paso TX, 296
"The Enchanted Bluff" (Cather), 50
Ernst, Oswald H., 186
Erwin, James B., 321
Estabrook, Henry D., 147
Executive Order No. 24, 285

407

Index

Favela, Juan, 314
"The Fear That Walks by Noonday" (Cather), 355
Fechet, E. G., 159
Fetterman Massacre, 371n41
Field, Allan W., 159
Fierro, Rodolfo, 300
Fifteenth Cavalry, 229
Fifth Cavalry, 100
First Mesa, 5
First New Mexico Infantry, 88
First Philippine Republic, 243
First Regiment of the Missouri State Militia, 30
Flagstaff, AZ, 4
Flanders Field, 353
Fleming, L. J., 170, 173
Fletcher, Henry P., 274
Fletcher, John, 42, 43
Fling, Fred Morrow, 149
Forbes, Cameron, 278, 285
Forsyth, James W., 122
Fort Assinniboine, 20, 164, 168, 169, 175, 185
Fort Bayard, 20, 74, 85, 93, 322
Fort Benton MT, 170
Fort Bliss, 300, 301, 310, 317
Fort Craig, 94
Fort Defiance AZ, 2, 3, 18
Fort Lyon, 101
Fort McKinney, 128
Fort Missoula, 172
Fort Myer, 155
Fort Niobrara, 128, 130, 135
Fort Sam Houston, 20, 349
Fort Sheridan, 135
Fort Stanton, 20, 81, 88, 89, 94, 96, 97, 105, 106, 137, 279, 368n9
Fort Sumner, 100–101
Fort Verde, 15
Fort William McKinley, 270, 271, 272, 288, 336
Fort Wingate, 20, 86, 100, 101, 104
Fort Yates, 117
Fremont, Elkhorn & Missouri Valley Railroad, 114, 128
Funke Opera House, 138

Funston, Frederick R., 315, 316, 319, 333, 334, 335, 339–40
Ganoe, William A., 342
García, Calixto, 206
Garrett, Pat, 90
"Garryowen" (song), 128
George V, 351
George VI, 353
Gere, Frances, 208
Gerhardt, David (fictional character), 356
Geronimo, 71, 75, 76, 77, 78, 167, 200, 322, 323
Ghost Dance, 113, 118, 119, 122, 127
Ghost Dance Uprising, 20, 200, 296
Ghost Shirt, 122
Gibbons, Floyd, 324
Glenn Springs, 334
Gomez, Felix, 337–38
Goodnight-Loving Trail, 90
Gordon, William W., 287
Grand Canyon, 1, 2, 4, 7, 8, 15–17, 19, 105
Grant, Fred, 184
Grant, Ulysses, III, 347
Grant, Ulysses S., 62, 65, 71
Grant Hall (UNL), 143
Greasy Grass, 111, 124, 164
Great Falls MT, 171, 172
Great Plains, 110, 111
Griscom, Lloyd, 259
Guaun, Philippines, 240
Guerrero, 326
Guillén, Genovevo Rivas, 337

Hance, John, 2, 15–16, 362n32
Hanna, Mark, 177
Hannibal and St. Joseph Railroad, 26
Harbord, James G., 222
Havana, Cuba, 197
Hawkins, Feather, 40
Haymarket Square (Lincoln NE), 137
Hayward, William, 145, 149
Hearst, William Randolph, 195
Hein, Otto, 186
heliographic system, 80–82
Hell Yet-Suey (Apache scout), 323
Helmick, Eli, 239

Index

Henry, Guy V., 201
The Hesperian, 142, 146, 153, 155, 374nn44–45
Hickok, James "Wild Bill," 34
Holden, Jonas, 197
"Hold the Fort" (hymn), 4, 13–14
Holmdahl, E. L., 333
Holtzclaw, Clifton, 32–36, 99
Homestead Act, 293
Hopper, James, 330
Hotchkiss guns, 122, 123, 210
Hotel Aguana (Juárez), 333
Hotel Paso del Norte (El Paso), 333
Howard, Oliver Otis, 62, 366n3
The Howitzer, 189
How the Other Half Lives (Riis), 256
Howze, Robert, 326
Huerta, Victoriano, 297
"Hundredth Night Show," 189
Hunter, Hubert S., 305
Hurst, James, 346
Husk, Carlo, 300
Hyde Park Methodist Episcopal Church (Chicago), 221, 379n26

Iligan, Philippines, 229
Infantry and Cavalry School (Fort Leavenworth KS), 106
International Mark Twain Society, 353
International Mining Company, 334
Irish National League, 148
Iron Tail. *See* Beard, Dewey

James, Frank and Jesse, 31, 37
Jicarillas, 88
Jim Crow, 51, 166
Johnson, Alvin, 144, 151
Jolo, Philippines, 285
Jones, Jonathan, 32
Jornada del Muerto, 81
Joubert, Papa and Madame (fictional characters), 356
Judge Advocate General Department, 178, 191
juramentados, 228, 237, 250, 283–84

Kaibab Forest, 15
kampilans, 227, 238, 247, 285

Keams, Tom, 4
Keams Canyon, 2, 3, 18
Kemper, Steve, 11
Kendell, Henry M., 101, 102
Kettle Hill, Cuba, 209, 212, 213, 214, 216
Kicking Bear, 112, 113, 119, 125, 127
Kingsbury, Henry P., 271
Knights of Columbus, 343
krises, 227, 247, 285

Laclède, Pierre, 26
Laclede MO, 28, 44, 47, 67, 136, 166, 355, 356; description of, 30–31; Holtzclaw raid on, 31; impact of Civil War on, 36, 39; post–Civil War growth of, 47
Laclede Negro School, 51
Laclede News, 58
Lake Butig (Philippines), 240
Lake Lanao (Philippines), 229, 230, 233–34, 237, 240
Lakotas, 124, 172, 218
Lamont, Daniel S., 158
Lanao District, Philippines, 279
Lanckton, Frank, 233, 280, 282, 296
Landor, Henry Savage, 246
Langhorne, George T., 334
Lansing, J. F., 372n3
Lansing Theatre, 138
lantakas, 239
Las Cienegas, 332
Las Guásimas, 206
Latour, Father Jean Marie (fictional character), 319
Lawton, H. W., 211, 213
Lee, Fitzhugh, 196
L'Enfant, Pierre Charles, 182
Leona, 204, 206
Letterman Army Hospital, 307
Library of Congress, 182
Lincoln NE, 72, 98, 100, 102, 135, 137, 138, 152, 163, 178, 254, 350
Lincoln NM, 89
Lingard, Lena (fictional character), 140
Lippincott, Aubrey, 328
Lisnet, Frank, 91
Literary Digest, 351
Little Bighorn battle, 111, 124, 164

Index

Little Colorado River, 8, 12
Lomax, Henry, 31, 40
London Mail, 246
Long, John D., 196, 198
"Long Walk," 101
Lozano, Ismael, 328
Lumbayanague Rancheria (Philippines), 240
Lusitania, 301
Luzon, Philippines, 254

MacArthur, Arthur, 254, 261–62, 263
MacArthur, Douglas, 254
Maciu, Philippines, 237, 239, 240–41
Madero, Francisco Indalecio, 297–98
Madison Square Garden, 184, 214
Magdalena Mountains, 94
Magoon, Charles E., 157, 160, 164, 178, 257, 260
Maguire, C. L., 190
Maine, USS, 193, 196–97, 198
malpais, 1, 6, 8, 10, 13
Mance, Henry, 80
Manderson, Charles, 134
Mangus, 78, 79
Mangus Coloradas (Mangus's father), 367n36
Mangus Springs, 79
Manibilang, Ahmai, 230, 232–33, 234, 235
Manila American, 268–69
Manila Times, 244
Marahui, Philippines, 232, 250
Marietta, Shelley, 354
Marshall, George C., 354
Marti, Jose, 194
Martinelli's, 71
Mary Powell, 71
Mata Ortiz pottery, 321
Maxim-Nordenfelt mountain howitzers, 239
Maxwell, Pete, 90
McCarty, Henry (Billy the Kid), 90, 137
McClernand, Edward J., 204, 263
McCook, Alexander, 106
McKinley, William, 157, 183, 195, 198, 199, 203, 215, 218, 221, 223

McLaughlin, James, 113, 114, 117
McNair, Lesley J., 347
Meiklejohn, George D., 157, 160, 183, 191, 199, 200, 201, 204, 216, 219, 221, 222–23, 226, 227, 249
Merritt, Wesley, 62
Mesa, Antonio, 327
Mescaleros, 88, 89
Meuse-Argonne Offensive, 350
Mexican International Railroad, 320
Mexico North-Western Railroad, 320
Miles, Nelson A., 77, 91, 94, 114, 115, 116, 117, 125, 127, 164, 172, 176, 179, 184, 185, 200, 202, 203, 218, 236, 242, 322, 348
Military Division of the Missouri, 114
Mills, Samuel M., Jr., 185, 186
Mimbres Mountains, 81
Mindanao, Military Department of, 20, 234
Mindanao, Philippines, 225, 226, 227–51, 278–94
Miniconjous, 119
Minus (Indian packer), 3, 8, 9, 14–15, 17–18
Missouri mules, 83
Missouri State Normal School, Kirksville, 54–55
Mizner, J. K., 177
Moenkopi Wash, 8, 17
Mogollon Mountains, 78
Monotolth (Apache scout), 323
Moqui Indian Reservation, 2
Moquis, 107
Morey, Lewis S., 337–38
Moro Province, 20, 254, 277
Moros, 19, 226–27, 285
Morrill Act, 138
Morrison, Jasper, 169
Mountain Pleasant Garden Club, 148
Mounted Service School (Fort Riley KS), 287
Muñoz, Juan, 312
My Ántonia (Cather), 28, 42, 140
My Experiences in the World War (Pershing), 352

Index

Namiquipa, 326
Nampeyo, 5
Napoleon III, 48
National Competitive Drills, 153
National Guard. *See* Organized Militia (National Guard)
Navajo Church (rock formation), 102
Navajos, 4, 100–101, 107, 251
Nave, Jim, 32
New Mexico Military Institute, 91
Newscome, Fred, 304
New York Times, 351
New York Tribune, 331
New York World, 287
Nez Perce, 164
Nez Perce War, 165
Northern Great Plains, 111
North Missouri Railroad, 26
North Platte NE, 99
Northwest Territory, 24
Nueva Casas Grandes, 344

Oato, Philippines, 248
Obregón, Alvaro, 300, 333
O'Connor, Richard, 96, 318
Ojos Azules Ranch, 332
Omaha Cup, 154
Omaha NE, 122, 135
O'Neill, Buckey, 15
One of Ours (Cather), 150, 209, 355
O Pioneers! (Cather), 296
Oraibi (Hopi village), 2, 5, 18
Ord, Jules, 213–14, 215
Organized Militia (National Guard), 329, 335, 341, 347
Orozco, Pascual, Jr., 297
Orr, Anne (Boswell), 273, 303

Paddock, Richard B., 88, 96, 97, 178, 377n31
Palmer, Frederick, 57
Palomas Land & Cattle Company, 314
Panama-Pacific International Exposition, 302
Pandapatan, Philippines, 234–35, 243
pandita, 228
Panic of 1873, 48–49
Pantaun, Philippines, 240

pan y palo, 296
Paquimé (Casas Grandes), 320–21, 326
Parang, Philippines, 234
Parral, Chihuahua, 327, 328–29
Patterson, Robert U., 248
Patton, Anne "Nita," 388n15
Patton, George, 317, 324, 332–33, 347, 388n15
Pecos Plains, 90
Penn, Julius Augustus, 82, 88, 96, 106
Perry, John, 66
Pershing, Anna May (JP's sister), 28, 97, 143, 178, 308
Pershing, Anne (JP's second child), 273, 304
Pershing, Anne Elizabeth (Thompson) (JP's mother), 26, 33, 36, 41, 43, 46, 49, 254
Pershing, Christena (Milliron) (JP's great-grandmother), 25
Pershing, Daniel (JP's great-grandfather), 25
Pershing, Elizabeth (Davis) (JP's grandmother), 25
Pershing, Francis Warren, 276, 304, 307, 352, 391n4
Pershing, Frederick (JP's brother), 39
Pershing, Frederick (Pfoerschin) (JP's great-great-grandfather), 24–25
Pershing, Grace (Paddock) (JP's sister), 28, 97, 143, 178
Pershing, Helen Elizabeth (JP's first child), 267, 304
Pershing, Helen Frances (Warren), 286, 289, 295, 301, 352, 356; and birth of first child, 267; and birth of second child, 273; and birth of third child, 276; and birth of fourth child, 282; and courtship with JP, 257, 259–60; death of, 303–5; description of, 256; marriage of, to JP, 260; meets JP at Fort Myer hop, 255; in Philippines, 271–73, 277–94; response of, to accusation of JP having Filipino mistress, 270
Pershing, James (JP's brother), 35, 44, 49, 55, 56, 134, 222, 261

411

Pershing, John Fletcher (JP's father), 25; as civic leader in Laclede, 43, 47; death of, 266; expands business following Civil War, 39; as logger, 26; meets JP's wife, 261; move of, to Chicago, 134; move of, to Lincoln, 72; move of, to St. Louis, 26; operates wholesale business, 178; as opposed to slavery, 31; partnership of, with Stone and Jennings, 26; as postmaster of Laclede, 30; as produce broker, 26; racial attitudes of, 46; as railroad section manager, 26; in Republican politics, 39; as storekeeper in Laclede, 30; sutler appointment of, 30; as traveling salesman, 48, 51; as Union supporter during Civil War, 31; as victim of Holtzclaw raid, 33–34

Pershing, John Joseph: accused of having a Filipino mistress, 268; adolescence of, 40; as aide to Nelson Miles, 179; and Anne Patton, 388n15; appointed brevet captain of volunteers, 220; appointed post commander at Iligan, Philippines, 229; approach of, to Moros, 229–30; asks Senator Warren for Frankie's hand in marriage, 259; and Bacolod campaign, 246; and birthdate controversy, 366n1; birth of, 28; and birth of first child, 267; and birth of second child, 273; and birth of third child, 276; and birth of fourth child, 28; as "Black Jack," 191; books in childhood home of, 41; brothel established by, 344; and Bud Bagsak campaign, 288–89; and Bud Dajo campaign, 286; builds infrastructure in Mindanao, 291–92; buries juramentados with pigs as deterrent, 284; cadets' tribute to, 374n51; at Camp Vicars, 236; captures horse thieves, 104; childhood activities of, 45, 47; childhood education of, 41; and Civil War, 27, 29; as college student at Kirksville, 54; commands Tenth Cavalry in Cuban combat, 215; and comparison of Moros to American Indians, 238; considers leaving the army to practice law, 157, 178; courtship of, with Frankie, 257, 259–60; and Crees, 173–75; death of, 354; death of father of, 266; death of mother of, 254; decision of, to remain in army, 106; description of, as a cadet at West Point, 67; description of, as a youth, 40; and Distinguished Service Cross, 290; early family history of, 23–25; and exposure to guns as a youth, 44; first trip of, to Europe, 224; formative years in the West of, summarized, 136; Fort Bayard (NM) posting of, 74; Fort Stanton (NM) posting of, 88, 106; Fort Wingate (NM) posting of, 100; as general of the armies, 351, 390n56, 391n7; and Ghost Dance campaign, 120; and hazing at West Point, 377n47; health issues of, 275; and heliographic system, 80–81; and Holtzclaw raid, 34–35; and horses, 67; hosts Mindanao trade fair, 281; and Lake Lanao, 250; and Lakota scouts, 131; and lawsuit against *New York World*, 287; leaves for Tokyo, 261; lessons learned by, at Fort Bayard, 82; lessons learned by, during 1880s postings, 127; lessons learned by, during Punitive Expedition, 347; lessons learned by, in Cuba, 219; and machine guns, 264, 367n4; marriage of, to Frankie, 260; marriage of parents of, 27; Medal of Honor denied to, 290; meets Arthur and Douglas MacArthur, 254; meets Buffalo Bill, 99–100; meets Theodore Roosevelt, 184; memoirs of, published, 352; as military governor of Moro Province, 277–94; as Moro dato, 244; Moro strategy of, compared to Petraeus's FM 3-24, 382n50; mother of, described, 27; Philippines posting of (1899–1903), 225–51; Philippines posting of (1907–8), 270–73; Philippines posting of (1909–13), 277–94; and prison reform, 292; and professional buffalo hunters, 111; profes-

Index

sional development of, in New Mexico, 95–96; promoted to brigadier general, 267; promoted to first lieutenant, 149; promoted to major general, 267, 343; and Pulitzer Prize, 352; and Punitive Expedition, 315–48; and "rabbit hunts" as field training, 92, 172, 271, 322, 331; reapplies for assignment at University of Nebraska, 134; receives law degree, 149; and religion, 41–42, 43, 282–83, 306, 384n19; restructures UNL's cadet program, 144; and Russo-Japanese War, 262–66; and Silver Star, 219; and Sixth Cavalry, 70; smoking habit of, 275; teaches at African American school, 51–52; teaches at Prairie Mound, 52–53; training program introduced by, 342; transfer of, to El Paso TX, 296; transition of, to manhood, 50; trek of, to Grand Canyon, 1–19; and trench warfare, 264; with U.S. Army's General Staff, 255; views of, on Native Americans, 87–88; views of, on race, 46, 166, 168, 206; at West Point, 61–70, 186, 190; West Point entrance exam of, 57; and women, 66, 169

Pershing, John Warren, III (JP's grandson), 391n4
Pershing, Joseph M. (JP's grandfather), 25
Pershing, Maria Elizabeth (Weygandt) (JP's great-great-grandmother), 25
Pershing, Mary Elizabeth (Bessie) (JP's sister), 28, 55, 56, 254, 266, 308
Pershing, Mary Margaret (JP's fourth child), 282, 304
Pershing, Richard W. (JP's grandson), 391n4
Pershing, Rose and Ruth (JP's twin sisters), 39
Pershing, Ward, 39, 178, 376n30
Pershing Auditorium (Lincoln NE), 391n2
Pershing Republican League, 351
Pershing Rifles, 151, 161, 200
Philippine Insurrection, 226
Philippines, 20, 21, 87, 96, 158, 201, 203, 222, 223, 225–51, 254, 262, 264
Pine Ridge Reservation, 113, 119, 126, 132
Pittsburgh Leader, 208
Placido, Padre Tel, 231
Platt, Rutherford, 233
Poe, John, 90
Prairie Mound School, 52, 150
Presidio, San Francisco, 20, 302, 303–5
Proctor, Redfield, 134–35
The Professor's House (Cather), 139, 180
prostitutes, 344
Pulitzer, Joseph, 195
Punitive Expedition, 20, 91, 95, 315–48; hampering of, 341; impact of, on Pancho Villa, 346; and training program, 342; U.S. casualties in, 340

Quantrill, William C., 31
Queen Victoria, 171
querida system, 269

Rapid City SD, 114
Ravel, Sam, 312
Red Cloud (Lakota warrior), 111, 112, 119, 132, 371n41
Red Cloud NE, 28
Red Cross, 390n58
Red Legs, 34, 99
Red Tomahawk, 118
Remington, Frederic, 115–16, 167, 177
Resco, Micheline, 352, 354
Riel, Louis, 169
Riis, Jacob A., 256
Robinson, Dave, 46
Robinson, Martha, 46
Rodney, W. H., 284, 386n13
Roosevelt, Franklin D., 290, 353, 354
Roosevelt, Theodore 1, 15, 160, 184, 201, 202, 206, 208, 214, 215, 255, 256, 260, 263, 267, 269, 349
Root, Elihu, 208, 242, 250, 263
Rosebud Reservation, 112, 128
Rosecrans, William S., 67
Rosita, Coahuila, 334
Rough Riders (First U.S. Volunteer Cavalry), 201, 206, 214, 215, 221, 268, 378n16

Index

Round Table, 148
Royal Arsenal (Woolwich, England), 224
Ruggles, Mr. (showman), 6
Russo-Japanese War, 19, 263, 264–66, 271

Sajiduciman, 243–44
Salvation Army, 343
Sam (Indian guide to Grand Canyon), 3, 8, 14
San Francisco Chronicle, 304–5
San Francisco Mountain, 4
San Geronimo, 326
Sangre de Cristo Mountains, 73
San Juan Hill (Cuba), 209, 211, 215, 216
San Miguelito Ranch, 332
Sanno, J. M., 172, 176
San Ramon (Filipino prison), 292
Santa Cruz de Villegas, 328
Santa Maria River, 324
Santiago, Cuba, 202, 209, 210, 217
Santo Clara Canyon, 340
Santo Domingo Ranch, 336–37
Sargent, Herbert, 379n42
Scott, George, 93
Scott, Hugh L., 286, 315, 329, 333, 335, 344
Scott, Walter, 150
The Scouts of the Prairie (stage play), 368n26
Scout's Rest (William Cody ranch), 99
Second Anglo-Afghan War, 80
Sedalia and Baxter Springs Trail, 37
Seventh Cavalry, 76, 121, 122, 124, 125, 128, 316, 331
Shafter, William R., 202, 207, 211, 213, 217
Shangreau, John, 121
Sheldon, George L., 153
Sheridan, Phil, 70
Sherman, John, 179
Sherman, William Tecumseh, 65, 74, 167, 179
Shinn, Zellar H., 270
Short Bull, 112, 113, 119, 125
Shoshones, 113
Siberia (Pacific Mail steamer), 253
Sides, Hampton, 11
Sierra Blanca Mountains, 89, 91
Signal Corps, 323
Sigsbee, Charles D., 193, 197
Sikyátki pottery, 5

Silver City NM, 73, 79, 85
Sitting Bull, 111, 113, 114, 117–18, 124, 164
Sixth Cavalry, 70, 75, 85, 100, 101, 108, 115, 116, 117, 126, 128, 271
Slocum, Herbert, 313–14
Smith, Gene, 269, 317
Smith, Joseph, 111
Smithsonian Institution, 110, 182
Smythe, Donald, 21, 36, 160
The Song of the Lark (Cather), 4, 16
Sonora, 297
Sooky (Pershing family cook), 46
Southwestern Division, 258
Spanish-American War, 19, 20, 21, 157, 160, 201, 218, 226
Spilsbury, Lem, 337, 339
Spurgeon, Charlie, 54–55
Standing Rock Reservation, 111, 113, 114, 117
Stanton, Henry, 88
Stevenson, Tom, 129
St. Louis Post-Dispatch, 268
St. Mihiel, battle of, 19
Stotsenburg, John Miller, 1–19, 105, 363n42, 375n58
St. Peter, Godfrey (fictional character), 139
Sultan of Sulu (stage play), 381n25
Sulu News, 293
Sumner, E. V., 120
Sumner, Samuel S., 224, 239, 244, 250, 258
Swobe, Thomas, 269

Taft, William Howard, 260, 269
Taglibi, Philippines, 288
Tampico, Mexico, 298
Taraca cotta, 250
Tenth Cavalry, 133, 165, 167, 170, 176, 191, 199, 201, 202, 203, 204, 209, 211, 214, 215, 216, 217, 268, 316, 326, 328, 336, 376n30
Texas, USS, 217
Thayer, John M., 99
Third Mesa AZ, 5
"Three Green P's," 88, 178, 347
Thunder Bull, 132
Thurston, John M., 183

Index

Time magazine, 354
Tomkins, Frank, 326
Toulmin, H. A., Jr., 322, 324
Trans-Mississippi West, 24, 109
"The Treasure of Far Island" (Cather), 242–43
Treaty of Portsmouth, 263
trench warfare, 264–65
Tres Hermanas, 310
Treviño, Jacinto, 335, 345
Truchas Mountains, 73
Trump, Donald, 386n15
Tuba City AZ, 2, 6–7, 17
Twain, Mark, 68

University Hall (UNL), 139, 140, 372n5
University of Cincinnati College of Law, 147
University of Missouri Law School (Columbia MO), 54
University of Nebraska–Lincoln, 28, 86, 97, 98, 102–3, 134, 136, 138, 141, 149, 151, 155, 158, 161, 163, 171, 187, 190, 200, 226, 253, 349, 350, 355, 356

Valencia, Pablo, 10
Valle de Zaragoza, 327
Valverde, battle of, 100
Vandiver, Frank, 99, 172, 213, 215, 232, 275
Varsity Rifles, 153, 161
Veracruz, Mexico, 299
Vicars, Thomas A., 235
Vickers machine guns, 245, 383n54
Villa, Francisco "Pancho," 20, 73, 91, 95, 203, 297, 299–301, 308, 309, 310–13, 342, 349
vintas, 232, 249

Walker, Norman, 305–6
Walker Lake (NV), 109, 112
Walpi (Hopi village), 2, 5, 361n7
Walter Reed Army Hospital, 354, 356
Warren, Francis Emory (JP's father-in-law), 20, 255–56, 257, 260, 267, 295, 301, 307, 349, 385n37
Washington DC, description of (1890s), 180–83
Wasumaza. See Beard, Dewey
Weasel Bear, Louise, 123
West, Parker, 263
Western Reserve, 24

West Point (U.S. Military Academy), 1, 61–70, 158, 163, 253
Weyler, Valeriano, 195, 196
Wheeler, Claude (fictional character), 209, 356
Wheeler, Joe, 212, 214
White Lance, 123
Whitside, Samuel M., 121
Wilson, David, 109
Wilson, Henry H., 156
Wilson, Henry Lane, 298
Wilson, Jack, 109
Wilson, Tug, 53
Wilson, Woodrow, 298, 309, 315, 316, 329, 345
Wingate, Benjamin, 100
The Winning of the West (Roosevelt), 184
Wint, T. J., 213
Wood, Junius B., 342
Wood, Leonard, 221, 267, 271, 278, 285, 286, 293, 379n27
Wooten, William P., 189
World War I (Great War), 19, 21, 22, 23, 69, 107, 145, 150, 160, 185, 189, 202, 203, 208, 214, 217, 219, 222, 245, 258, 265, 272, 281, 317, 321, 343, 347
Wounded Knee, battle (massacre) of, 20, 121–24, 133, 200, 210
Wovoka, 109, 111–12
Wright, Maud, 311
Wright, William M., 65

Yellow Bird, 122
"Yellow Legs," 103
Ygnacio, Joaquina, 268, 270
Ygnacio, Petronilla, 268
Yockelson, Mitchell, 78
Young, B. M., 202
Young, Charles, 329
Younger, Cole, 37
Younger brothers, 31, 364n20
Young Men's Christian Association (YMCA), 343

Zamboanga, Philippines, 225, 228, 268, 277–78, 281
Zapata, Emilio, 314, 341
Zunis, 100, 103, 251